Lecture Notes in Computer Science 3110

Commenced Publication in 1973
Founding and Former Series Editors:
Gerhard Goos, Juris Hartmanis, and Jan van Leeuwen

Ari Juels (Ed.)

Financial Cryptography

8th International Conference, FC 2004
Key West, FL, USA, February 9-12, 2004
Revised Papers

 Springer

Volume Editor

Ari Juels
RSA Laboratories
174 Middlesex Turnpike, Bedford, MA 01730, USA
E-mail: ajuels@rsasecurity.com

Library of Congress Control Number: 2004108443

CR Subject Classification (1998): E.3, D.4.6, K.6.5, K.4.4, C.2, J.1, F.2.1-2

ISSN 0302-9743
ISBN 3-540-22420-3 Springer-Verlag Berlin Heidelberg New York

Springer-Verlag is a part of Springer Science+Business Media

springeronline.com

© IFCA/Springer-Verlag Berlin Heidelberg 2004
Printed in Germany

Typesetting: Camera-ready by author, data conversion by Olgun Computergrafik
Printed on acid-free paper   SPIN: 11300311   06/3142   5 4 3 2 1 0

Preface

The 8th Annual Financial Cryptography Conference was held during 9–12 February 2004 in Key West, Florida, USA. The conference was organized by the International Financial Cryptography Association (IFCA).

The program committee, which comprised 25 members, reviewed 78 submissions, of which only 17 were accepted for presentation at the conference. This year's conference differed somewhat from those of previous years in its consideration of papers devoted to implementation, rather than purely conceptual research; one of these submissions was presented at the conference. This represented a movement in the conference toward practical problems and real-world perspectives as a complement to more traditional academic forms of research.

In this spirit, the program included a number of excellent invited speakers. In the opening talk of the conference, Jack Selby threw down the gauntlet, describing some of the achievements of the PayPal system, but also enumerating reasons for the failures of many elegant e-cash schemes in the past. Ron Rivest, in contrast, described an emerging success in the cleverly conceived Peppercoin micropayment system. Jacques Stern enlightened us with his experience in the cryptographic design of banking cards in France. Simon Pugh unveiled some details of a new generation of wireless credit card. Finally, in deference to the many consumers in the world lacking either techno-savvy or technological resources that we often too easily take for granted, Jon Peha described a fielded banking system that avoids reliance on conventional financial infrastructures. Thanks to all of these speakers for rounding out the conference with their expertise and breadth of vision.

The conference also included a panel, moderated by Andrew Patrick, on usability and its impact on security. This was a salutary and engaging reminder of how security means much more than cryptography alone.

I wish to thank the program committee for their diligence and care in reviewing papers, and in some cases for providing highly detailed comments to submitters. I would also like to thank the external referees who lent help in reviewing papers: Danny Bickson, Liad Blumenreich, Julien Brouchier, Dario Catalano, Benoit Chevallier-Mames, Pierre-Alain Fouque, Zvika Guterman, Helena Handschuh, Stanislaw Jarecki, Ofer Margo, Nick Mathewson, Pascal Paillier, Elan Pavlov, Ludovic Rousseau, Yaron Sella, and Jessica Staddon.

Thanks to the IFCA directors and officers for their guidance in conference arrangements. I am grateful to Moti Yung for chairing the rump session, an evening of short, informal presentations on ideas in the making or the breaking. Thomas Herlea of KU Leuven was very helpful as administrator of the conference submission server. Also thanks to Hinde ten Berge, who served as General Chair, overseeing not only the local arrangements for this conference, but also the publication of the preproceedings.

Finally, thanks to all of the contributors of the scientific papers to the conference. As in previous years, participants enjoyed not only mentally stimulating presentations, but also the ample sunshine – a nearly forgotten delight for many delegates from northern countries.

From its beginning, Financial Cryptography has been something of a haven for cryptographic mavericks and a meeting-point for researchers, scientists, financiers, and hands-on implementers. As the conference matures, let us look to see its early spark of originality continue to thrive in the conference hall and on the beaches.

April 2004   Ari Juels

Financial Cryptography 2004

Program Chair

Ari Juels   RSA Laboratories, USA

Program Committee

Masayuki Abe   NTT Laboratories, Japan
David Birch   Consult Hyperion, UK
Roger Dingledine   The Free Haven Project, USA
Niels Ferguson   MacFergus, The Netherlands
Philippe Golle   Stanford University, USA
Tim Jones   Simpay, UK
Marc Joye   Gemplus, France
Kwangjo Kim   ICU, Korea
Arjen Lenstra   Citicorp, USA and
                                   Technische Univ. Eindhoven, The Netherlands
Helger Lipmaa   Helsinki Univ. of Tech., Finland
Dahlia Malkhi   Hebrew Univ., Israel
David Naccache   Gemplus, France
Tatsuaki Okamoto   NTT Laboratories, Japan
Benny Pinkas   Hewlett-Packard, USA
Nicole Pohl   Franklin and Marshall College, USA
David Pointcheval   CNRS-École Normale Supérieure, France
Bart Preneel   K.U. Leuven, Belgium
Avi Rubin   Johns Hopkins University, USA
Vitaly Shmatikov   SRI International, USA
Adam Shostack   Informed Security, Canada
Sean Smith   Dartmouth College, USA
Rebecca Wright   Stevens Institute of Technology, USA
Moti Yung   Columbia University, USA

General Chair

Hinde ten Berge

Sponsors

Silver Sponsors   nCipher and NTT DoCoMo USA Labs
Bronze Sponsor   RSA Labs
In-Kind Sponsor   Consult Hyperion

Financial Cryptography 2004 was organized by the International Financial Cryptography Association (IFCA).

Table of Contents

Panel Session: Building Usable Security Systems

Invited Talk

Auctions and Lotteries

Game Theoretic and Cryptographic Tools

Mix Networks and Anonymous Communications

Analyzing the Success and Failure
of Recent e-Payment Schemes
(Abstract)

Jack R. Selby*

Clarium Capital Management LLC
San Francisco, CA, USA
jack@clariumcapital.com
www.clariumcapital.com

The advent of the Internet was believed to be a critical factor in accelerating the ease of distribution and overall adoption of "E-Payment" schemes. However, the "dot-com" boom of the late 1990's yielded few successful new payment systems. Instead, many recurring problems plagued the Internet-based schemes, and an examination of these persistent pitfalls suggests necessary changes in approach for future "E-Payment" entrepreneurs.

By a very wide margin, PayPal, Inc. represents the most successful new "E-Payment" scheme hatched during the Internet boom. With more than 30 million users and a profitable business model, PayPal today is owned fully by eBay after a $1.4 billion dollar acquisition (concluded in October 2002). Why did PayPal succeed when others failed?

First, PayPal designed a new payment scheme specifically for a clear demand from buyers and sellers. Specifically, PayPal addressed the inefficiencies endemic with paper (checks, money orders, et al) payments. Additionally, PayPal focused on the expensive nature of credit card processing, especially for small and medium enterprises (SMEs) which often struggle to afford the fixed cost and fraud component of processing plastic payments. Second, PayPal tapped a market of tremendous size and scope - the online auction market. Markets like eBay enabled PayPal to spread rapidly and scale as a business model (spread fixed costs across rapid top-line revenue growth). Finally, PayPal mastered many of the operation complexities that doomed many of its competitors, in particular fraud prevention and customer service.

Why did other new payment schemes fail? Some premised their businesses on "partnerships" with financial institutions for distribution agreements. These arrangements often became mired in bureaucracy while running afoul of the "not invented here" syndrome common within the industry. Other new payment schemes developed technologies without any regard for real consumer or merchant demand. These "over-engineered" applications, while elegant in design, failed to translate to practical and useful improvements over current payment options.

---

* Managing Director, Clarium Capital LLC. Former Senior Vice President and Corporate Officer of PayPal, Inc. (NASDAQ: PPYL)

A. Juels (Ed.): FC 2004, LNCS 3110, p. 1, 2004.
© IFCA/Springer-Verlag Berlin Heidelberg 2004

Peppercoin Micropayments

Ronald L. Rivest

Computer Science and Artificial Intelligence Laboratory
Massachusetts Institute of Technology
Cambridge, MA 02139
rivest@mit.edu

Abstract. We present the "Peppercoin" method for processing micropayments efficiently. With this method, a fraction of the micropayments received are determined, via a procedure known as "cryptographic selection," to qualify for upgrade to a macropayment. The merchant deposits the upgraded micropayments as macropayments, and merely logs locally the non-qualifying micropayments. In this manner, the merchant transforms a large collection of small micropayments into a smaller collection of macropayments, of the same total expected value. The merchant pays much less for processing the resulting macropayments, since there are fewer of them. Consumers are billed for exactly the amount they spend, based on auxiliary information recorded in each micropayment. The method is highly secure, and compatible with existing payment mechanisms such as credit cards.

1 Introduction

The Peppercoin micropayment system is due to Micali and Rivest [MR02]; we refer the reader to their original paper for more details. Here we give only a high-level description of the method.

For this paper, a "micropayment" is any payment that is small enough that processing it is relatively costly, as a percentage of the overall transaction value. Given that typical credit card processing fees may be twenty-five cents per transaction, we may consider a "micropayment" to be any payment under $10.

We view the introduction of efficient micropayments into the world of internet e-commerce as potentially as significant as the invention of metal coins by the Lydians in 640 B.C. Coins turned out to be a signficant market enabler – the first retail markets evolved soon thereafter.

Today, it is clear that small electronic payments will soon become commonplace. Not only to pay for music downloads (note the recent success of Apple's iTunes), but also for other digital downloads and other digital goods and services. Small electronic payments will begin to replace metal coins and small paper bills for real-world purchases as well.

Efficient processing is essential for a successful micropayment method; it makes no sense to charge twenty-five cents to process a ten-cent payment!

Other important factors include ease-of-use, security, and compatibility with the existing payment infrastructure.

A. Juels (Ed.): FC 2004, LNCS 3110, pp. 2–8, 2004.

2   Aggregation Methods

The key to efficient processing of micropayments is, of course, the *aggregation* of many small micropayments into a few larger macropayments. We distinguish four levels of potential aggregation, of increasing efficiency.

2.1   No Aggregation

When no aggregation is done, each payment, no matter how small, makes its way around the entire payment cycle, from purchaser to merchant to merchant (acquiring) bank to consumer (issuing) bank to consumer (for billing). [Or the equivalent, depending on whether this is a debit or credit system.] Having every party touch every payment in this manner is extremely inefficient and costly. Chaum's Digicash system [Cha83] is an example of a payment system with no aggregation. (To be fair, the emphasis of his design was on anonymity rather than efficiency for micropayments.)

2.2   Session-Level Aggregation

With session-level (also known as merchant-level) aggregation, the merchant collects several small payments from a given consumer – say all of those spent by that consumer during one day – and submits a macropayment representing the aggregate amount due at the end of the day or session. This method only works sometimes: when the consumer makes repeated small purchases at the same merchant within a short time period; it doesn't work in general. PayWord [RS97] is an example of a method based on session-level aggregation.

2.3   Aggregation by Intermediation

Another approach to provide aggregation is to create a new intermediary that all consumers and merchants must interact with in order to process micropayments. This intermediary attempts to keep track of all micropayments made by each consumer at any participating merchant, and then submit for processing by the ordinary banking system only payments that represent the entire amount spent by that consumer during the given time period, or the entire amount to be received by a given merchant during that time period. This approach still requires handling of each payment by the intermediary, who is tasked with replicating the functionality of the entire existing banking system, at lower cost! Clearly, the way towards success should be by *reducing* the amount of mechanism and processing involved, not by *increasing* it!

2.4   Universal Aggregation

The "Peppercoin" method uses *universal aggregation*, which we sometimes also call *cryptographic selection* or *many/many/many* aggregation, since it aggregates smoothly across many consumers, many merchants, and many payment service providers.

With universal aggregation, each participating merchant processes micropayments directly, using special cryptographic software.

The software first checks the validity of the micropayment – for example, by checking the consumer's digital signature on that micropayment. If the micropayment is valid, the merchant then completes the transaction and delivers the purchased goods to the consumer.

The software then checks whether the micropayment "qualifies for an upgrade" (to a macropayment). If the micropayment does not qualify for an upgrade, the merchant merely logs the micropayment, and need do no further processing. If the micropayment does qualify for an upgrade to a macropayment, then the merchant will deposit that micropayment *as a macropayment* with his bank.

The size of the resulting macropayment will be a fixed system parameter, such as $10 or $20.

The fraction of micropayments that qualify for such an upgrade depends on the size of the micropayments. For example, for ten-cent micropayments and a $10 macropayment size, approximately one in every 100 micropayments will qualify for such an upgrade to a $10 macropayment.

It is easy to see that the merchant expects to receive the same amount on the average, since one hundred ten-cent micropayments has the same net value as one ten-dollar macropayment.

Indeed, the merchant should be very happy with such a procedure, since he is now only paying a single transaction processing fee (for the ten-dollar macropayment) instead of one hundred transaction processing fees (for each of the micropayments). Universal aggregation turns what was probably a money-losing proposition into a profitable operation for the merchant!

The qualification procedure is cryptographic in nature, so that neither the consumer nor the merchant can affect the decision as to whether a particular micropayment will qualify for upgrade. The qualification procedure depends upon the merchant's digital signature on data derived from the micropayment, so that other parties, such as the merchant's and consumer's banks, can check that a given micropayment did indeed qualify for upgrade.

While one may loosely think of the qualification procedure as selecting a given micropayment for upgrade "with a certain probability," the qualification procedure is in fact deterministic and not randomized – the merchant's digital signature method will be a deterministic signature method.

It is important to note that each micropayment is tested for qualification for upgrade *independently* of each other micropayment. The merchant does not need to keep any sort of records of previous transactions, cumulative amount spent by each consumer, or the like; this simplicity permits very elegant and clean implementations for the merchant.

When a particular micropayment qualifies for an upgrade to a macropayment, and is turned in for a $10 deposit by the merchant, who pays the merchant the

$10? It may be awkward to bill the consumer, since it may be his very first micropayment.

The Peppercoin system ensures that a consumer is never billed for more than he has spent. This is accomplished by having each micropayment indicate the total cumulative value of the consumer's expenditures to date. The consumer's bank sees these values every so often, when it sees micropayments from the consumer that have been upgraded to macropayments, and can thus incrementally bill the consumer appropriately. The consumer's bank thus acts as a financial "buffer" between the cash outlays to merchants and the receipts from the consumer, in a manner very similar, but not identical, to what happens with standard credit card processing. The cryptographic nature of the qualification process ensures that the cash flows of the consumer's bank will (almost exactly) balance, as they grow in value. The use of cryptography – based on digital signatures by consumers and merchants – also prevents various forms of fraud of one or two parties against the other(s).

Universal aggregation excels for processing micropayments, since the micropayments exist as such only in the hands of the consumers and merchants, who are in any case involved with other transaction details as well. Deposits made by the merchant are solely in the form of macropayments. Consumers are only billed for the amount they have spent at *all* merchants over the billing period (e.g. one month), which will not be a micropayment (for most consumers). There is no intermediary involved who has to handle every payment. Thus, universal aggregation provides a clean and simple way to extend an existing payment system, such as a credit-card system, to the realm of micropayments.

3   Other Issues

3.1   Ease of Use

The basic Peppercoin method can be implemented in a variety of ways, to maximize ease-of-use for the consumer in a given situation. For example, while the basic Peppercoin method requires that each consumer have digital signature capability, one can easily eliminate this requirement by having a party trusted by the consumer sign the payments for him as a proxy; this might be a natural approach in a web-services environment.

The Peppercoin method can also be implemented so that it feels to the consumer as a natural extension of his existing credit-card processing procedure, further increasing consumer acceptance and ease-of-use.

3.2   Scalability

The Peppercoin micropayment system scales easily to very large implementations, since all of the "real work" involving micropayments is handled by the consumer and merchant directly, and since the system works naturally with a variety of financial institutions representing the consumer and the merchant.

3.3   Non-interactivity

The Peppercoin method is *non-interactive* in the sense that a Peppercoin micropayment can be emailed or transmitted directly from consumer to merchant. There is no need for the merchant to interact with the consumer during the payment process, or even to be on-line at the time of the payment.

This non-interactivity means, for example, that Peppercoin micropayments could conceivably be used in applications such as spam-prevention, where it has often been proposed that spam could be reduced by requiring a micropayment with each email sent.

3.4   Low-Cost Qualification Procedures

The simple universal aggregation method described above requires the merchant to compute a digital signature for every micropayment received. For some merchants, who are processing a very high volume of very low-priced goods, this may be a bit of a burden.

It is possible to reduce this computation cost considerably, by modifying the qualification procedure slightly. For example, it may depend only on the merchant's signature on the time of the micropayment, measured to the nearest minute. Then the merchant need only compute one digital signature per minute. A different approach to reducing computation time can be based on having the server compute a "Merkle tree" [Mer79] to hash together many micropayments, and then compute a digital signature on the root.

3.5   Variable-Sized Payments

Although this point may already be clear, we emphasize that the Peppercoin micropayment system handles micropayments of varying sizes in a smooth and efficient manner. The only relevant factor is the ratio between the macropayment size and the micropayment size. For example, if macropayments are ten dollars and a micropayment is ten cents, this ratio is one-hundred; in this case the qualification procedure ensure that one out of every one hundred ten-cent micropayments, on the average, qualifies for an upgrade to a macropayment. Thus, as an additional example, one-dollar micropayments would qualify for upgrade one out of every ten times, on the average, to a ten-dollar macropayment.

3.6   Revenue Variance

The merchant will see a dramatic reduction in his costs for processing transactions, since he is requesting processing for a small number of macropayments instead of a large number of micropayments.

But the merchant may worry that the qualification procedure might leave him nonetheless somehow at a disadvantage, since during a given period a unusually small number of micropayments might qualify for upgrade.

Fortunately, this worry is easily determined, with a little analysis, to be a non-issue. The cost-savings provided by Peppercoin, which provide a benefit to the merchant on *each and every* transaction, and which grow cumulatively in value as he processes more transactions, are going to overwhelm any "jitter" in the qualification decisions, which are unbiased. The following theorem is one example of such analysis, comparing a Peppercoin implementation which charges a fee of pT for processing each transaction of value T, versus another system that charges qT for processing each transaction of value T.

Theorem 1. *If a Peppercoin implementation which charges a fee of pT for processing each transaction of value T, while another system that charges qT for processing each transaction of value T, then once the total number of macropayments (qualifying micropayments) exceeds*

$$(5/(q-p))^2$$

the probability is 999,999 out of 1,000,000 that the merchant's net total receipts will be higher with Peppercoin than with the other system.

As an example, consider a scenario where a Peppercoin-based system offers to process ten-cent payments for a penny each (i.e., $p = 0.1$; quite feasible with Peppercoin), while competitor C offers to process them for three cents each (i.e., $q = 0.3$; very hard to achieve without using a selection procedure such as Peppercoin's). Thus, $q - p = 0.2$, and the merchant will almost surely be ahead with Peppercoin after only $(5/0.2)^2 = 625$ macropayments. This is a rather worst-case estimate, and the merchant is likely to be ahead with Peppercoin from the start.

4 Summary

The Peppercoin universal aggregation method for processing micropayments offers low-cost processing, even for very small payments, with a high-degree of security. It can be implemented in an easy-to-use manner that extends existing payment mechanisms.

More details can be found on the Web [Pep,Riv].

References

[Cha83] David Chaum. Blind signatures for untraceable payments. In R. L. Rivest, A. Sherman, and D. Chaum, editors, *Proc. Crypto '82*, pages 199–203, New York, 1983. Plenum Press.

[Mer79] Ralph Charles Merkle. *Secrecy, Authentication, and Public Key Systems*. PhD thesis, Stanford University, June 1979. Technical Report 1979-1; Information Systems Laboratory.

[MR02] S. Micali and R. L. Rivest. Micropayments revisited. In B. Preneel, editor, *Proc. Cryptography Track at RSA Conference 2002*, pages 149–263. Springer, 2002. Lecture Notes in Computer Science No. 2271.

[Pep]   Peppercoin web site. `http://www.peppercoin.com`.

[Riv]   Rivest web site. `http://theory.csail.mit.edu/~rivest`.

[RS97]   Ronald L. Rivest and Adi Shamir. PayWord and MicroMint–two simple micropayment schemes. In Mark Lomas, editor, *Proceedings of 1996 International Workshop on Security Protocols*, volume 1189 of *Lecture Notes in Computer Science*, pages 69–87. Springer, 1997. (Also available in Crypto-Bytes, volume 2, number 1 (RSA Laboratories, Spring 1996), 7–11, and at `http://theory.lcs.mit.edu/~rivest/RivestShamir-mpay.pdf`).

Microcredits for Verifiable Foreign Service Provider Metering

Craig Gentry and Zulfikar Ramzan

DoCoMo Communications Laboratories USA, Inc.
{cgentry,ramzan}@docomolabs-usa.com

Abstract. With the explosive growth of mobile communications, users may often access value-added services through foreign service providers. These providers will interact directly with users, later providing details to a user's home service provider regarding the services rendered; the home service provider, in turn, bills the user. One critical concern is that the foreign service provider might inflate the usage figures it furnishes to the home service provider. In this paper, we address this issue using a microcredit scheme. The scheme is efficient as the verification time required by the home service provider is only logarithmic in the number of microcredit transactions, and the verification time required by the foreign service provider is constant. Moreover, the communication complexity per microcredit transaction between the user and foreign service provider is also constant. The scheme uses QuasiModo trees, which have been previously applied to certificate revocation. It improves upon previous chain-based proposals and their tree-based analogues. As a byproduct, our scheme yields a micropayment protocol which is an improvement over tree schemes with respect to both communication complexity and time complexity (in both cases by a factor of approximately 2, amortized).

Keywords: Metering, Micropayments, Microcredits, QuasiModo trees.
Category: Research.

1 Introduction

As mobile wireless computing becomes more prevalent, home service providers (HSPs) will look to offer an ever-increasing number of value-added services to their customers. In many cases, these services will be offered through foreign service providers (FSPs), with whom some type of prior arrangement has been established. The FSP reports the amount of service accessed by the user to the HSP who, in turn, bills the user an amount commensurate with the usage. This type of situation occurs today in the case of cellular phone service where users who are roaming may connect through someone other than their home service provider. As the number of services begins to grow, so too will the number of FSPs. This phenomena will create an interesting security issue – namely, to what extent can the user and HSP trust the FSP?

SO MANY FSPS, SO LITTLE TRUST. Two critical security issues arise when a user $\mathcal{U}$ who has a prior relationship with the HSP accesses a service through the

A. Juels (Ed.): FC 2004, LNCS 3110, pp. 9–23, 2004.

FSP. The first is to prevent the FSP from overstating the amount of service $\mathcal{U}$ actually used. The second is to prevent $\mathcal{U}$ from accessing more service than he will later be billed for. These issues are critical since trustworthiness in FSPs will likely degrade with their proliferation. If the FSPs cheat, then not only are users victimized, but the ancillary dispute resolution costs incurred by the HSP might be prohibitively high. Likewise, if the users cheat, it could significantly cut into the profit margins of the FSPs who would otherwise resell their services at discounted wholesale prices to the HSP. Allegations of such cheating are not uncommon, even for large service providers [10].

NAÏVE SOLUTION. Using techniques from micropayments we can put forth a simple approach for addressing the above problem; for concreteness, we consider hash-chain based micropayment schemes [1, 15, 16, 19]. Recall that a length-preserving function f is said to be one way on its iterates if, for any i, given $f^i(x)$, it should be hard to find a pre-image z such that $f(z) = f^i(x)$, except with negligible probability. The user $\mathcal{U}$ computes a chain consisting of tokens or values: $x_0, \ldots, x_m$, where x_m is chosen at random from the domain of f and $x_i = f(x_{i+1})$ for $i \in \{0, \ldots, m-1\}$, and obtains the HSP's signature on $\langle x_0, m \rangle$. When $\mathcal{U}$ makes use of the service via the FSP, he provides it with $\langle x_0, m \rangle$ and HSP's signature. At each successive interval, such as when a certain amount of time passes or perhaps with each packet sent, $\mathcal{U}$ releases the next consecutive value in the chain. The FSP, having verified the HSP's signature, checks that the chain element hashes to the starting point x_0. Finally, when use of the service is terminated, the FSP provides the HSP with the last chain value it received. If x_t is the last value sent, then $\mathcal{U}$ is billed for using t intervals of service.

The above approach has several drawbacks. First, it imposes a burden on the HSP, since it not only has to compute a digital signature every time $\mathcal{U}$ wants to initiate a session with the FSP, but it also has to traverse the chain, which requires t invocations of f. Given that a single HSP may have millions of users, each of whom may access a service for a large number of intervals, it is clear that the above approach does not scale well. We present schemes where the HSP performs $\lfloor \log_2(t) \rfloor + 1$ hashes during the verification phase; note that this value is independent of the number of tokens m initially generated. Before proceeding, we explicitly identify some design goals.

DESIGN GOALS. We want a solution with the following security properties:

- Neither the FSP nor the HSP can overcharge $\mathcal{U}$. In particular, should there be any dispute, one or both parties can produce evidence that the user did indeed use the amount of service for which it is being billed.
- $\mathcal{U}$ cannot obtain more service than it will actually be billed for. In particular, should the user try to obtain extra service, the FSP should be able to detect this immediately and apply an appropriate policy, such as terminating the service – perhaps with some advance warning.

Furthermore, we would like to meet the following performance requirements:

- The FSP's workload, when allowing $\mathcal{U}$ access to service, should be $O(1)$ per microcredit transaction.

- $\mathcal{U}$'s workload, when accessing service through the FSP, should be $O(1)$ per microcredit transaction.
- The communication complexity between the FSP and $\mathcal{U}$ should be $O(1)$ per microcredit transaction.
- The HSP's workload, at billing time, should be much less than the actual service used; e.g., logarithmic, $O(\log t)$.
- The FSP's workload, when interacting with the HSP to provide billing information, should be much less than the actual service used; e.g., logarithmic, $O(\log t)$.
- The communication complexity between the HSP and FSP should be much less than the amount of service actually used; e.g., logarithmic, $O(\log t)$.

Note that, at billing time, the FSP must at least convey to the HSP the value t specifying how much service was used. Since t requires $O(\log t)$ bits to represent, the above performance requirements are essentially asymptotically optimal.

OUR CONTRIBUTIONS. We present a scheme that meets the above design goals. Communication complexity between the user and the FSP is between 1 to 2 hash outputs (20 to 40 bytes if we use SHA-1). The FSP performs one hash function computation. At the end, the FSP provides at most $\lfloor \log_2 t \rfloor + 2$ hash values to the HSP, where t corresponds to the amount of service used by $\mathcal{U}$. To achieve the lowest time and communication complexity, the FSP needs to store or cache $O(t)$ hash function outputs. The scheme uses QuasiModo trees which were introduced for efficient certificate revocation [4]. Finally, we observe that QuasiModo trees yield a micropayment scheme that is a strict improvement over other simple tree-based schemes with respect to both communication complexity and time complexity (in both cases by a factor of approximately 2, amortized).

We use the term *microcredits* to refer to our approach since users generate their own tokens, and are billed only after the service is rendered. As a result, users are not paying directly, but rather are on credit. Also, in a microcredit scheme, other performance parameters, such as the amount of effort required to reconcile accounts when the FSP interacts with the HSP after the service is rendered, are especially relevant.

RELATED WORK. While there is extensive work in the area of micropayments, a comprehensive literature review is beyond the scope of the present paper; however, an excellent survey can be found in the paper of Lipton and Ostrovsky [11]. Instead, we focus on micropayment schemes that are more germane to our work. One such family of schemes, as already described above, are those based on hash chains [1, 15, 16, 19]. Jutla and Yung's PayTree scheme [9] replaces the hash chains with trees. For m coins, a PayTree, in its most basic form, is an (almost) balanced binary tree with m leaves[1]. For each leaf, a secret random value is chosen, and the leaf is assigned a label corresponding to a cryptographic hash of that value. Each interior node is assigned a value corresponding to a

---

[1] For simplicity, one can assume that m is a power of 2 meaning that the tree is strictly binary, as was done in [9], but the generalization to non-powers is straightforward.

cryptographic hash of the values assigned to its children. A party wishing to use the scheme simply generates such a tree and commits to its root by signing it. The advantage of PayTree is that a single tree can be used for multiple merchants, where, in one variation, each merchant is constrained to using a given set of leaves for payment.

There is also a great deal of work specifically on the use of micropayment techniques within the mobile wireless setting [6, 17, 20, 21, 23]. The paper by Jakobsson et al. [6] proposes a probabilistic micropayment scheme for encouraging users in a multi-hop network to forward packets. The idea of probabilistic payment systems was independently suggested by Rivest [18] and Wheeler [22]; the general paradigm of not involving the bank in every transaction was proposed by Jarecki and Odlyzko [8] who audit transactions probabilistically, though the payments themselves are deterministic. The remaining schemes tend to use hash chain techniques and variations thereof. Our proposal improves upon these chain-based schemes especially when it comes to final billing as the HSP only needs to perform $O(\lfloor \log_2 t \rfloor + 1)$ compared with $O(t)$ work for a naïve chain based scheme and $O(\lfloor \log_2 m \rfloor + 1)$ for a naïve tree-based scheme, where t is the number of transactions and m is the number of initial tokens generated.

ORGANIZATION. The next section presents our microcredit scheme. Section 3 discusses the scheme's performance and security. The subsequent section describes the performance tradeoffs one achieves through variations on QuasiModo trees. Finally, section 5 describes various extensions related to probabilistic polling, micropayments, and achieving anonymity within a session.

2   Microcredits Using QuasiModo Trees

2.1   Preliminaries

MODEL AND NOTATION. We have a home service provider HSP, a foreign service provider FSP, and a user $\mathcal{U}$. We assume the existence of an open or closed public-key infrastructure in which HSP and $\mathcal{U}$ have public-private key pairs. For a party $P \in \{\mathsf{FSP}, \mathcal{U}\}$, its key pair is denoted $(\mathsf{Sk}_P, \mathsf{Pk}_P)$ where Sk_P is the private signing key for computing the signature on a message, and Pk_P is the public verification key corresponding to Sk_P. Let $\mathcal{DS} = (\mathsf{KG}, \mathsf{Sign}, \mathsf{Vf})$ denote a digital signature scheme that is secure against existential forgery under adaptive chosen message attack [5]. Here KG denotes the key generation algorithm, $\mathsf{Sign}(\mathsf{Sk}_P, M)$ denotes the signing algorithm which outputs a signature σ on message M under signing key Sk_P (the signing algorithm may be randomized), and $\mathsf{Vf}(\mathsf{Pk}_P, M, \sigma) \in \{0, 1\}$ denotes the verification algorithm which evaluates to 1 if the signature σ on message M is correct with respect to the public key Pk_P.

Let $\{0, 1\}^*$ denote the set of all bit strings. Let H denote a *cryptographic compression function* that takes as input a b-bit payload and produces a v-bit output. Our constructions require $b = 2v$ which can easily be achieved by padding well known constructs. The compression function may also be parameterized by a v-bit initialization vector or IV, which is fixed and publicly known; for convenience, we do not view the IV as an actual input to H so sometimes omit it from the argument list. In our schemes, we may assign a different hash function to each user by, for example, setting the IV or some other payload padding to be a function of the user's identity. We assume these cryptographic compression functions are *collision resistant*; that is, finding two distinct inputs $m_1 \neq m_2$ such that $H(\mathsf{IV}, m_1) = H(\mathsf{IV}, m_2)$ is difficult. A practical example of a compression function is seen in SHA-1 [14]; its output and IV length is 20-bytes and its payload is 64-bytes. In practice, the hash functions in our schemes will not operate on data larger than the compression function payload size. For simplicity, we use the term hash function instead of compression function, where it is understood that a hash function takes arbitrary length strings $\{0, 1\}^*$ and produces a fixed length output in $\{0, 1\}^v$. We use the symbol $\mathcal{H}$ to denote such a function. Hash functions are assumed to be both one way and collision resistant. Finally, for a real number ρ, $\lceil \rho \rceil$ denotes the smallest integer greater than or equal to ρ and $\lfloor \rho \rfloor$ denotes the largest integer less than or equal to ρ.

MERKLE TREES. One important notion is that of a *Merkle tree* [13], which can be described as follows. We start with λ (pseudo) random values $x_1, \dots, x_\lambda$ each of which is in $\{0, 1\}^n$. For simplicity, assume that λ is a power of 2. Let $\mathcal{H} : \{0, 1\}^{2n} \to \{0, 1\}^n$ be a cryptographic hash function that maps $2n$-bit strings to n-bit strings. The Merkle tree associated with $x_1, \dots, x_\lambda$ under hash function $\mathcal{H}$ is a balanced binary tree in which each node is associated with a specific value $\mathsf{Value}(v)$. There are λ leaves, and for each leaf ℓ_i, $\mathsf{Value}(\ell_i) = \mathcal{H}(x_i)$, $1 \leq i \leq \lambda$. Note that we abuse notation since the x_i are in $\{0, 1\}^n$, but the domain of $\mathcal{H}$ is $\{0, 1\}^{2n}$; in this case, we assume that $\mathcal{H}$ is padded appropriately. For an interior vertex v, let $\mathsf{C}_0(v)$ and $\mathsf{C}_1(v)$ denote its left and right children. Let $\circ$ denote the concatenation operation. Then, $\mathsf{Value}(v) = \mathcal{H}(\mathsf{Value}(\mathsf{C}_0(v)) \circ \mathsf{Value}(\mathsf{C}_1(v)))$.

Merkle trees may be used to digest data in digital signatures, where the message blocks are assigned as leaf values and the digest corresponds to the value associated with the root. Also, if the underlying compression function is collision resistant, then it is hard to find two different sets of starting values whose Merkle root value is identical [3, 12].

QUASIMODO TREES. QuasiModo trees were introduced for certificate revocation [4]. They ostensibly resemble Merkle trees except that the interior vertices are numbered. Our observation is that a subset of the internal nodes can be directly utilized in a micropayment scheme. The upshot is an improvement in both the time complexity and communication complexity compared to using a Merkle tree. We begin with m (pseudo) random values, $x_1, \dots, x_\lambda \in \{0, 1\}^n$. We assume, for convenience, that λ is a power of 2. The bottom tree layer has λ *only-children* vertices. Next, we place a depth $k + 1$ balanced binary tree on top of the bottom layer vertices. We now assign values to the vertices. The bottom level λ vertices take on the values $x_1, \dots, x_\lambda$ respectively. For the layer that is directly on top of the bottom layer, we assign the n-bit value $\mathcal{H}(x_i)$ to the ith such vertex. That is, if ℓ_i' is such a vertex, then $\mathsf{Value}(\ell_i') = \mathcal{H}(x_i)$, for $1 \leq i \leq \lambda$. For the remaining vertices v, $\mathsf{Value}(v) = \mathcal{H}(\mathsf{Value}(\mathsf{C}_0(v)) \circ \mathsf{Value}(\mathsf{C}_1(v)))$. Next, we color the tree vertices. Any vertex that is a left child or an only child is colored grey. The remaining nodes (including the root) are colored white. The grey vertices are then numbered top-down from left to right. That is, the number one is assigned to the left child of the root. The number two is assigned to the left child of the left child of the root. The number three is assigned to the left child of the right child of the root, and so on. We refer to the ith grey vertex by $\mathsf{gv}(i)$. Figure 1 provides an example of a QuasiModo tree that can be used for 15 microcredit transactions; the tree is compared to a Merkle tree which would require approximately 2 times as many vertices to achieve approximately the same aim.

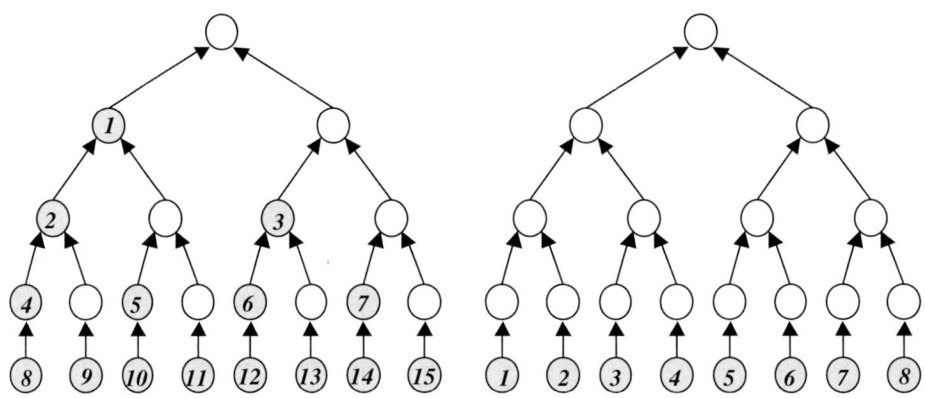

Fig. 1. On the left is a 23-vertex QuasiModo tree that can be used for 15 microcredit transactions; each interior node is assigned a value equal to the hash of its children's values. Each left child is numbered sequentially top-down, left to right. On the right is a 23-vertex Merkle tree. The basic part of the tree has 15 vertices; but 8 additional implicit vertices hang off the bottom. This tree can only be used for 8 microcredit transactions. By using interior vertices, we achieve almost twice as many microcredit transactions for the same size tree, yielding an overall efficiency improvement.

We also use the notion of the *co-nodes* for a given vertex in either a Merkle or QuasiModo tree. For a vertex v, $\mathsf{CoNodes}(v)$ is the set of siblings of the vertices on the path from v to the root. More formally, if $\mathsf{Sib}(v)$ and $\mathsf{Parent}(v)$ denote v's sibling and parent respectively, then:

$$\mathsf{CoNodes}(v) = \begin{cases} \emptyset & \text{if } v \text{ is the root} \\ \{\mathsf{Sib}(v)\} \bigcup \mathsf{CoNodes}(\mathsf{Parent}(v)) & \text{otherwise.} \end{cases} \quad (1)$$

Finally, for a set of co-nodes, we abuse notation by letting $\mathsf{Value}(\mathsf{CoNodes}(v))$ denote the values associated with the co-nodes of a vertex v.

Given the co-nodes, we may calculate the root value. Suppose that the value associated with $\mathsf{gv}(i)$ is v and suppose that the values of the siblings of all the vertices on the path from $\mathsf{gv}(i)$ to the root vertex are $v_1, \ldots, v_\ell$. Then, the root value can be calculated as h_ℓ where $h_1 = \mathcal{H}(v \circ v_1)$ and $h_i = \mathcal{H}([h_{i-1}, v_i])$ where $[h_i, v_i]$ equals $v_i \circ h_i$ if v_i is a left child or $h_i \circ v_i$ if v_i is a right child.

2.2   Our Microcredit Scheme

SET UP. During the one-time set-up phase, the following steps are performed:

1. HSP creates a public / private key pair $(\mathsf{Pk_{HSP}}, \mathsf{Sk_{HSP}})$. It provides the public key (out of band) to each user $\mathcal{U}$ and each foreign service provider FSP with which it does business.
2. Each user $\mathcal{U}$ generates a public / private key pair $(\mathsf{Pk}_{\mathcal{U}}, \mathsf{Sk}_{\mathcal{U}})$. It presents $\mathsf{Pk}_{\mathcal{U}}$ to HSP and proves that it knows the corresponding private signing key; this step can be accomplished by signing a series of challenge messages or by providing a zero-knowledge proof.
3. If $\mathcal{U}$ succesfully convinces HSP that it knows the signing key, and if the user is an authorized subscriber of HSP, then HSP first constructs certificate data $\mathsf{CertData}_{\mathcal{U}} = \langle \mathcal{U}, \mathsf{Pk}_{\mathcal{U}}, d_{exp}, d_{issue}, \Pi_{\mathcal{U}} \rangle$ where d_{exp} and d_{issue} are the date of expiration and the date of issuance of the certificate respectively, and $\Pi_{\mathcal{U}}$ is a policy specifying information regarding what services are authorized, and such information. The date of expiration can either be a numerical date or could specify that the certificate is valid for some number of time periods from the date of issuance (e.g., 365 days).
4. HSP computes $\sigma_{\mathcal{U}} = \mathsf{Sign}(\mathsf{Sk_{HSP}}, \mathsf{CertData}_{\mathcal{U}})$. It provides $\langle \sigma_{\mathcal{U}}, \mathsf{CertData}_{\mathcal{U}} \rangle$ to the user $\mathcal{U}$. Note that HSP effectively is the certificate authority in a closed public-key infrastructure.
5. $\mathcal{U}$ checks that $\mathsf{Vf}(\mathsf{Pk_{HSP}}, \mathsf{CertData}_{\mathcal{U}}, \sigma_{\mathcal{U}}) = 1$. If so, he accepts; if not, he informs HSP.

SERVICE USAGE. To use the service, $\mathcal{U}$ and FSP perform the following steps.

1. $\mathcal{U}$ estimates how much service he wishes to use in terms of the number of transactions that will take place. We denote this number by m. This estimate does not have to be accurate and the user can always generate additional microcredit tokens as we will see. Performance improves with accuracy, though the user is better off overestimating rather than underestimating.
2. $\mathcal{U}$ creates a QuasiModo tree with $(m+1)/2$ leaves (which correspond to m grey vertices). Let r denote the root of the tree. The user computes $\sigma_r = \mathsf{Sign}(\mathsf{Sk}_{\mathcal{U}}, \mathsf{FSP}, \mathsf{Value}(r))$. It sends $\langle \mathsf{Value}(r), \sigma_r, \mathsf{CertData}_{\mathcal{U}}, \sigma_{\mathcal{U}} \rangle$ to FSP and makes an official service request.
3. FSP examines $\Pi_{\mathcal{U}}$ to ascertain that $\mathcal{U}$ indeed can use the service in question. Next, FSP verifies that $d_{issue} < d_{exp}$ on the certificate data $\mathsf{CertData}_{\mathcal{U}}$. Finally, it checks if the signatures of HSP and $\mathcal{U}$ are valid. If these check out correctly, it grants the service request. Otherwise, it follows an appropriate policy, like refusing service. Also, if the certificate scheme incorporates some revocation mechanism, then the certificate's status should be checked. The process by which that is done is essentially orthogonal to the present scheme.
4. At each period i, if the user wishes to continue service, it provides FSP with the ith microcredit token $\mathsf{Value}(\mathsf{gv}(i))$ as well as $\mathsf{Value}(\mathsf{Sib}(\mathsf{gv}(i)))$ (if the latter exists).

5. FSP computes $hv = \mathcal{H}(\mathsf{Value}(\mathsf{gv}(i)) \circ \mathsf{Value}(\mathsf{Sib}(\mathsf{gv}(i))))$, if $i \leq (m-1)/2$, or simply $hv = \mathcal{H}(\mathsf{Value}(\mathsf{gv}(i)))$ otherwise. If i is even, FSP checks if $hv = \mathsf{Value}(\mathsf{gv}(i/2))$. Otherwise, it checks if $hv = \mathsf{Value}(\mathsf{Sib}(\mathsf{gv}((i-1)/2)))$. Observe that FSP can perform these computations since it received $\mathsf{Value}(\mathsf{gv}(i/2))$ and $\mathsf{Value}(\mathsf{Sib}(\mathsf{gv}((i-1)/2)))$ at iteration $\lfloor i/2 \rfloor$. If these checks succeed, FSP accepts $\mathcal{U}$'s token. Otherwise, it rejects the token and applies an appropriate policy, like terminating service, perhaps with some advance warning.

If $\mathcal{U}$ runs out of tokens, he creates another QuasiModo tree, signs the root, and provides the relevant information to FSP. This results in an extra signature computation and verification, so is not desirable. However, since hashing is much less expensive than signing, $\mathcal{U}$ can take precautions by generating a larger number of coins, with minimal penalty[2].

BILL RECONCILIATION.   To reconcile and appropriately bill $\mathcal{U}$, the following steps are taken.

1. Suppose service ends after t intervals. Then FSP has received $\mathsf{Value}(\mathsf{gv}(t))$. It transmits $\langle t, \mathsf{Value}(r), \sigma_r, \mathsf{Value}(\mathsf{gv}(t)), \mathsf{Value}(\mathsf{CoNodes}(\mathsf{gv}(t))), \mathcal{U} \rangle$ to HSP. Note that FSP received the co-node values in earlier iterations.
2. HSP first determines whether the user was allowed to access the service in question, and checks to see that he has a valid certificate. Next, it checks that $\mathsf{Vf}(\mathsf{Pk}_{\mathcal{U}}, \mathsf{FSP}, \mathsf{Value}(r), \sigma_r) = 1$. Finally, HSP computes the root of the QuasiModo tree using the co-nodes it received, and it checks that this root matches the root value that FSP provided. If these computations check out, HSP bills $\mathcal{U}$ for t intervals of service from FSP. In theory these checks should not fail since HSP is effectively performing the identical steps that FSP performed earlier. But of course, in practice, something else may go wrong. So, should any checks fail, HSP would follow some appropriate policy; for example, HSP and FSP may determine what caused the failure. If it was because FSP accepted an incorrect token, or failed to perform a computation correctly, then FSP may be penalized.

DISPUTE RESOLUTION.   If there is a billing dispute in the sense that a user claims to be billed for more service than was utilized, then both HSP and FSP can provide a proof of the correct amount by presenting $\langle t, \mathsf{Value}(r), \sigma_r, \mathsf{Value}(\mathsf{gv}(t)), \mathsf{Value}(\mathsf{CoNodes}(\mathsf{gv}(t))) \rangle$. We later show that if the root value computed utilizing $\mathsf{Value}(\mathsf{gv}(t))$ and $\mathsf{Value}(\mathsf{CoNodes}(\mathsf{gv}(t)))$ matches $\mathsf{Value}(r)$, and $\mathsf{Vf}(\mathsf{Pk}_{\mathcal{U}}, \mathsf{Value}(r), \sigma_r) = 1$ then, it either follows that $\mathsf{Value}(\mathsf{gv}(t))$ was known to FSP or HSP, or that a collision was found in $\mathcal{H}$. Assuming that $\mathcal{H}$ is collision resistant, it must be the case that FSP or HSP received $\mathsf{Value}(\mathsf{gv}(t))$. Since this value was secretly generated by $\mathcal{U}$ and not revealed previously, it must be the case that the user transmitted it.

---

[2] Observe that one distinct advantage of using QuasiModo trees is that verification time is proportional to the logarithm of the grey vertex number. If one were to try using regular trees, then the verification time would be proportional to the *entire height* of the tree. The latter will be larger if the user generates many more coins than he eventually uses.

3   Discussion and Analysis

PERFORMANCE. Our microcredit scheme is efficient in terms of both computation and communication, especially when Quasimodo trees are used. If $\mathcal{U}$ spends t microcredits from a single hash tree with FSP during a session, then at the end of the session, FSP only needs to store at most $\lfloor \log t \rfloor + 2$ node values corresponding to the values of the tth grey vertex and its co-nodes, regardless of the size of the full hash tree. Similarly, FSP's transmission of the tth microcredit to HSP consumes $O(\log t)$ bandwidth, and HSP can verify the microcredit using $O(\log t)$ computation. With an m-token Merkle trees, FSP would have to store $1 + \log_2 m$ values. Note that $m \geq t$. Moreover, m is an upper bound on the number of tokens the user believes he will use.

Now, we compare the bandwidth consumption of using QuasiModo trees versus Merkle trees. For m microcredit tokens, the corresponding QuasiModo tree has $(3m + 1)/2$ vertices (since there are $(m + 1)/2$ leaves and m interior nodes); if all tokens are spent, the total number of proof node values transmitted is $(3m - 1)/2$ since we do not have to count the root. For m transactions, the amortized proof size is $3/2 - 1/2m$ hash values per transaction. Assuming caching we will always send exactly 2 values for the first $(m - 1)/2$ transactions and 1 value for the remaining $(m + 1)/2$ transactions. For a simple Merkle-tree we have $3m - 1$ vertices; where $2m - 1$ vertices are part of the basic tree, and m vertices are attached to the bottom of the tree. Again, ignoring the root value, the total number of proof node values transmitted is $3m - 2$. Thus, the amortized proof size of m transactions is $3 - \frac{2}{m}$. Therefore, the improvement factor of using QuasiModo trees is $2 - \frac{2}{3m-1}$ which approaches 2 as m increases. In practice, however, the effects may be more pronounced for two reasons. The first is that the above improvement factor assumes that all m microcredit tokens are spent. Recall, however, that in our scheme the user generates a QuasiModo tree where the number of encoded tokens is an upper bound on what he wishes to spend. For a QuasiModo tree only one or two values are sent even if this upper bound is never reached, whereas for a Merkle-tree based scheme, the penalty is more severe since the proof size is related to the tree height. The second reason is that Merkle tree proof sizes vary with each iteration – going up to $1 + \log_2 m$. This variance is more likely to increase the packet count and hence the transmission time; we discuss this concept in more detail shortly.

Next, let us compare the time complexity of verifying QuasiModo proofs versus Merkle-tree proofs. As we observed, for m tokens either one or two values are sent, so we only require a single call to a cryptographic compression function to verify it, assuming that FSP caches the hash values it receives. We compute the total proof verification time for a Merkle tree as follows. For each of the m vertices attached to the bottom of the tree, one compression function call is required. Next, for the vertices above the bottom, one compression function call is required for each interior node. Since there are $m - 1$ such nodes, $m - 1$ compression function calls are required. The total number of calls is thus $2m - 1$. So, the improvement factor from using QuasiModo trees is $2 - \frac{1}{m}$ which approaches 2 as m gets large.

A potential drawback of the QuasiModo approach is that FSP has to cache many of the hash values $\mathcal{U}$ transmits in order to achieve $O(1)$ time complexity for verification. In the worst case, for a QuasiModo tree with m grey vertices, FSP may have to cache $(m+1)/2$ vertex values (corresponding to the values of the vertices one level from the bottom). For reasonable parameters values, this might not be a problem. For example, suppose that there are 5,000 users, each of whom are simultaneously looking to access 2047-units of service from FSP. These numbers are conservative since an FSP might be accessed in a manner that is local to a smaller population group, such as via a base station, so the number of simultaneous users is unlikely to be 5,000; moreover since 2047 transactions at 5-second intervals would provide close to three hours of continuous service, it is even less likely that all 5,000 users will want this much service (especially in the mobile setting). If we use SHA-1 as the underlying hash function (with a 20-byte output), then in the absolute worst case, FSP would have to cache $(2047 + 1)/2 \times 5000 \times 20$ bytes – which is approximately 100MB. This amount is negligible (on the order of $1/50^{th}$ of 1%) with respect to the cache size on a carrier-grade server, which is usually on the order of several hundred gigabytes.

Observe that a micropayment or microcredit approach using pure hash chains only requires one hash value to be transmitted per microcredit, and only requires that FSP store a single hash value and that only a single hash value is transmitted between FSP and $\mathcal{U}$; however, HSP's costs are considerable: its computation cost is $O(t)$ per user. When you consider that a sizeable service provider may have millions of users, and when you imagine a situation in which a token is sent for every packet transmitted or for every few seconds of service, the resulting computation is enormous. Also, we remark that saving 20-bytes of communication, as one may sometimes achieve in a chain-based scheme while desirable, in theory, is unlikely to lead a direct performance improvement in practice. In particular, as observed by [4], communication complexity, in practice, is measured by the number of packets transmitted rather than bits transmitted. Consider that the average sized TCP packet is 536-bytes (after removing 20-bytes each for the TCP and IP packet headers) and packet sizes up to approximately 1500 bytes (the maximum ethernet packet size) are reasonable especially if some form of path maximum transmission unit detection has taken place to ensure that the packets will not get fragmented. So, with packet sizes that are much larger than 20-bytes, it is likely that one can find a place for the hash value without requiring the transmission of any extra packets.

SECURITY ANALYSIS. We will prove the following two theorems regarding the security properties of interest. We assume that adversaries are resource bounded and can neither compromise the security of the underlying signature scheme $\mathcal{DS}$ nor can they find collisions or pre-images in the hash function $\mathcal{H}$, except with negligible probability.

Theorem 1. *Assuming that $\mathcal{H}$ is a one-way collision-resistant hash function and that $\mathcal{DS}$ is a secure signature scheme,* FSP *will not be able to overcharge the user, except with negligible probability.*

Proof. (Sketch) We first consider the slightly more complex case that $\mathcal{U}$ did not use all the microcredit tokens it generated. Suppose $\mathcal{U}$ used t units of service, but FSP tried to pass a charge of $t + \Delta$. FSP would then need to transmit

$$\langle t + \Delta, \mathsf{Value}(r), \sigma_r, \mathsf{Value}'(\mathsf{gv}(t + \Delta)), \mathsf{Value}'(\mathsf{CoNodes}(\mathsf{gv}(t + \Delta))), \mathcal{U} \rangle$$

to HSP, and have HSP accept it as valid. Assuming that $\mathcal{DS}$ is a secure signature scheme, it follows that to overcharge the user, FSP must construct its own vertex values that may not correspond to actual values computed by $\mathcal{U}$ at those vertices. Here $\mathsf{Value}'(\mathsf{gv}(t + \Delta))$, and $\mathsf{Value}'(\mathsf{CoNodes}(\mathsf{gv}(t + \Delta)))$ denote these spurious values. However, HSP uses these values to compute the root and matches it against r. Let $v = \mathsf{Value}'(\mathsf{gv}(t + \Delta))$ and let $r_1', \ldots r_\ell'$ denote the values of the co-nodes ordered along the siblings of the vertices on the path from the vertex to the root. First note that if ℓ is greater than the depth of the original tree, then that implies FSP inverted $\mathcal{H}$ at a random point, which we assume to be infeasible. So, let us suppose ℓ is bounded by the depth of the original tree. Now, let $r_1, \ldots, r_\ell$ denote the *actual values* corresponding to what $\mathcal{U}$ generated in the tree. If for all $i \in \{1, \ldots, \ell\}$, it holds that $r_i = r_i'$, then it follows that FSP correctly computed a pre-image of $\mathcal{H}$ since $\mathcal{U}$ never revealed all the r_i. This event only happens with negligible probability since $\mathcal{H}$ is a one-way collision-resistant cryptographic hash function.

So, suppose that the r_i and r_i' are not all equal. In that case, we can show that FSP is able to compute a collision in $\mathcal{H}$. Now, because the r_i' can verified as hashing to root, it follows that the root value can be calculated as h_ℓ' where $h_1' = \mathcal{H}(\mathsf{Value}'(\mathsf{gv}(t + \Delta))) \circ r_1')$, and $h_i' = \mathcal{H}([h_{i-1}', r_i'])$ for $i \in \{1, \ldots, \ell\}$. Likewise, the same root value can be calculated as h_ℓ where $h_1 = \mathcal{H}(\mathsf{Value}(\mathsf{gv}(t + \Delta)) \circ r_1)$, and $h_i = \mathcal{H}([h_{i-1}, r_i])$. Moreover, because both calculations should yield the same committed root value, it follows that $h_\ell = \mathsf{Value}(r) = h_\ell'$. Now since the r_i and r_i' are distinct, but $h_\ell = h_\ell'$, it follows that there is some index $j \in \{1, \ldots, \ell\}$ for which $h_j' = h_j$, but $(h_{j-1}, r_j) \neq (h_{j-1}', r_j')$. In that case, we have a collision since by definition

$$\begin{aligned} h_j' &= \mathcal{H}([h_{j-1}', r_j']) \\ &= \mathcal{H}([h_{j-1}, r_j]) \\ &= h_j. \end{aligned}$$

However, the inputs to $\mathcal{H}$ are distinct. We have therefore violated the collision-resistance property of $\mathcal{H}$, which can only happen with negligible probability. In the remaining case where $\mathcal{U}$ used up all microcredit tokens, the only mechanism for overcharging is to produce a spurious vertex that is one level below the actual leaf. The value for such a vertex constitutes a preimage for the leaf value. Since the leaf value is picked randomly, it would follow that FSP inverted $\mathcal{H}$ at a random point, which only happens with negligible probability, by one-way-ness.

Theorem 2. *Assuming that $\mathcal{H}$ is a one-way collision-resistant hash function and that $\mathcal{DS}$ is a secure signature scheme, $\mathcal{U}$ will not be able to use services for which he has not otherwise paid, except with negligible probability.*

Proof. (Sketch) This property is easy to verify since the user must present a well-formed token at each interval; any attempt to use more service than is paid for would imply that a well-formed microcredit token *was not* sent at a given interval. In such a case, FSP would immediately identify it and follow the appropriate policy.

4   Tradeoffs

MICROCREDIT SIZE VS. VERIFICATION TIME (FOR HSP). In a Quasimodo tree, the kth microcredit consists of $O(\log k)$ node values and may be verified in $O(\log k)$ time; a hash chain has constant size, but requires $O(k)$ verification time. We can find tradeoffs in between by replacing each node in a binary tree with a hash chain. If each chain has length ℓ, we get a hybrid Quasimodo / hash-chain microcredit scheme, where the size of the kth microcredit is at most $1 + \log(k/\ell)$ and the verification time is at most $\ell \log(k/\ell)$.

TREE TRAVERSAL BY THE USER. One potential shortcoming of QuasiModo trees when using breadth-first enumeration of the nodes is that "tree traversal" is somewhat expensive for $\mathcal{U}$. At one extreme, $\mathcal{U}$ may cache all of the node values so that each microcredit is ready to transmit without any recomputation. At the other extreme, $\mathcal{U}$ may cache no node values; however, in the worst case, computing a microcredit requires $O(n)$ recomputation. In between these extremes, we can view the tree as consisting of $L = (\log n)/h$ levels, where each level consists of subtrees of height h. Instead of enumerating individual nodes breadth-first, we may order the subtrees in a breadth-first manner, adjusting the numbering of individual nodes accordingly. Such an enumeration allows a $O(h2^h) : O(n/2^{2h})$ memory-computation tradeoff. Although this may be reasonable for some values (especially for small values of L like 2 or 3) this does not compare favorably with the tradeoff elegantly achieved by Jakobsson et al. [7] for traversing Merkle trees – namely, $\frac{3}{2} \log^2 n / \log \log n$ memory and $2 \log n / \log \log n$ computation.

It turns out that, using QuasiModo trees, one can improve upon Jakobsson et al.'s tradeoff. To do this, the nodes of the tree are numbered according to a pre-order traversal; that is, the parent is numbered first, then the left descendants, and then right descendants. The kth microcredit consists of the kth node's children, along with the kth node's co-nodes. This enumeration retains the benefit of unit transmission cost for $\mathcal{U}$ and unit verification cost for FSP, but it is possible that the kth microcredit's verification path is longer than $\log k$.

The tree is traversed using essentially the same approach as in [7], except that each output requires only one unit of the *TREEHASH* algorithm for each subtree (rather than two units). At a very intuitive level, the reason is that QuasiModo trees, unlike Merkle trees, make full use of internal nodes. For a tree in which computing the root node value requires n hashes, QuasiModo squeezes out n microcredits, while Merkle trees only get $\lfloor \frac{n+1}{2} \rfloor$. This doubling carries over into the traversal algorithm computation, so that QuasiModo requires half the computation per microcredit.

5   Extensions

INCORPORATING POLLING.   We may incorporate polling into our schemes to lower computational effort, at an increased risk of fraud, in two places. First, when FSP receives microcredits from $\mathcal{U}$, it can choose whether to immediately verify each token according to some probability (this does not apply to the first and last tokens, which should always be verified). If $\mathcal{U}$ tries to cheat, then at the very least, he will either be caught when the last token is verified, or there will at least be some prior valid token that can be used to bill $\mathcal{U}$. If FSP keeps track of such user behavior, it can tailor the polling probability dynamically.

We may also incorporate polling into the bill reconciliation phase. In particular, suppose s users have finished accessing the service through FSP. Suppose further that the roots on the QuasiModo trees they generate are $r_1, \ldots, r_s$, respectively and that the amount of service they use is $t_1, \ldots, t_s$, respectively. At bill reconciliation time, FSP first sends $\langle \mathsf{Value}(r_1), t_1 \rangle, \ldots, \langle \mathsf{Value}(r_s), t_s \rangle$ to HSP. Next, HSP picks a set of k indices $i_1, \ldots, i_k \in \{1, \ldots, s\}$ and sends these to FSP. Finally, FSP transmits

$$\langle t_{i_j}, \mathsf{Value}(r_{i_j}), \sigma_{r_{i_j}}, \mathsf{Value}(\mathsf{gv}(t_{i_j})), \mathsf{Value}(\mathsf{CoNodes}(\mathsf{gv}(t_{i_j}))), \mathcal{U}_j \rangle,$$

for $j \in \{1, \ldots, k\}$. These constitute the values he was prepared to send HSP anyway; however because he sent $\langle \mathsf{Value}(r_1), t_1 \rangle, \ldots, \langle \mathsf{Value}(r_s), t_s \rangle$ in the first phase, he *committed* himself. Now, HSP verifies the transmitted values as he normally would. If any of these checks fail, he will request the remainder and possibly penalize FSP. If there is later a dispute that arises from one of $\mathcal{U}_{i_1} \ldots, \mathcal{U}_{i_s}$, it can by handled by HSP directly. If, on the other hand, there is a dispute for another user, HSP can then request the information regarding that user from FSP. If FSP cheated, then it will be caught now since it already *committed* to $r_1, \ldots, r_s$. On the other hand, if FSP is honest, it will be able to produce the usage proof for the other user.

MICROPAYMENTS USING QUASIMODO. We may directly use QuasiModo trees in a micropayment scheme. The advantage of such a scheme over, say, Payword is that the computation required by the bank to validate coins sent by a merchant is only logarithmic in the number of coins spent, rather than linear. At the same time, the communication complexity between the merchant and user is constant, as is the time complexity of the work the merchant and user both have to do.

PAYTREE USING QUASIMODO. Paytree [9] extends Payword [19] to allow a single tree and signature to be used for multiple merchants. In one variation, specified in the original paper, each leaf of the tree is a PayWord hash chain associated with a single merchant. Obviously, we can reduce the bank's verification time if each merchant is, instead, associated with a QuasiModo subtree of the Paytree.

CUSTOMER ANONYMITY. If $\mathcal{U}$ uses a conventional signature scheme, and $\mathcal{U}$'s public signing key is certified in a normal fashion, then $\mathcal{U}$'s transactions with FSP are not anonymous. If we wish to achieve some degree of anonymity between

$\mathcal{U}$ and FSP, we may do so through the use of *group signatures;* for example, we may use the scheme of [2], which is the current state of the art. Then, each user $\mathcal{U}$ registers with HSP, who acts as a group manager, to establish its signing key. We may have separate classes of group public keys corresponding to different credit levels. When requesting service from FSP, $\mathcal{U}$ signs the root of a hash tree with its signing key. FSP can check that $\mathcal{U}$ is indeed in the group managed by HSP, and that HSP has given $\mathcal{U}$ sufficient credit; so, it can accept microcredits from $\mathcal{U}$ up to that amount. On the other hand, because a group signature scheme is used, FSP will not know $\mathcal{U}$'s identity. At bill reconciliation time, FSP will, as usual, relay $\mathcal{U}$'s signature to HSP, who can then "open" the signature to determine $\mathcal{U}$'s identity and charge the account accordingly.

If it is really desired, the customer can achieve anonymity even with respect to HSP if HSP signs the root value using a blind signature. With such a micropayment scheme, the customer can then give these coins to an FSP without fear that HSP and FSP can collude to map transactions to customers.

However, we stress that in both cases, there is some degree of *linkability* between individual transactions in a given session since all the hash values are anchored to the root of the same tree. However, between sessions themselves, there is no linkability.

VARIATIONS ON QUASIMODO TREES. One can imagine slight variations on QuasiModo trees. For example, instead of having a binary tree, one can have a k-ary tree. We could not find any meaningful advantage to such an approach since the number of co-nodes for a vertex is proportional to the tree degree. Thus, for a k-ary tree, the ith grey vertex will have proof size $O(k \log_k i)$.

Another variation is to apply a different coloring of the vertices. In our case we colored every left child, however, we may instead pick a child arbitrarily and color it grey, while making its sibling white. One can extend our schemes to this setting.

In a similar vein, we may want to consider a different numbering of the grey vertices. For example, if we number vertices depth first rather than breadth first, then FSP only has to cache at most $O(\log_2 m)$ values where m is the size of the tree. However, the disadvantage of this approach is that the deeper the vertex, the longer the associated proof – with the maximum proof size being $O(\log_2 m)$ for a leaf. By numbering breadth first, we may never have to present leaf vertices in a microcredit transaction.

Acknowledgements

We thank Alejandro Hevia and Ravi Jain for a number of helpful discussions on the microcredits scheme and for comments on early drafts of this manuscript. We also thank Markus Jakobsson, Helger Lipmaa, and Stuart Stubblebine for helpful discussions at the conference. We finally thank the anonymous referees for a number of excellent and thoughtful comments.

References

1. R. Anderson, H. Manifavas, and C. Sutherland. A Practical Electronic Cash System. Manuscript, 1995.
2. G. Ateniese, J. Camenisch, M. Joye, and G. Tsudik. A Practical and Provably Secure Coalition-Resistant Group Signature Scheme. In *Proc. of CRYPTO 2000.*
3. I. Damgård. A Design Principle for Hash Functions. In *Proc. of CRYPTO '89.*
4. F. Elwailly, C. Gentry, and Z. Ramzan. QuasiModo: Efficient Certificate Validation and Revocation. In *Proc. of Public-Key Cryptography 2004.*
5. S. Goldwasser, S. Micali, and R. L. Rivest. A Digital Signature Scheme Secure Against Adaptive Chosen-Message Attacks. *SIAM Journal on Computing,* 17(2):281–308, 1988.
6. M. Jakobsson, J-P.Hubaux, and L. Buttyan. A Micropayment Scheme Encouraging Collaboration in Multi-Hop Cellular Networks. In *Proc. of Financial Cryptography '03.*
7. M. Jakobsson, T. Leighton, S. Micali, and M. Szydlo. Fractal Merkle Tree Representation and Traversal. In *Proc. of the Cryptographer's Track, RSA Conference, '03.*
8. S. Jarecki and A. Odlyzko. An Efficient Micropayment System Based on Probabilistic Polling. In *Proc. of Financial Cryptography '97.*
9. C. Jutla and M. Yung. PayTree: Amortized Signatures for flexible Micropayments. In *Proc. of USENIX workshop on Electronic Commerce, '96.*
10. S. Labaton. MCI Faces Federal Fraud Inquiry on Fees for Long-Distance Calls. *New York Times,* 2003. July 27.
11. R. J. Lipton and R. Ostrovsky. Micro-Payments via Efficient Coin Flipping. In *Proc. of Financial Cryptography '98.*
12. R. Merkle. One-way hash functions and DES. In *Proc. of CRYPTO '89.*
13. R. Merkle. Protocols for Public-Key Cryptography. In *Proc. IEEE Symposium on Security and Privacy, '80.*
14. National Institute of Standards. FIPS 180-1: Secure Hash Standard. 1995.
15. T. Pedersen. Electronic Payments of Small Amounts. In *Proc. of Security Protocols Workshop, '96.*
16. T. Pedersen. Electronic Payments of Small Amounts. Technical Report 495, DAIMI PD, Aarhus University, August 1995.
17. M. Pierce and D. O'Mahony. Micropayments for Mobile Networks. In *Proceedings of European Wireless, '99.*
18. R.L. Rivest. Electronic Lottery Tickets as Micropayments. In *Proc. of Financial Cryptography, '97.*
19. R.L. Rivest and A. Shamir. PayWord and MicroMint–Two Simple Micropayment Schemes. *CryptoBytes (RSA Laboratories),* 2(1), 1996. Proc. of Security Protocols Workshop '96.
20. H. Tewari and D. O'Mahony. Multiparty Micropayments for Ad-Hoc Networks. In *Proc. of IEEE Wireless Communications and Networking Conference, '03.*
21. H. Tewari and D. O'Mahony. Real-Time Payments for Mobile IP. *IEEE Communications,* 41(2):126–136, 2003.
22. D. Wheeler. Transactions Using Bets. In *Proc. Security Protocols Workshop, '96.*
23. J. Zhou and K-Y. Lam. Undeniable Billing in Mobile Communication. In *Proc. of MOBICOM, '96.*

A Privacy-Friendly Loyalty System
Based on Discrete Logarithms over Elliptic Curves

Matthias Enzmann, Marc Fischlin⋆, and Markus Schneider

Fraunhofer Gesellschaft (FhG), Institute for Secure Telecooperation (SIT)
Dolivostr. 15, D-64293 Darmstadt, Germany
firstname.lastname@sit.fraunhofer.de

Abstract. Systems for the support of customer relationship management are becoming increasingly attractive for vendors. Loyalty systems provide an interesting possibility for vendors in customer relationship management. This holds for both real world and online vendors. However, beside some potential benefits of a loyalty system, customers may also fear an invasion into their privacy, and may thus refuse to participate in such programs. In this paper, we present a privacy-friendly loyalty system to be used by online vendors to issue loyalty points. The system prevents vendors from exploiting data for the creation of customer profiles by providing unconditional unlinkability of loyalty points with regard to purchases. In the proposed system, we apply the difficulty for the computation of discrete logarithms in a group of prime order to construct a secure and privacy-friendly counter. More precisely, all computations are carried out over special cryptographic groups based on elliptic curves where the decisional Diffie-Hellman problems can be solved easily while the computational Diffie-Hellman is believed to be hard.

1 Introduction

The World Wide Web has evolved to a business platform with worldwide reach and 24h/7 service for selling various kinds of goods. Presently, more than 600 millions of people have access to this business platform and thus, are potential customers for online vendors. Naturally, every online vendor's interest lies in attracting new customers and increasing the base of loyal customers. Since loyal customers create regular revenues, the goal of online vendors, as well as real-world vendors, is to turn occasional customers into loyal ones. Thus, in the past, online and real-world vendors have introduced loyalty programs, e.g., frequent flyer programs or online consumer reward systems.

Aside from customer retention, another incentive for vendors is to learn more about their customers to exploit this information for purposes, such as customer profiling, data mining, or direct marketing. Thus, from the customer's perspective, loyalty programs have two sides. On the one hand, customers value the financial benefits, on the other hand, they may fear an infringement of their privacy. Hence, if privacy concerns outweigh the expected benefits from the loyalty program the vendor's strategy for attracting and retaining customers will fail. Thus, if privacy is a barrier for customers to

---

⋆ Now at Department of Computer Science and Engineering, University of California, San Diego, USA. Most of work done while at Fraunhofer-Institute for Secure Telecooperation.

A. Juels (Ed.): FC 2004, LNCS 3110, pp. 24–38, 2004.

participate in the program, it may be worthwhile for vendors to reconsider their strategy of collecting personal data. Indeed, according to [18, 22], there are many customers that are concerned about their privacy in electronic commerce scenarios. Thus, privacy-friendly loyalty systems might be of particular interest to vendors in order to gain a competitive advantage.

In this work, we deal with loyalty systems in which customers receive points from vendors for their purchases. Points can be redeemed at the vendor's in exchange for a reward. Usually, a reward can be obtained when a customer has reached a pre-defined number of loyalty points.

In order to enhance privacy for the customers, the vendor must not be able to generate consumer profiles by linking customers' transactions through the loyalty program. Thus, it is our goal to prevent the vendor from using loyalty points to link any two customer transactions. Hence, when points are handed in by the customer, it is not possible for the vendor to determine the purchases in which the points were obtained. Of course this is only meaningful if there is no other linking information available to the vendor outside the loyalty system. In addition to unlinkability of points to transactions, there are security requirements with respect to unforgeability of points and preventing that the same points are redeemed more than once.

The privacy-friendly loyalty system presented here uses an efficient variant of blind signatures which are based on discrete logarithms in groups of prime order. All computations are done in special cryptographic groups based on elliptic curves that allow to decide easily whether three given group elements form a Diffie-Hellman triple, while both the computational Diffie-Hellman and the Discrete Logarithm problem are conceivably intractable [19, 20]. We propose a counter-based solution in which multiplications in the elliptic curve are iteratively applied for each loyalty point that is issued. As it turns out, this yields more efficient solutions than with straightforward application of blind signatures (called token-based system), yet it also entangles the design and security analysis. Furthermore, in contrast to such a token-based system, the proposed counter-based system prevents different customers from pooling their loyalty points since values of different counters cannot be added up. In the redeem transaction, the counter which represents the loyalty points collected by a customer can be efficiently verified in one step by the vendor. The proposed loyalty system provides unconditional unlinkability of loyalty points with regard to purchases.

The paper is organized as follows. Section 2 gives some background on loyalty systems. In section 3 we define essential privacy and security requirements for loyalty systems. Section 4 provides necessary background on elliptic curves and proposes the protocols of our loyalty system. In section 5, we consider the properties of the proposed system. Related work is discussed in section 6, before we draw some conclusions.

2   Loyalty Programs

A loyalty program is a structured marketing effort which rewards, and therefore encourages, loyal behaviour of customers, which is hopefully beneficial to the vendor [28]. We say that a customer is loyal if she has a strong attitude to a certain vendor over its competitors. The motivation of vendors for adopting a loyalty program is, in general, twofold. First, vendors want to retain present customers and stimulate repeated purchase behaviour which would guarantee regular future earnings. And second, they want to learn more about their customers in order to refine their business strategy.

In general, the basic conditions for loyal customer behaviour in the real world are different from the electronic world [26]. Connecting to a vendor's site is as easy as connecting to its competitor's site. This is in contrast to the real world where barriers exist, such as geographical distance or an existing inter-personal relationship between customer and shop personnel, that may prevent customers from instantly switching vendors. Thus, online vendors must be even more interested in loyalty programs than their real-world counterparts.

There are different types of loyalty programs, e.g., reward systems and virtual communities. Reward systems give program members a financial incentive. They can be classified according to the time the reward is given relative to the purchase. There are immediate reward systems, e.g., price promotions or rebates through membership credit cards, and delayed reward systems, e.g., point collecting programs like frequent flyer miles or "buy 10 get one free". Virtual communities focus on social and service aspects, e.g., online discussion panels on product related problems.

There are some variants for point-based loyalty programs. The number of points awarded to the customer may depend on the monetary value of a purchase, e.g., one point for each Euro spent, or it may depend on specific types of products, e.g., after having bought 10 mp3 files one can download one for free. Furthermore, we can categorize point programs according to the way points are collected. In a token-based approach, for each awarded point a token is issued, e.g., chips issued by a supermarket, while in a counter-based approach the number of points to be obtained is added to the current point balance, e.g., frequent flyer miles.

Members of loyalty programs have a greater propensity to be loyal to the vendor and also have an increased usage frequency compared to non-members [28]. Furthermore, it can be assumed that members are less willing to try offers of competing vendors, even when negative experiences with the vendor occur since these effects are moderated by the loyalty program membership [5]. According to [14], loyalty program members are also less price sensitive, spend more money and are more likely to pass on positive recommendations than non-members.

The customer information gathered in loyalty programs can be used by the vendor for direct marketing, data mining, and customer profiling in order to promote products, infer new customer data, and optimize their range of products, respectively. This means that vendors have a large consumer database where they record every single transaction of their customers. Thus, common loyalty programs do not look so bright anymore from the customer's perspective since they may see this monitoring as an invasion to their privacy. In this context, customers may fear losing control over their personal data, since vendors may disclose their data to other parties. Clearly, customer loyalty strongly depends on the customers' trust in the vendor. Thus, if customers are convinced that they participate in a privacy-friendly loyalty program their loyalty may even increase. In this paper, we propose a point-based loyalty system which may lead to increased customer loyalty due to enhanced privacy.

3   Requirements

When designing electronic loyalty systems, both customers' and vendors' interests need to be taken into account. There are requirements such as customer privacy and security regarding the unforgeability of loyalty points that must be considered. In the following, we describe requirements that a loyalty system must fulfill.

Privacy. Customers have the fundamental requirement to protect their privacy. In our context, this means that it should not be possible for the vendor to create customer profiles from the awarding and redeeming processes of loyalty points. More precisely, it should not be possible for the vendor to link any two customer transactions by means of the loyalty system. This includes both awarding or redeeming transactions. This means, given a redeeming transaction, the vendor should be prevented from linking it to the corresponding awarding transactions and to other redeeming transactions of the same customer. And likewise, given an awarding transaction, the vendor cannot link it to awarding and redeeming transactions of the same customer. Note that we focus only on the loyalty systems' properties that are necessary to achieve unlinkability. Clearly, linkability may be possible outside the loyalty system. However, preventing this is out of scope of this work. In order to achieve unlinkability for electronic purchases in general, additional technologies have to be used, e.g., unlinkability of search and order phases proposed in [16], payment systems that allow the customer to remain anonymous with respect to the vendor [12, 9], anonymity networks as in [11, 27], or privacy-friendly delivery in case of hard goods similar to the approach proposed in [15].

Security. The security requirements considered here can be summarized as *system integrity*. The property of system integrity in the context of a point-based loyalty system means that no other party beside the vendor should be able to create valid loyalty points. We have several aspects of system integrity that need to be considered.

Unforgeability. Loyalty points may only be created by the vendor himself, i.e., customers should not be able to produce them. At the very least, the vendor should be able to tell false points from genuine ones.

Double-spending detection. In contrast to real-world loyalty points, their electronic counterparts can be easily copied and are indistinguishable. As a consequence, parties may try to hand-in copies of loyalty points at the vendor's. Thus, we require that it must be *detectable* whether loyalty points have been spent before.

Pooling prevention. In general, vendors do not want different customers to pool their loyalty points in order to jointly achieve the redeem threshold. Thus, the loyalty system should prevent successful pooling, e.g., it should be impossible for two users to transform their individual counter values of, say, 5 into a joint counter of 10. Note that this does not address the problem of colluding customers sharing a counter; the latter cannot be prevented in systems with perfect privacy.

4   Construction of the Loyalty System

In this section, we present the counter-based loyalty system. Before presenting the protocols, we introduce the specific type of elliptic curves our scheme relies on and some important facts. Using these curves allows customers in our construction to verify the validity of issued loyalty points as will become clear later.

4.1 Elliptic Curves

Elliptic curves provide an alternative to well-known groups based on modular arithmetic over the integers. Compared to cryptographic operations like RSA over $\mathbb{Z}_N^*$ or Diffie-Hellman over $\mathbb{Z}_p^*$ elliptic curves usually offer smaller key sizes at a comparable security level. Nonetheless, our motivation for basing our protocol on elliptic curves stems from a recently discovered property of some of these curves. Namely, we deploy special elliptic curves for which the *computational* Diffie-Hellman problem (given g, g^a, g^b determine g^{ab}) is believed to be intractable, whereas the *decisional* Diffie-Hellman problem (given g, g^a, g^b, g^c decide if $g^c = g^{ab}$) is known to be easy[1]. Such elliptic curves have been suggested only recently [19, 20] but have immediately gained a lot of attention because of their usefulness for the design of cryptographic protocols, e.g., [6, 7, 4, 13].

The decision procedure for elliptic curves separating the computational and the decisional Diffie-Hellman problem is usually based on the so-called Weil or Tate pairing. These pairings can be carried out efficiently and allow to decide whether a given tuple constitutes a correct DH triple or not. We omit further technical details as they are irrelevant for the conceptual design of our loyalty system here. Nonetheless, we remark that such curves have already been investigated quite well, in particular with respect to

- appropriate choices of such groups in light of efficiency and security (note that the computational DH problem must still be intractable for the group) [20, 7];
- fast computation of the pairing functions [6, 1, 17], i.e., fast verification of putative DH triples (g^a, g^b, g^c);
- hashing into the curve [7]; that is, how to define a hash function H mapping bit strings to the group.

Since we merely apply these properties we refer to these works for details. For an introduction to elliptic curves see [25].

4.2 Protocols

The loyalty scheme consists of two protocols, the *issue* and *redeem* protocol. Both protocols involve two parties, the vendor and the customer. The goal of our construction is to achieve the unlinkability of issue and redeem and also the unlinkability of any two issue transactions and any two redeem transactions.

Initialization. The system is set up as follows. The vendor chooses an appropriate elliptic curve for which the decisional Diffie-Hellman problem can be decided efficiently but for which the computational Diffie-Hellman problem is presumably hard. The order of the group should be a sufficiently large prime q for which we will later specify another condition, namely, that $q - 1$ does not have small prime factors (see Section 5.3). Let g be a generator of this curve. From now on, unless otherwise noted, it is understood that all computations are done in the curve.

---

[1] We use the multiplicative notation for the elliptic curve generated by g.

Customer		Vendor
choose $s \in_R \mathbb{S}_n$		choose $v \in_R \mathbb{Z}_q^*$
compute $c_0 := H(s)$	$\xleftarrow{g,V}$	publish $g, V := g^v$

Fig. 1. Initialization

The vendor randomly selects a value $v \in \mathbb{Z}_q^*$ and computes $V = g^v$. He publishes (g, V) (and a description of the curve) as his public key and keeps v private. The customer chooses a random serial number s from some finite set $\mathbb{S}_n$. This serial number will act as an identifier for her future loyalty points, and serial numbers should be chosen such that collisions do not occur. After that, the customer binds to s by computing her initial counter $c_0 := H(s)$, where H is some cryptographic hash function mapping to the group. This hash function should be specified and published by the vendor, too. The initialization process is depicted in Figure 1.

Issue. When the customer is to be credited with a loyalty point, she randomly chooses r_i from $\mathbb{Z}_q$. Then, she blinds her current counter value c_{i-1} by computing $b_i := c_{i-1}g^{r_i}$ and sends b_i to the vendor. The vendor raises b_i to the v-th power and returns the result. Next, the customer computes the unblinding factor V^{-r_i} and subsequently derives $b_i^v V^{-r_i} = c_{i-1}^v$. After that, the customer verifies that the vendor has sent a correct value. To do so she checks whether (c_{i-1}, V, c_{i-1}^v) is a valid DH triple by running the efficient test for the curve. Note that, in general, this validity test is intractable for groups like $\mathbb{Z}_p^*$. If the verification here succeeds then the customer sets $c_i := c_{i-1}^v$ and stores (i, c_i). The issue protocol is shown in Figure 2.

Customer		Vendor
choose $r_i \in_R \mathbb{Z}_q$;		
compute $b_i := c_{i-1}g^{r_i}$;	$\xrightarrow{b_i}$	
	$\xleftarrow{b_i^v}$	compute b_i^v;
compute unblinding factor V^{-r_i};		
unblind b_i^v		
$\qquad b_i^v V^{-r_i} = c_{i-1}^v g^{r_i v} V^{-r_i}$		
$\qquad\qquad = c_{i-1}^v g^{r_i v} g^{-r_i v}$		
$\qquad\qquad = c_{i-1}^v$;		
verify (c_{i-1}, V, c_{i-1}^v) DH triple?;		
set $c_i := c_{i-1}^v$;		

Fig. 2. Issue protocol in the customer's i-th purchase

Redeem. If the customer has reached some redeeming threshold, i.e., has gathered enough points to hand them in for a reward, she may execute the redeem protocol shown in Figure 3. There, the customer sends her serial number s, the number of collected loyalty points n, and the counter value c_n. The vendor validates this triple by checking that c_n is in fact $c_0^{v^n}$ for $c_0 = H(s)$.

In order to prevent customers from redeeming the same counter more than once, the vendor checks if s is already stored in his database of redeemed serial numbers. If this is not the case the vendor stores the new serial number s — alternatively, the serial number's hash value $H(s)$ may be stored and checked, respectively. Eventually, if all checks are completed successfully the vendor sends the reward to the customer.

Customer	Vendor

$$\xrightarrow{\ (s,n,c_n)\ }$$

$\qquad$ verify $c_n \overset{?}{=} H(s)^{v^n}$;

$\qquad$ s not yet stored in database?;

$\qquad$ grant reward if verification successful;

Fig. 3. Redeem protocol

Note that if the serial numbers would be used directly, i.e., without applying the hash function or some similar measure, then the vendor might be easily tricked into accepting a forged counter. Specifically, given two correct counter values $c_n = s^{v^n}$, $c'_n = (s')^{v^n}$ for some n it is easy to derive a third counter $c_n c'_n = (ss')^{v^n}$ for serial number ss'.

5   Properties

5.1   Privacy

Privacy of the customer follows easily from the fact that the element b_i in the issue protocol is uniformly and independently distributed since the values of r_i are chosen independently. This also holds if the vendor knows the serial number s and all data derived from s like $c_0 = H(s)$, $c_1 = c_0^v$, etc. This means that any two issue transactions cannot be linked by the vendor provided that there is no additional information that can be used for linking purposes. The same holds for the linkability of issue and redeem transactions. No execution of the issue protocol can be assigned to a specific customer then, even after revealing (s, n, c_n) in the redeem protocol and even if the vendor has unlimited computational power.

5.2   Security

To claim security properties of our loyalty system we first have to specify the attack scenario and successful attacks. Afterwards, we show that our system achieves the desired properties.

We remark that the vendor in our system can easily thwart double spending by keeping track of used serial numbers s and by rejecting claims for previously submitted ones. As for the unforgeability and pooling prevention we prove security of our scheme based on the intractability of a new problem, called the incremental Diffie-Hellman (iDH) problem. This problem is related to the classical Diffie-Hellman problem as well as to the previously proposed one-more RSA and one-more Discrete Logarithm problems for proving Chaum's blind signature and its discrete-log variant to be secure [2, 4]. Although we were unable to reduce some standard cryptographic problem to this new problem, our reduction enables us to investigate the security of our system by considering a pure mathematical problem and hiding the details of the protocol. Indeed, we will also provide some discussion about the hardness of the iDH problem below.

Attack Model. The attack model is as follows. We assume that the adversary controls several customers and coordinates their activities. Note that this covers "less malicious" cases where, say, some adversarial users act individually. The adversary is allowed to run issue protocols with the honest vendor and finally engages in a redeem protocol execution. The goal of the adversary is to claim more points than issued in total to these users.

There is a subtlety in the formalization of the adversary "redeeming more points than issued". Recall the example of two users both having already 5 individual points and then trying to combine their points to a joint counter value of 10. In this case 10 points have already been issued indeed. Hence, the two adversarial users actually do not redeem more points than earned before, yet they illicitly pool them. The definition of pooling prevention should capture such misbehavior. We therefore augment the attack model by so-called scheduled users in addition to the controlled users.

A scheduled user is basically an autonomous customer following the protocol honestly. The adversary merely schedules the actions of this user, i.e., determines when this user runs the initialization or issue protocol. More precisely, the adversary can perform three operations with scheduled users. First, the adversary can create a new scheduled user during the attack. This new user immediately follows the prescribed initialization protocol, i.e., chooses a serial number s and computes $c_0 := H(s)$. The user goes idle until the adversary wakes him up again. Second, the adversary may call a scheduled user and ask him to step the counter. In this case the user runs the issue protocol with his current counter value and returns to an idle state again. We assume that the scheduled user also stores the intermediate values in addition to the current counter value (i.e., previous blinding and counter values)[2]. Third, at any time the adversary may corrupt a scheduled customer which then becomes a controlled user; the adversary gets all the previously stored information and the current counter value, and from now on coordinates all the user's activities. Note that the adversary still controls the set of corrupted users in addition to such scheduled customers.

We count the issued points as follows. For each scheduled user we individually count the number of issue protocol invocations for this user (until the user becomes corrupted or the attack ends). If a controlled customer starts an issue execution then we increment the adversary's global count instead. By this, we have an individual number n_{cust} of invocations for each customer cust (possibly $n_{cust} = 0$ if the customer has been corrupted right away or has never run the issue protocol), and a global number n_{adv}

---

[2] Usually, honest users are supposed to delete such information. However, reliable erasure is in general hard to achieve and the adversary may later be able to recover the values from the user's hard disk. Thus, a conservative approach is to presume that the user in fact saves the values explicitly.

of invocations with fully controlled customers. We now say that the adversary *breaks the system* if the adversary successfully claims strictly more than $n_{adv} + \max\{n_{cust}\}$ points for some user, where the maximum is over all customers cust appearing during the attack.

Note that the lower bound itself, $n_{adv} + \max\{n_{cust}\}$, can trivially be reached by any adversary scheduling a customer $\max\{n_{cust}\}$ times and then corrupting the customer (thereby taking over its counter) and performing n_{adv} subsequent runs of the issue protocol by herself (using the corrupted customer's counter as her starting counter). Claiming more than $n_{adv} + \max\{n_{cust}\}$ points captures the cases where (a) the adversary manages to add at least one additonal point that was not issued by the vendor to some counter, (b) two or more customers manage to pool their counters, or (c) a combination of both.

In how far do scheduled users reflect pooling attacks? In the example of two customers merging their counter values of 5, one may think of these users as scheduled users. The adversary then corrupts them and tries to redeem 10 points. In this simple attack we have $\max\{n_{cust}\} = 5$ and $n_{adv} = 0$ and, according to the definition, the adversary breaks the system if she manages to redeem 6 or more points for some user (by pooling both counter values, yielding 10 points, or by increasing the counter by at least one point using some other means).

The Incremental Diffie-Hellman Problem. The incremental Diffie-Hellman problem is to find $n \geq 1$ and $g^{v^{n+1}}$ for given group elements g and $V = g^v$ (where v is unknown). To facilitate the task one is allowed to query a special Diffie-Hellman oracle $\mathrm{DH}_{g,V}(\cdot)$ computing X^v for inputs X. Yet, the condition is that the oracle can only be queried at most $n - 1$ times, e.g., to compute g^{v^3} from g, g^v one may make a single call to the oracle. Specifically:

Definition 1 (incremental Diffie-Hellman problem). *Let g be a generator of a group of prime order q and $V = g^v$ be a random element in this group. Given g, V and access to an oracle $\mathrm{DH}_{g,V}(X) = X^v$ the incremental Diffie-Hellman (iDH) problem is to come up with an element Z and an integer $1 \leq n < \mathrm{ord}_{\mathbb{Z}_q^*}(v) - 1$ such that*

$$Z = g^{v^{n+1}}$$

and such that the oracle $\mathrm{DH}_{g,V}(\cdot)$ has been queried at most $n - 1$ times.

The upper bound on the integer n rules out trivial solutions. Else, $Z := V$ would for example be a correct claim for any multiple n of the order $\mathrm{ord}_{\mathbb{Z}_q^*}(v)$ of v in $\mathbb{Z}_q^*$ because $g^{v^{n+1}} = g^v = Z$. For our scheme we therefore choose a sufficiently large order for v; see Section 5.3 for details.

Unforgeability and Pooling Prevention. The incremental Diffie-Hellman problem reduces to the security of our scheme in the random oracle model. To show this we present an iDH algorithm that uses a successful forger for our loyalty system as a subroutine. In order to use the forger in this way, the iDH algorithm will set up a "virtual" environment for the forger by impersonating the vendor and inserting the input for the iDH problem. As the experiment looks like a real interaction with the vendor from the forger's perspective, the forger will claim more points than issued in the experiment if she would do so in an actual attack. But any solution in the experiment will immediately give a solution for the iDH problem. We conclude that each forger for our protocol must implicitly solve the iDH problem.

In the experiment we will model the hash function H mapping serial numbers to group elements as a so-called random oracle [3]. That is, we assume that H acts as a random function: it maps inputs to uniformly and independently distributed group elements, repeating answers for previously queried inputs. Note that the idealized random oracle model merely provides some heuristic evidence that the scheme is indeed secure; refer to [10] for a discussion. Therefore, in Section 5.3 we also present a modification which completely forges random oracles but which essentially preserves the efficiency (with only a negligible loss in the initialization protocol).

We next specify the construction of the iDH algorithm from an arbitrary forger. For this, the iDH algorithm first tries to guess the maximum $N_{\text{cust}} := \max\{n_{\text{cust}}\}$ of issued points for scheduled users in the upcoming experiment. This value is usually bounded by a parameter N representing the system's maximum of redeem points. Instructively, think of N as 10 or $1,000$.

To guess $N_{\text{cust}} = \max\{n_{\text{cust}}\}$ the iDH algorithm picks a uniformly distributed value between 0 and N. The forger's view in the following simulation is independent of this choice, and the iDH algorithm thus hits the right value with probability $1/(N+1)$. If, on the other hand, the guess later turns out to be incorrect the iDH solver will stop with failure instead. The overall success probability of the iDH algorithm therefore decreases by a factor of $1/(N+1)$ compared to the forger. From now on, we condition on the event that the iDH algorithm selects the correct N_{cust}.

We describe the simulation of the forger. The iDH algorithm is given g and V and access to the oracle, and has predicted N_{cust}. It first computes $g^{v^2}, g^{v^3}, \ldots, g^{v^{N_{\text{cust}}+1}}$ by iteratively querying the oracle, starting with V. This can be done with N_{cust} queries. It next starts the simulation of the forger by providing g, V as the public key of the vendor. The emulation proceeds as follows:

- Whenever the forger queries the hash function H about some serial number s, i.e., adds another *controlled user* to the system, then the iDH algorithm chooses $w_s \in \mathbb{Z}_q$ at random and returns V^{w_s} (or returns the previously given answer if this serial number has been queried before).
- If the forger initiates the issue protocol for a controlled user and submits a value b to the virtual vendor then the iDH algorithm calls the DH oracle to derive b^v and answers on behalf of the vendor with this value.
- If the forger adds another *scheduled user* to the system then the iDH algorithm chooses a number s and sets $H(s) := V^{w_s}$ for a random value $w_s \in \mathbb{Z}_q$ (or returns the previously given answer if this serial number has appeared before). The iDH algorithm from now on impersonates this scheduled user with values s and $c_0 = H(s) = V^{w_s} = g^{w_s v}$.
- If the forger asks a scheduled user to step the counter then the iDH solver fetches the current counter value $c_{i-1} = g^{w_s v^i}$ and runs a simulation of the issue protocol:
  - Take $g^{v^{i+1}}$ from the pre-computed list of powers. Note that, by assumption, i does not exceed the correct guess N_{cust} and therefore $g^{v^{i+1}}$ must be in this list.
  - On behalf of the customer select $r_i \in \mathbb{Z}_q$ at random and compute $b_i := c_{i-1} g^{r_i}$.

- On behalf of the vendor compute V^{r_i} and $(g^{v^{i+1}})^{w_s}$ and reply with

$$b_i^v = V^{r_i}(g^{v^{i+1}})^{w_s} = V^{r_i}c_{i-1}^v.$$

Store $c_i = g^{w_s v^{i+1}}$ and r_i in the name of the customer. Note that all the values, including c_i and r_i, are distributed identically to an execution between a scheduled user and the vendor in an actual attack.
- If the forger corrupts a scheduled user the iDH algorithm hands over all the previously stored values on behalf of this customer and stops impersonating this user.

When the forger finally redeems a counter value Z and $n \geq 1$ for some serial number s then the iDH algorithm computes $w_s^{-1} \bmod q$ and outputs $Z^{w_s^{-1}}$ and n and stops[3].

Note that the answers of the iDH algorithm are identical to those of the genuine vendor and the simulated hash function evaluation yields uniformly distributed values like the random oracle. This means that the view of any forger in the experiment is the same as in an actual attack, and if the forger is able to redeem more points in reality then she succeeds in the simulation with the same probability (under the condition that the iDH solver has guessed N_{cust} in advance).

Finally, it remains to be shown that the construction above turns any forgery in the experiment into a solution to the iDH problem. For this note that, for a successful redemption,

$$Z^{w_s^{-1}} = \left(g^{w_s v^{n+1}}\right)^{w_s^{-1}} = g^{v^{n+1}}$$

Furthermore, $n > \max\{n_{\text{cust}}\} + n_{\text{adv}}$ which implies

$$n \geq \max\{n_{\text{cust}}\} + n_{\text{adv}} + 1$$

Since the iDH algorithm has queried its oracle exactly $\max\{n_{\text{cust}}\} + n_{\text{adv}}$ times this means that $Z^{w_s^{-1}}$ and n constitute a valid solution to the iDH problem. Therefore, we have presented an algorithm solving the iDH problem whenever the forger succeeds and the initial guess is right.

As for the exact security of our loyalty system we note that, according to common practice, the running time of the attacker comprises her own steps and the ones of honest parties during the attack. But then the running time of the derived algorithm iDH differs only marginally from the one of the attacker, i.e., the iDH algorithm initially computes the powers g^{v^i} via the oracle and also performs some additional computations when simulating answers of the vendor. Our reduction hence shows that if the adversary breaks the loyalty system in t steps with probability ε, then there is an algorithm solving the iDH problem in time $t' \approx t$ and with probability $\frac{1}{N+1}(\varepsilon - \frac{2}{q})$.

On the Hardness of the iDH Problem. It remains to argue the intractability of the iDH problem. We are not aware of any reduction from well-established problems like the Discrete Logarithm problem or the canonical Diffie-Hellman problem. Still, we

---

[3] There is a very small probability that $w_s = 0$ which has no inverse in $\mathbb{Z}_q$, or that the forger successfully claims a counter value for a number s that has not been passed to the hash function before. However, both probabilities are equal to $1/q$ and we thus neglect them for the analysis.

give a brief discussion about the intractability of the iDH problem and its relationship to similar problems.

The algorithm's task is to find some $n \geq 1$ and $g^{v^{n+1}}$ after having made at most $n-1$ calls to the oracle. *Under the condition that the algorithm never queries the oracle* the canonical Diffie-Hellman problem can be reduced to this problem and our problem is hence believed to be infeasible. Namely, without the help of the oracle the algorithm computes a variant of the Diffie-Hellman function, $g^v \mapsto g^{v^n}$ for unknown v and some $n > 1$. This function, however, has the same power as the classical DH function for n's of order $O(\sqrt{\log q})$, refer to [24, 21].

As for the power of the oracle queries, note that the iDH problem is related to another problem from computational complexity. Namely, it is believed that computation of powers V^{2^n} requires n *sequential* squarings and that there is no efficient improvement allowing a faster parallel computation. This problem has been applied in cryptography before to derive protocols with critical time release properties [8].

In our case the constant 2 in the computation of V^{2^n} is replaced by the unknown value v, even hampering the task. Hence any successful iDH algorithm that, in addition to the oracle calls, only performs operations which are independent of the input would give rise to a new algorithm deriving powers V^{v^n} with less than n exponentiations (using some preprocessing).

In conclusion, we cannot prove that the iDH problem is as hard as, say, the computational Diffie-Hellman problem. However, the discussion above indicates that straightforward algorithms for the problem do not work and that more sophisticated algorithms would be required to solve the problem —if it can be solved efficiently at all.

5.3 Efficiency and Implementation Issues

To implement the protocol one has to pick an appropriate elliptic curve with a pairing function and define a hash function mapping strings to random group elements. We refer to [20, 6, 7, 1, 17] for such choices. Indeed, it is not hard to see that we can eliminate the hash function (and the random oracle model in the security proof) if we let the vendor choose a random value c_0 for the customer in an initialization step. The unforgeability now follows from the hardness of the iDH problem alone.

The variant with the vendor choosing the serial number can also avoid accidental collisions which may happen when customers select the serial numbers, even if the collision probability is very small. Unfortunately, this variant has some drawbacks as well. First, it requires an additional interaction to get a new serial number for initializing a new counter. Second, requesting a serial number might be correlated with a purchase/issue transaction. This may allow the vendor to link the redeem transaction with the counter's first issue transaction. Furthermore, in this variant the vendor learns that no issue transaction prior to the creation of the serial number is related to the user. In summary, the creation of serial numbers by the vendor has some disadvantages regarding privacy. Another drawback is that a malicious customer could repeatedly request serial numbers from the vendor without really using them. Since each serial number can only be issued once, this may lead to an unnecessary waste of serial numbers.

Recall that we also require the order of the vendor's secret v in the multiplicative group $\mathbb{Z}_q^*$ to be quite large. This can be accomplished by letting $q - 1$ have only large prime factors. Specifically, for $q \approx 2^{160}$ it suffices to let $q - 1$ consist only of prime factors larger than 40 bits. Then any element $v \neq 1$ has order at least 2^{40} in $\mathbb{Z}_q^*$ which is sufficient for all practical purposes. Since $g^{v^n} = g^{v^{n+i \cdot \mathrm{ord}_{\mathbb{Z}_q^*}(v)}}$ for any $i \geq 0$, an adversary may claim higher counter values $n + i \cdot \mathrm{ord}_{\mathbb{Z}_q^*}(v)$ instead of n. But this can be tackled by defining a maximum counter value which is obviously smaller than $\mathrm{ord}_{\mathbb{Z}_q^*}(v)$, i.e., larger counter values will not be accepted in the redeem protocol. The vendor may publish this bound on the maximum number of points as part of the system parameters.

We address the vendor's effort for the verification in the redeem protocol. Note that the vendor first calculates $w := v^n \bmod q$ over $\mathbb{Z}_q^*$ and then $H(s)^w$ in the elliptic curve and finally compares it with the given c_n. Altogether these are only two exponentiations, and thus improves efficiency over the verification of n blind signatures in the token-based case. To decrease this effort further the vendor can also pre-compute and store powers of the universal value v, especially if all customers are likely to claim points for a fixed value, like $n = 10$. Verification of a claim then essentially boils down to a single exponentiation.

The proposed solution has an efficiency drawback in a model that allows customers to be issued more than one loyalty point in one purchase. If a customer should obtain $m > 1$ points in one purchase, the issue protocol has to be carried out m times.

6   Related Work

Much work has been done by economic and marketing experts in the field of loyalty systems, e.g., see [5, 28, 14]. Furthermore, there has been lots of work stressing the importance of privacy for electronic commerce, e.g., see [18]. A common goal of proposals for privacy enhancing systems in the area of electronic commerce is to prevent certain parties from linking activities of the same customer. In typical commercial relationships, there are many possibilities to link customer transactions. For instance, in the area of payment systems, the unlinkability of widthdrawal and desposit has been considered [12, 9]. In [16], a solution to establish the unlinkability of the customer's search and order phases has been proposed. In this context, we provide a solution to guarantee that unlinkability achieved by other techniques still holds when using a loyalty system.

Other work regarding technical proposals for loyalty systems can be found in [23]. In this work, an infrastructure based on smart cards is proposed which allows individuals to introduce their own currencies or loyalty systems. However, they do not deal with the problem of achieving privacy in loyalty systems. Another proposal for a loyalty system was presented in [29]. In this work, the authors respect the privacy aspect. However, the goal of the system was not to provide unlinkability of transactions. The solution is based on pseudonymity, and thus provides a weaker form of privacy protection.

7   Conclusion

We have presented a privacy-friendly loyalty systems that does not allow vendors to link customers' transactions. The presented approach basically consists of a counter for loyalty points secure against forging and linking of transactions. The counter is increased in a blind signatures protocol exploiting the problem to compute discrete logarithms in groups of prime order. In the redeem phase, the counter can be verified efficiently in one step, regardless of the number of loyalty points that have been collected. Loyalty systems can provide an important strategy for vendors' customer relationship management to retain customers and to increase the incentive for repeated buying. The privacy property of our proposal may attract customers that usually refuse to become members of a loyalty program since they fear infringements of their privacy.

References

1. Paulo S.L.M. Baretto, Hae Y. Kim, Ben Lynn, Michael Scott. Efficient algorithms for pairing-based cryptosystems. In *Advances in Cryptology - CRYPTO 2002 – 22th Annual International Cryptology Conference, Proceedings*, LNCS 2442. Springer Verlag, 2002.
2. M. Bellare, C. Namprempre, D. Pointcheval, M. Semanko. The one-more-RSA-inversion problems and the security of Chaum's blind signature scheme. In *Journal of Cryptology*, Vol. 16, No. 3, 2003.
3. Mihir Bellare, Phillip Rogaway. Random oracles are practical: A paradigm for designing efficient protocols. In *Proceedings of the 1st ACM conference on computer and communications security (CCS '93)*, November 1993.
4. Alexandra Boldyreva. Efficient threshold signatures, multisignatures and blind signatures based on the Gap-Diffie-Hellman-group signature scheme. In *Public Key Cryptography (PKC) 2003*, LNCS 2567. Springer Verlag, 2003.
5. Ruth N. Bolton, P. K. Kannan, Matthew D. Bramlett. Implications of loyalty programs and service experiences for customer retention and value. *Journal of the Academy of Marketing Science*, 28(1), 2000.
6. Dan Boneh, Matthew Franklin. Identity based encryption from the Weil pairing. In *Advances in Cryptology - CRYPTO 2001 – 21st Annual International Cryptology Conference, Proceedings*, LNCS 2139. Springer Verlag, 2001.
7. Dan Boneh, Ben Lynn, Hovav Shacham. Short signatures from the Weil pairing. In *ASIACRYPT 2001, 7th International Conference on the Theory and Application of Cryptology and Information Security, Proceedings*, LNCS 2248. Springer Verlag, 2001.
8. Dan Boneh, Moni Naor. Timed commitments (extended abstract). In *Advances in Cryptology - CRYPTO 2000 – 20th Annual International Cryptology Conference, Proceedings*, LNCS 1880. Springer Verlag, 2000.
9. Jan Camenisch, Jean-Marc Piveteau, Markus Stadler. An efficient fair payment system. In *1st ACM Conference on Computer and Communications Security (CCS'96)*. ACM Press, 1996.
10. Ran Canetti, Oded Goldreich, Shai Halevi. The random oracle methodology, revisited. In *Proceedings of the thirtieth annual ACM symposium on Theory of computing (STOC 1998)*. ACM Press, 1998.
11. David Chaum. Untraceable electronic mail, return addresses, and digital pseudonyms. *Communications of the ACM*, 24(2), February 1981.
12. David Chaum. Privacy protected payments: Unconditional payer and/or payee untraceability. In *Smart Card 2000, Proceedings*. North Holland, 1989.
13. Yevgeniy Dodis. Efficient construction of (distributed) verifiable random functions. In *Public Key Cryptography (PKC) 2003*, LNCS 2567. Springer Verlag, 2003.
14. Grahame R. Dowling, Mark Uncles. Do customer loyalty programs really work? *Sloan Management Review*, 38(4), 1997.
15. Matthias Enzmann, Claudia Eckert. Pseudonymes Einkaufen physischer Güter. In *Sichere Geschäftsprozesse, Tagungsband zur Arbeitskonferenz Elektronische Geschäftsprozesse*. IT Verlag für Informationstechnik, 2002.

16. Matthias Enzmann, Thomas Kunz, Markus Schneider. Privacy protection through unlinkability of customer activities in business processes using mobile agents. In *3rd International Conference on Electronic Commerce and Web Technologies (EC-Web 2002)*, LNCS 2455. Springer Verlag, September 2002.

17. Steven D. Galbraith, Keith Harrison, David Soldera. Implementing the Tate pairing. In *Algorithmic Number Theory, 5th International Symposium, ANTS-V, Proceedings*, LNCS 2369. Springer Verlag, 2002.

18. Donna L. Hoffman, Thomas P. Novak, Marcos Peralta. Building consumer trust online. *Communications of the ACM*, 42(4), April 1999.

19. Antoine Joux. A one round protocol for tripartite Diffie-Hellman. In *Algorithmic Number Theory, 4th International Symposium, ANTS-IV, Proceedings*, LNCS 1838. Springer Verlag, 2000.

20. A. Joux, K. Nguyen. Separating Decision Diffie-Hellman from Diffie-Hellman in cryptographic groups. Cryptology ePrint Archive, Report 2001/003, 2001. http://eprint.iacr.org/.

21. Eike Kiltz. A tool box of cryptographic functions related to the Diffie-Hellman function. In *INDOCRYPT 2001, Second International Conference on Cryptology in India, Proceedings*, LNCS 2247. Springer Verlag, 2001.

22. Alfred Kobsa. Tailoring privacy to users's needs. In *User Modeling 2001 (UM 2001), 8th International Conference, Proceedings*, LNAI 2109. Springer Verlag, 2001.

23. David P. Maher. A platform for privately defined currencies, loyalty credits, and play money. In *Financial Cryptography, Second International Conference (FC'98), Proceedings*, LNCS 1465. Springer Verlag, 1998.

24. Ueli M. Maurer, Stefan Wolf. Diffie-Hellman oracles. In *Advances in Cryptology - CRYPTO '96 – 16th Annual International Cryptology Conference, Proceedings*, LNCS 1109. Springer Verlag, 1996.

25. Alfred J. Menezes. *Elliptic Curve Public Key Cryptosystems*, volume 234 of *The Kluwer International Series in Engineering and Computer Science*. Kluwer Academic Publishers, 1993.

26. Gina Colarelli O'Connor, Robert O'Keefe. The Internet as a new marketplace: Implications for consumer behaviour and marketing management. In M. Shaw, R. Blanning, T. Strader, A. Whinston, (eds), *Handbook on Electronic Commerce*. Springer Verlag, 2000.

27. Michael G. Reed, Paul F. Syverson, David M. Goldschlag. Anonymous connections and onion routing. *IEEE Journal on Selected Areas in Communications — Special Issue on Copyright and Privacy Protection*, 16(4), 1998.

28. Byron Sharp, Anne Sharp. Loyalty programs and their impact on repeat-purchase loyalty patterns. *International Journal of Research in Marketing*, 14(5), December 1997.

29. Arrianto Mukti Wibowo, Kwok Yan Lam, Gary S.H. Tan. Loyalty program scheme for anonymous payment systems. In *Electronic Commerce and Web Technologies*, LNCS 1875. Springer Verlag, 2000.

Addressing Online Dictionary Attacks
with Login Histories and Humans-in-the-Loop
(Extended Abstract)

S. Stubblebine[1] and P.C. van Oorschot[2]

[1] Stubblebine Research Labs, Madison, NJ, USA
[2] Computer Science, Carleton University, Ottawa, Canada

Abstract. Pinkas and Sander's (2002) login protocol protects against
online guessing attacks by employing human-in-the-loop techniques (also
known as Reverse Turing Tests or RTTs). We first note that this, and
other protocols involving RTTs, are susceptible to minor variations of
well-known middle-person attacks, and suggest techniques to address
such attacks. We then present complementary modifications in what we
call a history-based protocol with RTT's. Preliminary analysis indicates
that the new protocol offer opportunities for improved security, improved
user-friendliness (fewer RTTs to legitimate users), and greater flexibility
(e.g. in customizing protocol parameters to particular situations).

1 Introduction

Recent interest has arisen in tests which distinguish humans from computers, and
in using such tests to ensure human involvement in a wide range of computer-
based interactions. The idea is to find simple tasks which are relatively easily
performed by a human, but which appear difficult or infeasible for automated
programs to carry out – for example, visually recognizing distorted words. Mechanisms involving such tests have been referred to as *human-in-the-loop protocols*,
mandatory human participation schemes, and *Reverse Turing Tests* (RTTs) [19,
5, 22].

One specific purpose for which RTT challenges have been proposed is protecting web sites against access by automated scripts. RTTs are currently being
used to protect against database queries to domain registries, to prevent sites
from being indexed by search engines, and to prevent "bots" from signing up for
enormous numbers of free email accounts [5]. They have also been proposed for
preventing more creative attacks [4].

Our main interest in RTTs is their use to protect web servers against online
password guessing attacks (e.g. online dictionary attacks). The idea is that automated attack programs will fail the RTT challenges. A specific instance of such
a protocol was recently proposed by Pinkas and Sander [20] (see §3). While this
protocol appears to be quite simple, closer inspection reveals it to be surprisingly
subtle and well-crafted. Simpler techniques preventing online dictionary attacks
are not always applicable. For example, account lock-out after a small number

A. Juels (Ed.): FC 2004, LNCS 3110, pp. 39–53, 2004.
© IFCA/Springer-Verlag Berlin Heidelberg 2004

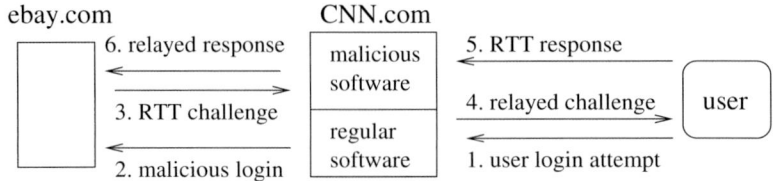

Fig. 1. RTT Relay Attack

of failed password attempts may result in unacceptable side effects, such as increased customer service costs for additional telephone support related to locked accounts, and new denial of service vectors via intentional lock-out of other users [24]. Another standard approach is to use successively longer delays as the number of successive invalid password attempts on a single account increases. This may lead to similarly unacceptable side effects.

In this paper, we begin by noting that many RTT-based protocols, including that of Pinkas and Sander, are vulnerable to an *RTT relay attack*: RTT challenges may be relayed to possibly unsuspecting parties, who generate responses which are then relayed back to the challenger. We explore this threat and mechanisms to address it, and propose additional (orthogonal) enhancements to the Pinkas-Sander protocol.

This paper is organized as follows. §2 presents the RTT relay attack. §3 discusses background context and assumptions, including a reference version of the basic RTT-based login protocol. §4 presents a new variation, with enhancements aimed towards usability, security against online dictionary attacks, and parameter flexibility. §5 discusses standard techniques to augment general RTT-based login protocols to prevent, detect or deter attacks including the relay attack. §6 provides background and a summary of related work. §7 contains concluding remarks.

2   RTT Relay Attack

A relay attack (see §6) may be carried out on online protocols involving an RTT by relaying the RTT challenge to an auxiliary location or "workforce" which generates responses, which are relayed back to the challenger. The original RTT target thus escapes computing RTT responses.

One attack variant might proceed as follows (see Fig. 1). Assume there are two web sites[1]. The first, say ebay.com, is assumed to be the target of regular online dictionary attacks, and consequently requires correct responses to RTT challenges before allowing access. The second, say CNN.com, is a popular high volume web site, which for our purposes is assumed to be vulnerable to compromise. The attack begins with an adversary hacking into the CNN.com site and installing attack software.

---

[1] The authors have no affiliation with ebay.com or CNN.com, and no reason to believe either site is insecure. These sites are used as examples simply due to their popularity.

Upon a user initiated HTTP connection to CNN.com, the attack software receives the request and initiates a fraudulent login attempt to ebay.com. The attack software, presented with an RTT challenge from ebay.com, redirects it to the CNN.com user connection, instructing that user to answer the RTT to get access to CNN.com. (Many users will follow such instructions: most users are non-technical, unsuspecting, and do as requested.) The CNN.com user responds to the RTT challenge. The attack software relays the response to ebay.com, completing the response to the challenge to the fraudulent login attempt. In conjunction with replying to eBay's RTT challenge, after a sufficient number of passwords guesses (e.g. dictionary attack), an eBay account password can be cracked. The procedure is repeated on other accounts, and the attack program summarizes the online dictionary attack results for the adversary.

The attack is easy to perform if the adversary can control *any* high volume web site – e.g. a popular legitimate site the attacker compromises (as above), or an owned malicious site to which traffic has been drawn, e.g. by illegally hosting popular copyrighted content, a fraudulent lottery, or free software. A related attack involves attack software which relays RTTs to groups of human workers ("sweatshops"), exploiting an inexpensive labor pool willingly acting as a mercenary RTT-answering workforce. An unconfirmed real-world variant reported [21] to involve an "adult web site" requiring users to solve RTTs before being served the content; presumably those running the site relayed the answers to gain access to legitimate sites which posed the original RTT in the hope of preventing automated attacks. Our discussion of mechanisms to counteract such threats continues in §5.

3   Background, Constraints, Assumptions, and Objectives

For reference, Fig. 2 provides a simplified description of the original RTT-based login protocol (for full details, see [20]). The system parameter p is a probability which determines the fraction of time that an RTT is asked, in the case that an invalid userid-password pair is entered. In the case of a successful login, the protocol stores a cookie on the machine from which the login occurred; the cookie contains the userid (plus optionally an expiration date), and is constructed in such a way (e.g. using standard techniques involving symmetric-key encryption or a MAC) that the server can verify its authenticity.

For context, we next state a few assumptions and observations relevant to both the original and new protocols. We begin with a basic constraint.

Constraint 1: Account Lock-out Not Tolerable. We are interested in protocols for systems where locking-out of user accounts after some number of failed login attempts is not a viable option. (Otherwise, online login attacks are easily addressed – see §1.)

Trust Model Assumptions: Trusted Host and Ephemeral Memory. We assume that client computers, and any resident software at the time of use, are trusted (e.g. no keyboard sniffers or malicious software run on the machine). This is standard for (one-factor) password-based authentication protocols – otherwise,

```
1   fix a value for system parameter p, 0 < p ≤ 1 (e.g. p = 0.10)
2   user enters userid/password
3   if (user PC has cookie) then server retrieves it
4   if (entered userid/password pair correct) then
5     if (cookie present & validates & unexpired & matches userid) then
6         login passes
7     else % i.e. cookie failure
8         ask an RTT; login passes if answer correct (otherwise fails)
9     endif
10  else % i.e. incorrect userid/password pair
11    set AskAnRTT to TRUE with prob. p (otherwise FALSE) †
12    if (AskAnRTT) then
13        ask an RTT; wait for answer; then say login fails
14    else
15        immediately say login fails
16    endif
17  endif
```
   † This setting is a deterministic function of the userid/password pair [20]

Fig. 2. Original RTT-based Login Protocol (simplified description)

the password is trivially available to an attacker. For similar reasons, we assume client software leaves no residual data on user machines after a login protocol ends (e.g. memory is cleared as each user logs out). In practice it is difficult to guarantee these assumptions are met (e.g. for borrowed machines in an Internet cafe); but without them, the security of almost all password protocols seems questionable.

Observation 1: Limited Persistence by Legitimate Users. A typical legitimate user will give up after some maximum (e.g. $C = 10$) of failed logins over a fixed time period, after which many will check with a system administrator, colleague or other source for help, or simply stop trying to log in. Large numbers of successive failed logins, if by a legitimate user, may signal a forgotten password or a system availability issue (here login failures are likely not formally recorded by the system); or may occur due to an attacker, as either a side effect of attempting to crack passwords, or intentionally for denial-of-service in systems susceptible to such tactics.

Observation 2: Users Will Seek Convenience. If a login protocol is necessary to access an online service, and users can find a similar alternate service with a more convenient login (though possibly less secure), then many users will switch to the alternate service. User choices are rarely driven by security; usability is usually a far greater factor, and poor usability typically leads to loss of business.

These observations lead us to our usability goal; we state it informally.

Usability Goal – Minimal Inconvenience to Users. Relative to standard userid-password schemes, we wish to minimize additional inconvenience experienced by a user.

As usual, the usability goal must be met in a tradeoff with security, and we have a two-part security goal. One part is protecting specific accounts (e.g. certain users may be more concerned about, or require more, protection; or a service provider may worry more about specific accounts – say those with high sales ratings, or high account values). The second is protecting all accounts in aggregate (e.g. a web service provider might not want *any* user accounts misappropriated to host stolen software; a content service provider might want to protect access to content available to authorized subscribers).

Security Goal – Control Access to both Specific Accounts and Non-specific Accounts. Constrain information the adversary learns from trial password guesses before being "stopped" by an RTT challenge in the context of fully-automated attacks directed towards a specific account (single-account attack) and towards any account (multi-account attack).

In practice, for authentication schemes based on user-selected passwords, prevention of unauthorized access cannot be 100% guaranteed for a specific account or all accounts in aggregate, due to the non-zero probability of correctly guessing a password, and the ubiquity of poor passwords. Nonetheless, the quality of a login protocol may be analyzed independent of particular password choices, and this is what we pursue. For a given password, we are interested in how effectively a given protocol allowing online interaction prevents extraction of password-related information. As little information as possible should be leaked.

Requiring mandatory human participation increases the level of sophistication and resources for an attack. If RTTs are effective and RTT relay attacks are countered (e.g. by means such as embedded warnings – see §5.1), then constraining information leaked before being "stopped" by an RTT challenge is an important security characteristic of a password-based login protocol.

4   History-Based Login Protocol with RTT's

Here we modify the original protocol, intending to both improve the user experience and increase security, e.g. to increase the percentage of time that an adversary is challenged with an RTT, without further inconveniencing legitimate users[2]. The modifications do not themselves prevent RTT relay attacks (§2), but are complementary to those in §5 that do, and can thus be combined. We also provide analysis of the new protocol.

4.1   New Protocol

We assume familiarity with the original protocol (§3). The new protocol is given in Fig. 3. Line changes from the original protocol (Fig. 2) are: lines 7.1-7.6 replace 8; and 11.1 replaces 12. The new protocol with failed-login thresholds $(b_1 = 0, b_2 = \infty)$ behaves the same as the original protocol.

---

[2] One might try to improve usability by allowing a small number of trial passwords per userid without triggering an RTT. While this reduces security only minorly for a single-account attack (see §4.2), the problem is greater with multi-account attacks.

1   fix values for $0 < q \leq 1$ (e.g. $q = 0.05$ or 0.10) and integers $b_1, b_2 \geq 0$
2   user enters userid/password
3   **if** (user PC has cookie) **then** server retrieves it
4   **if** (entered userid/password pair correct) **then**
5   **if** (cookie present & validates & unexpired & matches userid) **then**
6   login passes
7   **else** % i.e. cookie failure
7.1   set AskAnRTT to TRUE if account is in owner mode (otherwise FALSE)
7.2   **if** (AskAnRTT) OR (*FailedLogins[userid]* $\geq b_1$) **then**
7.3   ask an RTT; login passes if answer correct (otherwise fails)
7.4   **else**
7.5   login passes
7.6   **endif**
9   **endif**
10 **else** % i.e. incorrect userid/password pair
11   set AskAnRTT to TRUE with prob. q (otherwise FALSE) †
11.1 **if** (AskAnRTT) OR (*FailedLogins[userid]* $\geq b_2$) **then**
13   ask an RTT; wait for answer; then say login fails
14   **else**
15   immediately say login fails
16   **endif**
17 **endif**
   † This setting is a deterministic function of the userid/password pair [20]

Fig. 3. New Protocol (History-based Login Protocol with RTT's). *FailedLogins[userid]* is set to the userid's number of failed logins in a recent period T, and updated (not shown). See §4.1 re: handling cookies and definition of owner mode

We next discuss some differences between the new and original protocols, including: cookie-handling (related to owner and non-owner mode) – cookies are now stored only on trustworthy machines; per-user tracking of failed logins; and setting failed-login thresholds. The idea of dynamically changing failed-login thresholds has been previously mentioned [20, §4.4-4.6]; we detail a concrete proposal and comparison.

Handling cookies. The original protocol stores a cookie on any device after successful authentication; the new protocol does not. Optional user input controls cookie storage similar to web servers using a login page checkbox asking if users want to "remember passwords", e.g. "Is this a trustworthy device you use regularly? YES/NO". This part of the page appears if no cookie is received by the server. Upon a YES response, a cookie is pushed to the user device only after the user successfully authenticates (requiring a successful RTT response, if challenged). This cookie approach reduces exposure to cookie theft vs. the original protocol, with negligible usability downside because the question appears on the same screen as the login prompt (default answer NO).

The original protocol requires that cookies be tracked by the server and expire after a limit of failed login attempts with the particular cookie [20, §4.5]. We follow a similar approach. Each time a login fails (e.g. lines 7.3, 13, and 15), we increment the failed login count associated with the cookie if a valid cookie was received. If the cookie exceeds a failed login threshold, we invalidate it. Line 5 includes a check that the cookie hasn't been invalidated. The *cookie failure threshold* is the number of failed logins allowed before a cookie is invalidated. We recommend setting this to the minimum of b_1 and b_2.

Definition of owner, non-owner. A user is more likely to login from "non-owned" devices when traveling (e.g. borrowing an Internet access device in a library, guest office, conference room, or Internet cafe). Also, a user submitting a login request which does not include a cookie is likely to be using a non-owned device. As a consequence of how cookies are handled, we can assume (with small error) that a user is on a non-owned device if their most recent successful login does not include a cookie. We initially define a user account to be in *"owner"* mode, and expect an account to be in owner mode most of the time if most of the time they use their regular device (e.g. one of the devices they own). An account transitions to *"non-owner"* mode when a login is successfully authenticated without the server receiving a valid cookie (Fig. 3, line 7.5), and returns to owner mode after a specified time-out period W (e.g. 24 hours) or a successful login with a cookie present. The timeout period is restarted, and the account remains in non-owner mode, if there is another cookieless successful login. The time-out period reduces the number of accounts in non-owner mode, which lowers the security risk; accounts in non-owner mode are more susceptible to multi-account dictionary attacks (see §4.2).

Tracking failed logins. We define *FailedLogins[userid]* to be the number of failed login attempts for a specific userid within a recent period T (e.g. 30 days). Here *failed login attempts* includes: non-responses to RTT challenges, incorrect responses, failed userid-password pairs, and outstanding authentication attempts (e.g. the adversary may simultaneously issue multiple login attempts; one strategy might be to issue a very large number, and respond to only a subset of resulting RTT challenges, perhaps being able to exploit some "weak sub-class" of RTTs for which computer-generated responses are feasible).

Setting the failed-login thresholds (bounds b_1, b_2). Low values for b_1, b_2 maximize security at the expense of usability (e.g. for users who frequently enter incorrect passwords). A reasonable bound may be $b_1, b_2 \leq 10$ (perhaps larger for large T). In the simplest case the protocol bounds b_1, b_2 are fixed system variables; in a more elaborate design, they (and q) are dynamic and/or set on a per-user basis (varying for a particular userid, based on a history or profile and possibly subject to system wide constraints e.g. maximum bound on b_2). For example, certain users who regularly enter a password incorrectly might be given a higher failed-login threshold (to increase usability) compared to users who almost always enter correct passwords. If it is expected or known from a historical profile that a user will log in L times over a period T, and that say 5% of legitimate login attempts fail, then b_2 might be set somewhat larger than $(0.05) * L$ (e.g. $T = 30$ days, $L = 100$, $b_2 = 5$). Over time, per-user rates of legitimate logins (e.g. mistyped or forgotten/mixed up passwords, perhaps more frequent on unfamiliar machines) can be used to establish reasonable thresholds. To simplify presentation, updating of per-user table entries *FailedLogins[userid]* in Fig. 3 is not shown. Note that while per-user values require server-side storage when these values cannot be user-stored via cookies, a small amount of per-user server-side storage is already required in both the original and new protocol to ameliorate cookie theft (see above). (Optionally, setting the RTT challenge probability q on a per-user basis also allows flexibility for tuning usability and security on a per-account basis.)

4.2   Comparitive Analysis – Security and Usability

For a comparitive analysis of the new protocol with the original protocol, we first focus on the analysis for a single account, with respect to security and usability. We generally follow the assumptions from the original protocol [20], including that passwords are from a fixed set (dictionary) of cardinality N, and that for analysis purposes they are equally probable. The probabilities p and q are as defined in the protocols.

Discussion of Security (Single-Account Attacks). To aid our single-account security analysis, we use the following questions (and assume for now no cookie theft, i.e. an attacker knows a userid but has no corresponding cookie). For a single user account, for the original and new protocols, what is the ... Q1: expected number of passwords eliminatable from the space, answering no RTT's? Q2: expected number of RTT's an attacker must answer to correctly guess a password? Q3: probability of a confirmed correct password guess for attacker willing to answer c RTT's?

The answers summarized in Table 1 are based on the best attack strategies known to us[3]. For Q2 and Q3, perhaps surprisingly, this involves an attacker simply answering the first c RTT's sent[4]. Since better attack strategies may exist, e.g. our answers to Q3 should be interpreted as lower bounds, albeit under conditions favorable to the attacker: we assume that failed login counts are 0 at the start of an attack.

Some observations follow. Rows Q1 and Q2 indicate that the number of passwords that an attacker is able to eliminate "for free" (without any RTT's) is substantially greater in the original protocol[5]. A second observation favoring the new protocol is evident from rows Q3b and Q3c: the probability of a successful attacker guess in the new protocol (on the order of $1/N$) is generally significantly smaller than in the original (on the order of $1/pN$), except that when b_2 is relatively large the new protocol's behaviour effectively becomes that of the original, with probability c/qN matching the table entry c/pN for the Original Protocol; when b_2 is small, $b_2 + c$ is less than c/q, so the probability in the new protocol is better, i.e. less than the original.

---

[3] Currently, we make a simplifying assumption: an account is in one of the two modes.
[4] Additional details on attack strategies and Table 1 will be provided in the full paper.
[5] For the new protocol, these figures are per time period T. However for a sophisticated multi-period attack, the new protocol remains better (fewer passwords are eliminatable), assuming $p = q$, unless at least N/b_2 time periods are used (e.g. about 1600 years for $T = 1$ month, $N = 100\,000$ and $b_2 = 5$).

Table 1. Tabular data for comparitive analysis (single-account attack). q is used for p in the new protocol to emphasize possible use of different values ($p = q$ is also possible).

Question	Original Protocol	New Protocol	
		Account Mode	
		Owner	Non-owner
Q1	$(1-p)N$	$z_1 = (1-q)b_2$	$z_2 = \max(b_1, (1-q)b_2)$
Q2	$\frac{1}{2}pN$	$\frac{1}{2}(N - z_1) \approx N/2$	$\frac{1}{2}(N - z_2)$
Q3a ($c = 0$)	0	0	b_1/N
Q3b ($c = 1$)	$1/pN$	$(1 - (1-q)^{b_2+1})/qN$	$(b_1 + 1)/N$
Q3c ($c \geq 2$)	c/pN	$\min(\frac{c}{q}, b_2 + c)/N$ †	$(b_1 + c)/N$

†Upper bound

Table 2. Fraction of the time a legitimate user must answer an RTT ($1.0 = 100\%$). As in Table 1, q is used in place of p in the new protocol.
†After the failed login bound is crossed in the new protocol, in several cases – e.g. on incorrect passwords, and correct passwords without valid cookies – RTT's occur more frequently (i.e. 100% of the time after the bound is crossed within period T). However for accounts in owner mode we expect a large number of users select a "Remember password" option (standard in many applications) which stores passwords locally on their regular machines. No failed passwords are expected from such users; but note their failed login thresholds may still be crossed due to attacker activities.

	Original Protocol	New Protocol	
		Account Mode	
		Owner	Non-owner
Incorrect password	p	q†	q†
Correct password - valid cookie	0	0	0
Correct password - no valid cookie	1.0	1.0	0†

Note: for both $c = 1$ and $c \geq 2$, the table gives a probability (i.e. an expectation over a large number of runs). The new protocol has a guaranteed upper bound on the probability: $(b2 + c)/N$.

According to row Q3a, for an attacker unwilling to answer any RTTs, the security is the same in both protocols except we relax security (i.e. to b_1/N) for some small number of accounts in non-owner mode to improve usability (see usability improvement in Table 2, bottom row).

A security analysis for multi-account attacks (wherein an attacker's goal is to break into any one of many accounts, not necessarily a specific account) and parallel login attacks (wherein an attacker may try to simultaneously login to one userid a large number of times on different servers) is left for the full version of this paper.

Discussion of Usability. For comparing usability between the original and the new protocols, Table 2 notes the proportion of time a legitimate user is queried with an RTT on entering a correct or incorrect password, with and without a valid cookie. A case of particular focus for the new protocol is the legitimate "travelling user", who generally operates with an account in non-owner mode and without a valid cookie. The new protocol is significantly more user-friendly to such users. We also believe that such users are typically more likely to enter incorrect passwords (see discussion in caption of Table 2), and therefore increasing usability in this case is significant as one would expect that "incorrect password" cases occur far less often in owner mode.

Also related to usability – the value of the parameter q may be reduced in the new protocol without loss of security, due to the use of the failed login bound b_2 and depending on its value relative to q (see Table 1). This further increases usability in the incorrect password case, independent of the discussion in the paragraph above.

Discussion of Cookie Theft. The above analysis assumes that no cookie theft occurs; here we make a few observations in the case cookie it does.

1. *New Protocol.* If a cookie is stolen, then within the cookie's validity period, under the recommended cookie failure threshold, the attacker gets $\min(b_1, b_2)$ password guesses on the userid. The attack we consider is one where the attacker quits all guesses that return an RTT, and having a good cookie, hopes to reach line 6 with a lucky guess[6].
2. *Original Protocol.* Similarly, the attacker gets free guesses up to the cookie failure threshold. A correct password guess on any of these trials allows a successful login without having to answer an RTT.

Comments. (a) It is less likely that a cookie is stolen under the new protocol, since they reside in fewer places – e.g. cookies of the original protocol would show up in airport Internet rooms. (b) A combined cookie and non-cookie attack against a single account is less likely to be successful in the new protocol, primarily because the attacker can reduce the password space to a p-fraction in the original protocol even before using the stolen cookie (see related discussion on questions Q1 and Q2).

5   Additional Techniques Augmenting RTT-Based Authentication

Here we propose a number of techniques to augment the original protocol (Fig. 2), without changing its basic functionality. This includes addressing RTT relay attacks (§2). These techniques are intended primarily to improve security, and are independent of (orthogonal to) the changes proposed in §4. We present them briefly without additional analysis.

5.1   RTT with Embedded Warning

Here we propose a simple method to prevent RTT relay attacks. A drawback of the proposal is that it requires some thought on behalf of users (which is, in

---

[6] This attack may take place in conjunction with one that reduces the password space without answering an RTT, or one where the adversary answers c RTTs.

some cases, unfortunately unrealistic). However, we believe the general idea may be adapted to significant advantage.

The general idea is to rely upon self-awareness of legitimate users to prevent unwitting participation in an RTT relay attack. One approach is to make RTT challenges user-directed by incorporating a user's specific userid *within the RTT itself*. Preferably, removing this information is of comparable difficulty as answering the RTT itself.

For example, as part of answering a text RTT, a portion of the text is a userid field[7], which the user is warned to compare to their own userid, thereby confirming that the RTT is targeted specifically at them (within the embedded warning the user is instructed to not answer the RTT if the match fails). As an additional optional feature, the RTT might also contain an embedded short "help URL", for a site giving further instructions on the use of this type of RTT.

This idea is analogous to the now generally accepted, and recommended, practice in authentication protocols of putting party identifiers within the protected (i.e. signed or MAC'd) region of protocol messages. It is also analogous to the typical automated check, when using secure browser cookies, that cookies match a particular userid or IP address; and to the matching userid check in the original protocol (line 5, Fig. 2).

5.2   Notification Regarding Failed Logins

Here we propose a simple method to detect automated dictionary attacks and trigger counter-active measures[8]. Once a small threshold (e.g. 3-10) login failures occurs for any single account, an automated, out-of-band communication (e.g. email) is sent to an address-on-record of the associated legitimate user. If the failed logins resulted from the user's own actions, the user will be aware of the failures and can safely ignore the message; otherwise, it signals malicious activity, and may lead the user to take such actions as to request[9] changes to server-side user-specific login protocol parameters (see §4), or to change their own password to a more secure password using the normal change password method.

As an alternative, albeit less desirable[10], after some larger number of failed logins (e.g. 25), the system might automatically reset the user's password to a computer-generated secure password emailed to the user. This would prevent a user's typically weak self-chosen password from being cracked through standard dictionary attacks. (Depending on the security policy in use, the user might be allowed to change the password back to a weak one if they wish, but at this point they may also be motivated to follow recommended password rules.)

---

[7] A variant instead includes the name of the site being visited, with similar explanation. (An anonymous referee suggested this.) The choice between web site name and userid could be made dynamically, e.g. selecting the shorter of the two.

[8] This expands on administrators manually sending out-of-band messages [20, §4.4].

[9] For example, through an authenticated channel such as an email to an un-advertised pre-arranged address, or a hidden URL provided in the email alert to the user.

[10] This may raise customary issues related to system-generated passwords and system-initiated password changes. If used, this alternative must be crafted so as not to generate additional customer service calls, which are not tolerated within our scope.

This proposal is less effective against multi-target attacks, and *slow-channel dictionary attacks* wherein an automated program tries passwords on a certain account after there is likely to have already been a successful login attempt (e.g. waiting for a random but minimal delay, such as one-day intervals). In some systems, an attacker can confirm if a user has logged in recently (e.g. an eBay user), and mount only a limited number of trial password guesses some fixed period after each such successful login. This proposal may nonetheless be helpful, and other parameters may limit the success of slow-channel attacks. A small amount of per-user server-side state is needed, but the original protocol has a similar requirement to address cookie-theft [20, §4.5]. A remaining drawback of this proposal is degraded usability (additional user attention is required).

5.3   Consuming Client Resources
Using Zero-Footprint Software Downloads

We propose that login protocol variants (e.g. see §4) be augmented by known techniques requiring that clients solve "puzzles" consuming client resources, and return answers prior to the server verifying a login. This follows research lines to combat junk mail (e.g. [8, 1]) and denial-of-service attacks [15]. Another augmenting technology is to harden passwords with auxilliary protocols that can interact directly with the server [11].

Since functionality for performing client puzzles is not resident in standard client software (e.g. browsers), this proposal requires allowing Java applets, Javascript, or other zero-footprint downloads. We no longer agree with dismissing special client-side software outright (cf. [20]); rather, we see opportunity for advantageous use. Though perhaps worrisome, most users and organizations now operate under the assumption that Java, and certainly Javascript, are turned on[11]. Nonetheless, since popular web services should work for 100% of potential users, to accommodate those who cannot use zero-footprint software, RTT-based login protocols can be designed as follows. Client puzzles (or the like) are sent to users. For those unable to answer the puzzles for any reason (in some case the server may learn this *a priori*), the protocol branches to a path replacing the puzzle by an (extra) RTT. This RTT will be less convenient to the user (requiring user attention, vs. machine resources), but we expect this to be a relatively small percentage of users, and therefore viable.

6   Background and Related Work

The RTT relay attack of §2 is related to general classes of *middle-person attacks* and *interleaving attacks* involving an active attacker inserting itself between legitimate parties in a communications protocol, and/or using information from one instance of a protocol to attack a simultaneous instance. Such attacks

---

[11] These are in fact the settings that result from the Internet Explorer default ("medium" security), and which we expect remain unchanged by most users.

are well-known in cryptographic protocols and have a long history ([6, 7]; [18, pp.530-531]).

For example, challenge-response protocols have long been used to identify military aircraft in *identify-friend-or-foe* (IFF) systems. IFF challenges from enemy challengers have reportedly been forwarded in real-time to the enemy's own planes, eliciting correct responses which were then successfully used as responses to the enemy's original challenges [2, pp.19-20]. Note that responses in such systems are typically automatic; the protocols do not involve entity authentication of the querying party.

Related to this is the well-known grandmaster postal-chess attack: an amateur simultaneously plays two grandmasters by post, playing white pieces in one game and black in the other, using the moves of his opponents against each other, resulting in an overall outcome better than the two losses he would have achieved on his own.

The term *strong authentication protocols* is often used for protocols designed to preclude attacks which first obtain appropriate data related to one or more protocol runs, and then proceed to crack passwords offline (i.e. without further interaction). This line of research began with the early work of Gong and co-authors [17, 12, 13]; Bellovin and Merritt's EKE protocol [3] then inspired a number of others (e.g. Jablon's SPEKE [14]; Wu's SRP [23]; see also [16]).

Offline exhaustive password-guessing attacks typically proceed by trying potential passwords in order of (perceived) decreasing likelihood. The most probable passwords are often in conventional dictionaries, or modified dictionaries specially tailored to this task. Offline attacks are thus often called *dictionary attacks*, although dictionaries are also used in online attacks (if account lock-out and time-delays are not used; see §2).

Use of system-generated passwords can provide higher security (by better password choices), but suffers severe usability issues. Pass*phrases* have also been proposed (e.g. see [27, 26]). Other approaches include system administrators running password-crack tools on their own systems (*re-active* password checking); enforcement of simple password rules or policies at the time of new password selection; and at such time, checking for its presence in large customized dictionaries built for this purpose (*pro-active* password checking, e.g. see Yan [25] for a recent summary).

7   Concluding Remarks

We expect that a large number of human-in-the-loop and mandatory human participation schemes, unrelated to the RTT-based login protocol discussed here, are also subject to the RTT relay attack of §2.

A major feature of our new protocol (§4) is the additional flexibility and configurability, including failed login thresholds and potentially lower RTT challenge probabilities (e.g. for suitable b_2 lowering q does not decrease security). This allows the protocol to be tailored to match particular environments, classes of users, and applications; while determining the optimal parameters for specific user profiles appears non-trivial, we expect further analytical study will be fruitful. Another new aspect is storing cookies only on trustworthy machines. As mentioned earlier, the new protocol can be parameterized to give the original protocol as a special case. While the configurability does complicate protocol implementation somewhat, we note that a number of the parameters which are optionally dynamic can be managed by automated tools; thus the additional human administrative costs are relatively minor. For example, an automated tool can keep a running ratio of successful logins to failed logins for the entire system, and alter system wide (or account-specific) parameter q, or system-wide (or account-specific) failed login thresholds b_1 and b_2, based on this ratio. A significant improvement of our protocol over prior work concerns protecting against relay attacks by forcing an RTT challenge on all login attempts after the number of failed logins reaches a threshold. Previous work enabled a significant fraction of the password space to be eliminated with an automated attack. Per-user failed-login counts (as used in Fig. 3) also provide protection against sweatshop attacks and RTT relay attacks, especially such attacks targeting a particular account. Note that embedding warnings within RTTs (§5.1) does not by itself protect against sweatshop attacks.

For practical protection in Internet-scale live systems, we recommend combining techniques from §5 with those of §4. We see a large number of ways to expand on the ideas of §4. In particular, we encourage others to explore the use of dynamic parameters (ideally managed by automated tools), and other ways to gain advantage by treating users logging in from non-owned devices (e.g. traveling users) different from those continually using their regular login machines.

Acknowledgements

We thank anonymous referees for helpful comments. The second author acknowledges the generous support of the National Sciences and Engineering Research Council of Canada for support as Canada Research Chair in Network and Software Security, and under an NSERC Discovery Grant.

References

1. M. Abadi, M. Burrows, M. Manasse, T. Wobber, "Moderately Hard, Memory-bound Functions", NDSS'03, San Diego, February 2003.
2. R. Anderson, *Security Engineering: A Guide to Building Dependable Distributed Systems*, Wiley, 2001.
3. S. Bellovin, M. Merritt, "Encrypted Key Exchange: Password-Based Protocols Secure Against Dictionary Attack", *Proc. IEEE Symp. Research in Security and Privacy*, Oakland, May 1992.
4. S. Byers, A. Rubin, D. Kormann, "Defending Against an Internet-based Attack on the Physical World", Workshop on Privacy in the Electronic Society (WPES'02), November 21 2002, Washington D.C.
5. CAPTCHA Project web site, http://www.captcha.net/ (first appeared: 2000).

6. W. Diffie, M. Hellman, "New Directions in Cryptography", *IEEE Trans. Info. Theory* vol.22 (1976), pp.644-654.
7. W. Diffie, P.C. van Oorschot, M.J. Wiener, "Authentication and Authenticated Key Exchange", *Designs, Codes and Cryptography* vol.2 (1992), 107-125.
8. C. Dwork, M. Naor, "Pricing via Processing or Combatting Junk Mail", *Lecture Notes in Computer Science 740 (Proceedings of CRYPTO'92)*, 1993, pp. 137–147.
9. Password Usage, Federal Information Processing Standards Publication 112, U.S. Department of Commerce, NIST, 1985.
10. Automated Password Generator, FIPS Pub 112, U.S. Dept. Commerce, 1993.
11. W. Ford, B. Kaliski, "Server-Assisted Generation of a Strong Secret from a Password", 9th Int'l Workshop on Enabling Technologi (WET-ICE 2000), IEEE, 2000.
12. L. Gong, "Verifiable-text attacks in cryptographic protocols", *1990 IEEE INFO-COM*, pp.686-693.
13. L. Gong, T. Lomas, R. Needham, J. Saltzer, "Protecting poorly chosen secrets from guessing attacks", *IEEE J. Selected Areas Comm.* vol.11 (1993), pp.648-656.
14. D. Jablon, "Strong password-only authenticated key exchange", *ACM Computer Communcations Review*, Oct.1996.
15. A. Juels, J. Brainard, "Client puzzles: A cryptographic defense against connection depletion attacks", *Proceedings of the 1999 ISOC Network and Distributed System Security Symposium*, pp.151-165, 1999.
16. C. Kaufman, R. Perlman, M. Speciner, *Network Security: Private Communication in a Public World*, Second Edition, Prentice Hall, 2002.
17. T. Lomas, L. Gong, J. Saltzer, R. Needham, "Reducing risks from poorly chosen keys", *Operating Systems Review* vol.13, pp.14-18 (presented at 1989 ACM Symp. on Operating Systems Principles).
18. A. Menezes, P. van Oorschot, S. Vanstone, *Handbook of Applied Cryptography*, CRC Press, 1997.
19. M. Naor, "Verification of a human in the loop or Identification via the Turing Test", unpublished manuscript, 1997. Online version available at: http://www.wisdom.weizmann.ac.il/~naor/PAPERS/human.ps
20. B. Pinkas, T. Sander, "Securing Passwords Against Dictionary Attacks", *2002 ACM Conf. on Computer and Communications Security*, Wash. D.C.
21. L. von Ahn, Eurocrypt'03 presentation of [22], 6 May 2003, Warsaw, Poland.
22. L. von Ahn, M. Blum, N. Hopper, J. Langford, "CAPTCHA: Using Hard AI Problems for Security", *Eurocrypt'03* proceedings, Springer-Verlag, LNCS 2656 (2003).
23. T. Wu, "The secure remote password protocol", Internet Society *1998 Network and Distributed System Security* symposium (NDSS'98).
24. T. Wolverton, Hackers find new way to bilk eBay users, CNET news.com 03/25/02.
25. J. Yan, "A Note on Proactive Password Checking", *Proc. 2001 ACM New Security Paradigms Workshop*, New Mexico, USA, Sept.2001.
26. J. Yan, A. Blackwell, R. Anderson, A. Grant, "The Memorability and Security of Passwords – Some Empirical Results", Tech. Report 500, Computer Lab, Cambridge, 2000. http://www.ftp.cl.cam.ac.uk/ftp/rja14/tr500.pdf.
27. P. Zimmermann, *The Official PGP User's Guide*, MIT Press, 1995.

Call Center Customer Verification
by Query-Directed Passwords

Lawrence O'Gorman, Amit Bagga, and Jon Bentley

Avaya Labs Research, Basking Ridge, NJ, USA
{logorman,bagga,jbentley}@avaya.com

Abstract. We introduce an authentication framework called Query-Directed Passwords (QDP) that incorporates the convenience of authentication by long-term knowledge questions and offers stronger security than from traditional types of personal questions. Security is strengthened for this scheme by imposing several restrictions on the questions and answers, and specifying how QDP is implemented in conjunction with other factors. Four QDP implementations are examined for call center applications. We examine the security and convenience of one of these implementations in detail. This implementation involves client-end storage of questions in a computer file or a wallet card, and follows a basic challenge-response authentication protocol.

1 Introduction

> *"Good morning, Alice, and thank you for phoning ABC Finnacial. For customer verification purposes, please tell me your: social security number, mother's maiden name, date of birth, name of first pet, ..."*

The amount of information in the request above may be exaggerated, but the scenario is not. We experience similar customer verification procedures at the beginning of many call center sessions, especially those dealing with health insurance and personal finances. Yet, the practice of using personal data for authentication is troubling. Is knowledge of Alice's date of birth a good piece of information to use for security? If so, should Alice schedule her birthday party far away from the true birth date so that no one can learn this "secret" information? And should Alice give her social security number to any call center agent who asks? Not only may she have privacy concerns with this, but if social security number is used for verification to many call centers, isn't this like re-using a password for different hosts, which we are advised not to do?

It is clear why a password is not ideal for call center customer verification: the customer cannot remember yet another password. However, are personal knowledge questions good substitutes? Let's compare the two. A password is a secret shared by a user and an authenticating host. In contrast, personal knowledge like your social security number and date of birth is not a shared secret and can be learned by an attacker through some amount of investigative effort. A password can be changed if compromised. However, you can't change your mother's maiden name. With passwords, we are instructed to use different ones for different hosts to eliminate cross-attacks. However, there are only a few examples of personal knowledge that are traditionally used for authentication so the need to reuse them rises with each new host to which we register. Worse yet, because these personal-knowledge questions are known for particular hosts (e.g., host X always uses mother's maiden name), these become standing

A. Juels (Ed.): FC 2004, LNCS 3110, pp. 54–67, 2004.

targets for an attacker to learn this information about customers. To avoid standing target questions, some verification procedures require the user to create questions of their own (e.g., "What is my first pet's name?"). However, there is a danger here that users may choose questions poorly. Choosing a poor question is similar to choosing a weak password that can be guessed or found by dictionary search. For these and other reasons, authentication by these personal-knowledge types of questions is not currently a good substitute for passwords. So, why is it still widely used? It is because memorized passwords are forgotten [1-4] and personal knowledge is not.

There are alternatives to knowledge-based authentication by password or personal knowledge [5]. Tokens, such as smart cards can store or create strong passwords without the need for memorization. However, for customer applications, there is a significant expenditure to provide tokens and readers to all customers. Biometrics suffers the same cost drawback to provide scanners (readers) to customers, and also has reliability and logistic drawbacks (e.g., if a fingerprint is compromised, how do you change it? [6, 7]).

Because of deficiencies with these alternatives, we reexamine knowledge-based authenticators in this paper, and attempt to obtain a better balance of convenience and security for the call center customer application. If this better balance can be obtained, there are advantages to this type of authenticator. Like the biometric, users always have their personal knowledge. Unlike tokens and biometrics, a user doesn't need special readers for personal knowledge because computer keyboards and telephone keypads are the input device, and these are ubiquitous. And because no extra equipment is needed, personal knowledge authentication is inexpensive.

Because our application is call center authentication, where customers often need to authenticate infrequently and where ease-of-use is important, our work focuses not on memorized passwords but on responses to questions based on long-term knowledge. Although we have just criticized the traditional use of this type of authentication, our goal is to retain its inherent convenience and to improve upon its weak security. One way we attempt to attain a balance of convenience and security is by using not the traditional questions but a larger base of questions whose answers reside in a user's *permastore* memory [8]. Permastore describes a category of long-term memory that is persistent over a very long period of time up to a lifetime. This includes common personal facts like birth date, but there are other, perhaps trivial facts, like the color of car in which you learned to drive and your food preference as a child. In addition to the choice of questions, we strengthen security by creating a more rigorous framework for their use.

Attempts to make personal knowledge authentication stronger are not unique. Ellison et al. [9] propose a method, called *personal entropy*, to encrypt secrets or passwords via the answers to several questions. They base this upon Shamir's secret-sharing scheme [10], also called a (t,n)-threshold scheme, where a secret is distributed into n shares of which at least t of these is needed to reconstruct the secret. The n shares are encrypted and decrypted using hashed functions of the personal-knowledge questions and answers. The emphasis in this work is to offer the user fault tolerance by allowing her to forget the answers to some small number of questions, but still achieve successful authentication.

Frykholm and Juels [11] offer an approach, called *error-tolerant password recovery (ETPAR)*, with the similar goal of deriving a strong password from a sequence of answers to personal-knowledge questions. One portion of the method is similar to the personal entropy method, distributing the answers to questions in a vector that is used for encryption and decryption. However the ETPAR method achieves fault tolerance not by secret sharing but by using error-correcting codes in a scheme called *fuzzy commitment* [12]. The emphasis in this work is offering cryptographically strong security to defend against the computationally unbounded attacker. They describe an experiment on 9 users over a one-week period for their system-authored questions with open answers.

Our approach is similar to these previous works in at least two respects. We also use personal-knowledge questions and can achieve fault tolerance with multiple questions. However, there are also differences in our emphasis and approach. The previous papers emphasize the cryptographic underpinnings of the approaches, whereas our paper deals with details closer to the human end. One example of this is design and types of questions. Our approach deals only with system-guided questions and answers. Another difference is in the use of the approach. Whereas the previous papers presented schemes for password storage and recovery, our paper applies query-directed authentication to customer call center verification.

In Section 2, we introduce our method, called Query-Directed Passwords (QDP). We describe specifications for questions and answers that underlie this approach. In Section 3, we describe the call center application, beginning with requirements and then offering four implementations with different security and convenience tradeoffs. Security comparisons are made between implementations and we investigate one implementation, involving client-end storage of questions, in more detail. Conclusions and future work are discussed in Section 4.

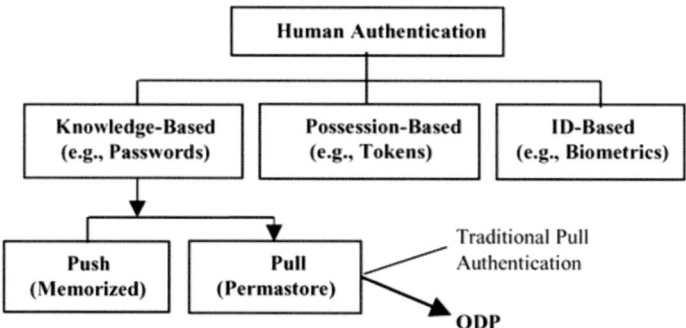

Fig. 1. Hierarchy of human authentication, showing query-directed passwords under the category of knowledge-based, pull-type authentication.

2   Query-Directed Passwords (QDP)

2.1   Background

User authentication can be divided into three categories (Fig. 1): knowledge-based (which includes passwords), possession-based (which includes tokens), and ID-based (which includes biometrics). In this paper, we further divide the knowledge-based category into "push" and "pull" passwords. The distinction is that a push-type password must be memorized by the user at registration. A pull-type password is recalled from the user's memory; since it is already in permastore memory, it does not need to be memorized first. All pull-type passwords are hint- or query-directed, however within this category we make a distinction between the traditional type and our approach. We call the first type *traditional pull-type authentication*, the stereotypical example being mother's maiden name. We call our approach *query-directed passwords*, or *QDP*. The distinction is not in an entirely different approach, but in the fact that QDP applies a formalism that constrains the types of questions and the procedure by which these questions are used.

We can describe three types of questions and answers for pull-type authentication. Examples are listed for each:

1. Open question and open answer (user creates the questions),
   - *What is the name of my first pet?*
2. Selectable question and open answer (system provides the questions for selection),
   - *What is my mother's maiden name?*
   - *What was the number of my childhood house?*
3. Selectable question and multiple-choice answer (system provides the questions and answers for selection),
   - *What color is the first family car I remember in childhood?*
     1) black, 2) white, 3) gray, 4) blue, 5) green, 6) red.
   - *How did I travel to my first paying job as a teen?*
     1) drove, 2) driven, 3) public transit, 4) carpool, 5) bike, 6) walk.

2.2 QDP Approach

In contrast to the traditional approaches of choosing a very limited number of personal questions or enabling the customer to create questions, we create QDP questions with strict guidelines. Instead of personal facts, QDP questions involve trivial facts or opinions such as, "Where is a wall clock in your house?" and "What type of apple do you prefer?" These are unlikely to be on your resume or in official personal records, so are more difficult for an attacker to learn. Instead of a few questions, QDP requires the user to select a number of questions (e.g., 5 to 15). This larger number of questions helps authentication in three ways: 1) different questions can be used for different hosts, 2) different questions can be used for different authentication sessions for the same host, and 3) if a question becomes compromised, it can be eliminated with still other questions to take its place. Instead of the system assigning questions, some that the user might consider to be private, the system offers questions for user selection, so that any questions considered private need not be selected. Below, we list specifications of QDP answers and questions:

1. Answers must be consistently and easily recalled by a user over time.
2. Answers must be discriminating of a user. The answer space must be fairly evenly distributed across the population and individual answers must be independent of one another.
3. Answers must not be easily guessed or learned.
4. Answers must not be considered confidential.
5. Questions offered for user selection must be fairly large in number, and the question selection must be fairly evenly distributed across the population.
6. Questions chosen by a user must be dispersed in type or topic.

Comparisons between traditional questions and QDP questions are shown in Table 1.

Table 1. Comparison between traditional pull-type authentication and QDP.

Traditional	QDP
A few traditional questions, or user-created	System offers pre-created questions for selection
Personal facts that may be learned by others	Trivial facts and opinions, difficult to learn by others
Few questions	Many questions
Can't be changed if compromised	Replace with another question if compromised
Mandatory information may be considered private	User selects non-confidential questions

Of the question and answer types described in Section 2.1, we restrict QDP usage to type 3 and a subset of type 2. The type 3, selectable question and multiple-choice answer, constitute the majority of a user's QDP questions. We call these *QDP multiple-choice questions*. It is straightforward to perform a security analysis upon this type because we know questions and permissible answers beforehand. Ideally, we also know population statistics such as frequencies of selected questions and answers that will help in security analysis.

QDP questions can also be a subset of type 2 questions, selectable questions and open answers, which involve particular questions with numeric answers. "What was the street number of my childhood house?" is an example of this. We call these *QDP numeric questions*, and these are often used where a traditional PIN would be used, the advantage of the QDP numeric question being that it is elicited from permastore with a query, so it is more easily recalled. In Section 4, we will briefly describe how we use information extraction techniques to guide a user toward a permissible question and answer of this type. The numeric restriction facilitates this analysis.

We do not use type 1 questions, open questions and open answers. This is because of the difficulty in automatically analyzing such questions and answers (the question would need to be understood by a computer as a precondition to security analysis).

Use of QDP multiple-choice questions alone does not provide the level of security required of most applications. If an authentication system were designed with 4 questions of 6 multiple-choice answers each, a brute force attacker would be able to guess the answer after $6^4 / 2 = 648$ guesses on average. If the attacker has some knowledge of the user or some knowledge of the distribution of answers, he could guess even more quickly. This is far less secure than for a 4-digit PIN, for which $10^4 / 2 = 5000$ is the average number of guesses needed. Therefore, the security story does not end with the QDP questions and answers. Our own use of QDP involves some other contributor to overall system security such as a second factor or a particular protocol to strengthen security. This is shown by the description of implementations in Section 3.

We have performed preliminary user testing of QDP and will report this elsewhere. One component of this testing was an experiment on answer recall rate over time. In a short-term test done weekly for 30 users from Avaya Labs over a 3-month period and longer term testing done 5-6 months after enrollment, users answered about 95% of individual questions correctly. With fault tolerance on the 5 to 8 questions asked per session, users successfully authenticated 98.5% of the attempts. This test was not meant to simulate a secure authentication application but to test whether users could recall answers to QDP-type questions at a high enough rate over time to be effective for authentication. We have since begun a pilot for password recovery whose purpose is security and whose population size is larger and more varied than for the preliminary test.

3   Call Center Application

QDP has properties that make it applicable to such tasks as computer password recovery and use of voiced password in a public area. In this paper, we focus on one application, call center authentication. Customer verification is common for financial- and health-related call centers. In this paper, we focus on *call* centers (implying just telephone communications) rather than *contact* centers (phone and Web communications). This is because the former presents a more constrained and challenging problem. The methods presented here can apply to the superset of contact center transactions as well.

3.1   Specifications

Security is the main objective in authentication, however an important consideration in specifying this application is that the authenticating person is a customer. Unlike employees, military personnel, or civil servants, there is little leverage to *make* customers do anything because they can switch to a competitor if they are dissatisfied. Therefore, a well-designed call center will offer both security *and* customer convenience. These call center specifications are listed below:

I. Security-Related Specifications:
   1. It should be difficult for an attacker to authenticate in place of the authorized customer.
   2. It should be difficult for potential attackers at the host-side to learn the customer's authentication information.
   3. Compromise detection and recovery are desirable.
   4. It should be difficult for an attacker to mount a successful denial of service attack.
   5. Progressively adjustable security strengths should be possible.

II. Customer-Related Specifications:
   1. It should be convenient with respect to time and memory effort for an authorized customer to authenticate.
   2. The customer's privacy should be respected.
   3. The customer should be allowed some fault tolerance to get a portion of the authentication response wrong but still to successfully authenticate.
   4. Verification should be possible via the numeric keypad of a telephone.
   5. Verification should also be possible by speaking into the telephone without worry that an eavesdropper can learn the authentication information.
   6. The scheme should be inexpensive on a per customer basis.

We describe these specifications below and examine how these are met for particular QDP implementations in Section 3.3.

Security specification 1 is the main purpose here, to safeguard confidential information and to prevent transactions by unauthorized persons. There are two types of client-side attackers: strangers and acquaintances. Strangers do not know anything about the customer prior to the attack. They can guess answers or first learn about the customer via whatever public means are available. Acquaintances (which span the range from an office colleague to a spouse) already know some things about the customer. With knowledge of the customer an acquaintance can mount an imposter attack.

Security specification 2 refers to host-side or insider attack. For instance, if a call center operation allows agents to see customer access PINs, then a dishonest agent could steal these for fraudulent use. In the world of computer administration, user passwords are usually transformed and stored via a 1-way hash function. In this way, even administrators with access to password files cannot easily learn user passwords because there is no direct transformation from the hashed value back to the password.

Security specification 3 states that some means of compromise detection and recovery is desirable. A bankcard, for instance, provides tangible means for detecting one form of compromise – when you can't withdraw money because your card is gone, it may have been stolen. Recovery involves canceling the card and obtaining a new one. In contrast, personal data are almost in a permanent state of "compromise" because many people know your date of birth, etc. Furthermore, compromise recovery is impossible with data such as date of birth.

Security specification 4 states that denial of service attacks should be difficult. One way to cause the system to deny service to a true customer is for someone to answer the questions incorrectly a number of times. Most systems will freeze the account after a number of failed attempts to prevent brute force attacks.

Security specification 5 allows fewer questions to be asked for a low-security application, and more for stronger security. Furthermore, even within a single session, the customer can start with a "default" security level, then be required to answer more questions if a transaction requiring higher than default level is requested. A single password does not meet this specification.

Customer specification 1 states that authentication should be convenient. Security and convenience often present conflicting specifications, so a compromise must be chosen. Since authentication includes both enrollment and verification, one can anticipate another tradeoff between these. For instance, a longer time spent to enroll diligently might save time later each time the customer verifies.

Customer specification 2 regards privacy, what information a person wants to keep confidential. But personal privacy concerns are different for different people. The system should be able to handle differences in privacy preferences.

Customer specification 3 sets query-directed authentication apart from passwords and other authentication options. If you forget a password, you will not be authenticated. There is no middle ground. The same is true if you lose a smart card or your voice fails to verify. However, if a customer forgets an answer to one or more authentication questions, we'd like to offer him some leeway to still authenticate. It is important to say that strength of security should not suffer here, so if for example a customer misses an answer, tolerance is not defined as simply asking more questions until he gets one right. The number of correct and incorrect answers must both be considered.

Customer specification 4 is a practical requirement for the targeted telephone medium. Although it might be convenient to speak an authentication response, speech recognition technology is still not reliable enough to correctly recognize all responses consistently, especially for unconstrained telephone speech (untrained speaker, unlimited vocabulary, random telephone line) [13], and for instances of high background noise. Therefore, basic interaction is by touch-tone key entry into an IVR (Interactive Voice Response) system.

Customer specification 5 allows the customer to speak authentication responses (in addition to keying them as just specified). However, the customer should not have to worry about an eavesdropper overhearing and using the information for attack. An example test of this is the following. A customer who works in an open office environment checks her financial information by phone each day. Specification 5 states that her office neighbors who can overhear these calls should not be able to learn information such as to subsequently impersonate her. A traditional voiced password would not meet this specification.

As many as possible of the adjectives used in the requirements above, "difficult," "easy," "fault tolerance," and "security strength" should be quantified. Security and convenience are not always measurable in an absolute sense, however we will attempt to compare relative merits among options below.

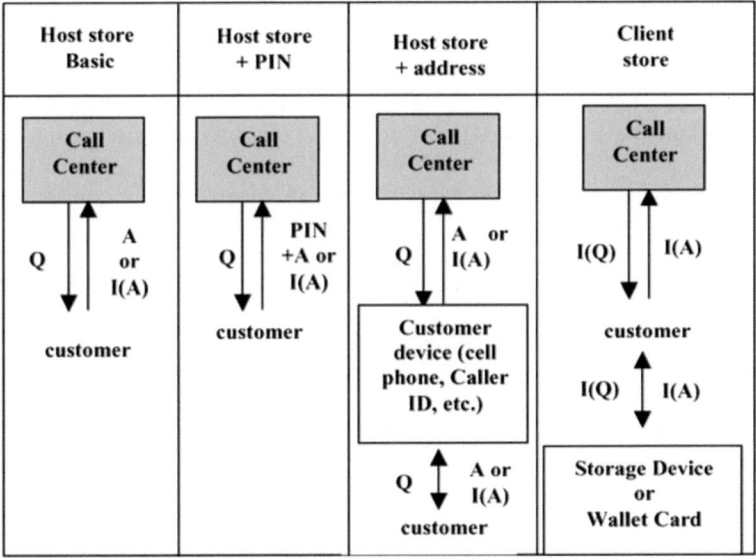

Fig. 2. The four options for call center authentication are illustrated. Questions Q or question indices I(Q) are sent by the call center. Answers A or answer indices I(A) are returned.

3.2 Implementations

We show four ways to implement QDP for call center authentication in Fig. 2 and describe these below.

3.2.1 Host Store – Basic. The basic host store implementation uses QDP alone in the procedure described in Section 2. This provides the least security among implementations. The customer phones the call center and is connected with the IVR system for performing authentication. After identifying herself by keying in an identity number, the system asks a random subset of the customer's enrolled questions. The customer responds by keying in the indices of chosen multiple-choice answers. If all of the answers are correct (or some pre-set portion of them), then the customer is successfully authenticated.

The basic implementation has a number of vulnerabilities. One is that any attacker can learn some questions selected by the customer just by phoning the call center and entering that person's (non-secret) identification number. After learning the questions, the attacker can make an effort to find the answers. So these questions become a standing target for an attacker. Another problem is the small keyspace. For example, if there are $k=4$ questions with $M=6$ multiple-choice answers each, this results in a keyspace of $6^4=1296$, which is guessable in 648 tries on average. This is not very strong security. Finally, personnel at the authenticating host can easily learn a customer's information. Questions and answers cannot be hashed as for computer passwords because (for one reason) a telephone has no computing power to perform this computation. They can be encrypted at the host, but are vulnerable when decrypted for use.

Notwithstanding these problems, the basic implementation of QDP is more secure than traditional pull-type authentication. For a client-end attacker to expose the customer's questions he could have the following strategy. Phone the call center to expose the k questions that are asked for a single authentication session; and answer these with random guesses, likely failing authentication. Endeavor to learn the answers to these k questions offline. Phone again and answer any previously exposed questions to which he has learned the answers, and expose new questions. Continue this process until authentication is successful. If the total number of questions a user has selected is n, then the minimum (worst case) number of sessions to expose all questions is n/k. For $n=15$ and $k=4$, the attacker would need at least 4 sessions to expose all questions, and could successfully attack in the next session if he learned all the answers. We can prevent an attacker from being able to expose all the questions by freezing the account after some number of failed questions. If an attempted attack is suspected in this case, then the exposed questions can be retired from those selected by the customer. This cannot be done with traditional pull-type authentication, where the number of potential questions is either fixed or very small.

The basic QDP scheme can prevent host-end personnel from learning questions and answers from one system, then using them on another. This is because questions are not as limited or few with QDP as traditional pull-type authentication. A customer can use a different set of questions and answers for different hosts. In contrast, there are a limited number of hosts where only mother's maiden name, social security number, and date of birth can be used.

3.2.2 Host Store Plus PIN. A weakness of the basic implementation is that an attacker can learn the customer's questions merely by entering into an authentication session. We can defend against this vulnerability by asking for a PIN before relaying the questions. If the entered PIN is correct, the system asks k questions selected by the customer. If the entered PIN is incorrect, then the system still asks k questions, but these are not necessarily the customer's selected questions but rather are a random selection from the N questions in the QDP database. In this way, an attacker cannot first learn the PIN by brute force attack, and then independently expose the questions. By posing the selected questions depending upon the correct PIN, this increases the keyspace from 10^4 *plus* 1296 for a 4-digit PIN and for four questions, to 10^4 *times* 1296, about 3 orders of magnitude greater.

The drawback of requiring a PIN is that the customer will now have to memorize something, and if she forgets will not be able to access her account. This is where a QDP numeric question can replace a traditional PIN for the convenience of the customer.

3.2.3 Host Store Plus Address. Instead of requiring the customer to use a PIN, we can keep the customer's selected questions confidential in another way. When the customer wants to authenticate, the questions are sent only to a previously registered communications device. If the customer registers the home phone number, then the caller identification can be used for this. The same is true for a cell phone or the address of a pager or wireless PDA. The degree of security depends on how easily an address is spoofed and how exclusively a customer maintains the device. We have built an application where the questions are sent as a text message to a cellular phone. This has two advantages. One is that the questions are sent only to the registered personal device. The other is that a customer can visually read text far faster than waiting for the same questions to be spoken.

3.2.4 Client Store. An inherent drawback to the host store QDP implementations described above is that they are vulnerable to host-side attack. An alternative to these is to store the questions not at the host but at the client.

Three parties are involved for enrollment in this client store protocol: customer, authentication host (call center, in this case), and QDP question server. The enrollment procedure is as follows. The customer first accesses the QDP server, likely via the Web. This server contains a database of questions with multiple-choice answers. The questions have indices, q_i, $i = 1, ..., N$ and the answers have indices, a_j, $j = 1, ..., M$. The only peculiarity of this database is that question and answer indices are reordered in a random way for each enrollment session. That is, a particular question and particular answer will likely have different indices for different visits to the database. The customer does not identify herself, but selects questions and downloads them to a file on her computer or prints them out. She mentally chooses answers to her selected questions – but doesn't circle the answers or indicate them in any other way. The last step of the enrollment is for the customer to send to the authenticating host a file that contains the question indices and the customer's chosen answer indices.

The verification procedure is straightforward. The customer identifies herself whereupon the authenticating host queries the customer with randomly chosen question indices from enrollment. The customer looks up in her file what questions correspond to those indices and answers with the indices of her answers. If the customer answers all correctly, or a number within some pre-determined tolerance, then she successfully authenticates.

The customer file is a rudimentary codebook. It contains a list of codewords, which are the question indices, and corresponding decoded "plaintext", which are the answer indices. However, only one of the M answer indices per question is correct. The true codebook owner possesses the "key" to this codebook by having knowledge of the answers to the questions. Therefore, to succeed at authentication, a person needs two things. One is the codebook and the other is the "key."

3.3 Security

3.3.1 Implementation Comparisons. Table 2 shows how well the different implementations of Section 3.2 meet specifications of Section 3.1.

Table 2. Shows how well different QDP call center implementations meet specifications listed in Section 3.1. A "Y" indicates that specification is met; "N" indicates specification is not met; "–" indicates specification is met under some circumstances and not under others.

	Host Basic	Host + PIN	Host + address	Client
Security Specifications:				
1. resist client attack	–	Y	Y	Y
2. resist host attack	N	N	Y	–
3a. offer compromise detection	N	N	–	Y
3b. offer compromise recovery	Y	Y	Y	Y
4. resist denial of service attack	N	N	Y	Y
5. offer adjustable security	N	Y	Y	Y
Customer Specifications:				
1. convenient	Y	Y	–	–
2. privacy respected	Y	Y	Y	Y
3. fault tolerance	Y	Y	Y	Y
4. numeric keypad input	Y	Y	Y	Y
5. voice input without eavesdroppers	Y	–	Y	Y
6. inexpensive	Y	Y	–	Y

The "host store – basic" implementation is the least taxing of the customer. If the user selects QDP questions that she can always remember, there is no extra effort needed. However, a major drawback of this implementation is that it has less resistance to client attack than the other implementations. This is because an attacker can learn the customer's questions by phoning repeatedly, then either learning or guessing answers to these questions.

The "host store plus PIN" implementation requires the next least effort of the customer. A drawback of this implementation is that, if an eavesdropper can hear a customer's PIN, he can then obtain questions and attack the system in the same way as for the basic implementation. We can strengthen the host plus PIN implementation by requiring the PIN to be entered via the keypad and by using a number of QDP numeric questions that are chosen randomly across authentication sessions.

The "host store plus address" implementation requires the customer to have some device, whether home phone with Caller ID or cell phone. There is expense involved if the customer does not otherwise have one of these, and this requirement is potentially inconvenient because the user must have, or be at, this device when authenticating. This implementation meets all security specifications except compromise detection.

The "client store" implementation compares well among these implementations. It has similar security to the "host store plus address" implementation, but a major advantage is that it entails no device expense. Since this is a "what you know" and "what you have" combination, the customer will be inconvenienced if she forgets the paper or file on which the indices are written. It is vulnerable to a host attack because the host stores indices for each question and answer. However, indices can easily be changed periodically, and they are different for different hosts to reduce the danger of cross-host attack.

3.3.2 Client Store Security.

The client store implementation has some attractive properties of user convenience and security. We examine security of this scheme in more depth in this section.

The client store verification procedure follows a challenge-response protocol. The server sends a challenge vector, which is a set of k question indices. The customer looks up each question by its index, chooses an answer, and returns the index of the answer. The customer returns k answer indices in total. A straightforward way to number the answer indices is sequentially from 1 to M for each multiple-choice question. However, if this is done, the potential answer keyspace is only M^k. For example, for $M=6$ choices and $k=4$ questions, this is $6^4=1296$. A stronger security scheme is to use random numbers for the multiple-choice answer indices. Now, the answer keyspace can be arbitrarily high, with the tradeoff that the customer must enter longer numbers for each answer. For example, if each answer index is chosen randomly from the range $[0, ..., 99]$, then the potential keyspace increases to $100^4=10^8$; if the range is $[0, ..., 999]$, then the keyspace is $1000^4=10^{12}$.

If an attacker steals the wallet card containing the customer's selected questions, then vulnerability increases. In this case, using random number answer indices adds nothing to the security strength because the attacker knows the potential answer index for each question. For $M=6$ choices and $k=4$ questions, the keyspace is 1296. However, just like a physical house key, the wallet card provides evidence of compromise detection. When the customer finds it is missing, she should notify the call center of this, whereupon the current questions will be cancelled.

We use the term, "poor man's token" for the client store implementation in which a wallet card (or piece of paper) stores the questions and multiple-choice answers. Like using a more expensive challenge-response security token, a customer can receive a random number challenge and return the appropriate random number response. However, there is one significant difference between the electronic token and the paper one. The electronic token has a very large number of challenges that it can respond to. Challenge numbers are typically 8 to 10 digit numbers, so the number of challenges is 10^8 to 10^{10}. In contrast, a wallet card holds n questions of which k of these are used in a session. There are $n!/(n-k)!$ permutations of questions, which for $n=15$ and $k=4$ is 32,760. This is not a large number of challenges, but is likely to be large enough to defend against direct replay attacks given the low frequency of call center authentications per customer. The easier attack is if an eavesdropper can learn the discrete question indices and corresponding answer indices, then he can successfully impersonate the customer. The eavesdropper could learn all answer responses in as few as n/k sessions, or 4 sessions for our example. This attack can succeed if authentication is performed over a channel in plaintext. Telephone transmission is usually in plaintext, since the terminal has no computing power to perform encryption, however capture of an analog telephone transmission requires physical presence to tap the telephone line. In contrast, data network eavesdropping does not require physical presence. So, any transmission of authentication information via data channels should be encrypted. The SSL (Secure Sockets Layer) protocol is commonly used for communications between contact centers and customers on the Web.

4   Conclusions and Future Work

We can conclude from the implementations proposed and from the results of preliminary user testing that the QDP approach to call center customer verification is promising. However, since much of this work is for the purpose of improving customer convenience, the real proof of this will only be found when the scheme is used in a full-scale system. We are in the process of implementing a version of the client store implementation for password recovery use within Avaya. This application has a call center component where users can obtain aid in recovering their password over the telephone.

A number of areas require more investigation for this approach. One involves statistics of the QDP multiple-choice questions. Specification 2 in Section 2.2 listed uniformity of the question and answer spaces and independence of answers to be important for discriminating among users. We have done smaller-scale tests on these statistics showing a fairly good spread of selections (to be reported in another paper). However, no question or answer spread will be perfectly uniform, so we are investigating different weighting schemes to identify and correct for questions and answers that may give an attacker advantage due to non-uniform selection.

Another area of current work is important for the QDP numerical questions. Since the answers are open, we need a proactive method (such as in [14]) for recognizing "good" or "poor" answers. For example, the question, "What is my current telephone number?" is a poor question because an attacker can easily learn the answer. However, the question, "What is Fido's telephone number?" is a better question because an attacker would have difficulty associating a dog's name with the owner's telephone number. We are working on a method that employs information extraction techniques to search for question and answer associations in telephone directories and in general web searches, and prohibit a user from choosing questions that could be associated easily with answers by an attacker.

There are other open issues that will become clearer with further testing, longer experience, and use in real applications. Memory recall has only been tested over 5 months. Will users still recall their answers consistently over longer periods of time? Our current database of 200 questions was authored with some reading into the psychology of memory, however we are not experts in this area. Can questions be better designed? And, no security proposal is complete until opened to the security of security experts and the abuse of potential attackers. Will the QDP approach offer the combination of better convenience along with stronger security as proposed?

This paper investigates call center customer verification using an authentication scheme involving personal-knowledge questions, called Query-Directed Passwords (QDP). QDP is shown to differ from traditional personal-knowledge authentication schemes (e.g., "What is your mother's maiden name?") due to a QDP framework that adheres to strict requirements on the types, number, and use of questions. This framework provides stronger security while maintaining the inherent convenience of the traditional approach. Four implementations for call center customer verification are described here. These four implementations differ in how and where the QDP questions are stored. One of the most secure implementations involves a 3-party enrollment protocol and client-side storage of the questions on a computer file or on a wallet-card. This offers the stronger security of a challenge-response protocol along with other advantages such as compromise detection and low cost.

References

1. R. Morris, K. Thompson, "Password security: A case history," *Comm. ACM*, Vol. 22, no. 11, Nov. 1979, pp. 594-597.
2. D.C. Feldmeier and P.R. Karn, "UNIX password security – ten years later," *Advances in Cryptology – CRYPTO '89 Proceedings*, Springer-Verlag, 1990, pp. 44-63.
3. S. M. Furnell, P. S. Dowland, H. M. Illingworth, P. L. Reynolds, "Authentication and supervision: A survey of user attitudes," *Computers and Security*, Vol. 19, no. 6, 2000, pp. 529-539.
4. J. Yan, A. Blackwell, R. Anderson, A. Grant, "The memorability and security of passwords – some empirical results," TR 500, University of Cambridge, Computer Laboratory, Sept. 2000, http://www.cl.cam.ac.uk/TechReports/UCAM-CL-TR-500.pdf
5. L. O'Gorman, "Comparing Passwords, Tokens, and Biometrics for User Authentication," *Proc. IEEE*, Vol. 91, No. 12, Dec. 2003, pp. 2019-2040.
6. L. O'Gorman, "Seven issues with human authentication technologies," *IEEE Workshop on Automatic Identification Advanced Technologies*, New York, March 2002, pp. 185-186.
7. C. Dorai, N. K. Ratha, R. Bolle, "Dynamic behavior analysis in compressed fingerprint videos," *IEEE Trans. Circuits and Systems for Video Technology*, Special Issue on Video-Based Biometrics, Oct. 2003.
8. H. P. Bahrick, "Semantic memory content in permastore: Fifty years of memory for Spanish learned in school," *J. of Exp. Psychology: General*, 113 (1), 1984, pp. 1-29.
9. C. Ellison, C. Hall, R. Milbert, B. Schneier, "Protecting secret keys with personal entropy," *J. of Future Generation Computer Systems*, 16 (4), Feb. 2000, pp. 311-318.
10. Shamir, "How to share a secret," Comm. of the ACM, Vol. 22, No. 11, Nov. 1979, pp. 612-613.
11. N. Frykholm, A. Juels, "Error-tolerant password recovery," in P. Samarati, ed., *Eighth ACM Conference on Computer and Communications Security*, ACM Press. 2001, pp. 1-8.
12. Juels, M. Wattenberg, "A fuzzy commitment scheme," in G. Tsudik, ed., *Sixth ACM Conf. Computer and Communications Security*, ACM Press, 1999, pp. 28-36.
13. J. Fiscus, W. M. Fisher, A. Martin, M. Przybocki, D. S. Pallett, "NIST Evaluation of Conversational Speech Recognition over the Telephone," Speech Transcription Workshop, Maryland, May, 2000. http://www.nist.gov/speech/publications/
14. M. Bishop, D. V. Klein, "Improving system security via proactive password checking," Computers and Security, Vol. 14, no. 3, 1995, pp. 233-249.

Cryptography and the French Banking Cards: Past, Present, Future

Jacques Stern

Dépt d'Informatique, ENS – CNRS, 45 rue d'Ulm, 75230 Paris Cedex 05, France
Jacques.Stern@ens.fr
http://www.di.ens.fr/users/stern

Abstract. This is a brief summary of the invited lecture delivered during the conference. The interested reader is referred to [2] for more information.

1   Introduction

In 1967, a group of French banks decided to offer a credit card service, under the form of a mere plastic card. The device was later enhanced with a magnetic stripe in 1971. Although magstripe cards display some cryptographic data, they are quite vulnerable: using rather simple equipment, it is possible to capture the encoded data and manufacture a fake card.

In 1990, it was decided to improve the security of the card by adding a chip. Since november 1992, all cards issued by the French banks are chip cards.

2   The Cryptography of the French Banking Cards

Based on the chip, several mechanisms were introduced:

1. PIN code verification,
2. RSA authentication,
3. (triple)-DES authentication.

The PIN code is a four digit sequence that the card holder enters. It is verified either from its enciphered version present on the magnetic stripe, in which case both need to be sent to a data center by means of an on-line connection, or else by the chip itself.

RSA authentication is based on an RSA signature of the card number and other related data. It is read from the chip and verified by the terminal at the point of sale.

DES authentication is based on the result of a CBC-MAC computation on the transaction data, by means of a triple DES key which the chip holds. Although simple DES was used when chip cards were launched in 1990, it has now been abandoned and replaced by triple DES. Since verification requires knowledge of the card's key, it can only be performed through an on-line connection.

A. Juels (Ed.): FC 2004, LNCS 3110, pp. 68–69, 2004.
© IFCA/Springer-Verlag Berlin Heidelberg 2004

In 1998, the "Humpich case" received wide coverage from the press, following an "experiment" demonstrating the use of a fake card at an off-line vending machine. Cryptographers will agree that the experiment did not show that its author was a genius: based on overoptimistic evaluations on the hardness of factoring (see e.g. [3]), the designers had originally chosen to use an RSA modulus of 320 bit only! RSA moduli now in use are over 768 bits, and quickly moving to 1024 bits.

Following the above, it was understood that the security offered by the chip card in an off-line scenario was hampered by more subtle versions of the "yes card" fraud. Such cards return a yes answer when a PIN code is submitted and display a card number and RSA signature captured form a legitimate card. To counter the fraud, it is necessary to replace the "static" authentication offered by RSA signatures by a dynamic version based an a challenge/response mechanism. Such mechanism is offered as an option in the EMV standard [1], under the acronym DDA (Dynamic Data Authentication). Taking advantage of the adoption of EMV, it has been decided to implement DDA in the French banking cards. The author believes this is an unprecedented effort of using public key cryptography in mass devices.

3   The Future

With triple DES, RSA, and DDA on board, the French banking cards are reaching a high level of cryptographic sophistication. French people are usually surprised to discover that in most countries, credit cards have no chip... It is expected however that chips will spread out, at least in Europe. Of course, the progress of the factoring algorithms is closely followed by the banks, and larger key sizes are bound to appear. Why not elliptic curves some day?

References

1. EMVCo EMV 4.0 Specifications available at http://www.emvco.com/
2. J. Patarin. La cryptographie des cartes bancaires. *Pour la Science*, Juillet/Oct 2002, 66–68.
3. R. Rivest, A. Shamir, and L. Adleman. A Method for Obtaining Digital Signatures and Public Key Cryptosystems. *Communications of the ACM*, 21(2):120–126, February 1978.

PayPass Security and Risk

(Abstract)

Simon Pugh

MasterCard International Inc.

MasterCard provides internationally accepted debit and credit payment programs. These programs provide cost-effective solutions that enable transactions to be performed in a wide variety of acceptance environments.

Until now, to conduct payment transactions at a Point of Sale (POS) terminal, physical contact was required between the card and the terminal. This physical contact would be made by:

- swiping a magnetic stripe (for magnetic stripe cards)
- inserting a chip card into a reader (for contact chip cards).

MasterCard is extending its product range to include "proximity technologies". These technologies enable terminals and cards to exchange data without physical contact.

Proximity technologies include a wide variety of wireless technologies such as Radio Frequency IDentifier (RFID) transponders, Bluetooth, Infrared, Wireless Fidelity (WiFi), and contactless chip cards (based on the ISO/IEC 14443 standard). Each of these technologies has a unique operational range and mode of operation. Depending on the technology used, cardholder devices can make payments at distances of up to 10 meters from the POS terminal.

MasterCard PayPass is the first program to be implemented under the MasterCard Proximity Payments Program. MasterCard selected the ISO/IEC 14443 standard for contactless cards. Using this technology, issuers can implement the standard in a card form that supports MasterCard or Maestro. MasterCard PayPass transactions use the same MasterCard network messages, rules and policies as magnetic stripe or contact chip transactions. This means issuers can build on their existing network.

A contactless card uses the electromagnetic field generated by the terminal to power its chip. Modulation of this electromagnetic field enables an exchange of data between the card and the terminal, typically up to a range of 10 cm (4 inches).

MasterCard PayPass provides a simpler way to pay, and is ideal in payment environments where speed and convenience are crucial, (for example, fuel pumps, vending machines, quick service restaurants, and convenience stores). MasterCard PayPass supports both magnetic stripe and contact chip acceptance environments. MasterCard will offer two PayPass implementation options, each of which is aimed at a specific target market:

A. Juels (Ed.): FC 2004, LNCS 3110, pp. 70–71, 2004.

- PayPass – Mag Stripe – this is aimed at the magnetic stripe market, complementary to the magnetic stripe technology, and uses the current magnetic stripe processing infrastructure
- PayPass – M/Chip – this is aimed at the contact chip market, complementary to the contact chip technology, and uses the current contact chip infrastructure.

The design of PayPass included a number of security features to mitigate the risk from new threats to the transaction integrity from the introduction of proximity technology. These include eavesdropping on transactions as well as remote "pickpocketing" of the card data. It also addresses measures to prevent the creation of counterfeit magnetic stripe cards, or the misuse of PayPass card data for e-Commerce transactions.

The Vector-Ballot e-Voting Approach

Aggelos Kiayias[1] and Moti Yung[2]

[1] Computer Science and Engineering, University of Connecticut
Storrs, CT, USA
aggelos@cse.uconn.edu
[2] Computer Science, Columbia University
New York, NY, USA
moti@cs.columbia.edu

Abstract. Looking at current cryptographic-based e-voting protocols, one can distinguish three basic design paradigms (or approaches): (a) Mix-Networks based, (b) Homomorphic Encryption based, and (c) Blind Signatures based. Each of the three possesses different advantages and disadvantages w.r.t. the *basic properties* of (i) efficient tallying, (ii) universal verifiability, and (iii) allowing write-in ballot capability (in addition to predetermined candidates). In fact, none of the approaches results in a scheme that simultaneously achieves all three. This is unfortunate, since the three basic properties are crucial for efficiency, integrity and versatility (flexibility), respectively. Further, one can argue that a serious business offering of voting technology should offer a flexible technology that achieves various election goals with a single user interface. This motivates our goal, which is to suggest a new *"vector-ballot" based approach* for secret-ballot e-voting that is based on three new notions: *Provably Consistent Vector Ballot Encodings*, *Shrink-and-Mix Networks* and *Punch-Hole-Vector-Ballots*. At the heart of our approach is the combination of mix networks and homomorphic encryption under a single user interface; given this, it is rather surprising that it achieves much more than any of the previous approaches for e-voting achieved in terms of the basic properties. Our approach is presented in two generic designs called "homomorphic vector-ballots with write-in votes" and "multi-candidate punch-hole vector-ballots"; both of our designs can be instantiated over any homomorphic encryption function.

1 Introduction

There are three basic paradigms for cryptographic secure ballot elections. The first method is based on mix-networks where the tallying officials move the ballots between them and permute them in the process while changing their representation (e.g., partially decrypting them). Methods for doing this robustly and correctly have been designed in the last 20 years, starting with the initial work of Chaum [7]. In practical implementations, this approach in its fully robust form (i.e., proving the correctness of the shuffling) is still considered a slow tallying process, even though there have been several steps toward more efficient designs,

A. Juels (Ed.): FC 2004, LNCS 3110, pp. 72–89, 2004.

see e.g. [33, 6, 20, 24, 1, 26, 18]. The second method is based on homomorphic encryption (started by Benaloh [9, 4, 3], and then followed by many other works including [12, 10, 35, 16, 13, 2]). In this general approach the ballots are encrypted and then "compressed" via a homomorphic encryption scheme into a tally. This compression property allows fast tallying, and is what makes this approach attractive. However the drawback is that pure "compressible" homomorphic encryption is not suitable to deal with write-in ballots. In fact, compression of the write-in ballots content is *not possible* since, information theoretically, if this content has no redundancy (which is always possible in the write-in ballots case) compression will ruin it. A third approach is based on blind signatures, [17], and relies on the voters obtaining a certified secret ballot from the authorities by employing the blind signature module. This enables them to embed any form of ballot (including write-in). Subsequently, this approach requires the employment of an anonymous channel between the voter and the tallying authorities, to hide the identity of the user at the "ballot casting stage." This requirement may be inhibiting and thus people have suggested to combine this approach with the mix-net one so that the "anonymous channel" is implemented formally. Furthermore, while the previous paradigms support universal verifiability which assures robustness, this approach relies on tallier – voter interaction and does not support it.

In recent years, due to the aftermath of the USA 2000 presidential election debacle as well as other initiatives, e-voting technology has gained high level of interest (see [21]). One effort that took place is the joint Caltech-MIT electronic voting project. Rivest, who participated in this project, has raised the question whether it is possible to incorporate write-in ballots in homomorphic encryption based elections in a way that will still maintain its advantages and keep some of its computational gains. In fact, Rivest's question raises the more general concern that the cryptographic paradigms optimize different goals, and business wise it may be smart to combine them under a single user interface and hope to retain some of their individual advantages and to try to gain more by a combinational approach.

Homomorphic Vector-Ballot with Write-in Votes. Motivated by this question and issues, we started by attacking the problem of allowing write-in ballots as follows: since homomorphic encryption elections are based on a summation register (ciphertexts are modular-multiplied together which effectively sums-up the ballots under the encryption), write-in ballots need to be read individually.

To incorporate a write-in choice into a homomorphic encryption based scheme, we suggest the design of a composed ballot or a "vector ballot" that is cast by each user, and is either a regular (predetermined candidate) ballot or a write-in one with indistinguishable external representation in either case. This is the base of the vector-ballot approach. This sounds simple, but if done in a straightforward fashion this may give voters more "free choice" in ballot representation and in cheating, and it may also give more ways to distinguish between users' ballots. Thus, this new design leads to new concerns regarding ballot validity and ballot uniformity. In particular, it leads us to the simple yet crucial notion of *provably consistent vector ballot encodings*, which assures that in spite of the extended scenario the ballot is nevertheless legal, i.e. the voter is forced to either select a write-in, or a predetermined choice, but *not* both at the same time. Further, whenever the voter makes one of the two choices, she is forced to enter a "neutral" value in the other portion of the vector ballot. The added validation proofs by the voter makes the ballot longer, however this price (constant increase in validity proof) is reasonable given the enhancement (to be described below) it enables. The ballot representation looks the same regardless of whether the user votes for a predetermined candidate or casts a write-in ballot. After the ballot casting, the vector ballot is split into a "supposedly regular portion" and a "supposedly write-in portion" and they are processed (tallied) independently.

What we have described so far is a combination of two voting approaches: homomorphic encryption based and mix-net based. While this is important (as it allows the unification under the same user-interface of the efficient homomorphic encryption based voting with the write-in "friendly" mix-net voting), by itself the resulting scheme as a whole is not more efficient than the two individual approaches (and clearly the real bottleneck is the slow tallying robust mix-net approach).

It is thus, perhaps surprising that our approach that is based on the vector ballots has the potential to achieve more efficient tallying than any previous proposal for e-voting that allowed write-in ballots and is universally verifiable at the same time. The two major points that allow this are explained below:

1. The predetermined candidate portions of all ballots can be compressed using the efficient homomorphic encryption based tallying.
2. The write-in portions of all ballots are based on an indicator and a write-in portion. Based on such indicators we show that they can be processed using the new efficient method of *shrink-and-mix* that we propose. The method takes advantage of the fact that the vector ballots are based on homomorphic encryption and the fact that, usually, *most* of the voters select one of the predetermined candidates. Thus, using the compressibility of indicators we can eliminate a great number of unused neutral write-in portions. We note that in a typical scenario, the method achieves a five-fold improvement over stand alone mix-network based election (and this will be a noticeable factor in practice, since the gain is within the system's performance bottleneck component).

Further, the two tallying procedures above are independent. Thus, the tallying can be performed in two phases. An *on-line* phase can just perform the homomorphic encryption tallying process of the predetermined candidate portions. This is a very efficient mechanism. In most cases the actual tally and winner(s) can be declared based on the these regular votes only and the slower tallying of the write-in portions can, in this case, be done *off-line* and a later time. Typically, the winner will be one selected among the leading predetermined candidates of the established parties, whereas, say, Mickey Mouse (a popular write-in candidate in US elections) can afford waiting a bit longer till he knows the actual number of votes he won.

The above is the first construction within the vector-ballot approach. It shows how we achieve simultaneously the basic properties of universal verifiability and support for write-in ballots together with an efficient tallying procedure. Comparison to previous election paradigms is given in Figure 1.

Multi-candidate Punch-Hole Vector-Ballot. A modular extension of our new approach employs our notion of *punch-hole vector ballots* which enables a more suitable scheme for voting with a large number of predetermined candidates. It extends the functionality of our vector-ballot encodings (and thus write-ins can still be incorporated). The method introduces a multitude of c summation ciphertext registers, one per candidate, while earlier schemes packed all the candidate tallies into a single summation register. Note that the vector ballot portions in the ballot design correspond to various candidates and to the corresponding summation registers. Note further that a ballot needs to have a consistent valid encoding and the voter has to prove this validity. This is different from the simplistic multi-election ballot in [4].

Employing separate registers relaxes the burden of participants by allowing them to deal with smaller ciphertexts. The gain is especially noticeable in case of many candidates. To formalize the ciphertext summation register size requirement, we introduce the notion of "capacity" of an homomorphic encryption function, which measures how many integers can be represented as plaintexts within a given summation register. Our punch-hole vector ballot design requires the capacity of the underlying encryption to be only n (the number of voters), instead of n^c required for a single summation register used previously. In fact, all leading proposed election methods in the literature that employ summation registers, [10, 16, 13], and allow for n voters and c candidates, indeed, require capacity of n^c. Note that this may cause problems in selecting the security parameter when the number of candidates is very large: e.g., if the security parameter is 768 bits, this restricts the capacity to 2^{768}, and if the number of candidates is large, e.g. $c = 50$, and the voting population close to $35,000$, then the capacity *cannot* contain the summation register.

An important and substantial gain in efficiency of tallying, results from the new approach when applied over the ElGamal encryption. The recovery of the final tally requires only time $O(cn)$ which is *polynomial in the number of candidates*, instead of $O(n^c)$ which is exponential in c, as is the case in the state of the art discrete-log based scheme of [10]. We remark that this exponential gain is traded against a quadratic – rather than linear – (in c) work done for validity checking of ballots; this is a reasonable price to pay for such a gain.

2   Preliminaries

REQUIREMENTS FOR VOTING SCHEMES. A voting-scheme needs to fulfill a variety of requirements. A brief presentation of these requirements follows.

Secrecy. Ensures the security of the contents of ballots. This is typically achieved by relying on the honesty of a sufficient number of the participating authorities and at the same time on some cryptographic intractability assumption. In

Approaches	Efficient Tallying	Univ. Verifiability	Write-ins
Homomorphic Encryption	$\sqrt{}$	$\sqrt{}$	$\times$
Mix-networks	$\times$	$\sqrt{}$	$\sqrt{}$
Blind-Signatures	$\sqrt{}$	$\times$	$\sqrt{}$
Vector-Ballot approach	$\sqrt{}$	$\sqrt{}$	$\sqrt{}$

Fig. 1. A comparison of our new approach with previous work with respect to the following three important properties: (i) *efficient-tallying*: tallying does not require the application of a robust-mix to the total number of ballots; (ii) *universal-verifiability*: any interested third party may verify that the election protocol is executed correctly; (iii) *write-ins*: voters are allowed to enter write-in votes

particular, any polynomial-time probabilistic adversary that controls some arbitrary number of voters and a number of authorities (below some predetermined threshold) should be incapable of distinguishing which one of the predetermined choices a certain voter selected or whether the voter entered a write-in. In all voting schemes, once a certain number of votes have been aggregated into a partial tally, secrecy is not mandatory, e.g., once the votes of a precinct have been aggregated it is ok to reveal the partial tally (in fact in many cases it is not even desired to keep the partial tallies secret, if some regional statistics are to be extracted from the election results). Thus, voter secrecy will have an associated *Privacy Perimeter b* which will refer to the smallest number of votes that need to be aggregated into a partial tally before some information about the partial tally can be revealed; we will talk of secrecy with b-perimeter in this case. A more formal discussion of secrecy is deferred to the full version of this paper.

Universal-Verifiability. Ensures that any party, including an outsider, can be convinced that all valid votes have been included in the final tally.

Robustness. Ensures that the system can tolerate a certain number of faulty participants.

Fairness. It should be ensured that no partial results become known prior to the end of the election procedure.

Another property, which we do not deal with here explicitly, is **Receipt-Freeness** [5, 34, 27, 22, 25]. Standard techniques that use re-randomizers (see e.g. [2]) can be readily employed in our schemes to allow this property.

HOMOMORPHIC ENCRYPTION SCHEMES. An encryption scheme is a triple $\langle \mathcal{K}, \mathcal{E}, \mathcal{D} \rangle$. The key-generation $\mathcal{K}$ is a probabilistic TM which on input a parameter 1^w (which specifies the key-length) outputs a key-pair pk, sk (public-key and secret-key respectively). The encryption function is a probabilistic TM $\mathcal{E}_{\mathsf{pk}} : \mathbb{R} \times \mathbb{P} \to \mathbb{C}$, where $\mathbb{R}$ is the randomness space, $\mathbb{P}$ is the plaintext space, and $\mathbb{C}$ the ciphertext space. When $\mathbb{P} = \mathbb{Z}_a$ for some integer a, we will say that the encryption function has "*additive capacity*" (or just capacity) a. The basic property of the encryption scheme is that $\mathcal{D}_{\mathsf{sk}}(\mathcal{E}_{\mathsf{sk}}(\cdot, x)) = x$ for all x independently of the coin tosses of the encryption function $\mathcal{E}$. If we want to specify the coin tosses of $\mathcal{E}$ we will write $\mathcal{E}_{\mathsf{pk}}(r, x)$ to denote the ciphertext that corresponds to the plaintext x when the encryption function $\mathcal{E}_{\mathsf{pk}}$ makes the coin tosses r. Otherwise we will consider $\mathcal{E}_{\mathsf{pk}}(x)$ to be a random variable. For homomorphic encryption, we assume additionally the operations $+, \oplus, \odot$ defined over the respective spaces $\mathbb{P}, \mathbb{R}, \mathbb{C}$, so that $\langle \mathbb{P}, + \rangle$, $\langle \mathbb{R}, \oplus \rangle, \langle \mathbb{C}, \odot \rangle$ are groups written additively (the first two) and multiplicatively respectively.

Definition 1. *An encryption function $\mathcal{E}$ is homomorphic if, for all $r_1, r_2 \in \mathbb{R}$ and all $x_1, x_2 \in \mathbb{P}$, it holds that $\mathcal{E}_{\mathsf{pk}}(r_1, x_1) \odot \mathcal{E}_{\mathsf{pk}}(r_2, x_2) = \mathcal{E}_{\mathsf{pk}}(r_1 \oplus r_2, x_1 + x_2)$.*

We will consider two examples of Homomorphic Encryption schemes: "additive ElGamal" and Paillier Encryption. Both have been employed in the design of e-voting schemes in the past, see [10] and [13, 2] respectively (which are also the current state-of-the-art schemes in the homomorphic encryption based approach). We define them below:

Additive ElGamal Encryption. It is defined by a triple $\langle \mathcal{K}, \mathcal{E}, \mathcal{D} \rangle$: the key-generation $\mathcal{K}$ outputs the description of a finite multiplicative group $\mathcal{G}$ of prime order q, with three generators $\langle g, h, f \rangle$ which are set to be the public-key of the system pk; the secret-key sk is set to the value $\log_g h$. For a public-key $\langle g, h, f \rangle$ the encryption function $\mathcal{E}(r, x)$ equals the tuple $\langle g^r, h^r f^x \rangle$, and the domains $\mathbb{P} := \mathbb{Z}_q$, $\mathbb{R} := \mathbb{Z}_q$ and $\mathbb{C} := \mathcal{G} \times \mathcal{G}$. The operations $+, \oplus$ are defined as addition modulo q and the operation $\odot$ is defined as point-wise multiplication over $\mathcal{G} \times \mathcal{G}$. The decryption function $\mathcal{D}$ for a secret-key $\log_g h$ given $\langle G, H \rangle$ it returns $H/G^{\log_g h}$, and then it performs a brute-force search over all possible values f^x to recover x. Observe that $\langle \mathbb{P}, + \rangle, \langle \mathbb{R}, \oplus \rangle$ and $\langle \mathbb{C}, \odot \rangle$ are all groups, and the encryption $\mathcal{E}$ is homomorphic with respect to these operations. Finally notice that the capacity of $\mathcal{E}$ is q.

Paillier Encryption. [28]. It is a triple $\langle \mathcal{K}, \mathcal{E}, \mathcal{D} \rangle$, defined as follows: the key-generation $\mathcal{K}$ outputs an integer N, that is a product of two safe primes, and an element $g \in \mathbb{Z}_{N^2}^*$ of order a multiple of N. The public-key of the system pk is set to $\langle g, N \rangle$ and the secret-key sk is set to the factorization of N. For a public-key $\langle g, N \rangle$, the encryption function $\mathcal{E}(r, x)$ equals the value $g^x r^N (\mathrm{mod}\ N^2)$ and the domains $\mathbb{P} := \mathbb{Z}_N$, $\mathbb{R} := \mathbb{Z}_{N^2}^*$, and $\mathbb{C} := \mathbb{Z}_{N^2}^*$. The operation $+$ is defined as addition modulo N, and the operations $\oplus, \odot$ are defined as multiplication modulo N^2. The decryption function $\mathcal{D}$ for a secret-key p, q it operates as follows: first it computes $\lambda := \lambda(N)$ the Carmichael function of N, and given a ciphertext c, it returns $L(c^\lambda (\mathrm{mod} N^2))/L(g^\lambda (\mathrm{mod} N^2))$ where $L(u) = \frac{u-1}{N}$ and L is defined over the set of integers $\{u \mid u \equiv 1 (\mathrm{mod}\ N)\}$. Again, observe that $\langle \mathbb{P}, + \rangle, \langle \mathbb{R}, \oplus \rangle$ and $\mathbb{C}, \odot \rangle$ are all groups, and the encryption $\mathcal{E}$ is homomorphic with respect to these operations. Finally notice that the capacity of $\mathcal{E}$ is N.

PROOFS OF KNOWLEDGE. Proofs of knowledge are protocols between two players, the Prover and the Verifier. In such protocols there is a publicly known predicate Q for which the prover knows some witness x, i.e. $Q(x) = 1$. The goal of such protocols is for the prover to convince the verifier that he indeed knows such witness. We will concentrate on "3-move" protocols for which the prover acts in the first and third move, and the verifier challenges in the second move with a random value from the proper domain (see [11]). Conversations in such protocols will be of the form $\langle a, c, r \rangle$, and the verifier will accept provided that a, c, r satisfy some conditions given as part of the specifications of the protocol. Proofs of knowledge can be made *non-interactive* by employing the Fiat-Shamir heuristics, [15] (and then, security is shown in the random-oracle model, or alternatively assuming a beacon, [32]). If the predicate Q accepts a non-interactive zero-knowledge proof, and an agent possesses a witness for Q that he wants to prove knowledge of, we will say that the agent "writes a proof for Q." Proofs of knowledge of the above type can be combined in "AND" and "OR" fashion in an efficient manner.

PROOFS OF KNOWLEDGE FOR HOMOMORPHIC ENCRYPTION. Let $\langle \mathcal{K}, \mathcal{E}, \mathcal{D} \rangle$ be a homomorphic encryption scheme. Below, we identify useful proof protocols (which have been used in various settings and environments).

Proof of Knowledge of Properly Formed Ciphertext for a Public Plaintext. A useful proof of knowledge in the context of e-voting is a proof that shows that a ciphertext that encrypts a publicly known plaintext is properly formed. We define the predicate $Q_{\text{cipher}}^{m,V}$ as follows $Q_{\text{cipher}}^{m,V}(r) = 1$ if and only if $\mathcal{E}_{\text{pk}}(r, m) = V$. We remark that proofs of knowledge for the two homomorphic encryptions that we consider here (additive ElGamal, and Paillier) are standard and can be done efficiently.

Proof of Knowledge for a Random Shuffle. Observe that using a homomorphic encryption scheme one can "re-randomize" a ciphertext C by computing $C' := \mathcal{E}_{\text{pk}}(0) \odot C$ (i.e., C' is uniformly distributed over all ciphertexts that correspond to the plaintext of C). Suppose now that $C_1, \ldots, C_k$ is a sequence of ciphertexts and $C'_1, \ldots, C'_k$ is a random re-encrypted permutation of these ciphertexts. We define a predicate $Q_{\text{shuffle}}^{C_1,\ldots,C_k,C'_1,\ldots,C'_k}$ so that $Q_{\text{shuffle}}^{C_1,\ldots,C_k,C'_1,\ldots,C'_k}(r_1, \ldots, r_k, \pi) = 1$ if and only if $C'_{\pi(j)} = \mathcal{E}_{\text{pk}}(r_j, 0) \odot C_j$, for $j = 1, \ldots, k$.

A straightforward approach for a proof for $Q_{\text{shuffle}}^{C_1,\ldots,C_k,C'_1,\ldots,C'_k}$ would require $\mathcal{O}(k^2)$ space. Discovering more efficient proofs is a very active area of research (as such proofs constitute the basic operation of a robust mix-network, a fundamental primitive for elections based on mixes) and several papers provided sophisticated techniques of shortening the proof as well as relaxing the robustness model to allow more efficient implementations, [20, 24, 26, 18]. Two of the most efficient recent protocols are that of [18] and [26], that allow $\mathcal{O}(k)$-size proofs with relatively small constant.

THRESHOLD HOMOMORPHIC ENCRYPTION SCHEMES. A (t, m)-threshold homomorphic encryption scheme is a triple $\langle \mathcal{K}, \mathcal{E}, \mathcal{D} \rangle$ so that $\mathcal{K}$ is a protocol between a set of participants $A_1, \ldots, A_m$, that results in the publication of the public-key pk and the sharing of the secret-key sk so that any t of them can reconstruct it. Additionally, $\mathcal{D}$ is also a protocol between the participants $A_1, \ldots, A_m$ that results in the decryption of the given ciphertext in a publicly verifiable manner (i.e. each participant writes a proof that he follows the decryption protocol according to the specifications). Both Additive ElGamal and Paillier encryptions have threshold variants, see [30, 31, 19] and [16, 13] respectively.

3   The Vector Ballot Approach

The participants in our schemes are the voters $V_1, \ldots, V_n$, the authorities $A_1, \ldots,$ A_m, and the bulletin board server which is responsible for maintaining an authenticated communication transcript. Voter eligibility as well as basic ciphertext processing operations are also handled by the bulletin board server. Our voting approach is divided in four major steps: **Setup, Ballot-Casting, Tallying, Announcement of the Results.**

In our approach, every encrypted ballot is in fact a "vector-ballot" that has three coordinates: the first is a ciphertext that contains possibly one of the predetermined election choices, the second is a flag-ciphertext that encrypts the information whether the voter selects a write-in choice or not; finally, the third coordinate possibly contains a write-in choice. A proof of "consistent ballot encoding" will be broken into a number of "consistency arguments" and will ensure that the vector ballot is formed properly (i.e., it either contains a predetermined choice in the first coordinate or a write-in choice in the last coordinate and furthermore the "flag" value is encrypted consistently). The tallying phase has two independent phases: (i) tallying the non-write-in election results using the homomorphic encryption function properties; (iia) shrinking the number of write-in votes using the flag-ciphertexts; (iib) employing a mix-net over the shrunk write-in ballot sequence. The general overview of these procedures is presented in Figure 2. We describe our approach in detail in the following subsections.

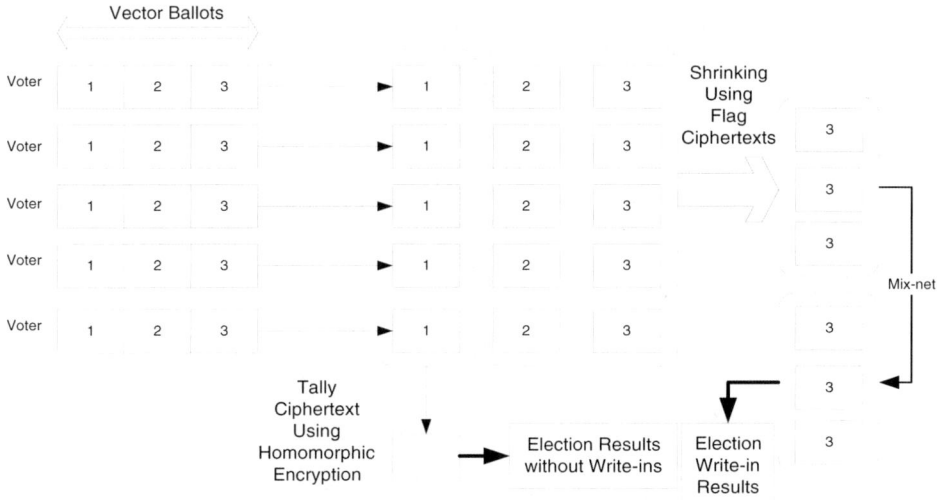

Fig. 2. The Vector-Ballot E-Voting Paradigm

3.1   Setup and Capacity Assumption

In our approach we will employ a threshold homomorphic encryption function $\langle \mathcal{K}, \mathcal{E}, \mathcal{D} \rangle$. We will also employ the necessary assumption regarding the capacity of the encryption function:

Capacity Assumption. The capacity of the encryption function satisfies $a > M^c$ where c is the number of candidates, and M an integer with $M > n$ (the number of voters).

Setup. The authorities $A_1, \ldots, A_m$ execute the protocol $\mathcal{K}$ which results in the publication in the bulletin board of the public-key pk. At the same time the secret-key sk is shared amongst the authorities $A_1, \ldots, A_m$.

3.2   Ballot-Casting Step

Each eligible voter gets authorized to the bulletin board and reads the public-key pk of the system. The set of choices is defined as Choices $:= \{1, M, M^2, \ldots, M^{c-1}\}$ where M is an integer with the property $M > n$.

Formation the Vector-Ballot. Each voter V_i publishes a vector ballot $\langle C_1[i], C_2[i],$ $C_3[i] \rangle$. If the voter wishes to select one of the predetermined choices of the election she selects $C_1[i]$ to be an encryption of one of the values in the set Choices while $C_2[i], C_3[i]$ are encryptions of 0; in particular $C_1[i] := \mathcal{E}_{\mathsf{pk}}(M^{\ell_i - 1})$ where $\ell_i \in \{1, \ldots, c\}$ is the personal choice of the voter, and $C_2[i] := \mathcal{E}_{\mathsf{pk}}(0), C_3[i] := \mathcal{E}_{\mathsf{pk}}(0)$. If the voter wishes to enter a write-in ballot she selects $C_1[i]$ to be an encryption of 0, $C_2[i]$ to be an encryption of 1, and $C_3[i]$ to be an encryption of some string string_i which is the voter's write-in entry. Formally, $C_1[i] := \mathcal{E}_{\mathsf{pk}}(0)$, $C_2[i] := \mathcal{E}_{\mathsf{pk}}(1)$ and $C_3[i] := \mathcal{E}_{\mathsf{pk}}(\mathsf{string}_i)$. Together with her vector ballot the voter must publish a proof of "consistent ballot encoding." In particular V_i writes a proof for the following predicate:

$$\left((Q_{\mathsf{cipher}}^{1, C_1[i]} \vee Q_{\mathsf{cipher}}^{M, C_1[i]} \vee \ldots \vee Q_{\mathsf{cipher}}^{M^{c-1}, C_1[i]}) \wedge Q_{\mathsf{cipher}}^{0, C_2[i]} \wedge Q_{\mathsf{cipher}}^{0, C_3[i]} \right) \vee (Q_{\mathsf{cipher}}^{0, C_1[i]} \wedge Q_{\mathsf{cipher}}^{1, C_2[i]})$$

The above proof can be done *efficiently* as discussed in section 2, since it is an AND/OR composition of the proof of knowledge for the predicate $Q_{\mathsf{cipher}}^{m, V}$ which can be done quite efficiently for either of the two homomorphic encryption functions that we consider. Moreover it only adds a small constant overhead compared to proofs of previous homomorphic-encryption based voting schemes.

Regarding the above proof of consistent ballot encoding it is easy to prove the following lemma:

Lemma 1. *The only ballot encodings for* $\langle C_1[i], C_2[i], C_3[i] \rangle$ *allowed are:*

(i) *The second ciphertext encrypts a 0, the first ciphertext contains a value from the set* Choices *and the third ciphertext encrypts a 0.*

(ii) *The second ciphertext encrypts a 1, the first ciphertext encrypts a 0 and the third ciphertext is unrestricted.*

3.3   Tallying Step

The Non-write-in Part. The vector ballots are parsed so that the first component is collected and the sequence of ciphertexts $C_1[1], \ldots, C_1[n]$ is formed. The "tally ciphertext" is defined as $C_{\text{tally}} = C_1[1] \odot \ldots \odot C_1[n]$. It is easy to see that due to the homomorphic property and the capacity assumption, C_{tally} is a ciphertext that hides a value T that satisfies $T = \sum_{i \in V} M^{\ell_i}$ (as an integer), where $V \subseteq \{1, \ldots, n\}$ is the set of voters that did not select the write-in option. Observe that if $k_0, \ldots, k_{c-1}$ are the tallies won by each of the c candidates, it holds that $T = k_0 + k_1 M + \ldots + k_{c-1} M^{c-1}$, and $k_0, \ldots, k_{c-1} < M$, i.e., if we write T as an integer in base M we can obtain the counts for each candidate.

Dealing with the Write-Ins – Shrink-and-Mix Networks. Write-in ballots are not "compressible" into a single ciphertext like regular ballots and thus they have to be mixed and revealed one by one. Nevertheless our approach allows for a significant efficiency improvement that we call a **Shrink-and-Mix** network. A shrink-and-mix network for voting is a mix-network that attempts to shrink the input ballot sequence prior to the mix procedure in order to gain efficiency. (Indeed gaining efficiency in settings where it is possible is crucial, given the state of the art of Mix networks, see [20]). Shrink-and-mix is a concept that naturally binds to our approach that combines write-in ballots with regular homomorphic encryption based e-voting. This is because in our approach the following unique properties are true:

1. Most voters will not cast a write-in ballot, but rather select one of the predetermined choices of the election.
2. There is a way to employ the homomorphic properties of the encryption function to test whether a small batch of encrypted vector ballots contains a write-in without violating the privacy of the voters (given security perimeter b).
3. There is a way to find the exact number of write-in votes prior to opening them, without violating the secrecy of the voters (given security perimeter b).

Justification. For item *1*, observe that in most settings the write-in option will be used sparingly by the voters who will typically select one of the predetermined candidates for the election. For item *2*, recall that in the vector-ballot approach, each vector ballot $\langle C_1[i], C_2[i], C_3[i] \rangle$ contains a "flag-ciphertext" (the value $C_2[i]$) that encrypts the value 0 or 1 depending on whether the voter voted with one of the predetermined choices (in $C_1[i]$) or entered a write-in (in $C_3[i]$). Suppose now that we have a set of voters $i_1, \ldots, i_b$ and we want the authorities to check whether one of them entered a write-in without violating the privacy of the voters. Then, simply the authorities collect the flag ciphertexts from the vector ballots of these voters $C_2[i_1], \ldots, C_2[i_b]$ and decrypt the ciphertext $C_{i_1, \ldots, i_b} := C_2[i_1] \odot \ldots \odot C_2[i_b]$. Now observe that the decryption of $C_{i_1, \ldots, i_b}$ is the number of write-in votes entered by the voters $\{i_1, \ldots, i_b\}$ and thus the authorities are capable of deducing whether there is a write-in entry among the ciphertexts $\{C_3[i_1], \ldots, C_3[i_b]\}$.

For item *3*, observe that the ciphertext $C_{1,\ldots,n} := C_2[1] \odot \ldots \odot C_2[n]$ is an encryption of the number of write-in votes. Thus if the authorities wish to find efficiently the exact number of write-ins they have to compute $C_{1,\ldots,n}$ and decrypt it (recall that linear computations in the number of voters constitute practically optimal complexity for the tallying phase).

Given the above properties we can now describe the shrink-and-mix method which is divided in two separate stages (perhaps not surprisingly named): (a) shrink and (b) mix.

Shrink Stage. First we describe the shrink stage in detail below:

`Functionality` *Input*: the sequence of all vector-ballots. Let $V \subseteq \{1, \ldots, n\}$ be the subset of voters that entered a non-write-in ballot and denote by V' the set $\{1, \ldots, n\} - V$ (the subset of voters that entered a write-in).

`Output`: a set V^* such that $V' \subseteq V^* \subseteq \{1, \ldots, n\}$.

`Initialize`. The authorities $A_1, \ldots, A_m$ compute the number of write-ins h (feasible by item *3* above). Let p denote the probability that an arbitrary voter enters a write-in defined as $p := h/n$. Let b be the desired privacy perimeter for the elections.

`Shrink`. Let $\sigma := \langle C_2[1], \ldots, C_2[n] \rangle$ be the sequence of the second components of all ballot vectors and let V^* initially defined to $\{1, \ldots, n\}$. The authorities divide σ into n/b batches so that each batch contains b ciphertexts. Since the probability of an arbitrary voter to enter a write-in is p it follows that the probability that a batch contains no write-in is $(1 - p)^b$. The authorities test whether each one of the n/b batches contains a write-in or not (as described in the item *2* above). If the batch of flag-ciphertexts that corresponds to the voters $\{i_1, \ldots, i_b\}$ does not contain a write-in we modify $V^* = V^* - \{i_1, \ldots, i_b\}$. Assuming that each batch is independent from the other, it follows that the expected number of batches without a write-in is $\frac{n}{b}(1 - p)^b$, so the expected size of V^* will be $n - n(1 - p)^b$. Observe that the correctness of the shrink stage (i.e. $V' \subseteq V^* \subseteq \{1, \ldots, n\}$) follows easily. The closeness of V^* to V' can be calibrated by lowering the parameter b.

Mix Stage. The mix-stage follows.

`Functionality` *Input*: A sequence of ciphertexts $\sigma^* := \langle G[i] \rangle_{i=1,\ldots,n^*}$, where $n^* = |V^*|$, V^* is the output of shrink and $\langle G[1], \ldots, G[n^*] \rangle = \langle V_3[i] \mid i \in V^* \rangle$.

`Output`: a sequence of ciphertexts $\langle G'[i] \rangle_{i=1,\ldots,n^*}$ so that there is a permutation π on $\{1, \ldots, n^*\}$ that satisfies $G'[i]$ is a random re-encryption of $G[\pi(i)]$.

`Mix`. The authorities $A_1, \ldots, A_m$ execute a "robust mix" for the sequence of ciphertexts $\sigma^* = \langle G[1], \ldots, G[n^*] \rangle$. This can be accomplished by employing any existing robust-mix method, [20, 24, 26, 18]. The most straightforward robust mix technique has each authority re-encrypting each ciphertext $G[i]$ and permuting the whole sequence randomly to obtain the sequence $\langle G'[1], \ldots, G'[n^*] \rangle$ and also writing a proof for $Q_{\text{shuffle}}^{G[1],\ldots,G[n^*],G'[1],\ldots,G'[n^*]}$. Note that authorities perform the above steps in sequence by acting on the output of the previous authority.

We remark that robust mixes are expensive in terms of computation and space, for this reason the shrink stage that our model allows can be crucial for the improvement of the efficiency of the mixing. The *shrink ratio* for a shrink-and-mix network is the expected reduction percentage of the given sequence of ciphertexts $\langle C_3[i] \rangle_{i \in V^*}$ i.e., the fraction $(n - |V^*|)/n$. Observe that it holds that $(n - |V^*|)/n = (1 - p)^b$ and thus the shrink ratio equals is $(1 - p)^b$ (employing average-case analysis). To illustrate the gain we obtain using the shrink-and-mix network consider the following scenario: in many elections it is reasonable to expect a write-in probability $1/100$, so by setting the privacy perimeter $b = 20$ (which is reasonable for the privacy of the voters in most settings) we obtain a shrink ratio of approximately 0.81, which means that 81% of the ciphertexts will be discarded prior to the execution of the robust mix. This translates to a significant gain in the efficiency of the mixing procedure.

3.4   Announcement of the Results

First the authorities announce the results for the non-write-in part of the election (in fact, this step can be performed prior to the execution of the shrink-and-mix network). The authorities $A_1, \ldots, A_m$ execute the protocol $\mathcal{D}$ on the ciphertext C_{tally} to reveal the the value T. Due to the properties of the value T it holds that if T, as an integer, is written in base M, then the tallies for each candidate are revealed (cf. section 3.3); note that due to the capacity assumption there will be no wrap-arounds during the computation of the tally ciphertext C_{tally}.

Subsequently the authorities execute the shrink-and-mix network (and frequently this will be done after the winner of the election is already determined from the non-write-in votes) and then they execute the protocol $\mathcal{D}$ for each of the ciphertexts $G_*[1], \ldots, G_*[n^*]$ that belong to the output of the shrink-and-mix network. This will reveal all the strings string_i for $i \in V^*$, where V^* is the output of the shrink stage. Since $V' \subseteq V^* \subseteq \{1, \ldots, n\}$ all entered write-ins will be revealed (with, perhaps, a number of 0's that correspond to the ciphertexts that were entered by the voters in $V^* - V'$). When $\text{string}_i = 0$ the entry will be removed from the write-in vote listing (recall that "0" is not considered a valid write-in vote). The final elections results consist of the counts for each of the pre-determined candidates as well as counts for the write-in selections.

3.5   Properties of the Paradigm

Efficiency. First note that our vector-ballot approach can be readily instantiated over the two homomorphic encryption functions (additive ElGamal or Paillier) that we describe in section 2.

The Voters' Perspective. The activity of each voter in the vector-ballot approach includes the following operations: after the setup phase each voter must be authenticated to the bulletin board server. The bulletin board server maintains the listing with all eligible voters. After authentication, the voter reads from the bulletin board the public-key of the authorities and all other information that is pertinent to the election, i.e., the listing of predetermined candidates. The voter privately decides on one of the predetermined candidates or to a certain write-in choice and publishes her encrypted ballot which consists of the three ciphertexts as described in section 3.2. Further she needs to publish the proof of consistent ballot-encoding. This is done by writing in the bulletin board the non-interactive zero-knowledge proof as described in section 3.2. This proof has size linear to the number of predetermined candidates and can be generated very efficiently for the two homomorphic encryption schemes that we consider.

The Authorities' Perspective. The work of the authorities is divided in two separate stages. (i) Before ballot-casting the authorities execute the **Setup** stage of the election that requires them to run the key-generation protocol of the employed threshold homomorphic encryption scheme. (ii) After the ballot-casting phase the authorities proceed to the tallying phase. The aggregation of the non-writein part of voters' encrypted ballots is a linear operation in the number of voters that employs the homomorphic property of the underlying encryption scheme. Observe that this task can be arbitrarily distributed to any number of entities. Given the aggregated ciphertext the authorities decrypt it by executing the decryption protocol of the underlying homomorphic encryption scheme; this reveals the counts for the predetermined candidates. It is highly likely that a winner of the election can be already determined at this stage. Subsequently, the authorities execute the shrink-and-mix protocol. This requires the authorities to execute a robust-mix protocol, but *only* over the encrypted writein ballots that remain after the shrinking phase. The shrinking phase by itself is efficient as it is only linear in the number of encrypted ballots. Subsequently the execution of the robust-mix is performed in the shrunk writein encrypted ballot sequence which allows a significant gain as it is argued in section 3.3. Furthermore any robust mix can be used in a black-box fashion by our shrink-and-mix method; thus we can take advantage of any sophisticated robust shuffling protocol, e.g. the schemes of [20, 24, 26, 18].

Comparison to Previous Work. We first observe that the efficiency of our scheme is comparable to previous approaches in the homomorphic encryption based election. In fact the only difference is the small constant overhead that is introduced in the part of the voter since she has to provide a proof of a consistent ballot encoding. In previous homomorphic encryption based solutions the "proof of ballot-validity" is also linear in the number of candidates; note that this cannot be improved further if we use encrypted-ballots coupled with a "1-out-of-c" non-interactive zero-knowledge proof (which has by definition length linear in c). Going beyond the homomorphic-encryption approach, our approach allows the incorporation of writein votes. In this respect, we first observe that our schemes achieve universal-verifiability, unlike the previous writein approach based on blind signatures. When compared to the mix-network approach, we also employ a "robust-mix" but we do so with a significant gain compared to the previous mix network protocols: indeed since the great majority of the voters will not cast a write-in vote, our *shrink-and-mix* approach will achieve a *five-fold*[1] improvement in many typical scenarios. This is a very significant improvement in any practical implementation.

Security. Regarding the security properties of our scheme we make the following claim: The e-voting approach described above satisfies secrecy with b-perimeter, universal-verifiability, robustness and fairness provided that (i) less than t authorities are malicious, (ii) the underlying homomorphic encryption scheme is semantically secure, (iii) participants can consult a beacon for the purpose of generating challenges for the zero-knowledge proofs.

Justification. First we argue about Universal-verifiability: a third party auditor can verify that all votes have been counted by performing the following three steps: (i) *verifying the non-writein part*: the auditor recomputes the tally ciphertext C_{tally} from the first portion of every voter's vector-ballot and verifies that the authorities decrypted C_{tally} properly by checking the non-interactive zero-knowledge proof of decryption; (ii) *verifying the shrinking phase*: the auditor recomputes all ciphertexts $C_{i_1,\ldots,i_b}$ that were used in the shrinking stage of the shrink-and-mix network and verifies their decryption as in (i). (iii) *verifying the robust mix*: the auditor checks all mixing proofs given by the shuffling authorities during the mixing procedure. Regarding fairness, we observe that no partial sum can be revealed to any third party due to the semantic-security of the homomorphic encryption function and the zero-knowledge properties of the proofs of consistent ballot encodings. Regarding robustness observe that it is guaranteed unconditionally for voters: any eligible voter may fail without having any impact on the protocol; furthermore, any number of authorities below the threshold t may fail without affecting the protocol. Note that we do not deal with failures explicitly affecting the bulletin board server which is a formalism used in a black-box fashion in all the cryptographic e-voting literature, [3]. Finally, secrecy with b-perimeter of our scheme is justified based on the semantic security of the underlying homomorphic encryption scheme. A formal treatment of the security properties is deferred for the full version of the paper.

4   Punch-Hole / Write-In Ballots

In settings where the number of candidates c and the number of voters n is large it could be the case that it might be detrimental (in terms of efficiency) to use any scheme based on the homomorphic encryption approach ([10, 16, 13]) as well as our approach of the previous section. This is because the capacity assumption (employed by all the above protocols) mandates that the capacity a of the encryption function satisfies the condition $a > n^c$. Even worse if the additive ElGamal instantiation is used (as e.g. in the case of the scheme of [10]) the tallying phase would require a brute-force step proportional to n^c which is very expensive. For such cases we introduce an alternative generic vector ballot

---

[1] Assuming writein probability of $1/100$, see section 3.3.

design for our e-voting approach that is capable of dealing with such settings very efficiently. In the variant of our approach of this section, the ballot of each voter consists of $c + 2$ ciphertexts (instead of 3) and the only allowed ballot encodings are the following (i) encrypt a single "1" in the first c ciphertexts and "0" everywhere else, or (ii) enter a write-in ballot in the last ciphertext, encrypt a "0" in the first c ciphertexts and encrypt a "1" in the $(c + 1)$-th ciphertext (which plays the role of the "flag-ciphertext"). The encoding can be thought of as "punch-hole/write-in" voting because the voter either "punches" a hole in the first c locations (by voting "1") or enters his write-in choice in the last location. In the remaining we briefly explain the approach, mentioning only the cases where there is significant difference from our paradigm of section 3. More details will be provided in the full version.

First we note that the capacity assumption will be relaxed as follows:

Relaxed Capacity Assumption. The capacity a of the encryption function satisfies $a > n$ (the number of voters).

Formation the Vector-Ballot. Each voter V_i publishes a vector ballot $\langle C_1[i], C_2[i], \ldots, C_{c+1}[i], C_{c+2}[i]\rangle$. If the voter wishes to select one of the predetermined choices $\{1, \ldots, c\}$ of the election she selects $C_{\ell_i}[i] := \mathcal{E}_{\mathsf{pk}}(1)$, where $\ell_i \in \{1, \ldots, c\}$ is her choice, and then sets $C_\ell[i] := \mathcal{E}_{\mathsf{pk}}(0)$ for all $\ell \in \{1, \ldots, c + 2\} - \{\ell_i\}$. On the other hand, if the voter wishes to enter a write-in she selects $C_{c+2}[i] := \mathcal{E}_{\mathsf{pk}}(\mathsf{string}_i)$ where string_i is her write-in choice, and sets $C_{c+1}[i] := \mathcal{E}_{\mathsf{pk}}(1)$ as well as $C_\ell[i] := \mathcal{E}_{\mathsf{pk}}(0)$ for $\ell = 1, \ldots, c$. Together with her vector ballot the voter publishes a proof of a consistent vector ballot encoding to ensure that her ballot is formed properly. More specifically this is done as follows:

(Consistency Argument #1) V_i shows that the first $c + 1$ locations of her vector ballot contain only a single 1 among c 0's; this is accomplished as follows: V_i publishes a random re-encrypted shuffle of the $c + 1$ ciphertexts $C_1[i], C_2[i], \ldots, C_{c+1}[i]$ denoted by $\langle C'_1[i], C'_2[i], \ldots, C'_{c+1}[i]\rangle$ and proves its correctness. Then, the voter opens all ciphertexts $C'_\ell[i]$ (by showing their coin-tosses); this allows any third party to verify that the plaintexts encrypted in $C'_1[i], \ldots, C'_{c+1}[i]$ are exactly a single 1, among c 0's; due to the zero-knowledge proof this shows that the same is true about the corresponding ciphertexts in the vector-ballot; note that due to the zero-knowledge properties of the shuffle this step does not reveal any information about the location of the 1.

(Consistency Argument #2). The voter shows that either the two last ciphertexts in the vector ballot encrypt 0, or that the $(c+1)$-th ciphertext encrypts a 1, i.e., V_i writes a proof for the predicate $(Q_{\mathsf{cipher}}^{0, C_{c+1}[i]} \wedge Q_{\mathsf{cipher}}^{0, C_{c+2}[i]}) \vee (Q_{\mathsf{cipher}}^{1, C_{c+1}[i]})$

It is easy to verify that the above consistency arguments enforce the intended ballot-encodings. In the tallying phase, the vector ballots are parsed so that the first c components are collected and the c sequences of ciphertexts $C_\ell[1], \ldots, C_\ell[n]$ are formed for $\ell = 1, \ldots, c$. We define c "tally ciphertexts" as $C_{\mathsf{tally}}^\ell = C_\ell[1] \odot \ldots \odot C_\ell[n]$. It is easy to see that due to the homomorphic property C_{tally}^ℓ is a ciphertext that hides a integer value T_ℓ that equals the number of votes that were won by the predetermined election candidate $\ell \in \{1, \ldots, c\}$.

Decrypting these ciphertexts reveals the votes accumulated by each predetermined candidate. Dealing with the write-in part of each vector-ballot is as in the paradigm of section 3.

Security and Efficiency. The security of the punch-hole/write-in version of our paradigm can be argued in similar terms as the main paradigm. Regarding efficiency, the main difference between the punch-hole paradigm and the general vector-ballot paradigm is that the encrypted ballot contains $c + 2$ ciphertexts instead of 3. While this may sound as a substantial increase in space it is not so: indeed, the security parameter in the vector-ballot paradigm (as well as in any homomorphic encryption scheme) must have a linear dependency on c, whereas the security parameter in the punch-hole approach is independent of c. Thus the two approaches do not differ (in the asymptotic sense) in terms of space. In terms of time-efficiency, the punch-hole approach requires more work from the voter in the proof of the vector-ballot consistency, but it yields a significant gain from the fact that the security parameter does not have to be proportional to the number of candidates and that tallying (as described below) can be done very efficiently over additive ElGamal encryption — in fact, an exponential gain.

Exponential Gain for the Additive-ElGamal Instantiation. Observe that when the above protocol approach is instantiated with additive ElGamal encryption the announcement of the results requires c brute-force searches of a space of size n instead of a brute-force step of a space of size n^{c-1} as it is the case with previous ElGamal-based encryption-schemes (e.g. [10]). This emphasizes further the usefulness of the "punch-hole" approach to increase the efficiency of the system. We remark that this significant gain is independent of the addition of the writein part of the election and in fact it can be also executed in the non-writein setting of [10].

Remark. It has been brought to our attention that a scheme related to the punch-hole approach (without the combination of vector-ballots/ write-in votes, though) appeared in the Ph.D. Thesis of M. Hirt [23].

Acknowledgement

We thank Ron Rivest for his motivating question regarding homomorphic encryption and writein ballot combination and to Pierre-Alain Fouque for getting it to our attention and for related discussions.

References

1. Masayuki Abe and Fumitaka Hoshino, *Remarks on Mix-Networks Based on Permutation Networks*, PKC 2001.
2. Olivier Baudron, Pierre-Alain Fouque, David Pointcheval, Guillaume Poupard and Jacques Stern, *Practical Multi-Candidate Election system*, In the Proceedings of the ACM Symposium on Principles of Distributed Computing (PODC), 2001.
3. Josh Benaloh, *Verifiable Secret-Ballot Elections*, PhD Thesis, Yale University, 1987.

4. Josh Benaloh and Moti Yung, *Distributing the Power of a Government to Enhance the Privacy of Voters*, In the proceedings of the ACM Symposium on Principles of Distributed Computing (PODC), 1986.
5. Josh Benaloh and Dwight Tuinstra, *Receipt-Free Secret-Ballot Elections*, STOC 1994.
6. Dan Boneh and Philippe Golle, *Almost Entirely Correct Mixing With Applications to Voting*, 9th ACM-CCS Conference, 2002.
7. David Chaum, *Untraceable Electronic Mail, Return Addresses, and Digital Pseudonyms*, Communications of the ACM 24(2): 84-88, 1981.
8. David Chaum, *Elections with Unconditionally-Secret Ballots and Disruption Equivalent to Breaking RSA*, Eurocrypt 1988.
9. Josh D. Cohen (Benaloh) and Michael J. Fischer, *A Robust and Verifiable Cryptographically Secure Election Scheme*, FOCS 1985.
10. Ronald Cramer, Rosario Gennaro and Berry Schoenmakers, *A Secure and Optimally Efficient Multi-Authority Election Scheme*, Eurocrypt 1997.
11. Ronald Cramer, Ivan Damgård and Berry Schoenmakers, *Proofs of Partial Knowledge and Simplified Design of Witness Hiding Protocols*, Crypto 1994.
12. Ronald Cramer, Matthew K. Franklin, Berry Schoenmakers and Moti Yung, *Multi-Autority Secret-Ballot Elections with Linear Work*, Eurocrypt 1996.
13. Ivan Damgård and Mats Jurik, *A Generalisation, a Simplification and Some Applications of Paillier's Probabilistic Public-Key System*, PKC 2001, pp. 119-136.
14. Alfredo De Santis, Giovanni Di Crescenzo, Giuseppe Persiano, Moti Yung, *On Monotone Formula Closure of SZK*, FOCS 1994.
15. Amos Fiat and Adi Shamir, *How to Prove Yourself: Practical Solutions to Identification and Signature Problems*, Crypto 1986.
16. Pierre-Alain Fouque, Guillaume Poupard and Jacques Stern, *Sharing Decryption in the Context of Voting or Lotteries*, Financial Cryptography 2000.
17. Atsushi Fujioka, Tatsuaki Okamoto and Kazuo Ohta: *A Practical Secret Voting Scheme for Large Scale Elections*, ASIACRYPT 1992.
18. Jun Furukawa and Kazue Sako, *An Efficient Scheme for Proving a Shuffle*, CRYPTO 2001, pp. 368-387.
19. Rosario Gennaro, Stanislaw Jarecki, Hugo Krawczyk and Tal Rabin, *Secure Distributed Key Generation for Discrete-Log Based Cryptosystems* Eurocrypt 1999.
20. P. Golle, S. Zhong, D. Boneh, M. Jakobsson and A. Juels, *Optimistic Mixing for Exit-Polls*, Asiacrypt 2002.
21. Dimitris Gritzalis (Ed.), **Secure Electronic Voting**, Advances in Information Security, Volume 7, Kluwer 2002.
22. Martin Hirt and Kazue Sako, *Efficient Receipt-Free Voting Based on Homomorphic Encryption*, Eurocrypt 2000.
23. Martin Hirt, *Multi-Party Computation: Efficient Protocols, General Adversaries, and Voting*, Ph.D. Thesis, ETH Zurich, 2001.
24. Markus Jakobsson, Ari Juels and Ronald L. Rivest *Making Mix Nets Robust for Electronic Voting by Randomized Partial Checking*, USENIX Security Symposium 2002, pp. 339-353.
25. Byoungcheon Lee and Kwangjo Kim, *Receipt-Free Electronic Voting Scheme with Tamper-Resistant Randomizer.* ICISC 2001.
26. C. Andrew Neff, *A verifiable secret shuffle and its application to e-voting*, ACM Conference on Computer and Communications Security 2001, pp. 116-125.
27. Tatsuaki Okamoto, *Receipt-Free Electronic Voting Schemes for Large Scale Elections*, Workshop on Security Protocols, 1997.

28. Pascal Paillier, *Public-Key Cryptosystems Based on Composite Degree Residuosity Classes*, Eurocrypt 1999.
29. Choonsik Park, Kazutomo Itoh and Kaoru Kurosawa, *Efficient Anonymous Channel and All/Nothing Election Scheme*, Eurocrypt 1993.
30. Torben P. Pedersen, *A threshold Cryptosystem without a Trusted Third Party*, Eurocrypt 1991.
31. Torben P. Pedersen, *Distributed Provers and Verifiable Secret Sharing Based on the Discrete Logarithm Problem*, PhD Thesis, Aarhus University 1992.
32. Michael Rabin, *Transactions protected by beacons*, Journal of Computer and System Sciences, Vol. 27, pp 256-267, 1983.
33. Kazue Sako and Joe Kilian, *Secure Voting Using Partially Compatible Homomorphisms*, Crypto 1994.
34. Kazue Sako and Joe Kilian, *Receipt-Free Mix-Type Voting Scheme - A Practical Solution to the Implementation of a Voting Booth*, Eurocrypt 1995.
35. Berry Schoenmakers, *A Simple Publicly Verifiable Secret Sharing Scheme and its Applications to Electronic Voting*, Crypto 1999.

Efficient Maximal Privacy in Boardroom Voting and Anonymous Broadcast

Jens Groth[1,2]

[1] BRICS*, University of Aarhus, Ny Munkegade bd. 540, 8000 Århus C, Denmark
[2] Cryptomathic A/S**, Jægergårdsgade 118, 8000 Århus C, Denmark
jg@brics.dk

Abstract. Most voting schemes rely on a number of authorities. If too many of these authorities are dishonest then voter privacy may be violated. To give stronger guarantees of voter privacy Kiayias and Yung [1] introduced the concept of elections with perfect ballot secrecy. In this type of election scheme it is guaranteed that the only thing revealed about voters' choices is the result of the election, no matter how many parties are corrupt. Our first contribution is to suggest a simple voting scheme with perfect ballot secrecy that is more efficient than [1].
Considering the question of achieving maximal privacy in other protocols, we look at anonymous broadcast. We suggest the notion of perfect message secrecy; meaning that nothing is revealed about who sent which message, no matter how many parties are corrupt. Our second contribution is an anonymous broadcast channel with perfect message secrecy built on top of a broadcast channel.

1 Introduction

Voting schemes are legion in the cryptographic literature. Common for most of them is that they rely on some authorities to conduct the election. Furthermore, if a large group of authorities is dishonest then individual votes may be revealed. To some extend this is unavoidable, some degree of privacy violation is inherent in any election; a group of voters may subtract their own votes from the result and thereby obtain some information about the remaining voters' choice. In terms of privacy, the best we can hope for is to ensure that nobody can deduce more about the distribution of honest voters' votes than what can be deduced from the result and knowledge of dishonest voters' choices. We call this type of security perfect ballot secrecy.

Kiayias and Yung [1] introduced the notion of perfect ballot secrecy together with self-tallying and dispute-freeness. Self-tallying means there is no need for authorities to tally the votes. Once all votes have been cast, the result can be tallied and verified by anybody. Dispute-freeness says that anybody may

---

* Basic Research in Computer Science (www.brics.dk),
  funded by the Danish National Research Foundation.
** www.cryptomathic.com

A. Juels (Ed.): FC 2004, LNCS 3110, pp. 90–104, 2004.

verify that indeed the parties do follow the protocol. In other words, it is public knowledge whether a party performed correctly or tried to cheat.

Kiayias and Yung [1] presented a self-tallying dispute-free voting scheme with perfect ballot secrecy with security based on the Decisional Diffie-Hellman (DDH) assumption. Later Damgård and Jurik [2] suggested a somewhat similar scheme based on the Decisional Composite Residuosity (DCR) assumption [3]. Both schemes work in the random oracle model and assume an authenticated broadcast channel; in the present paper, we use this model too.

Kiayias and Yung [1, 4, 5] rely on a method they call zero-sharing for achieving maximal privacy. Not only do they build a voting protocol from this, but they also suggest protocols for anonymous vetoing and simultaneous disclosure of secrets.

Our contributions. Our first contribution is a new voting scheme that has the same security properties as [1, 2] but is simpler and more efficient. We base our scheme on the DDH assumption, i.e., ElGamal encryption, but the same ideas can be used in combination with the DCR assumption. The reason for this choice is that it is easy to generate in a distributed manner suitable groups where the DDH assumption is well founded. Distributed generation of a suitable group for the DCR assumption is more complicated [6].

Our second contribution is to construct an anonymous broadcast channel with perfect message secrecy, i.e., no matter which parties are dishonest, they are not able to tell among the honest senders who sent a particular message. This scheme is related to voting in the sense that using this anonymous channel to cast votes gives us a self-tallying voting scheme with perfect ballot secrecy, but it may of course also have many other applications.

1.1   Model

Throughout the paper, we assume all parties have access to an authenticated broadcast channel with memory. We imagine this in the form of a message board that all parties can access. Each party has a special designated area where he, and nobody else, can write. No party can delete any messages from the message board. One way of implementing such a message board would be to have a central server on the Internet handling the messages. We discuss this further in Section 4.

When considering security of the protocols we imagine that there is an active polynomial time adversary $\mathcal{A}$ trying to break them. $\mathcal{A}$ is static, i.e., from the beginning of the protocol it has control over a fixed set of parties.

The parties in the protocol work semi-synchronously; the protocol proceeds in phases and in each phase parties may act in random order. We let the adversary decide when to change to the next phase. Since the protocols we design are intended for use with a small number of participants, we find this to be a reasonable assumption. Should several parties by accident happen to execute their action at the same time anyway, then it is quite easy to recover.

2   Self-tallying Voting Scheme with Perfect Ballot Secrecy

2.1   Security Definitions

The requirements we want the voting scheme to satisfy are the following.

Perfect ballot secrecy: This is an extension of the usual privacy requirement. In a voting scheme with perfect ballot secrecy the partial tally of a group of voters is only accessible to a coalition consisting of *all* remaining voters. This is the best type of anonymity we can hope for in elections where we publish the result, since a coalition of voters may of course always subtract their own votes.

Self-tallying: After all votes have been cast, it is possible for anybody, both voters and third parties, to compute the result.

Fairness: Nobody has access to a partial tally before the deadline. We will interpret this demand in a relaxed way such that it is guaranteed by a hopefully honest authority.

Dispute-freeness: This notion extends universal verifiability. A scheme is dispute-free if everybody can check whether voters act according to the protocol or not. In particular, this means that the result is publicly verifiable.

2.2   The Voting Protocol

The basic idea. To quickly describe our idea let us use an analogue with the physical world. Assume a group of people want to vote yes or no to a proposal. To do this the voters take a box with a small slot and each voter puts a padlock on the box. Taking turns the voters one by one drop a white (yes) stone or a black (no) stone into the box and remove their padlock. When the last voter has removed his padlock, they may open the box and see the result of the election. The protocol has perfect ballot secrecy since the box cannot be opened before all honest voters have cast their vote, and thus any honest voter's vote is mixed in with the rest of the honest voters' votes.

Overview of the protocol. For simplicity, we first describe the protocol in the honest-but-curious setting, i.e., corrupted voters may leak information but follow the protocol. For simplicity, we also assume there are just two candidates that the voters can choose between.

Initialization: First, the voters agree on a group G_q of order q where the DDH problem is hard. Let g be a generator for G_q.

All voters now select at random an element in $\mathbb{Z}_q$. Each voter j keeps his element x_j secret but publishes $h_j = g^{x_j}$.

Casting votes: Voters may vote in any adaptively chosen order, however, for simplicity we assume in this example that they vote in the order $1, 2, \ldots, n$. Let their choices be $v_1, v_2, \ldots, v_n \in \{0, 1\}$.

The election now proceeds like this:

1. Voter 1 selects at random $r_1 \in \mathbb{Z}_q$ and publishes $(g^{r_1}, (\prod_{i=2}^{n} h_i)^{r_1} g^{v_1})$.
2. Voter 2 selects at random $r_2 \in \mathbb{Z}_q$ and computes $(g^{r_2}, (\prod_{i=2}^{n} h_i)^{r_2} g^{v_2})$. Multiplying this to the first vote, he gets $(g^{r_1+r_2}, (\prod_{i=2}^{n} h_i)^{r_1+r_2} g^{v_1+v_2})$. With his knowledge of the secret key x_2, he may peel of a layer of this ElGamal encryption of the partial result. In other words, he computes $(g^{r_1+r_2}, (\prod_{i=3}^{n} h_i)^{r_1+r_2} g^{v_1+v_2})$. He publishes this on the message board.
3. Voter 3 performs the same type of operations as voter 2. He ends up publishing $(g^{r_1+r_2+r_3}, (\prod_{i=4}^{n} h_i)^{r_1+r_2+r_3} g^{v_1+v_2+v_3})$ on the message board.

$\vdots$

n. Voter n performs the same type of operations as the previous voters. When he is done, his output is $(g^{\sum_{i=1}^{n} r_i}, g^{\sum_{i=1}^{n} v_i})$.

Tallying: From the last voter's output we can read off $g^{\sum_{i=1}^{n} v_i}$. We compute the discrete logarithm, this is possible since the exponent is at most n, to get $\sum_{i=1}^{n} v_i$. This is the number of 1-votes in the election.

The full protocol. The protocol as described is not fair, it is possible for the last voter to know the result before casting his own vote. As in [1] we deal with this by saying that a special election authority must act like a voter and cast a zero-vote in the end. Since it is a zero-vote, it does not affect the result. On the other hand, the perfect ballot secrecy of the voting scheme ensures that up to this point nobody but the authority can know any partial tally. Therefore, if the authority is honest then the voting scheme is fair.

To go beyond the honest-but-curious assumption and deal with all kinds of adversaries all we have to do is to add zero-knowledge proofs of knowledge of correctness. These proofs will be the typical 3-move honest verifier proofs (Σ-protocols [7]), where using the Fiat-Shamir heuristic we can make very efficient non-interactive zero-knowledge proofs. Security of the protocol will be proved in the random oracle model [8].

We wish to support a set W of possible votes. Let us write the c candidates in W as candidates as $0, \ldots, c-1$. We do this by encoding candidate number i as $(n+1)^i$. From a sum $\sum_{i=1}^{n} v_i$ of votes with this encoding we can read off the number of votes on each candidate. To compute the result, we have to compute the discrete logarithm of $g^{\sum_{i=1}^{n} v_i}$. With n voters and c candidates, the number of possible results is $\binom{c+n-1}{c-1}$. With a small number of voters or a small number of candidates, it is possible to compute the discrete logarithm. If we have a larger number of voters and candidates, we may use a cryptosystem similar to the one in [2]. This allows computing discrete logarithms efficiently, but on the other hand the key generation becomes much more complicated. Alternatively, we may use the anonymous broadcast protocol we present in the next section.

The full protocol can be seen in Figure 1.

Performance. Let n be the number of voters, c be the number of candidates, and k be the security parameter. We assume that $n^c \leq q$.

Voting Protocol

Setup: The voters agree on a suitable group G_q of order q where the DDH assumption holds. Let g be a generator for G_q.

Key Registration: Voter i selects at random $x_i \in \mathbb{Z}_q$ and sets $h_i = g^{x_i}$. He publishes h_i and makes a proof of knowledge of x_i, $\mathrm{PK}[x_i : h_i = g^{x_i}]$. Any voters who did not supply a key are removed from the list of eligible voters. Set the current state of the election to be $(1,1)$.

Voting: Voter i wishing to cast a vote $v_i \in W$ downloads the current state of the election (u,v), and verifies the correctness of keys and all votes cast up to now. Then he selects r_i at random from $\mathbb{Z}_q$, sets $U = ug^{r_i}$ and $V = vu^{-x_i}(\prod_{j \in T} h_j)^{r_i} g^{v_i}$, where T is the set of remaining voters. He broadcasts (U,V) as the new state of the election together with a zero knowledge proof of knowledge
$\mathrm{PK}[(r_i, v_i, x_i) : h_i = g^{x_i} \wedge U = ug^{r_i} \wedge V = vu^{-x_i}(\prod_{j \in T} h_j)^{r_i} g^{v_i} \wedge v_i \in W]$,
i.e., a proof that he knows r_i, v_i, x_i making his vote correct.

Tallying: After all voters have cast their votes the state (u,v) has $v = g^{\sum_{i=1}^{n} v_i}$. The discrete logarithm $\sum_{i=1}^{n} v_i$ can be computed if there are not too many voters and candidates, and from this the result can be extracted.

Fault-correction: If some voters abstained from voting it is possible that the remaining voters still want to carry out the election. In that case, they can repeat the voting step with the now reduced set of voters. They may gain a factor $\log c$ in efficiency by proving that they cast the same vote as in the first voting phase instead of proving from scratch that the vote belongs to W.

Fig. 1. The voting protocol

For each voter it takes $\mathcal{O}(1)$ exponentiations to compute the key h_i and the associated proof. The size of the key is $\mathcal{O}(k)$. Verification of the n keys takes $\mathcal{O}(n)$ exponentiations.

In the voting phase, it takes $\mathcal{O}(\log c)$ exponentiations to compute the vote and the proof associated with it[1]. The vote has size $\mathcal{O}(k \log c)$. It takes $\mathcal{O}(n \log c)$ exponentiations to verify all the voters' proofs.

In comparison, the protocol in [1] lets the voter do $\mathcal{O}(n)$ exponentiations in the key registration phase, the key has size $\mathcal{O}(nk)$, and verification of the keys takes $\mathcal{O}(n^2)$ exponentiations. In the voting phase, the voter must do $\mathcal{O}(\log c)$ exponentiations, the vote has size $\mathcal{O}(k \log c)$, and it takes $\mathcal{O}(n \log c)$ exponentiations to verify all the votes.

---

[1] Let us sketch where the $\log c$ factor comes from. In the proof of correctness of a vote the voter has to argue that the encrypted vote is on the form $(1 + n)^i$ for $i \in \{0, \ldots, c-1\}$. Let $\{b_1, \ldots, b_{\lceil \log c \rceil}\}$ be a set of positive integers with the following property: for any number $1, \ldots, c - 1$ there is a subset where the numbers have this sum, and for no number larger than $c - 1$ is there a subset with elements having this sum. Write the vote as $(1 + n)^v = (1 + n)^{\sum_{i=1}^{\lceil \log c \rceil} a_i} = \prod_{i=1}^{\lceil \log c \rceil} (1 + n)^{a_i}$, where $a_1 = b_1 \vee a_1 = 0, \ldots, a_{\lceil \log c \rceil} = b_{\lceil \log c \rceil} \vee a_{\lceil \log c \rceil} = 0$. This shows that the vote can be built as a product of $\lceil \log c \rceil$ elements. It is possible to prove correctness of such elements and make proofs of products in $\mathcal{O}(1)$ exponentiations, giving a total of $\mathcal{O}(\log c)$ exponentiations.

The Kiayias and Yung protocol does have the advantage that many voters can vote at the same time, whereas we demand that they download the current state and use that in making their vote. Since the voting protocols are designed for self-tallying and demand that all voters participate we can only see them as being realistic in settings with few voters though. With few voters, we believe it is reasonable to assume that voters act one at a time; and even if they occasionally do not it is easy to correct.

2.3   Security

To argue perfect ballot secrecy of the voting protocol in Figure 1 we will show that a real-life execution of the protocol can be simulated with knowledge of the sum of the honest voters' votes only. To do so we define two experiments, a real-life experiment, and a simulation experiment.

Real-life experiment. In the real-life experiment the voters $V_1, \ldots, V_n$ have votes $v_1, \ldots, v_n$ that they want to cast. An adversary $\mathcal{A}$ tries to break the protocol. $\mathcal{A}$ has full control over a fixed set of corrupt voters and gets as input a string z. $\mathcal{A}$ controls the flow of the protocol, i.e., it decides when to shift to the next phase, and within each phase it can adaptively activate voters. Upon activation, a voter reads the contents of the message board, computes its input according to the voting protocol, and posts it on the message board. After an honest voter has been activated control is passed back to $\mathcal{A}$. Please note that $\mathcal{A}$ may choose not to activate a voter, in that case the voter does not get to submit a vote. Once the election is over $\mathcal{A}$ computes an output s and halts. The output of the experiment is $(s, \text{cont}, \text{result})$, where cont is the contents of the message board and result is the outcome of the election if this can be computed from cont.

We write $\mathbf{Exp}_{V_1,\ldots,V_n,\mathcal{A}}^{\text{real}}(v_1, \ldots, v_n, z)$ to denote the distribution of $(s, \text{cont}, \text{result})$ from the real-life experiment.

Simulation. In this experiment, a simulator $\mathcal{S}$ has to simulate the election. $\mathcal{S}$ gets as input a string z, including a list of corrupt voters. $\mathcal{S}$ controls the random oracle; this enables it to simulate zero-knowledge proofs. In the simulation, we let a trusted party $\mathcal{T}$ handle the message board as well as computation of the result. $\mathcal{T}$ learns the votes $v_1, \ldots, v_n$ and which voters are corrupt. In the key registration phase, the voting phase and the fault correction phase, $\mathcal{T}$ expects to receive also the witnesses when $\mathcal{S}$ submits a valid key or a valid vote on behalf of a corrupt voter. In particular, this means that $\mathcal{T}$ learns the plaintext vote whenever a corrupt voter tries to cast a vote. Due to the self-tallying property of the voting scheme, the honest voters' partial tally may be revealed at some point. We formulate the following rule for letting $\mathcal{T}$ reveal this partial tally to $\mathcal{S}$. First, $\mathcal{T}$ notes which honest voters did not participate in the setup phase or the key-registration phase. In the voting phase, if $\mathcal{S}$ is about to activate the last remaining honest voter then it may query $\mathcal{T}$ for the partial tally of the honest voters. Afterwards, we demand that $\mathcal{S}$ posts a vote on behalf of this simulated voter. After the election, $\mathcal{S}$ halts with output s. $\mathcal{T}$ computes the result using the plaintext votes and the honest voters votes, and outputs the contents of the message board and the result.

We write $\mathbf{Exp}^{\text{sim}}_{\mathcal{T},\mathcal{S}}(v_1, \ldots, v_n, z)$ to denote the distribution of $(s, \text{cont}, \text{result})$ in the simulation.

The simulator $\mathcal{S}$. $\mathcal{S}$ runs a copy of $\mathcal{A}$ and simulates everything that $\mathcal{A}$ sees, including the behavior of the honest voters. When $\mathcal{A}$ changes phase in the protocol so does $\mathcal{S}$. If $\mathcal{A}$ lets a corrupt voter post something on the message board, $\mathcal{S}$ verifies the proof. If the proof is valid, $\mathcal{S}$ uses rewinding techniques to extract the witness. It then submits the entire thing to $\mathcal{T}$. In particular, this means that the vote is submitted in plaintext to $\mathcal{T}$. If $\mathcal{A}$ activates an honest party in the key registration phase, $\mathcal{S}$ selects h_i at random and simulates the proof of knowledge of x_i. It submits h_i and the simulated proof to $\mathcal{T}$. If $\mathcal{A}$ activates an honest voter in the voting phase, and this is not the last remaining honest voter to vote, $\mathcal{S}$ picks (U, V) at random and simulates a proof of knowledge of the corresponding x_i, r_i, v_i. If the activated honest voter is the last honest voter to submit a vote, then $\mathcal{S}$ queries $\mathcal{T}$ for the partial tally of the honest voters. Knowing the witnesses for the corrupt voters' submissions it can then compute the partial tally of voters that have voted so far. Let S be the set of voters that have voted, including the voter to vote right now. Let T be the set of remaining eligible voters; all of them are corrupt. $\mathcal{S}$ picks U at random and computes $V = U^{\sum_{j \in T} x_j} g^{\sum_{i \in S} v_i}$. It then simulates the proof for having computed (U, V) correctly and gives it to $\mathcal{T}$. At some point the simulated $\mathcal{A}$ halts with output s. $\mathcal{S}$ outputs s and halts.

Lemma 1. *For any adversary $\mathcal{A}$ there exists a simulator $\mathcal{S}$ such that the distributions $\mathbf{Exp}^{\text{real}}_{V_1,\ldots,V_n,\mathcal{A}}(v_1, \ldots, v_n, z)$ and $\mathbf{Exp}^{\text{sim}}_{\mathcal{T},\mathcal{S}}(v_1, \ldots, v_n, z)$ are indistinguishable for all $v_1, \ldots, v_n, z$.*

Proof. We use the simulator $\mathcal{S}$ described above. To show indistinguishability we will go through a series of intermediate experiments $Exp_1, \ldots, Exp_3$. We then show that $\mathbf{Exp}^{\text{real}}_{V_1,\ldots,V_n,\mathcal{A}}(v_1, \ldots, v_n, z) \approx Exp_1(v_1, \ldots, v_n, z) \approx Exp_2(v_1, \ldots, v_n, z) \approx Exp_3(v_1, \ldots, v_n, z) \approx \mathbf{Exp}^{\text{sim}}_{\mathcal{T},\mathcal{S}}(v_1, \ldots, v_n, z)$.

Exp_1 works like $\mathbf{Exp}^{\text{real}}_{V_1,\ldots,V_n,\mathcal{A}}$ except whenever $\mathcal{A}$ submits a valid input on behalf of a corrupt voter. In these cases, we use rewinding techniques to extract the corresponding witnesses in expected polynomial time. This way for each key registration from a corrupt voter we know the corresponding exponent x_i, and for each vote we know the vote v_i as well as the randomness r_i and x_i. Having knowledge of the witnesses, we may now run the entire protocol using the trusted party $\mathcal{T}$ from the simulation experiment to control the message board. The outputs of the two experiments are the same, so indistinguishability is obvious.

Exp_2 works like Exp_1 except we simulate all proofs made by honest voters. Typically, these proofs are statistical zero-knowledge and then we get statistical indistinguishability between Exp_1 and Exp_2.

Let us consider Exp_2 a little further. Define $g_i = g^{r_i}$ and $h_{ij} = h_j^{r_i}$, where r_i is the randomness used by voter i. Consider the voting phase, denote at a given time S to be the voters that have cast votes already and T to be the voters that have not yet acted in this phase. The state at this time is

$$(u, v) = (\prod_{i \in S} g_i, (\prod_{i \in S} \prod_{j \in T} h_{ij}) g^{\sum_{i \in S} v_i}).$$

Since we are simulating the proofs, we do not need knowledge of x_i, r_i for honest voters. Therefore, to carry out Exp_2 we can first compute a table of the g_i's,h_j's and h_{ij}'s for the honest voters and then use these values.

Define Exp_3 to be Exp_2 where we choose the g_i's,h_j's and h_{ij}'s randomly from G_q. By a hybrid argument using the DDH assumption, the tables of these elements in Exp_2 and Exp_3 are indistinguishable. Therefore, the two experiments Exp_2 and Exp_3 are indistinguishable.

Remaining is the fact that we still use individual votes v_i from honest voters to perform the experiment. However, note that in the voting phase when an honest voter V_i updates from (u, v) to (U, V) he sets $U = ug_i$ and $V = v(\prod_{j \in S} h_{ji}^{-1})(\prod_{j \in T} h_{ij}) g^{v_i}$. The elements $\{h_{ij}\}_{j \in T}$ contain new randomness and therefore the vote v_i is perfectly hidden unless T has no honest voters, i.e., V_i is the last honest voter to vote.

These considerations lead us to modify Exp_3 the following way. An honest voter who is not the last honest voter to act in the voting phase computes the new state (U, V) by picking it at random in $G_q \times G_q$. An honest voter V_i who is the last honest voter to vote computes $\sum_{i \in S} v_i$, picks U at random from G_q and sets $V = U^{\sum_{i \in T} x_i} g^{\sum_{i \in S} v_i}$.

This modifies Exp_3 into $\mathbf{Exp}_{T,S}^{sim}$, so these two experiments are perfectly indistinguishable.   □

Lemma 1 says that the election can be simulated without knowledge of the honest voters' individual votes. Moreover, it forces the simulator to submit plaintext votes on behalf of corrupt voters, so their votes cannot be related to the honest voters' votes.

Theorem 1. *The voting protocol described in Figure 1 is self-tallying, dispute-free, and has perfect ballot secrecy. If the last voter is an honest authority that submits a zero-vote then the protocol is fair.*

Proof. It is easy to see that the protocol is self-tallying if all parties act according to the protocol, and the zero-knowledge proofs force the parties to act according to the protocol. Likewise, since the zero-knowledge proofs force parties to act according to the protocol it follows that the protocol is dispute-free. Perfect ballot secrecy follows from Lemma 1. Fairness follows from perfect ballot secrecy, since perfect ballot secrecy implies that we cannot compute any partial result before the authority submits its vote, and if honest the authority does not submit its vote before the end of the election.   □

2.4   A Veto Protocol

Kiayias and Yung suggested a veto-protocol in [5]. By this, we mean that any party may veto a proposal, however, it should not be possible to learn who vetoed the proposal or how many vetoed a proposal.

It is easy to implement such a veto protocol with the voting scheme we have suggested. We let acceptance of the proposal correspond to a 0-vote. On the other hand, a veto is a vote on a random element from $\mathbb{Z}_q$. This way, if nobody vetoed we get a tally, which is 0. On the other hand, if anybody vetoed, then we get a tally, which is a random number from $\mathbb{Z}_q$. Discrete logarithms are difficult to compute, however, we do not have to do that, all we need to do is to verify that $g^{\text{result}} \neq 1$.

One problem, which also pertains to the scheme in [5], remains with this scheme, since any vetoer knows his own random element and therefore he may check whether he is the only one who vetoed. To guard against that we may rely on the authority disclosing the result to raise (u, v) to a random exponent from $\mathbb{Z}_q^*$ before decrypting. This way it is impossible for any cheating vetoer to see whether he is the only one to veto the proposal.

3   Self-disclosing Anonymous Broadcast with Perfect Message Secrecy

3.1   Security Definitions

In this section, we deal with the possibility of building an anonymous broadcast channel on top of an authenticated broadcast channel. We want some strict security requirements to be satisfied. The security requirements are quite similar to those for self-tallying elections with perfect ballot secrecy but we rename the latter notion to stress that anonymous broadcast has many other applications than voting.

Perfect message secrecy: Knowledge of the set of messages to be broadcast is only accessible to a coalition of all remaining senders, and this knowledge does not include the connection between senders and messages. This means that a sender is hidden completely among the group of honest senders.
Self-disclosing: Once the last sender has submitted his message, anybody may see which messages were broadcast.
Fairness: Until the deadline is reached it is impossible to know what messages will be broadcast. Again, we will only demand fairness in a restricted sense, namely it will be ensured by a hopefully honest authority.
Dispute-freeness: It is publicly verifiable whether senders follow the protocol or not.

3.2   The Anonymous Broadcast Protocol

Physical analogue. The senders one after another enter a room alone. Bringing with them they take a box, all boxes look alike, and a padlock for each of the remaining senders. In the room, they write down their message, put it in the box, and lock the box with the padlocks corresponding to the remaining senders. Then they shuffle around the boxes so nobody can tell them apart. In the presence of the remaining senders, they now remove one lock from each box, namely the locks that fit their key. As the last sender removes the locks, the messages are revealed.

Idea in the protocol. We use similar ideas as we did in the voting protocol. Each voter encrypts his message with the keys of the remaining senders. This means that the message will not be revealed until all honest voters have been involved in the protocol and peeled off the layer of encryption corresponding to their secret key. The sender will rely on this last honest sender to anonymize his message with respect to all the honest senders.

Since the sender cannot know whether he is the last honest sender, he must also ensure himself that his message is mixed with the messages of the previous senders. Since ElGamal encryption is homomorphic, it is easy to permute and rerandomize (shuffle) all the ciphertexts made up to this point. Furthermore, efficient proofs of a correct shuffle exist, see [9–11].

Summarizing the protocol the method is as follows. The senders all register public keys just as in the voting protocol. When a sender wants to add his message to the pool, he encrypts it with the public keys of the remaining senders including his own key. Then he shuffles all the ciphertexts in a random way. Finally he peels of a layer of the encryption, namely he decrypts all the ciphertexts with respect to his own key. He proves in zero-knowledge that all these steps have been performed correctly.

The full protocol can be seen in Figure 2.

Performance evaluation. Key registration takes $\mathcal{O}(1)$ exponentiations for each sender, and each key has size $\mathcal{O}(k)$. To verify the correctness of the keys we use $\mathcal{O}(n)$ exponentiations.

With respect to message submission, we may use the efficient shuffle proofs of [9–11]. This way it takes $\mathcal{O}(n)$ exponentiations to compute the new batch of ciphertexts and the proofs, and such a batch has size $\mathcal{O}(nk)$. It takes $\mathcal{O}(n^2)$ exponentiations to verify all the senders' proofs.

Simultaneous disclosure. If we remove the shuffling part of our anonymous broadcast protocol, we get a simultaneous disclosure protocol. We can therefore compare our performance with the simultaneous disclosure protocol of [5], which uses $\mathcal{O}(n^2)$ exponentiations for each voter in the registration phase, and $\mathcal{O}(n)$ exponentiations for each voter in the message submission phase.

3.3   Security

To argue perfect message secrecy we show that the broadcast protocol can be simulated without knowledge of the individual messages. Very similar to the case of the voting protocol we therefore define a real-life experiment and a simulation experiment.

Anonymous Broadcast Protocol

Setup: The senders agree on a suitable group G_q of order q, where the DDH problem is hard. Let g be a generator for G_q.

The senders also set up suitable keys for commitment schemes that will be used in the zero-knowledge proofs to follow.

Key Registration: Sender i selects at random $x_i \in \mathbb{Z}_q$ and sets $h_i = g^{x_i}$. He publishes this public key together with a proof of knowledge of x_i.

Any senders who did not supply a public key are removed from the list of senders.

Message submission: Sender i wishing to send message $m_i \in G_q$.

Let S be the set of senders who already sent a message, including i, and let T be the set of senders who did not send a message. Let $\{(u_j, v_j)\}_{j \in S \setminus \{i\}}$ be the ciphertexts constituting the state.

Sender i first checks that all proofs of the previous senders are correct. Then he encrypts his message as $(u_i, v_i) = (g^{r_i}, (\prod_{j \in T \cup \{i\}} h_j)^{r_i} m_i)$. He picks at random a permutation π_i over S, permutes all ciphertexts $\{(u_j, v_j)\}_{j \in S}$ according to this permutation, and rerandomizes them into $\{(U_j, V'_j)\}_{j \in S}$. Finally, he removes the layer of encryption corresponding to his own private key. I.e., he computes $\{(U_j, V_j) = (U_j, V'_j U_j^{-x_i})\}_{j \in S}$.

He broadcasts this list of ciphertexts together with a proof of knowledge of having done all this correctly.

Broadcasting: The last senders' output contains V_j's that are the messages permuted according to the permutations selected by the senders.

Fault-correction: We do not have a clever fault correction algorithm; we simply start the protocol over again. Depending on the user requirements, we may now demand that the senders prove in zero-knowledge that they are submitting the same message as before.

Fig. 2. The anonymous broadcast protocol

Real-life experiment. We have parties $P_1, \ldots, P_n$ with messages $m_1, \ldots, m_n$ that they want to broadcast anonymously. An adversary $\mathcal{A}$ with input z controls a fixed set of these parties. $\mathcal{A}$ also controls the scheduling in the protocol, in other words, $\mathcal{A}$ decides when to proceed to the next phase, and within each phase $\mathcal{A}$ activates parties adaptively. When activated a party receives the contents of the message board, computes its input according to the protocol, and posts it on the message board. Control then passes back to $\mathcal{A}$. In the end, $\mathcal{A}$ outputs some string s and halts.

We denote by $\mathbf{Exp}^{\text{real}}_{P_1, \ldots, P_n, \mathcal{A}}(m_1, \ldots, m_n, z)$ the distribution of outputs (s, cont, messages) from the experiment, where cont is the content of the message board, and messages is a sorted list of messages from cont.

Simulation. Again, we have a trusted party $\mathcal{T}$ and a simulator $\mathcal{S}$. $\mathcal{T}$ controls the message board and has as input $m_1, \ldots, m_n$ and a list of corrupted parties. During the execution of the protocol it expects $\mathcal{S}$ to provide witnesses for correctness of the actions performed by corrupted parties. When only one honest party remains in the broadcast phase, S can query T for the set of messages $m_1, \ldots, m_k$ submitted by honest parties. After this S must then submit this honest party's broadcast to T. In the end, S halts with output s, and T outputs the contents of the message board and the set of messages submitted in lexicographic order.

We write $\mathbf{Exp}^{\mathrm{sim}}_{T,S}(m_1, \ldots, m_n, z)$ for the distribution of $(s, \mathrm{cont}, \mathrm{messages})$.

The simulator S. S runs a copy of A simulating anything A would see in a real-life execution, including the actions of the honest parties. Whenever A changes phase, so will S. If A lets a corrupt party submit something with a valid proof for the message board, S uses rewinding to extract the witness. This way, in the key registration phase S learns the exponent x_i, when corrupt party P_i registers key h_i. Likewise, when corrupt party P_i makes a broadcast, then S learns the randomizers used, the new message that was submitted, and the permutation π_i. After extracting the witness, S sends everything to the trusted party T. If A activates an honest party P_i in the key registration phase then S picks h_i at random and simulates a proof that it knows the exponent x_i. If A activates an honest party P_i in the message submission phase, and this is not the last honest party to act, S selects (u_i, v_i) at random from $G_q \times G_q$. For each $k \in S$, where S is the set of senders that have been active in the protocol, including P_i, S selects at random (U_k, V'_k) and (U_k, V_k). It then simulates proofs that it knows the message inside the (u_i, v_i) encryption, that it knows a permutation π_i and randomizers such that $\{(U_k, V'_k)\}_{k \in S}$ is a shuffle of $\{(u_k, v_k)\}_{k \in S}$, and that for each $k \in S$, (U_k, V_k) is the decryption of (U_k, V'_k) with key x_i used to form h_i. If the sender activated is the last remaining honest sender, S queries T for the list of messages for honest senders. Furthermore, it knows the messages submitted by corrupt parties. It labels in random order the messages $\{m_k\}_{k \in S}$. It picks (u_i, v_i) at random and picks at random (U_k, V'_k) for $k \in S$. Then for $k \in S$ it sets $V_k = U_k^{\sum_{j \in T} x_j} m_k$, where T is the set of (corrupt) senders that have not yet been activated. S simulates the proofs of correctness and submits it all to T. In the end the simulated A terminates with output s. S outputs s and halts.

Lemma 2. *For any adversary A there exists a simulator S such that the two distributions $\mathbf{Exp}^{\mathrm{real}}_{P_1, \ldots, P_n, A}(m_1, \ldots, m_n, z)$ and $\mathbf{Exp}^{\mathrm{sim}}_{T,S}(m_1, \ldots, m_n, z)$ are indistinguishable for all $m_1, \ldots, m_n, z$.*

Proof. The proof is similar to the proof for Lemma 1. We use the simulator described above. We define three intermediate experiments Exp_1, Exp_2 and Exp_3 and prove that $\mathbf{Exp}^{\mathrm{real}}_{P_1, \ldots, P_n, A}(m_1, \ldots, m_n, z) \approx Exp_1 \approx Exp_2 \approx Exp_3 \approx \mathbf{Exp}^{\mathrm{sim}}_{T,S}(m_1, \ldots, m_n, z)$.

Exp_1 is the real-life experiment where we use rewinding techniques to extract witnesses for valid actions that A lets corrupt parties make. Having the witnesses, we can then execute this experiment in the trusted message board model, giving T the witnesses to go along with the messages.

Exp_2 is a modification of Exp_1 where we simulate all proofs that honest parties make. Consider how an honest party P_i computes the new state $\{(U_j, V_j)\}_{j \in S}$, where S is the set of parties that have submitted their message.

Write T for the set of remaining parties that have not yet made a broadcast. P_i first selects r_i at random and sets $(u_i, v_i) = (g_i, (\prod_{j \in T \cup \{i\}} h_{ij})m_i)$, where $g_i = g^{r_i}$ and $h_{ij} = h_j^{r_i}$. Then P_i selects π_i as a random permutation over S, and computes the pairs $(U_k, V_k') = (u_{\pi_i^{-1}(k)}g_{ik}, v_{\pi_i^{-1}(k)} \prod_{j \in T} h_{ijk}\}_{k \in S}$, where $g_{ik} = g^{r_{ik}}$ and $h_{ijk} = h_j^{r_{ijk}}$, with the r_{ik}'s and r_{ijk}'s chosen at random from $\mathbb{Z}_q$. Finally, for $k \in S$ it sets $(U_k, V_k) = (U_k, V_k'U_k^{-x_i}) = (U_k, V_k \prod_{j \in S} h_{ji}^{-1})$. All this can be computed from a table of g_i's, h_j's, h_{ij}'s, g_{ik}'s, and h_{ijk}'s for the honest parties without knowing the underlying randomizers.

Exp_3 is a modification of Exp_2 where the g_i's, h_j's, h_{ij}'s, g_{ik}'s and h_{ijk}'s for honest parties are selected at random from G_q. By a hybrid argument using the DDH assumption, Exp_2 and Exp_3 are indistinguishable.

Looking at Exp_3, we notice that we might as well pick the elements u_i, v_i, U_k, V_k', V_k completely at random from G_q instead of bothering with picking a permutation π_i and inserting messages, as long as P_i is not the last honest party to broadcast a message. An honest party P_i that is the last honest party to broadcast a message chooses u_i, v_i, U_k, V_k' at random. It picks a permutation π at random and sets $V_k = U_k^{\sum_{j \in T} x_j} m_{\pi(k)}$ for $k \in S$. This last experiment is exactly what happens in the simulation so Exp_3 and $\mathbf{Exp}_{T,S}^{sim}$ are perfectly indistinguishable.   □

Theorem 2. *The protocol described in Figure 2 is a self-disclosing, dispute-free anonymous broadcast protocol with perfect message secrecy. If the last sender is an honest authority (who does not submit a message himself) then the protocol is fair.*

Proof. It is easy to see that the protocol is self-disclosing. The zero-knowledge proofs entail dispute-freeness. Perfect message secrecy follows from Lemma 2. Finally, fairness follows from the perfect message secrecy.   □

4   Various Comments

Reusing the public keys. In both the voting protocol and the anonymous broadcast protocol we may reuse the public keys in many instantiations of the protocols presented here, but some care must be taken. The reason to be careful is the fact we must be able to rewind and extract witnesses from proofs made by the adversary. In the simulation, however, we cannot rewind the trusted party T, so we must be careful that we never have to rewind past a point where T gives us a partial tally or partial set of honest senders messages. When only a single protocol is running this is no problem since in the zero-knowledge proofs we query the random oracle with the current state. When a partial result is released we always let an honest party act right after it, and this honest party injects some new randomness into the state. For this reason an adversary can not predict what the state will be after the release of a partial result, and therefore cannot make queries *before* the release of the partial result that it uses *after* the release of the partial result. This means that we never have to rewind back before the release of a partial result. When running multiple protocols we have to query the random oracle with the states of all protocols to guarantee not having to rewind back past a point where a partial result was released. If we do this, we may use the same public keys to run many protocols.

Universal composability. The statement of our lemmas is somewhat inspired by the universal composability framework of Canetti [12, 13]. However, we have *not* proved the protocols to be universally composable. In particular, we do not include a party $\mathcal{Z}$ to model the exterior environment. It is possible to make the protocols universally composable against non-adaptive adversaries by generating a key for a public key cryptosystem in the setup phase. After this we can in the key registration phase encrypt the keys x_i and prove to have done so in zero-knowledge. We can set this up so the simulator knows the corresponding secret key for the cryptosystem, and therefore it can make a straight-line extraction of the x_i's. Knowing the x_i's it can then extract votes and messages, and carry on the simulation without ever having to rewind. Unfortunately, the technique above may make the protocols considerably less efficient and we have therefore not pursued this option in the paper.

Flexibility in participation. It is easy to set up an election where only a part of the participants is allowed to participate. In that case, we simply ignore the public keys of those not allowed to participate in this instance of the protocol.

In the voting protocol, it is easy to include new voters that may participate in future election. We can choose the group $G_q \leq \mathbb{Z}_q$ specified by p, q, g in a publicly verifiable manner, e.g., chosen at random from the binary expansion of π, or chosen from a string of hashes on some random value. Considering uniform adversaries it would seem reasonable that this gives us a suitably hard group[2]. Since the new voter can trust this group, he simply needs to register a public key himself in order to join.

In the anonymous broadcast protocol, we may also include new senders. However, here the new senders have to beware of the risk that the commitment scheme may be chosen with a trapdoor known to the senders already registered. Therefore, the new sender will have to update this commitment key in a publicly verifiable way.

The authenticated broadcast channel. We do not need something fancy to form this channel. We may for instance assume that a central server stores all the data, and this central server may act like the authority too.

To ensure correctness of the data we will assume that all communication is signed with a digital signature. We cannot rely on a certification authority to issue these digital signatures in the strict setting we are working in. Instead,

---

[2] While it varies from group to group how hard it is to compute discrete logarithms, we do not know of any groups where the DDH problem can be efficiently solved, provided the groups are some subgroup of $\mathbb{Z}_p^*$ where q, p are suitably large primes. See also [14] on this issue.

each participant must certify each other participants public key. Since we assume only a few voters or senders are participating in the protocol, this is a reasonable burden to put on the participants.

Imagine now that the central server fails. Since everything is digitally signed, the participants may restore the state of the message board from their own data. They may now simply set up a new server to run the protocol. It is easy to modify the votes in a publicly verifiable manner such that the data fits the public key of the new authority.

References

1. Kiayias, A., Yung, M.: Self-tallying elections and perfect ballot secrecy. In: proceedings of PKC '02, LNCS series, volume 2274. (2002) 141–158
2. Damgård, I., Jurik, M.J.: A length-flexible threshold cryptosystem with applications. In: proceedings of ACISP '03, LNCS series, volume 2727. (2003) 350–364
3. Paillier, P.: Public-key cryptosystems based on composite residuosity classes. In: proceedings of EUROCRYPT '99, LNCS series, volume 1592. (1999) 223–239
4. Kiayias, A., Yung, M.: Robust verifiable non-interactive zero-sharing. In Gritzalis, D., ed.: Secure Electronic Voting. Kluwer Academic Publishers (2003) 139–151
5. Kiayias, A., Yung, M.: Non-interactive zero-sharing with applications to private distributed decision making. In: proceedings of Financial Crypto, LNCS series, volume 2742. (2003) 303–320
6. Algesheimer, J., Camenisch, J., Shoup, V.: Efficient computation modulo a shared secret with application to the generation of shared safe-prime products. In: proceedings of CRYPTO '02, LNCS series, volume 2442. (2002) 417–432
7. Cramer, R., Damgård, I., Schoenmakers, B.: Proofs of partial knowledge and simplified design of witness hiding protocols. In: proceedings of CRYPTO '94, LNCS series, volume 893. (1994) 174–187
8. Bellare, M., Rogaway, P.: Random oracles are practical: A paradigm for designing efficient protocols. In: ACM Conference on Computer and Communications Security 1993. (1993) 62–73
9. Furukawa, J., Sako, K.: An efficient scheme for proving a shuffle. In: proceedings of CRYPTO '01, LNCS series, volume 2139. (2001) 368–387
10. Neff, A.C.: A verifiable secret shuffle and its application to e-voting. In: ACM CCS '01. (2001) 116–125
11. Groth, J.: A verifiable secret shuffle of homomorphic encryptions. In: proceedings of PKC '03, LNCS series, volume 2567. (2003) 145–160
12. Canetti, R.: Security and composition of multi-party cryptographic protocols. Journal of Cryptology **13** (2000) 143–202
13. Canetti, R.: Universally composable security: A new paradigm for cryptographic protocols. In: FOCS 2001. (2001) 136–145
14. Gordon, D.M.: Designing and detecting trapdoors for discrete log cryptosystems. In: proceedings of CRYPTO '92, LNCS series, volume 740. (1992) 66–75

Usability and Acceptability of Biometric Security Systems

Andrew S. Patrick

Institute for Information Technology, National Research Council of Canada
1200 Montreal Rd., Ottawa, ON Canada K1A 0R6
Andrew.Patrick@nrc-cnrc.gc.ca

Biometrics are receiving a lot of attention because of the potential to increase the accuracy and reliability of identification and authentication functions. A lot of research has been done to assess the performance of biometric systems, with an emphasis on false acceptances and rejections. Much less research has been done on the usability and acceptability of biometric security systems. A number of factors are increasing the usability of biometric devices. The sensors are getting smaller, cheaper, more reliable, and designed with better ergonomic characteristics. The biometric algorithms are also getting better, and many systems include features to train the users and provide feedback during use. In addition, biometric devices are being integrated into associated security systems, such as access control and encryption services, to provide a seamless environment.

There are still a number of usability concerns, however. The accuracy of many biometric systems is still not high enough for some applications (i.e., matching against a very large database). Also, there is often a negative relationship between the accuracy of a biometric system and the convenience for use, with the most accurate systems (e.g., DNA, Iris, Retina) being the most awkward to use. Biometric devices also have continuing problems handling users with special physical characteristics, such as faded fingerprints, leading to high "failure to enroll" rates.

Concerning the acceptance of biometric security systems, factors that are making the systems more acceptable include technical interest, concerns about identity theft, government border-control initiatives, and the opportunity to reduce memory demands by replacing memorized passwords. Research has shown, however, that users are still wary of accepting biometrics because the benefits are not always evident, and the possibilities for misuse and privacy invasions are large and not understood. Nevertheless, a recent survey of Canadian citizens [1] found that 80% of the respondents think that biometric systems will be commonly used in the next 10 years.

Overall, widespread use of biometrics in security systems faces a number of fundamental challenges, not the least of which is that a biometric characteristic is not a secret, so there is always a risk of it being copied or forged. Including "vitality tests" that ensure the biometric is offered by a living person will be crucial to avoid these problems. Managing privacy impacts and ensuring personal control of biometric use will also be very important for promoting acceptance.

Reference

1. Citizenship & Immigration Canada: Tracking public perceptions of biometrics. 2003.
   http://www.cic.gc.ca/english/press/03/poll-biometrics-e.pdf

A. Juels (Ed.): FC 2004, LNCS 3110, p. 105, 2004.
© IFCA/Springer-Verlag Berlin Heidelberg 2004

Mental Models of Computer Security

L. Jean Camp

Kennedy School of Government
Harvard University
Cambridge, MA
jean_camp@harvard.edu

1   Introduction

Mental models that may be useful in communicating within security communities can communicate perverse incentives to naïve end users. When experts use models and metaphors in their own explanations and understanding of a systems, the metaphors are used to explain a particular element of a system based on a common understanding. When experts communicate to non-experts then those who are not expert then those end users take more than is intended by the expert.

Mental models research can enable effective communication of research. I discuss four possible approaches to computer security: medical infections, criminal behavior, economics failure, and warfare. If the models of computer scientists can be effectively communicated to end users then end user response may be enhanced. Without the ability to effectively communicate risk, no amount of technology will be empowering. I discuss the implications of each model for the end user, according to the implied responsibility of the end user.

Risk communication in the environmental sciences is well grounded in decades of practice. Many of the practices abandoned by environmental scientist continue to be used in attempt to communicate risk to computer users. These include enumerating all possible risks, attempting to make all those exposed to risk experts in the subject manner, and the use of confusing metaphors.

2   The Medical Model

In August of 2003, the computer security world already weary after a summer of headline-grabbing security problems rallied to defend systems against yet another internet worm, worm_blastMS. Although similar to previous blaster strains that exploited Windows RPC vulnerability, this "good worm" gained permissions through the security hole, then patched the infected system, preventing further malicious code from attacking. Although this worm still managed to bring down several networks due to a denial of service while the worm enforced patching, the security industry's response was mixed. Some systems were undeniable saved, suffering only patching, in an environment where far too many users failed to protect themselves. The best defense to the worm removed autonomy and control from those who had failed to patch their systems.

A. Juels (Ed.): FC 2004, LNCS 3110, pp. 106–111, 2004.

The medical model for malicious code is grounded in the patterns of diffusion of malicious code and infectious diseases, the importance of heterogeneity in the larger network, and again the importance of identification and response of a virus.

Blaster is an example of a virus with an pseudo-immune response. Blaster was designed to implement a DoS attack against windowsupdate.com. However, Microsoft moved this server.

The studies of network security have recently stressed the ecosystem of security.

A significant implication of public health is that there is a need for coordinated public response. however, the need for coordinated public response does not override the rights of individuals to make mistakes about their own health, even if that implies some risk to others. Public health also communicates to each person that the are likely to be targets. The individual risk model and the need for individual hygiene communicate individual responsibility as well as individual risk. No person believes they are not at risk for illness, unlike crime or warfare where there must be specific targeting.

3   The Criminal Model

The prosecutor in the Melissa virus case argues that this is "simply crime," arguing further that "Law enforcement can employ technology, too, and track down virus writers and hackers through the electronic fingerprints they invariably leave behind." (Smith, 2002). However, As of January of 2003 Norton antivirus offered 30,084 discrete virus descriptions and Symantec has recorded 4397 additional descriptions. virus or worms for which it has on-line descriptions including date of release and payload. There have been six prosecutions of authors of malicious code. These are described in this section, illustrating that there is little correlation between the severity of the violation and resulting prosecution. Severity may be measured in inherent damage by the payload or by the extent of the distribution; regardless there is no consistency.

There have been remarkable successes. Robert Morris was identified almost immediately as the creator of the first Internet worm, and was sentenced to three years probation. (Morris is now on the faculty at MIT). The worm also lead to the passage of the Computer Fraud and Abuse Act in the United States, The initiator of the SMEG family of virus' in 1995 received less generous treatment, arguably because there was no feasible possibility that he was engaged in research. Christopher Pile was the first person sentenced under the Computer Misuse Act in the United Kingdom and received an 18-month prison term.

Chernobyl has the most destructive payload yet recorded. Chernobyl destroys data by beginning at the disk sector zero and writing randomly generated data until the computer crashes. Before over writing the data Chernobyl corrupted the machines BIOS. The Taiwanese author of that virus Chen Ing-hau escaped prosecution because there had been no Taiwanese complaints against him. The virus was most destructive in South Korea and Hong Kong.

In contrast the author of the Melissa virus was sentenced to 20 months in prison, committed to community service, and fined.

Jan De Wit authored the Anna Kournikova and turned himself in. (The worm was named after the image file to which it was attached). He received 150 hours of community service. The worm's payload was self-reproduction via MS Outlook.

Onel de Guzman of the Philippines authored the "i love you" virus. The so-called Love Bug altered image files and template files, thus severely damaging the document on Windows-based web servers. It altered MP3 files. It added itself to all visual basic scripts. However, authoring such a virus was not a crime in the Philippines and thus the author remains free.

Four Israeli teenagers were arrested for developing The Goner in 2001. because of their age the final judgments against them are not public.

These six cases are the only recorded prosecutions for the release of a virus in the wild. The SoBig virus is believed to have originated in China, similarly other malicious rapid code could have been developed by any of a billion people.

Thus we have illustrated that the prosecution of malicious code has not proven successful. Yet this does not imply that the mental model of virus as crime cannot be used to better inform the population. In the last decade malicious code has been recognized as criminal and malicious behavior. There has been increased discussion of when malicious code can be socially acceptable (hacktivism references) with an understanding that it is criminal by default. This remarkable cultural change has been primarily in the computing population, and its use for the naive user will be explored.

If computer crime is considered strictly crime then the response to this crime has been inadequate and arbitrary. If Computer crime is criminal than the end user is responsible for taking particular actions in order to avoid making him or herself a specific target of opportunity. When computer crime is crime, then the end user has to experience him or her self as a potentially vulnerable target. The end users may be recruited into community policing, yet that requires providing the end user with the ability to recognize an attack.

4   The Warfare Model

That the warfare metaphor has been internalized is clear from the choice of terms used in network security, as well as the design.

Firewalls are perimeter defense technologies. Similarly intrusion detection is based on defense of a trusted interior and a trusted exterior. DMZs are another metaphor that embeds the concept of computer security as warfare.

Slammer represents both the potential and the problems with the warfare metaphor. Most individuals had no knowledge that they were at risk. Education was made more difficult as the initial response was, "I don't have a database - that is something for web servers."

Slammer illustrates the need for coordinated action, which is clearly an element of the war metaphor. The spread of Slammer could be easily detected at the network and thus could be completely stopped by blocking every 376-byte UDP packet to port 1434. In fact, two terrorist groups have claimed responsibility as would be appropriate in the warfare metaphor. However, in both cases technical flaws in their argument clearly disqualified the claimants.

The public health or epidemic model also suggests coordinated action. Law enforcement failed and there was no economic incentive.

Warfare metaphor is applicable in the critical need for speed in the response, the potential catastrophic results of a loss, and the focus on the control of resources.

In communicating the need for citizens to be alert, and the importance of individual action for collective security the warfare metaphor is powerful. However, the implication that the network is in a state of war implies that the individual may necessarily yield civil liberties. Warfare implies a temporary state and an identified state actor as initiator of an assault. Warfare is also a temporary state of affairs.

5   The Market Model

Security and network vulnerabilities can be seen as an economic failure. Security can be seen as a market failure, an externality (Camp & Wolfram, 2001). Computer security failures cause downtime and costs.

Three common ways in which security from one system harm another are shared trust, increased resources, and the ability for the attacker to confuse the trail. Shared trust is a problem when a system is trusted by another, so the subversion of one machine allows the subversion of another. (Unix machines have lists of trusted machines in .rhosts files). A second less obvious shared trust problem is when a user keeps on one machine his or her password and account information for another. The use of cookies to save authentication information as well as states has made this practice extremely common.

The second issue, increased resources, refers to the fact that attackers can increase resources for attacks by subverting multiple machines. This is most obviously useful in brute force attacks, for example in decryption or in a denial of service attack. Using multiple machines makes a denial of service attack easier to implement, since such attacks may depend on overwhelming the target machine.

Third, subverting multiple machines makes it difficult to trace an attack from its source. When taking a circuitous route an attacker can hide his or her tracks in the adulterated log files of multiple machines. Clearly this allows the attacker to remain hidden from law enforcement and continue to launch attacks. The last two points suggest that costs to hackers fall with the number of machines (and so the difference between the benefits of hacking and the costs increases), similar to the way in which benefits to phone users increase with the number of other phones on the network.

A fourth point is the indirect effect security breaches have on users' willingness to transact over the network. For instance, consumers may be less willing to use the Internet for e-commerce if they hear of incidents of credit card theft.

This is a rational response if there is no way for consumers to distinguish security levels of different sites.

Because security is an externality the pricing of software and hardware does not reflect the possibility of and the extent of the damages from security failures associated with the item.

Externalities and public goods are often discussed in the same breath (or at least in the same sections of textbooks). They are two similar categories of market failures. A common example of a public good is national security, and it might be tempting to think of the analogies between national security and computer security. National security, and public goods in general, are generally single, indivisible goods. (A pure public good is something which is both non-rival my use of it doesn't affect yours and non-excludable once the good is produced, it is hard to exclude people from using it.) Computer security, by comparison, is the sum of a number of individual firms' or peoples' decisions. It is important to distinguish computer security from national security (i.e. externalities from public goods) because the solutions to public goods problem and to externalities differ. The government usually handles the production of public goods, whereas there are a number of examples where simple interventions by the government have created a more efficient private market such that trades between private economic parties better reflect the presence of externalities.

SoBig is an exemplar of security as an externality. SoBig was motivated by the ability to subvert the computers of naive end users in order to implement fraud through phishing and spam. The creator of SoBog has not been detected by law enforcement. In fact, the lack of consideration of agency in computer crime laws creates criminal liability for those with computers subverted by SoBig as they are, in fact, spamming, phishing or implementing DoS attacks from their own home machines.

Such an attack had been previously identified as a theoretical possibility the year before it occurred in the First Workshop on the Economics of Computer Security.

The model of computer attacks as infection does not apply because the large financial motivation for creation of virus' are not addressed.

The model of computer crime as warfare fails in the SoBig example because the virus subverts but does not destroy. Conversely, 9/11 illustrates that the most effective attack against an advanced system is based on hijacking the system to leverage its destructive power. SoBig could be arguable leveraged as an effective terror attack.

What Is the Problem?

The different examples and metaphors suggest difference responses. Crime suggest investigation of every virus and worm. Crime also suggests minimal citizen responsibility with the possibility of neighborhood watch. The public health or metaphor implication requires coordinated public action with a fundamental requirement for retaining individual autonomy and civil rights. The criminal metaphor requires tracking and prosecution. The concept of warfare requires tight constraints on the network, with limited autonomy and top-down controls. Non-technical individuals will take all the implications of the metaphors. Therefore when communicating with policy makers, media, and non-technical users the computer security expert should consider which metaphor correctly communicates user expectations.

References

1. Anderson, 2002, Unsettling Parallels Between Security and the Environment Economics and Information Security Workshop, Berkeley, CA.
2. Schneier, 2002 Computer Security: It's the Economics, Stupid Economics and Information Security Workshop, Berkeley, CA.
3. Smith, 2002, "Melissa was 'a colossal mistake' says author", 2 May 2002, Sophos: Anti Virus for Business, http://www.sophos.com/virusinfo/articles/melissa2.html.
4. Camp & Wofford, "Pricing Security", Computer Emergency Response Team Information Survivability. Workshop
5. Varian, 2002, System Reliability and Free Riding. Economics and Information Security Workshop, Berkeley, CA.
6. Kephart, Chess, White, "Computer Networks as Biological Systems," IEEE SPECTRUM May 1993.

Visualization Tools for Security Administrators

William Yurick

NCSA Security Research
National Center for Supercomputing Applications (NCSA)
University of Illinois at Urbana-Champaign

System Administrators are users too! While the focus of human-computer interaction in security has to this point in time been on end-users, an important class of users who manage networked systems should not be ignored. In fact, system administrators may have more effect on security than individual users since they manage larger systems on behalf of users. End-users have become dependent upon the availability of services such as network-attached storage, authentication servers, web servers, and email gateways. These Internet-scale services often have thousands of hardware and software components and require considerable amounts of human effort to plan, configure, install, upgrade, monitor, troubleshoot, and sunset. The complexity of managing these services is alarming in that a recent survey of three Internet site showed that 51% of all failures are caused by operator errors [1].

Some of security administration is automated, however, the actual degree of automation is much lower than many people assume. Human operators are still very much in-the-loop. particularly during emergencies. Delay in the human-computer interface can adversely affect system security so an important goal is to enhance this interface to reduce the delay. Methods are needed to help security operators more quickly extract vital information from large amounts of data and translate this information into effective control actions.

Information visualization tools can aid in any situation that is characterized by large amounts of multi-dimensional or rapidly changing data and has rapidly emerged as a potent technology to support system administrators working with complex systems. The latest generation of visual data mining tools and animated GUIs take advantage of human perceptual skills to produce striking results – empowering users to perceive important patterns in large data sets, identifying areas that need further scrutiny, and enabling sophisticated decisions. But looking at information is only a start. Users also need to manipulate and explore the data, using real-time tools to zoom, filter, and relate the information – and undo if they make a mistake. In presentation and discussion I show successful examples of information visualization for security and hints of what is to come [2, 3]. My emphasis will be on examples of computer network intrusion detection and will highlight the challenges of providing universally usable interface designs.

A. Juels (Ed.): FC 2004, LNCS 3110, pp. 112–113, 2004.
© IFCA/Springer-Verlag Berlin Heidelberg 2004

References

1. David Oppenheimer et al, Why do Internet Services Fail, and What can be Done About it? 4th USENIX Symp. on Internet Technologies and Systems, March 2003.
2. W. Yurcik, J. Barlow, et al, "Two Visual Computer Network Security Monitoring Tools Incorporating Operator Interface Requirements," ACM CHI Workshop on Human-Computer Interaction and Security Systems, (HCISEC), 2003.
3. X. Yin, W. Yurcik, et al. "VisFlowConnect: Providing Security Situational Awareness by Visualizing Network Traffic Flows," Workshop on Information Assurance (WIA04) held in conjunction with the 23rd IEEE International Performance Computing and Communications Conference (IPCCC), 2004.

Secure Interaction Design

Ka-Ping Yee

University of California, Berkeley CA 94709, USA
ping@zesty.ca

1 The Role of User Expectations

Software correctness alone is not sufficient to achieve security, as some viruses and e-mail worms have demonstrated. For example, the Love Letter worm caused widespread damage even though it did not exploit any software flaws. It spread because users were unaware that attempting to view an attachment would damage their files and propagate the worm. User expectations are an essential part of the definition of computer security.

Users are constantly manipulating security policies through their interactions with computers. For instance, security expectations change, and hence security policies *should* change, whenever an application is installed, started, or stopped, and even when files are created, moved, or opened. So, merely upholding a *static* security policy is insufficient. Although much effort has been spent on methods for specifying security policies and formally assuring that programs will meet them, much more work is also required to understand how user expectations change over time and how to adjust policies accordingly.

2 Resolving the Conflict between Usability and Security

In most cases, security is not the primary purpose for using a computer. People use computers to communicate with friends, create art, manage money, prepare documents, and so on. Many of today's applications handle security issues by introducing security prompts that interrupt the main task or by expecting users to adjust settings on hidden option panels. That is to say, they present security as a secondary task. Whenever security is secondary, it opposes the usability of the primary task: users find it a distraction that they would rather ignore, avoid, or even defeat. Creating such a conflict ensures that the battle for security is lost even before it has begun.

But security measures need not necessarily make systems harder to use. The best security measures are incorporated into the user's workflow and become part of the user's main task rather than secondary tasks. Usability and security goals can be aligned by applying security mechanisms to accurately reflect the intent *already expressed* in user actions.

The security and usability communities have one important thing in common. They are both familiar with failed attempts to add security or usability as an afterthought to a completed design. Security practitioners know that true

A. Juels (Ed.): FC 2004, LNCS 3110, pp. 114–115, 2004.

security cannot be effectively added on to an existing system after the fact. Likewise, usability practitioners know that usability consists of much more than cosmetic touches added after a product is complete. Security and usability teams are likely to find themselves in conflict when either or both concerns have been treated as an afterthought. Systems that are designed without marginalizing either concern and incorporate both sets of considerations throughout the design process will yield the most successful results.

3 Suggested Design Principles

You may find the following guidelines helpful for thinking about designs for secure systems. When evaluating a system, ask whether the system meets these guidelines. If you discover a violation, the implications are probably worth some consideration. These principles are discussed and developed more detail in an earlier paper [1].

Path of Least Resistance. The most natural way to do any task should also be the most secure way.

Appropriate Boundaries. The interface should expose, and the system should enforce, distinctions between objects and between actions along boundaries that matter to the user.

Explicit Authorization. A user's authorities should only be provided to other actors as a result of an explicit user action understood to imply granting.

Visibility. The interface should allow the user to easily review any active authority relationships that would affect security-relevant decisions.

Revocability. The interface should allow the user to easily revoke authorities that the user has granted, whenever revocation is possible.

Expected Ability. The interface must not give the user the impression of having authorities that the user does not actually have.

Trusted Path. The interface must provide an unspoofable and faithful communication channel between the user and any entity trusted to manipulate authorities on the users behalf.

Identifiability. The interface should enforce that distinct objects and distinct actions have unspoofably identifiable and distinguishable representations.

Expressiveness. The interface should provide enough expressive power (a) to describe a safe security policy without undue difficulty; and (b) to allow users to express security policies in terms that fit their goals.

Clarity. The effect of any security-relevant action should be clearly apparent to the user before the action is taken.

References

1. Yee, Ka-Ping. *User Interaction Design for Secure Systems.* Proceedings of the International Conference on Information and Communications Security, 2002.

Bringing Payment Technology to the Unbanked
(Abstract)

Jon M. Peha*

Carnegie Mellon University and Ciphermint Inc.

Many companies have brought new Internet payment systems to market, and many have failed. Innovative technology is important, but obviously not sufficient. Technology must match consumer interests and the changing legal environment.

Cyphermint has developed an innovative Internet payment system called Pay Cash, and built a growing company to offer secure financial services. Cyphermint has distinguished itself by addressing the market needs of unbanked users, i.e. consumers in the US and around the world who are not adequately served by banks and credit card issuers. As a result, the system was developed for use from publicly-accessible user-friendly kiosks that support Internet shopping, bill payment, and other financial services, in addition to use from the typical Internet-connected PCs. These kiosks have so far been deployed across the United States and Canada.

The Pay Cash system [1] is based on the concept of electronic cash. Many talented researchers have sought ways to increase anonymity in such systems, sometimes at the expense of other traits desired by consumers or law-makers. Cyphermint responded to market demand and the events of September 11, 2001 by eliminating anonymity for US consumers, and more generally, by developing a flexible anonymity policy. This allows Cyphermint to accommodate user preferences and privacy and security laws that differ greatly from nation to nation. Moreover, even where accountability is considered more important than complete anonymity, privacy is always protected.

Pay Cash includes novel techniques to generate trustworthy records of all transactions, allowing it to reduce the costs of dispute resolution, and detect many forms of fraud. Dispute resolution is normally expensive, so this greatly reduces real transaction costs, especially with micropayments. The system also allows users to send a variable number of "electronic coins" in a single message, so both large and small amounts of money can be transferred efficiently.

References

1. Jon M. Peha and I. M. Khamitov, "Pay Cash: A Secure Efficient Internet Payment System," Proceedings of Fifth International Conference on Electronic Commerce, Oct. 2003. Also at www.ece.cmu.edu/ peha/papers.html

---

* Professor and Associate Director of the Center for Wireless and Broadband Networks, peha@cmu.edu, Carnegie Mellon University, Dept. of ECE, Pittsburgh, PA 15213, USA, www.ece.cmu.edu/p̃eha. Chief Technical Officer, Cyphermint Inc., www.cyphermint.com

A. Juels (Ed.): FC 2004, LNCS 3110, p. 116, 2004.
© IFCA/Springer-Verlag Berlin Heidelberg 2004

Interleaving Cryptography and Mechanism Design
The Case of Online Auctions

Edith Elkind[1] and Helger Lipmaa[2]

[1] Princeton University, Department of Computer Science,
35 Olden St, Princeton, NJ 08544, USA
elkind@cs.princeton.edu
[2] Helsinki University of Technology, Laboratory for Theoretical Computer Science
Department of Computer Science and Engineering, P.O.Box 5400, FI-02015 Espoo, Finland
helger@tcs.hut.fi

Abstract. We propose a new cryptographically protected multi-round auction mechanism for online auctions. This auction mechanism is designed to provide (in this order) security, cognitive convenience, and round-effectiveness. One can vary internal parameters of the mechanism to trade off bid privacy and cognitive costs, or cognitive costs and the number of rounds. We are aware of no previous work that interleaves cryptography explicitly with the mechanism design.

Keywords: auctions, cognitive costs, cryptography, mechanism design, privacy

1 Introduction

Traditionally, cryptography has been used to securify an existing auction mechanism – e.g., an English auction – by adding a layer of security and privacy on top of it. We show that introducing cryptography at the mechanism design level allows one to achieve many desirable properties. More precisely, we will concentrate on online auctions that can be organised over the Internet or a local wireless network. The bidders use software agents that do the computationally intensive parts of the bidding, while the human beings control the prices. Now, the software agents have, compared to the human beings, the necessary computing power and "willingness" to participate in more resource-consuming auction types. This increases the flexibility of mechanism design, making it possible for the sellers (auctioneers) to choose between auction mechanisms that are infeasible to implement in conventional auctions. In particular, it becomes possible to use public-key cryptography [DH76] to ensure both security (correctness in the presence of malicious sellers) and bid privacy.

At the expense of mitigated computational costs, the importance of other mechanism properties will grow in online auctions. *Cognitive costs* of computing one's valuation will dominate over the computational costs. Therefore, to further simplify participation in online auctions, it is desirable to devise an auction mechanism that neither requires the bidders to do an elaborated precomputation to calculate their precise valuation, nor extensive online calculations to react properly to the bidding strategies of other participants.

Security is another important concern in auctions. Auction fraud was the most common complaint to Internet Fraud Complaint Centre (IFCC) during the last years [CoI03].

A. Juels (Ed.): FC 2004, LNCS 3110, pp. 117–131, 2004.

The number of frauds could be decreased by using an auction mechanism with better security properties. For example, an online auction mechanism should be secure against a malicious seller and various possible attacks (shills, collusive bids, jump bidding). Additionally, only a minimal amount of information should be leaked to the seller or to the other bidders. Unfortunately, not all goals are achievable at the same time. As we will see in Section 3, one must trade off cognitive costs and resource-effectiveness, as well as cognitive costs and privacy. In particular, to have small cognitive costs, one should allow a large number of rounds, but also introduce some (otherwise unnecessary) privacy leakage.

We argue that a good auction mechanism should emphasise privacy and security against the seller over cognitive costs. Hence, when constructing an online auction mechanism, one should first make sure that the auction satisfies the desired allocation criteria, is secure against sellers and (almost-ideally) privacy-preserving. The next goal is to mitigate the cognitive costs as much as possible, without hurting security against the seller and bid privacy. For example, to minimise the (online) cognitive costs, it is desirable to have a non-manipulable mechanism – otherwise, the strategies of participating bidders might become arbitrarily complex. On the other hand, also some information about other bidders' valuations must be leaked for this purpose. Finally, one should make sure that the mechanism is sufficiently effective – that is, that it does not have more (and desirably, has less) rounds with human interaction than say proxy bidding, another auction mechanism tailored for agent-mediated online auctions, or require super-polynomial-time computations.

We will propose a new auction mechanism that is based on those guidelines, but we will also introduce parameters that make it possible to have a conscious trade off between the privacy and the cognitive costs, and between the cognitive costs and the number of rounds. We will discuss other desired and existing properties of (online) auctions in Section 3. There, we will point out why currently known mechanisms are less than ideal.

Briefly, every round of the new mechanism is a second-price auction (i.e., a Vickrey auction). This suffices to make the mechanism non-manipulable in the private value model, as well as in some interesting special cases of the common value model. Second, during every round only $m-1$ bids are revealed, where m is a public auction parameter. The revelation helps to alleviate cognitive costs (compared to a Vickrey auction), and the hiding of other bids protects privacy (compared to an English auction or proxy bidding). Third, this auction mechanism is parameterised by the cognitive error coefficient $0 \leq \varepsilon < 1$, that forces the bidders to precompute their values at least to some extent and thus has the potential to reduce the number of rounds. Additionally, the described mechanism is cryptographically protected, and includes some sensible finishing conditions that provide protection against shills and collusive bids. Some protection is also provided against jump bids.

The proposed mechanism has the same privacy properties as the cryptographically secured Vickrey mechanism (indeed, the choice $m = 2$ and $\varepsilon = 0$ results in a Vickrey auction), while the cognitive costs are comparable to the ones in English auctions. See Section 4 for a fuller description of the new mechanism, followed by detailed analysis. Finally, the new mechanism seems to be the first one that has been designed from scratch to provide security against the seller and bid privacy, and to minimise cognitive costs at the same time.

The difference from the well-known methodology of adding a cryptographic protocol on top of an existing mechanism is in that we are able to overcome some weaknesses of classical mechanisms. Therefore, our work has relevance to classical auction theory. We hope that it will stimulate more work in the direction of designing new auction mechanisms suited for online auctions. We also expect to see some convergence between the until-now separate lines of research on the game-theoretic, cognitive and cryptographic properties of auctions and of mechanisms in general.

Road-Map. Section 2 introduces some necessary cryptographic preliminaries. Section 3 gives a short overview of the different goals of auction mechanisms. Section 4 describes the new auction mechanism, followed by discussion and analysis. Section 5 explains the difference with related work.

2   Cryptographic Preliminaries

Public key cryptosystem is a triple $\Pi = (G_\Pi, E, D)$ of key generating, encryption and decryption algorithms. Commitment scheme $\Gamma = (G_\Gamma, C)$ is a tuple of key generating and commitment algorithms. We use standard notations like $E_K(m; r)$ and $C_K(m; r)$ to denote encryption/commitment of m by using a newly generated random value r. A public key cryptosystem Π (resp., a commitment scheme Γ) is *homomorphic* if $E_K(m_1; r_1)E_K(m_2; r_2) = E_K(m_1 + m_2; r_3)$ (resp., $C_K(m_1; r_1)C_K(m_2; r_2) = C_K(m_1 + m_2; r_3)$) for some r_3. For our purposes, we will use the homomorphic Damgård-Jurik cryptosystem [DJ01] that allows to flexibly encrypt large plaintexts. We will also use the homomorphic Damgård-Fujisaki (DF) statistically hiding and computationally binding integer commitment scheme [DF02] that allows to commit to arbitrary integers.

One can build efficient zero-knowledge arguments for a large class of languages by using an integer commitment scheme, as shown recently in [Lip03a]. In particular, there exist very efficient arguments for showing that (a) A committed number μ belongs to an arbitrary finite interval $[\ell, h]$. We call the corresponding argument a *range argument* and refer to [Lip03a] for precise proofs; and (b) A committed number has the form B^μ, where $\mu \in [\ell, h]$. We call the corresponding argument a *range argument in exponents* and refer to [LAN02,Lip03a] for a description. Due to the properties of the DF commitment scheme, the described zero-knowledge arguments will be statistically hiding and computationally convincing. This suits well the auction scenario, since one might want to have bid privacy for a long time, while the binding (and convincing) property is only needed for the duration of the auction.

We will also need to give range arguments (in exponents) for encrypted numbers. For this, we will assume that one accompanies all encryptions and operations on ciphertexts with similar commitments and operations on committed values. Now, when one needs to argue that the encrypted value satisfies some properties, one argues on the committed value instead, and then argues that the two values are equal. The latter argument is very standard.

3 Auction-Theoretic Goals for Mechanism Design

An auction mechanism is a protocol between the auction participants, with a motivational ingredient of monetary rewards for "proper" actions; in particular, it is required that nobody should have a negative payoff when following the auction mechanism. Some well-known mechanisms are English auctions (first-bid ascending auctions), Vickrey auctions (second-price sealed-bid auctions) and first-price sealed-bid auctions. We refer to [Kri02] for an overview of auction mechanisms. Auction theory usually assumes either the private value model (the bidders know their values or can compute them without using information about others' values) or the common value model (the valuation has a common component that is only partially known to bidders). We call a participant (either a bidder or the seller), who dutifully follows the auction mechanism and does not share her private information with other parties, *honest*.

An ideal auction mechanism should aim for the following properties. First, with respect to allocation, usually the goal is either *Pareto-efficiency* or *revenue maximisation*. The former is equivalent to maximising the social welfare, i.e., awarding the item to the bidder who values it most, while the latter corresponds to maximising the seller's profit. Sometimes, these two goals are in conflict, in which case a trade-off between them can be considered. Second, *resource-effectiveness*: The auction takes a small number of human-interacted rounds. The auction rules are sufficiently simple so that the seller and the bidders can follow them in "reasonable" time. Third, *security against the (malicious) seller*: The seller cannot increase the final price or change the winner without being caught. Fourth, *privacy*: No information about the bids of honest bidders is revealed, except the information that can be derived from the winner's identity and the contract price. Fifth, *minimal cognitive cost*: The cognitive cost of computing the valuation is small. Other properties are security against shills, collusive bids, jump bidding, etc [Kri02].

The cognitive cost of strategy planning is especially important in online auctions [UPF98,PUF98]. Since other participation costs decrease considerably due to the use of software agents, cognitive costs of computing one's valuation start to dominate. Therefore, it becomes important to decrease cognitive costs by devising an auction mechanism that neither requires the bidders to do an elaborated homework to compute their precise valuation and strategy, nor requires them to do extensive online calculations to react properly to the bidding strategies of other bidders. Such an auction mechanism should still have other desirable properties.

One must trade off between some of the mentioned properties. Clearly, the more information is leaked during an auction, the smaller is the cognitive cost. In most cases, this results in a higher seller's revenue [MW82] and possibly more efficient allocation in the presence of bounded-rational bidders. Usually, this means that multi-round actions with gradual information leakage are therefore revenue-maximising and also guarantee the best results for bounded-rational bidders. An interesting alternative approach was presented in [PWZ00], who constructed a two-round second-price sealed-bid auction PWZ mechanism with the same seller revenues as the English auctions, but with the drawback (from the privacy standpoint) that the two highest bidders of the first round – who continue in the second round – obtained the the distribution of first round losers' bids. The PWZ mechanism is resource-effective, and also slightly better than the Vickrey mechanism in cognitive cost. However, if the bidders are bounded-rational, then the PWZ mechanism is not Pareto-efficient, since all but 2 players do not get a second chance to revise their bids, and the remaining 2 players only get one more chance for it.

Proxy bidding is a designated online auction mechanism that assumes that all bidders use software agents with a fixed upper bound on the price. The agents participate in an English auction until this upper bound has been reached. Only after that the agents consult with their owner, who has to decide whether to continue to bid (by setting a new upper bound) or not (by passing). This can last many rounds, until the final price does not rise anymore. Clearly, proxy bidding has smaller cognitive costs than one-shot auctions, and on the other hand, has smaller participation costs (due to the smaller number of human-interactive rounds) than English auctions. Hence, proxy bidding offers a balance between the cognitive cost and the resource-effectiveness of the English and Vickrey auction mechanisms. This may explain the dominance of proxy bidding in Internet auctions: as early as in 1999, Lucking-Reiley surveyed 142 auction sites and found that 65 of them use a form of proxy bidding [Luc00, Section VIII.A].

However, even proxy bidding has its downsides. In particular, it does not solve the problem of revealed statistics even when cryptographically secured. (E.g., identities of persons who participate at every time moment, and therefore also partial information about their valuations, are revealed to the seller.) Moreover, if many bounded-rational people participate, proxy bidding can have a large number of rounds. So, while such a multi-round mechanism together with an adequate cryptographic protection increases privacy and efficiency compared to pure English auctions, it is still not ideal.

Bid Privacy and Security against Sellers. Clearly, a malicious seller can change the results of an auction to his benefit when it is not possible to verify his actions or when he obtains too much information about bidders' valuations. This is commonly seen as a reason why Vickrey auctions are not employed in practice [RTK90,RH95]. This observation has motivated a huge body of research on cryptographic Vickrey auction schemes, starting with [NS93]. Clearly, protecting privacy is important also in other auction mechanisms. However, the PWZ mechanism, proxy bidding and English auctions are (designed to be) "bad" from the privacy viewpoint, since they intentionally reveal the bid statistics to alleviate the cognitive cost.

We believe that a good auction mechanism should emphasise privacy and security against the seller over the cognitive costs. Our (informal) reasoning behind this belief is that it is easier to define what is the privacy (and what is a privacy leak) than to model the cognitive costs, as the latter vary widely from one bidder to another. For example, if instead of a single bid, information about two competing bids will be leaked, then this is certainly a privacy leak, but can bidders use this additional information to adjust their estimate of their own values? Probably yes, but how much exactly do they gain? If one cannot guarantee that a deliberate loss of privacy will decrease the cognitive costs, it is better not to lose any. (Cognitive cost *is* modelled in some publications [Par99,LS01], but there the authors are more concerned with the agents doing the computations, not the human beings.)

Cryptographic Auction Schemes. *Cryptographic auction schemes* are cryptographic algorithms to support specific mechanisms, that, when correctly followed by an honest party, ensure that certain well-defined privacy/security-against-the-seller properties will

Table 1. Comparison of different existing auction mechanisms and the new mechanism in the mentioned five categories: A "+" means that the mechanism performs well in this category, "(+)" means that the mechanism enjoys slightly better properties than the unmarked mechanisms, and "-" means that this property is undesirable by the design. The first column refers to efficiency in the private value model.

Mechanism	Pareto-e.	Round-effect.	Sec. against Auct.	Priv.	Cogn. c.
English	+			-	+
Dutch			+	+	
First-price		+	(+)	(+)	
Vickrey [Vic61]	+	+			
Proxy bidding	+	(+)		-	+
PWZ [PWZ00]	+	+		-	(+)
Secure Vickrey	+	+	+	+	
Secure proxy bidding	+	(+)	+	-	+
The new mechanism	+	(+)	+	+	+

be held w.r.t. her. In particular, a good auction scheme must ensure that neither a cheating seller nor cheating bidders can affect the allocation. Andrew Yao [Yao82] was the first to consider cryptographic (English) auctions. Cryptographic auction schemes for different auction mechanisms have been designed since then. (See [NPS99,LAN02] for some examples and an overview of the related literature.) In particular, cryptographic Vickrey auction schemes satisfy all desired properties that were described in the beginning of this chapter, except that they do not minimise the cognitive costs. The best cryptographic auction schemes guarantee security against the seller and privacy, to the extent required by the auction mechanism.

Summary of Auction Mechanisms. There are many well-known auction mechanisms, like English, Dutch, first-price sealed-bid and Vickrey [Vic61] auctions. (A description of these mechanisms can be found in [Kri02].) Different auction mechanisms satisfy different desiderata that are summarised in Table 1. (Note that we do not consider revenue maximisation: generally speaking, it is not achieved by any of the standard mechanisms, and also it requires more information about the bidders' valuations that we are willing to assume.) We do not know of any mechanism-scheme combination that satisfies all the previously described auction desiderata. Note that not all five desiderata, as described in the beginning of the current section, are equally important in all situations. Traditionally, one has mainly been stressing the first two properties. We will concentrate on online auctions, where the last three properties will gain in importance.

4   New Mechanism

4.1   High-Level Description

In this section, we describe the new cryptographically secured multi-round sealed-bid auction mechanism. Discussion and explanation will follow.

Notation. Let $P = \{v_1, \ldots, v_V\}$ be the set of possible valuations, e.g., $\{0.01, 0.03, \ldots, 0.90, 0.94, 1.00\}$; in practice, this means that some valuations are rounded off. The auction consists of the setup phase, rounds $1, \ldots, R$ (where R is not fixed in advance), and the closing phase.

Setup Phase. Assume that ϕ is a monotonic bijective function from P to the set of actual bids $[0, V - 1]$ that is sent – in a signed form – to the bidders by the seller S during the auction setup. (ϕ may be unknown by the auction authority A.) The mechanism is parameterised by public values $m \geq 2$ and $\varepsilon < 1$, selected by the seller S and announced to everybody before the auction. Intuitively, ε specifies to what degree the auction takes on the character of an English auction ($\varepsilon \to 1$) or a Vickrey auction ($\varepsilon = 0$), and m specifies the amount of deliberately leaked information. There are B bidders $1, \ldots, B$, one seller S and the auction authority A. Anybody can act as S (this means in particular that no trust can be put on S) while the authority is an established business party with a reputation history. The participants obtain a committing key, an encryption key and a signature key of the parties, with whom they will start to communicate. Otherwise, auctions are set up as usual, in particular by publicly announcing details such as the closing date.

Let $(X_1^r, \ldots, X_B^r)$ be the list of bids made in the rth round, $r \geq 1$, in non-increasing order, and let Y_i^r be the bidder who made the bid X_i^r. Note that $X_i^r \in [0, V - 1]$ for all r and i. We assume that $b_i = X_i^0 = 0$ and let (Y_i^0) be an arbitrary permutation of all bidders.

Auction Round $r \geq 1$. Before the first round, all bidders receive a signal s_i about their true values. At the beginning of the rth round, $r \geq 1$, the bidders compute an estimate $e_i^r \in P$ of their true private values that depends on their initial signal and on public information, obtained in the previous rounds. Intuitively, for rational agents it should be the case that $(1 - \varepsilon)v_i \leq e_i^r \leq v_i$. Bidders enter $b_i^r = \phi(\beta_i(e_i^r))$ into their software agent, where β is the ith strategy function. After that, the agents participate in a cryptographically secured sealed-bid auction protocol between bidders, the seller and the authority. Every bidder i submits an encryption of b_i^r, and argues in zero-knowledge that

$$\phi\left(\frac{1}{1-\varepsilon}\phi^{-1}(b_i^1)\right) \geq b_i^r \geq b_i^{r-1} \ . \tag{1}$$

At the end of rth round, the authority outputs a signed tuple $\mathrm{view}(r) := (X_2^r, \ldots, X_m^r; C_K(X_1^r; \rho^r))$ for a new random value ρ^r. The authority accompanies this with a non-interactive zero-knowledge argument that $\mathrm{view}(r)$ is correctly computed. All this is published in an authenticated manner to all bidders, who can do independent verifications.

Closing Phase. The auction lasts $R \geq 2$ rounds and stops iff $X_2^R = X_2^{R-1}$. (This is verified by all bidders by using the published zero-knowledge arguments.) The contract price will be X_2^R. Then Y_1^R is established by using another (interactive) cryptographic protocol. If there is a tie, one of the winners is selected by using, e.g., the equal probability rule.

4.2 Cryptographic Implementation

Every round of the new mechanism is a cryptographically secured 2nd-price auction where instead of only the second highest bid, $m - 1$ bids are revealed. Next, we outline some cryptographic implementation details. We will base our implementation on the LAN mth-price auction scheme [LAN02], although we stress that this is just an example cryptographic implementation. Additional tools [LAN02] can be employed to make the implementation secure against replaying attacks.

To simplify the zero-knowledge arguments, we will assume that bid 0 corresponds to some absolute minimal price $p_{\min}$, and that $\phi(x) = d \cdot \log_{1/(1-\varepsilon)} \frac{x}{p_{\min}}$ for some fixed d. (This same assumption makes also sense from the psychological and auction-theoretic viewpoints, see Section 4.3.) In this case, $\phi^{-1}(b) = p_{\min}(\frac{1}{1-\varepsilon})^{b/d}$, and the left side of (1) simplifies to the requirement that $(\frac{1}{1-\varepsilon})^{1+(b_i^1/d)} \geq (\frac{1}{1-\varepsilon})^{b_i^r/d}$, or $b_i^r \leq d + b_i^1$.

As in the LAN scheme, we will accompany all encryptions with corresponding commitments. Assume K is A's public key. In every round r, the ith bidder sends an encryption of $B^{b_i^r}$ to the seller S, by using an authenticated channel. This is accompanied by an efficient non-interactive statistical zero-knowledge (NISZK) argument that the bid was correctly formed [LAN02] (this is a range argument in exponents), and that (1) holds (this consists of two range arguments). These arguments can be shortened by using a different encoding function $Z_B(b_i)$ instead of B^{b_i} [Lip03a]. Both the bids and the NISZK arguments are stored on a cryptographic bulletin-board that is made publicly available to all bidders. (They can also simply be sent to all bidders.)

Next, the seller forwards the product of encrypted bids to the authority, who decrypts the bids, finds out the m highest bids and sends view(r) back to the seller over an authenticated channel; note that X_1^r is not revealed to the seller. This is accompanied with an NISZK argument that $C_K(X_1^r; \rho^r)$ commits to the highest bid, and that $(X_2^r, \ldots, X_m^r)$ are the next $m - 1$ highest bids (this can be done as a straightforward extension of the protocol from [LAN02] for proving that $\tilde{X}$ is the mth highest bid), and an NISZK range argument for either $X_2^r = X_2^{r-1}$ or $X_2^r > X_2^{r-1}$. After verifying the NISZK arguments, the seller posts view(r) together with the NISZK arguments and her own and authority's signatures on the bulletin-board. The bidders verify the signatures and the NISZK arguments. The bulletin-board contents (that is, the tuple $(C_K(b_1^r), \ldots, C_K(b_B^r), \text{view}(r))$ together with the signatures and NISZK arguments) is stored by all bidders.

In the closing phase, all bidders verify the correctness of closing and that the winning price was determined correctly (another range argument). Y_1^R can be established by using a method proposed in [Lip03b]: namely, all bidders and the seller participate in a proxy verifiable private equality test, after what the seller gets to know which bidder bid X_1^R without getting to know the value of X_1^R.

Alternative Cryptographic Implementations. Alternatively, one can implement the described auction mechanism by using Yao's model of general two-party computation [Yao82]. This would involve the design of a specific circuit that is suitable for the described mechanism, as successfully done by Naor, Pinkas and Sumner [NPS99] for mth-price auctions, although in the case of the new mechanism, the circuit will be considerably larger. It is also not immediately clear how to extend the Naor-Pinkas-

Sumner scheme efficiently to a multi-round scheme, where the number of rounds is not bounded. The LAN auction scheme is more communication-efficient (especially when the number of bidders is large), while the Naor-Pinkas-Sumner scheme, as corrected by [JS02], will not reveal any unwarranted information to A. Also, one can use any of the available mth-price cryptographic auction schemes that rely on threshold trust, although not all of them might be flexible enough to be used with the new mechanism. Finally, we share the viewpoint of [NPS99,LAN02] that threshold trust between > 2 machines, possibly operated by the (occasional and thus untrusted) seller himself is not sensible in most of the auction scenarios.

4.3   Discussion

The Rôle of ε. We call the bidders who are able to ε-approximate their true valuation ε-*rational*. Intuitively, one may assume that it is common knowledge that non-ε-rational rational bidders will not participate. A value of ε relevant in practice can be $0.1\ldots0.6$. Setting $\varepsilon \leftarrow 0$ would result in Vickrey auctions. A smaller ε will raise the time-efficiency of auctions and (as we will see) make the auctions less subject to jump bidding, while a greater ε has the potential to attract more bounded-rational bidders. However, if the seller wants to have a greater participation at the expense of risking to have longer auctions and jump bidding, she might even set $\varepsilon \leftarrow 0.999$.

The Function ϕ. As we already saw in Section 4.2, a suitable function ϕ can simplify the cryptographic implementation. The specific choice of ϕ proposed in Section 4.2 makes sense from both psychological and auction-theoretic viewpoint. Really, people are often thinking about the object's value on the logarithmic scale ("the first item is worth 3 times more than the second item") rather than on the linear scale. One should note, however, that this choice of function ϕ requires the seller to set a lower bound $p_{\min} = \phi^{-1}(0)$ and an upper bound $p_{\max} = \phi^{-1}(V - 1)$ on the selling price, although the difference between these two values can be made almost arbitrarily large, since $\phi^{-1}(V - 1)/\phi^{-1}(0) = (\frac{1}{1-\varepsilon})^{(V-1)/d}$. Assuming, say, that $\varepsilon = 0.95$, $V = 201$ and $d = 100$, this would make the price increase by 3% when bid is increased by 1, and we would have $p_{\max} \approx 400 p_{\min}$. This setting seems to be perfect for most auctions.

Equilibria. Setting $b_i^r > \phi(e_i^r)$ can occasionally result in negative payoffs. If the bidders are conservative then $\beta(e_i^r) \leq v_i$, so $b_i^r \leq \phi(v_i)$. Moreover, in many practically relevant cases the strategy of bidding strictly less than $\phi(e_i^r)$ is weakly dominated, so truth-telling results in a non-dominated equilibrium. For instance, if the bidders' values are private, i.e., the current price does not affect a bidder's estimate of the value, the usual argument for Vickrey auctions can be used to show that bidding $\phi(e_i^r)$ is a dominant strategy.

Moreover, truth-telling can be dominant in certain special cases of the common value model as well. In particular, we can show that this is the case for the "experts vs. amateurs" model. In this model, the valuation of the bidder i is of the form $v_i = w_i + T z_i$, where v_i, z_i are independently but not necessarily identically distributed random variables, and T is a random variable (same for all bidders) that can be equal to 0 or 1. Some bidders (let us call them experts) know the actual value of T, while others do not.

This model captures the markets in which some users (e.g., art dealers in an art auction) can determine whether the object being sold has some desired properties (e.g., whether a coin is fake or authentic), while others do not have this ability. In these markets, proxy bidding with a fixed deadline is susceptible to "sniping", i.e., experts bidding in the very last minute to prevent others from observing change in the posted price and adjusting their values (and hence their bids). This may result in inefficient allocation, and thus it is desirable to have a mechanism that does not encourage sniping.

Note that, intuitively, when $T = 1$, the experts may want to shade their bid to conceal this fact: it might be the case that when non-experts bid just w_i, the expert gets the object even though his own value is not particularly high, while if the others knew that $T = 1$, they would outbid him (in some sense, this is similar to sniping). Fortunately, we can show that because of our choice of finishing criteria our scheme does not have this problem, and, in fact, always achieves efficient allocation assuming conservative bidders.

Theorem 1. *Assume that all bidders are conservative, i.e., they avoid strategies that may lead to negative payoffs. Then conservative truthful bidding (experts bid $w_i + T z_i$, others bid w_i if they cannot determine T from the outcomes of the previous rounds, and $w_i + T z_i$ otherwise) is a Nash equilibrium, that is, no single bidder can gain by cheating.*

Proof. Consider the behaviour of bidder 1 in the first round assuming that everyone else bids truthfully. If bidder 1 is an amateur, or $T = 0$, the usual argument for Vickrey auctions applies. Now, suppose that $T = 1$. If bidder 1's truthful bid would not be the highest bid (assuming everyone else bids truthfully). Then bidder 1 cannot win the auction at a price that is lower than his value, so he might as well bid truthfully and lose. Hence, let us assume that bidder 1's truthful bid is higher than all other bids. Let $b = \max\{b_2^1, \ldots, b_n^1\}$. Suppose that bidder 1 decides to shade his bid. If he bids more than b (but less than his true value), the public information will be the same as in the case of truthful bidding, so this will not help. Alternatively, he can bid less than b, which means that he does not win the current round. Then, it might still be possible for everyone to derive that $T = 1$ (for instance, there may be several other experts who bid truthfully), so in the next round everyone will bid $w_i + T z_i$, and the setting is that of ordinary Vickrey auction. Finally, it might be the case that when bidder 1 cheats, others cannot be sure that $T = 1$. Then they will not change their bids, and unless bidder 1 bids more than b, the auction ends and he loses. To avoid that, he himself has to bid more than b in the second round, so we are back to square one.   □

Cognitive Cost. Our mechanism becomes Pareto-efficient as soon as all bidders are able to calculate their valuations with an arbitrary high but *a priori* known accuracy, given that the bidders are sufficiently rational to avoid a limited number of well-specified "bad" strategies. More precisely, one can easily prove the next theorem:

Theorem 2. *Assume that the underlying cryptographic implementation is secure. The described auction mechanism is Pareto-efficient with overwhelming probability if (a) The highest valuator is honest and in particular double-checks all zero-knowledge arguments and signatures, (b) The ith bidder never bids more than $\phi(v_i)$; and (c) The* *highest valuator does not set* $b_i^r \leq X_2^{r-1}$ *if* $v_i > \phi^{-1}(X_2^{r-1})$ [1], *(d) The highest valuator is ε-rational.*

Proof. Assume that bidder 1 had the highest valuation, and assume that (a) holds. Then it is known that after the closing $X_2^R = X_2^{R-1}$, and by (c), no bidder but 1 has a valuation higher than $\phi^{-1}(X_2^{R-1})$. By (a), the highest valuator still participates in the round R, and by (d), he is allowed to place a high enough bid. Finally, by (b), $v_{Y_1^R} > \phi^{-1}(X_2^{R-1})$ and thus Y_1^R is the highest valuator. $\square$

The virtue of this result is to make it precise when exactly the highest valuator will not obtain the item. In particular, it happens if his behaviour is in some sense quite irrational, the cryptographic implementation is insecure or other bidders are not conservative. In cryptography, it is important to give the security proofs under minimal assumptions, and our approach is the same. Moreover, all our assumptions are feasible.

Importantly, one can trade off cognitive cost and privacy by publishing the tuple $(X_2^r, \ldots, X_m^r)$, $m > 2$ instead of just X_2^r. Moreover, the mechanism can be generalised to reveal some other function of the bid vector, e.g., the number of bids exceeding a given threshold, the number of bidders who increased their bids compared to the previous round, etc., provided that this function can be efficiently computed in a secure manner. Depending on the structure of bidder's valuations, this can decrease the cognitive costs significantly, while having a negligible effect on privacy. This allows for an almost continuous tradeoff between the cognitive costs and the privacy. However, whenever a privacy leak can be quantified much more easily than the possible win in cognitive costs (and this usually the case), we would recommend to use the value $m = 2$.

Computational Efficiency. The two inequalities in Equation (1) are introduced, in particular, to increase the computational efficiency. The leftmost inequality enforces bidders to do at least some homework to estimate their valuation with precision ε. This can decrease the number of rounds. The rightmost inequality enforces the sequence (b_i^r) to be nondecreasing in r, and hence also helps to decrease the number of rounds. Bidding $b_i^r = b_i^{r-1}$ intuitively equals to passing: by doing so, one is guaranteed not to win at round r, unless his bid in round $r-1$ was the highest one. The chosen solution is superior to the one where the bidders can pass if their bids are not high enough, since in this case some of the private information of bidders will become public. (Additionally, it would make it possible the bidders to collude by signalling each other.)

One can additionally decrease the number of expected rounds by requiring that if b_i^r increases, then $\phi^{-1}(b_i^r) > (1+\delta)\phi^{-1}(b_i^{r-1})$ for some public value δ that may depend on the currently second highest bid X_2^{r-1}. This solution is common in English auctions, and can also be employed in conjunction with the described mechanism to achieve additional effectiveness. However, since we assume that the bidders are conservative, it also has the potential to decrease the revenues of the seller by a factor of $(1+\delta)$.

---

[1] We can make this assumption weaker, by assuming that he does not set $b_i^r \leq X_2^{r-1}$ if $v_i > (1+\delta)\phi^{-1}(X_2^{r-1})$ for some δ. Then the scheme will be δ-efficient, i.e., the value of the bidder who gets the object is within a factor of $1/(1+\delta)$ from the highest value.

4.4 Security Analysis

When a secure cryptographic implementation is used, the auction will be correct and privacy-preserving. Additionally, it will have some mechanism-centric properties that are not shared (say) by cryptographically secured English auctions.

We say that a bidder is *antisocial* if, maybe knowing that he cannot win, he bids more than his value solely to increase the contract price of other players [FB01]. That is, an antisocial bidder acts not to maximise his utility, but to minimise the utility of other players. We assume that antisocial bidders are conservative: that is, they will not bid more than the maximum of X_2^{r-1} and their own valuation. (They do not risk to come out with a negative payoff.) A *shill* is an antisocial bidder that is manipulated by the seller so as to drive up the price.

Theorem 3. *Suppose that the bidders' signals are sufficiently independent, namely, that from observing his own signal and the public information* $(X_2^{r-1}, \ldots, X_m^{r-1})$, *a bidder j cannot conclude with certainty that another bidder i has a value v_i such that* $\phi(v_i) > X_2^{r-1} + \delta$ *for a fixed value of δ. Then the proposed auction mechanism is secure against shills and antisocial bidders, as soon as all signatures and zero-knowledge arguments are verified.*

Proof. In the round r, knowing the value X_2^{r-1}, a shill j will make some bid $b_j^r > \phi(e_j^r)$. If $b_j^r \leq X_2^{r-1}$ then the second highest bid will not increase. Assume $b_j^r > X_2^{r-1}$. According to our assumption, j cannot be sure that his bid is lower than the highest bid, or that in the next round someone will be willing to bid more than b_r^j. So, there is a chance that he will have to pay the price himself, and, being conservative, he will refrain from submitting a bid that is higher than his value.   □

Security against Collusive Bids. For $m = 2$, the proposed auction mechanism is secure against collusive bids by the same reasons why it is secure against shills' bids: namely, the collusive bidders must bid more than the current highest bid to get their signal through. However, this also means that they might have to pay for the item. This is at least the case when the previous round highest bidder had approximated her value sufficiently precisely.

Security against Jump Bidding. English auctions are subject to jump bidding, where one bidder bids very high in the beginning of the auction just to scare other bidders away. Our previous argumentation that in the first-price auctions the bidders are not motivated to jump-bid does not clearly apply always – for example when Y_1 knows the approximate value of X_2.

While the described auction mechanism does not feature complete security against the jump bidding, it provides an approximate protection. First, being a second-price auction, it is secure against the case when one bidder jump bids, since only a (relatively moderate) X_2 would be published and other bidders would still have a chance to overbid it. Now, assume that at least two bidders jump bid, say bid within a fraction $1 - \delta \gg 1 - \varepsilon$ of their real valuations. In this case, $\phi^{-1}(X_2^1) \geq (1-\delta)V_2$, and the minimum price Y_1^1 has to pay is $\phi^{-1}(X_2^1) \geq (1 - \delta)V_2$ instead of V_2. This "worst" case would only happen in the case $\phi^{-1}(X_1^1) > V_2$, assuming that Y_2^1 would over-bid X_1^1 otherwise and that Y_1^1 and Y_2^1 do not collude.

Thus, in this case the highest valuator can get the item $1/(1-\delta) \ll 1/(1-\varepsilon)$ times cheaper than in the case when somebody else would also be doing the homework. The smaller is ε, the less can be gained by jump bidding. A cautious seller might have ε to be relatively low if she is afraid of jump bidding in the case when the richest client is also the most diligent. (Alternatively, she can just increase the initial price.) On the other hand, if rich but oblivious customers are to be expected, a larger ε will be more beneficial to the seller.

Adding another finishing criterion to the described auction mechanism makes it secure against nonconservative shills but insecure against jump bidding. Namely, if we say that the auction is finished if either $X_1^R = X_1^{R-1}$ or $X_2^R = X_2^{R-1}$, then a shill has an effect on the auction only when he bids more than X_1^{R-1} (and thus wins the auction). On the other hand, in this case a jump-bidder would be guaranteed to win the auction with his bid X_1^{R-1} unless a higher valuator will bid more than X_1^{R-1} (without knowing this value!) during the next round.

Security against Premature Finishing. A possible alternative to requiring everybody not to decrease their bids over time is to instead have the same scheme where this requirement is replaced by declaring Y_1^{R-1} as the winner of the auction whenever $X_2^R < X_2^{R-1}$. However, then the highest bidder Y_1^{R-1} could in some cases prematurely finish the auctions (and thus decrease the revenues of the seller) by bidding X_2^{R-1} in round R. In the case when only $Y_1^R = Y_2^{R-1}$ will bid $\geq X_2^{R-1}$ at round R, X_2^R will be equal to X_2^{R-1}. If Y_2^{R-1} bid less than X_1^{R-1} in round R, Y_1^{R-1} will obtain the item for $\phi^{-1}(X_2^{R-1})$, which might be less than the valuation of Y_2^{R-1}. The mechanism devised in this paper does not have this problem.

5   Comparison with Related Work and Conclusions

To our knowledge, the first paper to emphasise the cognitive costs in online auctions is by Parker, Ungar, and Foster [PUF98]. Their paper analysed the existing mechanisms from this perspective and concluded that English auctions are the best in the context of bounded rationality. A large body of research has followed. However, it mostly consisted of papers that did not actually propose new mechanisms, but instead suggested criteria for choosing between already existing and well-known mechanisms. Moreover, the emphasis of the above-mentioned papers is on fully autonomous agents, and it is assumed that the agents can somehow quantify their computational costs of regulating their beliefs. This is often not the case.

A completely different line of research has been focusing on the security against sellers and privacy properties of the online auctions. Various authors have been proposing a wide range of cryptographic schemes that guarantee security against sellers and privacy of various auction mechanisms under various assumptions, including and excluding threshold trust. Again, the focus has been on the existing mechanisms.

Our approach is different. We first asked what is relevant in online auctions. Our conclusion was that security against sellers and privacy are more important than cognitive costs (since those are hard to model precisely), while the latter is more important than the computational effectiveness (e.g., the number of rounds). We proposed a new mechanism that has all the mentioned properties, but puts emphasis on security over cognitive convenience, and on cognitive convenience over computational convenience. Moreover, the described mechanism makes it possible to trade off cognitive costs versus computational costs (by changing the parameter ε), and cognitive costs versus privacy (by increasing the amount of published data $(X_2^R, \ldots, X_m^R)$). It has long been argued that security issues and huge cognitive cost are two main reasons why non-manipulable auction mechanisms like the Vickrey auction are not widely used in practice. The scheme described in this paper mitigates both concerns and is non-manipulable whenever Vickrey auctions are.

The described mechanism can be used together with any reasonable cryptographic auction scheme. We described an implementation based on [LAN02], since we agree with its authors that avoiding threshold trust is more important than its bid statistics leakage to an established authority. Moreover, the scheme of [LAN02] is very efficient and easy to understand. A full description of, say, the Naor-Pinkas-Sumner [NPS99] auction scheme would have made the paper less modular. However, several other cryptographic schemes can be used here.

Finally, one can simplify the proposed mechanism-protocol interleaving in a straightforward way to obtain a secure proxy bidding protocol. To our knowledge, no cryptographic protocol to securify proxy bidding has been proposed before.

Acknowledgements

The second author would like to thank N. Asokan and Valtteri Niemi for fruitful discussions while writing the first version of this paper in 2001. A part of this work was done while the first author was visiting Helsinki University of Technology. This work was partially supported by Nokia research and the Finnish Defence Forces Research Institute of Technology.

References

[Bla02]   Matt Blaze, editor. *Financial Cryptography – Sixth International Conference*, volume 2357 of *Lecture Notes in Computer Science*, Southhampton Beach, Bermuda, March 11–14 2002. Springer-Verlag.

[CoI03]   National White Collar Crime Center and Federal Bureau of Investigation. IFCC 2002 Internet Fraud Report. Available at
`http://www1.ifccfbi.gov/strategy/IFCC_2002_IFCCReport.pdf`,
as of April 2003, 2003.

[DF02]   Ivan Damgård and Eiichiro Fujisaki. An Integer Commitment Scheme Based on Groups with Hidden Order. In Yuliang Zheng, editor, *Advances on Cryptology – ASIACRYPT 2002*, volume 2501 of *Lecture Notes in Computer Science*, pages 125–142, Queenstown, New Zealand, December 1–5 2002. Springer-Verlag.

[DH76]   Whitfield Diffie and Martin E. Hellman. New Directions in Cryptography. *IEEE Transactions Information Theory*, IT-22:644–654, November 1976.

[DJ01]   Ivan Damgård and Mads Jurik. A Generalisation, a Simplification and Some Applications of Paillier's Probabilistic Public-Key System. In Kwangjo Kim, editor, *Public Key Cryptography 2001*, volume 1992 of *Lecture Notes in Computer Science*, pages 119–136, Cheju Island, Korea, February 13–15 2001. Springer-Verlag.

[FB01]   Gerhard Weiß Felix Brandt. Antisocial Agents and Vickrey Auctions. In *Intelligent Agents VIII*, pages 335–347, Seattle, WA, USA, August 1–3 2001. Revised papers.

[JS02]   Ari Juels and Michael Szydlo. A Two-Server, Sealed-Bid Auction Protocol. In Blaze [Bla02], pages 72–86.

[Kri02]   Vijay Krishna. *Auction Theory*. Academic Press, 2002.

[Lai03]   Chi Sung Laih, editor. *Advances on Cryptology – ASIACRYPT 2003*, volume 2894 of *Lecture Notes in Computer Science*, Taipei, Taiwan, November 30–December 4 2003. Springer-Verlag.

[LAN02]   Helger Lipmaa, N. Asokan, and Valtteri Niemi. Secure Vickrey Auctions without Threshold Trust. In Blaze [Bla02], pages 87–101.

[Lip03a]   Helger Lipmaa. On Diophantine Complexity and Statistical Zero-Knowledge Arguments. In Laih [Lai03], pages 398–415.

[Lip03b]   Helger Lipmaa. Verifiable Homomorphic Oblivious Transfer and Private Equality Test. In Laih [Lai03], pages 416–433.

[LS01]   Kate Larson and Tuomas Sandholm. Costly Valuation Computation in Auctions. In Johan van Benthem, editor, *Eighth Conference of Theoretical Aspects of Knowledge and Rationality (TARK VIII)*, Certosa di Pontignano, University of Siena, Italy, July 8–10 2001. Morgan Kaufmann.

[Luc00]   David Lucking-Reiley. Auctions on the Internet: What's Being Auctioned, and How? *Journal of Industrial Economics*, 48(3):227–252, September 2000.

[MW82]   Paul R. Milgrom and Robert J. Weber. A Theory of Auctions and Competitive Bidding. *Econometrica*, 50(5):1089–1122, September 1982.

[NPS99]   Moni Naor, Benny Pinkas, and Reuben Sumner. Privacy Preserving Auctions and Mechanism Design. In *The 1st ACM Conference on Electronic Commerce*, Denver, Colorado, November 1999.

[NS93]   Hannu Nurmi and Arto Salomaa. Cryptographic Protocols for Vickrey Auctions. *Group Decision and Negotiation*, 2:363–373, 1993.

[Par99]   David C. Parkes. Optimal Auction Design for Agents with Hard Valuation Problems. In Alexandros Moukas, Carles Sierra, and Fredrik Ygge, editors, *Agent Mediated Electronic Commerce II, Towards Next-Generation Agent-Based Electronic Commerce Systems, IJCAI 1999 Workshop*, volume 1788 of *Lecture Notes in Computer Science*, pages 206–219. Springer-Verlag, 1999.

[PUF98]   David C. Parkes, Lyle H. Ungar, and Dean P. Foster. Accounting for Cognitive Costs in On-line Auction Design. In Pablo Noriega and Carles Sierra, editors, *Agent Mediated Electronic Commerce, First International Workshop on Agent Mediated Electronic Trading, AMET-98*, number 1571 in Lecture Notes in Computer Science, pages 25–40, Minneapolis, MN, USA, May 10 1998. Springer-Verlag. Selected papers.

[PWZ00]   Motty Perry, Elmar Wolfstetter, and Shmuel Zamir. A Sealed-Bid Auction that Matches the English Auction. *Games and Economic Behaviour*, 33(2):265–273, November 2000.

[RH95]   Michael H. Rothkopf and Ronald M. Harstad. Two Models of Bid-Taker Cheating in Vickrey Auctions. *Journal of Business*, 68(2):257–267, April 1995.

[RTK90]   Michael H. Rothkopf, Thomas J. Teisberg, and Edward P. Kahn. Why are Vickrey Auctions Rare? *The Journal of Political Economy*, 98(1):94–109, February 1990.

[UPF98]   Lyle H. Ungar, David C. Parkes, and Dean P. Foster. Cost and Trust Issues in On-Line Auctions. In *Agents'98 Workshop on Agent Mediated Electronic Trading (AMET'98)*, Minneapolis/St.Paul, MN, 1998.

[Vic61]   William Vickrey. Counterspeculation, Auctions, and Competitive Sealed Tenders. *Journal of Finance*, 16(1):8–37, March 1961.

[Yao82]   Andrew Chi-Chih Yao. Protocols for Secure Computations (Extended Abstract). In *23rd Annual Symposium on Foundations of Computer Science*, pages 160–164, Chicago, Illinois, USA, 3–5 November 1982. IEEE Computer Society Press.

Secure Generalized Vickrey Auction without Third-party Servers

Makoto Yokoo[1] and Koutarou Suzuki[2]

[1] NTT Communication Science Laboratories, NTT Corporation
2-4 Hikaridai, Seika-cho, Soraku-gun, Kyoto 619-0237 Japan
yokoo@cslab.kecl.ntt.co.jp
www.kecl.ntt.co.jp/csl/ccrg/members/yokoo/
[2] NTT Information Sharing Platform Laboratories, NTT Corporation
1-1 Hikari-no-oka, Yokosuka, Kanagawa 239-0847 Japan
suzuki.koutarou@lab.ntt.co.jp

Abstract. This paper presents a secure Generalized Vickrey Auction (GVA) scheme that does not require third-party servers, i.e., the scheme is executed only by an auctioneer and bidders. Combinatorial auctions, in which multiple goods are sold simultaneously, have recently attracted considerable attention. The GVA can handle combinatorial auctions and has good theoretical characteristics such as incentive compatibility and Pareto efficiency.

Secure GVA schemes have been developed to prevent frauds by an auctioneer. However, existing methods require third-party servers to execute the protocol. Having third-party servers that are operated by independent organizations is difficult in practice. Therefore, it is desirable that a protocol be executed by the participants themselves. However, if bidders take part in the execution of the auction procedure, a bidder might have an incentive to be an active adversary so that he manipulates the declarations of other bidders to become a winner or to decrease his payment. In our proposed scheme, we use a new protocol that can achieve the same outcome as the GVA. In this protocol, the procedure executed by a bidder affects neither the prices nor the allocation of the bidder. Therefore, a bidder does not have an incentive to be an active adversary.

Keywords: generalized Vickrey auction, combinatorial auction, mechanism design, game-theory.

1   Introduction

Combinatorial auctions have recently attracted considerable attention [15, 26, 29, 39, 40]. An extensive survey is presented in [9]. In contrast with conventional auctions that sell a single item at a time, combinatorial auctions sell multiple items with interdependent values simultaneously and allow the bidders to bid on any combination of items.

In a combinatorial auction, a bidder can express complementary/substitutable preferences over multiple bids. For example, in the Federal Communications

A. Juels (Ed.): FC 2004, LNCS 3110, pp. 132–146, 2004.

Commission (FCC) spectrum auction [20], a bidder could indicate his desire for licenses covering adjoining regions simultaneously (i.e., these licenses are complementary), while being indifferent as to which particular channel was awarded (channels are substitutable). By supporting such complementary/substitutable preferences, we can increase the bidder's utility and the revenue of the seller.

The Generalized Vickrey Auction (GVA) [35], which is also known as the Vickrey-Clarke-Groves (VCG) mechanism, is a generalized version of the well-known Vickrey auction [36] and one instance of the Clarke-Groves mechanism [8, 10]. The GVA can handle combinatorial auctions and has the following good theoretical characteristics.

Incentive Compatibility: For each bidder, truthfully declaring his[1] evaluation values is a dominant strategy, i.e., an optimal strategy regardless of the actions of other bidders.

Pareto Efficiency: If all bidders take the dominant strategy (i.e., at the dominant strategy equilibrium), the social surplus, i.e., the sum of all participants' utilities including the auctioneer, is maximized.

Individual Rationality: No bidder suffers any loss by participating in the auction.

Also, under certain assumptions, we can show that only the GVA can satisfy all of these properties while maximizing the expected revenue of the auctioneer [17].

Although the GVA has these good theoretical characteristics, even its simplest form, i.e., the Vickrey auction, is not yet widely used. As discussed in [25], the main difficulty in using the Vickrey auction is its vulnerability to an insincere auctioneer. For example, if the highest bid is $1,000 and the second highest bid is $500, then the payment of the winner becomes $500. However, if the auctioneer can somehow fabricate a dummy bid at $999, the auctioneer can increase his revenue to $999.

Another difficulty is that the true evaluation value is sensitive information that a bidder may not want to reveal [25]. For example, if a company wins in a public tender, then its bidding value, i.e., its true cost, becomes public, and the company may have difficulty in negotiating with sub-contractors.

The authors have developed a secure GVA scheme [34] that utilizes homomorphic encryption. However, this scheme requires that each bidder declare his evaluation values for all m^n possible allocations, where m is the number of goods and n is the number of bidders. This is inevitable for implementing the GVA in the most general case. However, for many auctions in the real world, we can assume the following two conditions.

No Allocative Externality: Each bidder is only concerned with the goods that are allocated to him, and he is indifferent to the allocations of other bidders.

Free Disposal: Goods can be discarded without any cost.

In this case, declaring his evaluation values for m^n possible allocations is grossly redundant, since his evaluation value is the same as long as the goods allocated

---

[1] We stick to personal pronoun "he" throughout this paper.

to him are the same. Also, he needs to declare his evaluation values only for the bundles in which he is interested.

The authors have developed secure Dynamic Programming (DP) protocols [33, 41]. In principle, by repeatedly solving winner-determination problems, we can obtain the results of the GVA. However, the disadvantage of these secure DP protocols, as well as the scheme presented in [34], is that they require third-party servers. These servers must be operated by independent organizations to avoid collusion among the servers. In practice, collecting a large number of such servers is very difficult. Therefore, it is desirable that the protocol be executed without such third-party servers. peer-to-peer network services that do not require central servers are becoming popular, since such services are more robust against various failures and are scalable. Similarly, for combinatorial auctions, it is desirable that the auction be executed only by participants, i.e., the auctioneer and bidders, without using third-party servers.

However, as described in [30], executing an incentive compatible mechanism in peer-to-peer networks is not trivial. If bidders take part in the execution of the auction procedure, even if the auction protocol is incentive compatible, a bidder might have an incentive to be an active adversary. For example, in the GVA, a bidder can manipulate the evaluation values of other bidders so that he would be a winner or his payment would decrease. We can avoid such manipulations by making the procedure publicly verifiable. However, this requires additional communication/processing costs.

In this paper, we develop a new auction protocol that can obtain the same outcome as the GVA. In this protocol, for each bidder, the price of each set of goods (bundle) is defined first, and then each bidder can choose a bundle that maximizes his utility based on these prices independently from the choices of bundles of other bidders. This protocol looks quite different from a standard GVA description, in which an allocation is determined first, then the payment is calculated. However, we show that our new protocol can obtain exactly the same outcome as the GVA.

The advantage of this new protocol is that its procedures can be distributed among bidders without giving them an incentive to be an active adversary. More specifically, in this protocol, the prices and allocation of bidder j is determined independently from the prices of bidder i. Therefore, if bidder j participates in the procedure for calculating the prices of bidder i, bidder j does not have an incentive to be an active adversary who manipulates the prices of bidder i.

For example, in the most simplest form of this protocol, in which a single unit of a single good is auctioned, the price of bidder i for the good is defined as the maximal evaluation value among all bidders other than i. Clearly, this protocol is identical to the Vickrey auction protocol. The task of calculating the price of bidder i can be distributed among other bidders, since even if bidder j manipulates bidder i's price (to increase the price), this manipulation does not affect the price of bidder j. Therefore, bidder j does not have an incentive to be an active adversary who manipulates the price of bidder i.

The rest of this paper is organized as follows. First, we give the standard description of the GVA in Section 2. Next, we describe our newly developed protocol that can obtain the same outcome as the GVA in Section 3. Then, we explain the details of the proposed secure GVA scheme in Section 4. Next, in Section 5, we describe the method for calculating the prices required in this protocol using dynamic programming (DP) [3]. Finally, we discuss the related works and remaining issues, including collusion among bidders, in Section 6.

2   Preliminaries: GVA

This section gives the standard description of the GVA. First, we define several terms and notations.

- $N = \{1, 2, \ldots, n\}$: a set of bidders
- $M = \{1, 2, \ldots, m\}$: a set of goods
- $u(i, B)$: the evaluation value of bidder i for bundle $B \subseteq M$
- We assume free-disposal, i.e., for all $B \subset B'$, $u(i, B) \leq u(i, B')$ holds.
- We assume quasi-linear utility, i.e., if bidder i obtains B by paying p_i, his utility is given by $u(i, B) - p_i$.
- $\boldsymbol{g} = (g(1), g(2), \ldots, g(n))$: a feasible allocation $\boldsymbol{g}$ for a set of goods M, where $g(i)$ represents the bundle allocated to bidder i, and the following two conditions hold: $\bigcup_i g(i) \subseteq M$, and for all $i \neq j$, $g(i) \cap g(j) = \emptyset$
- $G(M)$: a set of all feasible allocations of goods M.

In the GVA, for each bundle B, bidder i declares his evaluation value $v(i, B)$. Note that the declared evaluation value is not necessarily the same as the true evaluation value $u(i, B)$. The protocol selects a Pareto efficient allocation based on the declared evaluation values. More specifically, we choose an allocation $\boldsymbol{g}^* = (g^*(1), g^*(2), \ldots, g^*(n)) \in G(M)$ that maximizes the social surplus, i.e., the sum of evaluation values of all bidders. This means for any allocation $\boldsymbol{g} = (g(1), g(2), \ldots, g(n)) \in G(M)$, the following condition holds.

$$\sum_j v(j, g^*(j)) \geq \sum_j v(j, g(j)).$$

There might be multiple allocations that are Pareto efficient. In such a case, the GVA arbitrary selects one Pareto efficient allocation $\boldsymbol{g}^*$.

Next, the payment of bidder i is determined as follows. Let us assume $\boldsymbol{g}^*_{\sim i} = (g^*_{\sim i}(1), g^*_{\sim i}(2), \ldots, g^*_{\sim i}(n)) \in G(M)$ is an allocation that maximizes the social surplus except for i. Formally, it is defined as follows: for any allocation $\boldsymbol{g} = (g(1), g(2), \ldots, g(n)) \in G(M)$, the following formula holds.

$$\sum_{j \neq i} v(j, g^*_{\sim i}(j)) \geq \sum_{j \neq i} v(j, g(j)).$$

The payment of bidder i, i.e., p_i, is defined as follows.

$$p_i = \sum_{j \neq i} v(j, g^*_{\sim i}(j)) - \sum_{j \neq i} v(j, g^*(j)).$$

An intuitive explanation of this formula is as follows. The first term of this formula is the optimal social surplus except for i if bidder i would not have participated in the auction. The second term is the obtained social surplus except for i when bidder i does participate. Thus, p_i represents the decreased amount of the social surplus caused by the participation of bidder i, i.e., bidder i is required to compensate this decreased amount of utilities.

In the GVA, for each bidder i, declaring the true evaluation values, i.e., declaring $v(i, \cdot) = u(i, \cdot)$, is a dominant strategy, i.e., a best strategy to maximize his utility regardless of the actions of other bidders. This property is called *incentive compatibility*. The reason that the GVA is incentive compatible is explained as follows. Since the utility of i is quasi-linear, it can be represented as follows.

$$u(i, g^*(i)) - p_i = u(i, g^*(i)) - [\sum_{j \neq i} v(j, g^*_{\sim i}(j)) - \sum_{j \neq i} v(j, g^*(j))] \qquad (1)$$

$$= [u(i, g^*(i)) + \sum_{j \neq i} v(j, g^*(j))] - \sum_{j \neq i} v(j, g^*_{\sim i}(j)) \qquad (2)$$

The third term of formula (2) is determined independently from bidder i's declarations. Therefore, bidder i can maximize his utility by maximizing the sum of the first and second terms of formula (2). On the other hand, g^* is selected by maximizing $\sum_j v(j, g^*(j)) = v(i, g^*(i)) + \sum_{j \neq i} v(j, g^*(j))$. This means bidder i can maximize his utility by declaring $v(i, \cdot) = u(i, \cdot)$, i.e., by declaring true evaluation values.

Let us describe how the GVA works. Assume there are two goods 1 and 2 and three bidders 1, 2, and 3. The evaluation value for a bundle $u(i, B)$ is given as follows.

	{1}	{2}	{1,2}
bidder 1	6	0	6
bidder 2	0	0	8
bidder 3	0	5	5

In a Pareto efficient allocation, good 1 is allocated to bidder 1 and good 2 is allocated to bidder 3. The payment of bidder 1 is calculated as follows. Without considering bidder 1, the best allocation is to allocate both goods to bidder 2, and the social surplus except for bidder 1 is 8. When considering bidder 1, the social surplus except for bidder 1 at the Pareto efficient allocation is 5. Therefore, the payment of bidder 1, i.e., p_1, is given as $8 - 5 = 3$. Similarly, the payment of bidder 3 is given as $8 - 6 = 2$.

3   New GVA-Equivalent Protocol

In this section, we develop a new protocol that can achieve the same outcome as the GVA. In this protocol, as in the standard GVA, for each bundle B, bidder i

declares his evaluation value $v(i, B)$. Note that the declared evaluation value is not necessarily the same as the true evaluation value $u(i, B)$.

To simplify the protocol description, we introduce the following notation. For a set of goods $B \subseteq M$ and a set of bidders X, we define $V^*(B, X)$ as the sum of the evaluation values of X when B is allocated optimally among X. To be precise, let us represent the set of all feasible allocations of a set of goods B as $G(B)$, where for each $\boldsymbol{g} = (g(1), g(2), \ldots, g(n)) \in G(B)$, $\bigcup_{i \in X} g(i) \subseteq B$ and for all $i \neq j, g(i) \cap g(j) = \emptyset$ holds. $V^*(B, X)$ is defined as follows.

$$V^*(B, X) = \max_{\boldsymbol{g} \in G(B)} \sum_{j \in X} v(j, g(j)).$$

In this protocol, instead of determining the allocation first, we first determine the price of each bundle B for each bidder i. The price of bundle B for bidder i is defined as follows.

$$p_{i,B} = V^*(M, N \setminus \{i\}) - V^*(M \setminus B, N \setminus \{i\}). \tag{3}$$

Next, each bidder i chooses a bundle that maximizes his utility based on the prices, i.e., he chooses B_i^*, where $B_i^* = \arg\max_{B \subseteq M} u(i, B) - p_{i,B}$. Note that each bidder can choose a bundle that maximizes his utility independently from the choices of other bidders. To be more precise, if there exist multiple bundles that maximize his utility, then the protocol performs some adjustment so that the choices are consistent, but each bidder is still guaranteed to obtain one bundle that maximizes his utility.

It is obvious that this new protocol satisfies incentive compatibility. For bidder i, his prices are determined independently from his declaration. Also, he can choose the optimal bundle regardless of the choices of other bidders. Therefore, bidder i has no incentive to manipulate the prices of other bidders (which are dependent on his declaration). Since this protocol satisfies incentive compatibility, in the rest of this paper, we assume each bidder declares his true evaluation values $u(i, B)$. Thus, $V^*(B, X)$ can be represented as follows.

$$\max_{\boldsymbol{g} \in G(B)} \sum_{j \in X} u(j, g(j)).$$

This protocol is identical to the GVA, i.e., the following theorems hold.

Theorem 1. *A bundle B maximizes bidder i's utility if and only if for some $\boldsymbol{g}^*$, $g^*(i) = B$ holds.*

Theorem 2. *If B maximizes bidder i's utility, then $p_i = p_{i,B}$ holds.*

In proving these theorems, we use the characteristics described below. From the definition, the following formula holds.

$$\sum_{j \neq i} u(j, g_{\sim i}^*(j)) = V^*(M, N \setminus \{i\}).$$

Furthermore, for $\boldsymbol{g}^* = (g^*(1), g^*(2), \ldots, g^*(n))$, the following formula holds.

$$\sum_{j \neq i} u(j, g^*(j)) = V^*(M \setminus g^*(i), N \setminus \{i\}).$$

The proof of Theorem 1 is as follows. First, we show if for some $\boldsymbol{g}^*$, $g^*(i) = B$, then B maximizes bidder i's utility. More specifically, we derive a contradiction by assuming for some $\boldsymbol{g}^*$, $g^*(i) = B$ but bundle B does not maximize bidder i's utility. In this case, there exists another bundle B' and $u(i, B') - p_{i,B'} > u(i, B) - p_{i,B}$ holds.

$$p_{i,B'} = V^*(M, N \setminus \{i\}) - V^*(M \setminus B', N \setminus \{i\}).$$

$$p_{i,B} = V^*(M, N \setminus \{i\}) - V^*(M \setminus B, N \setminus \{i\}).$$

Therefore, the following formula holds.

$$u(i, B') + V^*(M \setminus B', N \setminus \{i\}) > u(i, B) + V^*(M \setminus B, N \setminus \{i\}).$$

However, the right side of this equation can be transformed as follows.

$$\begin{aligned} u(i, B) + V^*(M \setminus B, N \setminus \{i\}) &= u(i, g^*(i)) + V^*(M \setminus g^*(i), N \setminus \{i\}) \\ &= u(i, g^*(i)) + \sum_{j \neq i} u(j, g^*(j)) \\ &= \sum_j u(j, g^*(j)). \end{aligned}$$

The right side of this equation represents the social surplus at Pareto efficient allocation $\boldsymbol{g}^*$. On the other hand, the left side is the social surplus when allocating B' to bidder i and allocating other goods optimally among bidders other than i. This contradicts the assumption that $\boldsymbol{g}^*$ is Pareto efficient.

Next, we prove that if a bundle B maximizes bidder i's utility, then for some $\boldsymbol{g}^*$, $g^*(i) = B$ holds. More specifically, we derive a contradiction by assuming a bundle B maximizes bidder i's utility but for any $\boldsymbol{g}^*$, $g^*(i) \neq B$.

In this case, there exists bundle B', where $B' \neq B$, $B' = g^*(i)$, and $u(i, B) - p_{i,B} > u(i, B') - p_{i,B'}$ hold. Therefore, the following formula holds.

$$u(i, B) + V^*(M \setminus B, N \setminus \{i\}) > u(i, B') + V^*(M \setminus B', N \setminus \{i\}).$$

However, the right side of this formula represents the social surplus at Pareto efficient allocation $\boldsymbol{g}^*$, while the left side is the social surplus when allocating B to bidder i and allocating other goods optimally among bidders except i. This contradicts the assumption that $\boldsymbol{g}^*$ is Pareto efficient. □

Next, we prove Theorem 2. From Theorem 1, when B maximizes bidder i's utility, then for some $\boldsymbol{g}^*$, $g^*(i) = B$ holds.

$$\begin{aligned} p_i &= \sum_{j \neq i} u(j, g^*_{\sim i}(j)) - \sum_{j \neq i} u(j, g^*(j)) \\ &= V^*(M, N \setminus \{i\}) - V^*(M \setminus g^*(i), N \setminus \{i\}) \\ &= p_{i,B}. \end{aligned}$$

From the above, Theorem 2 is obtained. □

If there exist multiple Pareto efficient allocations, then multiple bundles can simultaneously maximize the bidder's utility. In this case, the protocol needs to adjust allocations so that the choices of bidders are consistent, i.e., no good is allocated to different bidders simultaneously. However, Theorem 1 states that any bundle B that is allocated to bidder i in a Pareto efficient allocation would maximize bidder i's utility. Therefore, by choosing any Pareto efficient allocation, we can find a way to adjust choices so that the choices of bidders are consistent and each bidder is guaranteed to obtain one of the optimal bundles.

Let us describe how this protocol works. In the identical setting of the previous example, the price of each bundle is calculated as follows.

	$\{1\}$	$\{2\}$	$\{1,2\}$
bidder 1	3	8	8
bidder 2	6	5	11
bidder 3	8	2	8

For example, when determining the prices for bidder 1, $V^*(M, N \setminus \{1\})$ is the optimal social surplus without considering bidder 1. This is equal to 8. When $B = \{1\}$, $V^*(M \setminus B, N \setminus \{1\}) = V^*(\{2\}, \{2,3\})$ means the sum of the evaluation values when good 2 is allocated optimally among bidders 2 and 3. The optimal allocation is allocating good 2 to bidder 3. Thus, $V^*(\{2\}, \{2,3\}) = 5$. Therefore, $p_{1,\{1\}} = 8 - 5 = 3$. When $B = \{2\}$, $V^*(M \setminus B, N \setminus \{1\}) = V^*(\{1\}, \{2,3\})$ is equal to 0, since neither bidder 2 nor 3 wants good 1 alone. Therefore, $p_{1,\{2\}} = 8 - 0 = 8$.

Given these prices, bidder 1 obtains good 1 at price 3, and bidder 3 obtains good 2 at price 2.

4   Secure GVA

In this section, we show how the new protocol presented in the previous section can be executed without third-party servers.

4.1   Economic Model of Bidders

We assume a bidder is rational, i.e., he tries to maximize his own utility. Furthermore, we make the following assumptions.

1. If a bidder has no incentive for acting dishonestly, i.e., his utility does not strictly increase by telling a lie or deviating from the protocol, then he will act honestly.
2. There is no way to enforce side-payments among bidders.
3. For each bidder, computation/communication costs for executing the protocol are negligible.

The first assumption is called ϵ-truthfulness [24]. Although this assumption might sound rather strong, it is natural if we assume the moral consciousness of a bidder provides a very slight preference toward acting honestly rather than acting dishonestly for nothing.

From the first and second assumptions, a bidder i cannot persuade another bidder j to do some action, unless doing so is profitable for bidder j. Therefore, a collusion of bidders is possible only when each participant in the collusion has strictly positive gain.

Also, from the first and third assumptions, a bidder will not neglect to execute the protocol simply due to laziness.

4.2   Proposed Scheme

The outline of the proposed scheme is as follows. Bidders N execute the following procedures. $n - 1$ bidders other than bidder i are assigned to calculate the prices for bidder i. We call these bidders $N \setminus \{i\}$ as price-calculators for bidder i.

1. Price-calculators $N \setminus \{i\}$ for bidder i perform a multi-party computation protocol [4] that is secure against *passive adversary*, to compute $\{(i, B, p_{i,B}) | B \subseteq M\}$ from secret input $u(j, B)$ of bidder $j \in N \setminus \{i\}$.
   Then, the result $\{(i, B, p_{i,B}) | B \subseteq M\}$ is published.
2. After the results $\{(i, B, p_{i,B}) | B \subseteq M\}$ for all i are published, the result of the auction is calculated as follows.
   Bidder i finds all bundles B_i^* that maximize his utility and publishes them. If there is conflict between these allocation, bidders adjusts bundle allocations so that they do not conflict with each other. As described in Section 3, we can always find consistent bundle allocations.
   Finally, the allocation $\{B_i^* | i \in N\}$ of goods and prices $\{p_{i,B_i^*} | i \in N\}$ are announced.

For this protocol, the following theorem holds.

Theorem 3. *If a bidder satisfies the above economic properties, this bidder executes the protocol honestly.*

The proof of Theorem 3 is as follows. In Step 1, if bidder j is a price-calculator for bidder i, the prices and the allocation of bidder i do not affect the prices or the allocation of bidder j, i.e., bidder j can obtain the optimal bundle regardless of the allocation of bidder i. Therefore, bidder j has no incentive to increase the prices of bidder i.

Also, since we assume there is no way to enforce side-payments among bidders, bidder j does not have an incentive to decrease the prices of bidder i. Furthermore, since we assume computation/communication costs for executing the protocol are negligible, bidder j does not have an incentive to neglect executing the protocol simply due to laziness.

Therefore, bidder j does not have an incentive to be an active adversary when calculating the price of bidder i. From above, bidder j will execute the protocol honestly, since he has no incentive to act dishonestly.

In Step 2, bidder i can maximize his utility by publishing all bundles B_i^* that maximize his utility. Therefore, bidder i does not have an incentive to manipulate the results. Although bidders adjust bundle allocations so that they do not conflict with each other, their utilities are the same for all possible combinations. Therefore, bidders do not have an incentive to manipulate the results. □

From Theorem 3, the following theorem holds.

Theorem 4. *If all bidders satisfy the above economic properties, the proposed protocol can unconditionally securely compute prices $\{(i, B, p_{i,B})|i \in N, B \subseteq M\}$ and auction result $\{B_i^*|i \in N\}$ against $t < (n-1)/2$ adversaries.*

The proof of Theorem 4 is as follows. By Theorem 3, price-calculators $N \setminus \{i\}$ for bidder i follow the protocol, so we can assume that adversaries are passive.

In step 1, since there are at most $t < (n-1)/2$ passive adversaries in $n-1$ price-calculators $N \setminus \{i\}$ for bidder i, a multi-party computation protocol [4] can unconditionally securely compute prices $\{(i, B, p_{i,B})|B \subseteq M\}$.

In step 2, bidders honestly calculate the auction result from published prices $\{(i, B, p_{i,B})|i \in N, B \subseteq M\}$. □

In the protocol, price $p_{i,B}$ is published. However, $p_{i,B}$ is obtained by aggregating many evaluation values of bidders. Therefore, it is difficult to precisely estimate each evaluation value from this information.

5   Efficient Price Calculation Using Dynamic Programming

In the previous section, we assume price-calculators calculate $p_{i,B}$ by directly applying formula (3). However, to calculate each of the first and second terms of formula (3), we need to solve a combinatorial optimization problem that is NP-complete [26]. Although the first term is common for all B, the second term must be calculated for each B. Note that we need to calculate $p_{i,B}$ for all bidders $i \in N$ and for all bundles $B \subseteq M$.

In this section, we describe an alternative method for calculating prices that is much more efficient than calculating $p_{i,B}$ directly using formula (3). This method utilizes dynamic programming (DP) [3] to incrementally calculate $V^*(B, N \setminus \{i\})$ for all $B \subseteq M$.

We assume each bidder j (except i) is declaring his evaluation value $u(j, B)$ for each bundle B in which he is interested. If bidder j has substitutable evaluation values, e.g., bidder j wants B_1 or B_2 but not both at the same time, we introduce a dummy good d. More specifically, we assume bidder j is interested in both $B_1 \cup \{d\}$ and $B_2 \cup \{d\}$. By introducing the dummy good, we can avoid allocating both B_1 and B_2 to bidder j at the same time. This must be done whenever $u(j, B_1) + u(j, B_2) > u(j, B_1 \cup B_2)$ holds.

Then, we create a node $(B, |B|)$ for each bundle $B \subseteq M$. $|B|$ is the number of goods included in B. Also, we create the following directed, weighted links for each bundle B in which bidder j is interested.

  - a link from node $(B, |B|)$ to terminal node $(\{\}, 0)$,
    where its weight $w((B, |B|), (\{\}, 0))$ is $u(j, B)$
  - for each $B', B'' \subseteq M$, where $B'' \subset B'$, $B' \setminus B'' = B$, and $|B''| \geq |B'|/2$,
    a link from node $(B', |B'|)$ to node $(B'', |B''|)$,
    where its weight $w((B', |B'|), (B'', |B''|))$ is $u(j, B)$

If there exists a bundle B in which nobody is interested, then we assume a dummy bidder j_d is interested in B, where evaluation value $u(j_d, B) = 0$. Also, if there exists a bundle B in which multiple bidders are interested, multiple links must be created between $(B', |B'|)$ and $(B'', |B''|)$. To avoid making the notation too verbose, in presenting the DP procedure, we assume there exists only one link between each pair of nodes.

We show an example of nodes and links, where $M = \{1, 2, 3\}$, in Figure 1. A circle is a node and the description within a circle represents $B, |B|$, where B is a bundle.

In this graph, the length of the longest path from node $(B, |B|)$ to terminal node $(\{\}, 0)$ represents the sum of the evaluation values when allocating goods B optimally to bidders other than i, i.e., $V^*(B, N \setminus \{i\})$.

Let us represent the length of the longest path from $(B, |B|)$ as $f((B, |B|))$. Then, $f((B, |B|))$ can be calculated by the following recurrence formula.

  - $f((\{\}, 0)) = 0$
  - $f((B, |B|)) = \max_{((B, |B|), (B', |B'|))}[w((B, |B|), (B', |B'|)) + f((B', |B'|))]$.

By using this formula, we can obtain $f((B, |B|))$ by starting from a node that has a smaller $|B|$. The price of bidder i for bundle B, i.e., $p_{i,B}$, is given as $V^*(M, N \setminus \{i\}) - V^*(M \setminus B, N \setminus \{i\})$. Therefore, $p_{i,B} = f((M, |M|)) - f((M \setminus B, |M \setminus B|))$.

We can use any MPC protocol to calculate the above formula to prevent leaking $w((B, |B|), (B', |B'|))$, which represents the evaluation value of a bidder. Besides using a general-purpose MPC protocol, we can use the specialized methods presented in [33, 41]. Note that we don't need to construct a graph for each $B \subseteq M$. Instead, we construct one graph for all $B \subseteq M$ and calculate $f((B, |B|))$ for all B in a single run of the DP procedure.

In using the DP procedure, we need to create a graph that consists of 2^m nodes to calculate the prices. If the number of goods m becomes large but the number of bundles in which each bidder is interested is relatively small, the graph contains exponentially many nodes, while most of the links are dummy links with zero weights. We are currently developing an efficient method for handling such graphs. One important special case of general combinatorial auctions is multi-unit auctions, in which multiple identical units of a good is auctioned. In this case, as described in [33], the DP procedure requires only $O(n \times m)$ nodes instead of 2^m nodes.

The advantage of using the DP method over calculating formula (3) for each bundle is clear, since we don't need to solve a combinatorial optimization problem for each B. On the other hand, in the DP method, for each B, $f((B, |B|))$ are published. However, $f((B, |B|))$ is obtained by aggregating many evaluation values of bidders. Therefore, it is difficult to precisely estimate each evaluation value from this information.

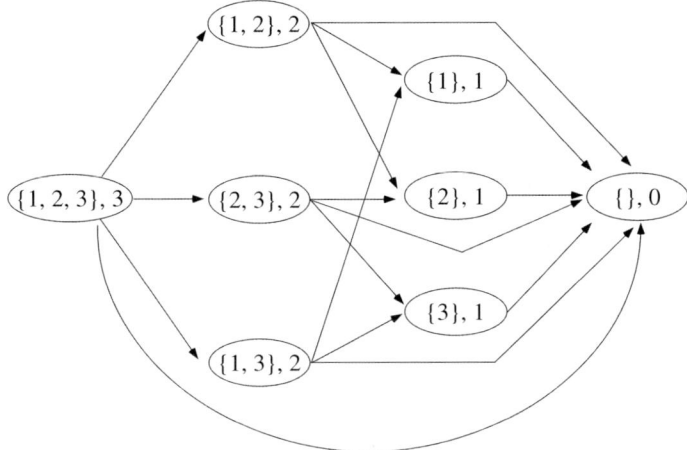

Fig. 1. Example of graph for Dynamic Programming

In the proposed scheme, each bidder declares his evaluation values only for the bundles in which he is interested. On the other hand, in the scheme described in [34], each bidder needs to declare his preference over m^n possible allocations, where n is the number of bidders and m is the number of goods. When the number of bidders n becomes large, the number of possible allocations becomes very large.

6   Discussions

Many works have been carried out for secure sealed-bid auctions[1, 2, 5–7, 11–14, 16, 18, 19, 21–23, 27, 28, 31, 33, 32, 37, 41]. In all of these schemes, however, the GVA has not been treated with the notable exceptions of [21] and [34]. Naor, Pinkas and Sumner [21] proposed a general method for executing any auction, including combinatorial auctions, based on a technique called the garbled circuit [38]. This method does not require interactive communications among multiple evaluators. However, designing a combinatorial circuit to implement the GVA as a whole is still an open problem, and the obtained circuit can be prohibitively large.

Suzuki and Yokoo [34] proposed a secure GVA protocol. However, as discussed in Section 1, this scheme requires that each bidder declare his evaluation values for all m^n possible allocations. Also, this scheme requires third-party servers.

By repeatedly applying the secure dynamic programming scheme [33, 41], we can determine the winner and payments of the GVA. However, if a bidder participates in the traditional procedure of the GVA, the bidder might have an incentive to be an active adversary.

When bidders take part in the auction procedure, an auctioneer might be concerned about collusion among bidders. Actually, the GVA protocol is vulnerable against collusions even if the auctioneer executes the auction procedure. For example, in the simplest form of the GVA, i.e., the Vickrey auction, bidder i, who has the highest evaluation value, can bribe the second highest bidder j to reduce j's declaration so that i's payment becomes smaller. One method to reduce the effect of collusion is to set reservation/minimum prices for each good. In our proposed scheme, this is possible if the auctioneer participates in the auction as a bidder. The auctioneer declares the price of each good, i.e., he is not willing to sell the good at less than that price.

7   Conclusions

In this paper, we developed a secure GVA scheme in which the GVA can be executed without using third-party servers, i.e., the scheme can be executed only by the auctioneer and bidders. We first developed a new auction protocol that can achieve the same outcome as the GVA. In this protocol, for each bidder, the price of each bundle is calculated first, and then each bidder can choose a bundle that maximizes his utility based on these prices independently from the choices of bundles of other bidders. In this protocol, the prices and allocation of bidder j are determined independently from the prices of bidder i. Therefore, if bidder j participates in the procedure for calculating the prices of bidder i, bidder j does not have an incentive to be an active adversary who manipulates the prices of bidder i.

References

1. M. Abe and K. Suzuki. M+1-st price auction using homomorphic encryption. *Proceedings of Public Key Cryptography 2002*, 2002.
2. O. Baudron and J. Stern. Non-interactive private auctions. *Proceedings of Fifth International Financial Cryptography Conference (FC-01)*, 2001.
3. R. Bellman. *Dynamic Programming*. Princeton University Press, Princeton, NJ, 1957.
4. M. Ben-Or, S. Goldwasser, and A. Wigderson. Completeness theorems for non-cryptographic fault-tolerant distributed computation. In *Proceedings of 20th ACM Symposium on the Theory of Computing*, pages 1–10, 1988.
5. F. Brandt. Fully private auctions in a constant number of rounds. In *Proceedings of Seventh International Financial Cryptography Conference (FC-2003)*, pages 223–238, 2003.
6. C. Cachin. Efficient private bidding and auctions with an oblivious third party. *Proceedings of 6th ACM Conference on Computer and Communications Security*, pages 120–127, 1999.
7. K. Chida, K. Kobayashi, and H. Morita. Efficient sealed-bid auctions for massive numbers of bidders with lump comparison. *Proceedings of ISC 2001*, 2001.
8. E. H. Clarke. Multipart pricing of public goods. *Public Choice*, 2:19–33, 1971.
9. S. de Vries and R. V. Vohra. Combinatorial auctions: A survey. *INFORMS Journal on Computing*, 15, 2003.
10. T. Groves. Incentives in teams. *Econometrica*, 41:617–631, 1973.

11. M. Harkavy, J. D. Tygar, and H. Kikuchi. Electronic auctions with private bids. *Proceedings of Third USENIX Workshop on Electronic Commerce*, pages 61–74, 1998.

12. A. Juels and M. Szydlo. A two-server, sealed-bid auction protocol. In *Proceedings of Sixth International Financial Cryptography Conference (FC-02)*, pages 72–86, 2002.

13. H. Kikuchi, M. Harkavy, and J. D. Tygar. Multi-round anonymous auction protocols. *Proceedings of first IEEE Workshop on Dependable and Real-Time E-Commerce Systems*, pages 62–69, 1998.

14. H. Kikuchi. (M+1)st-Price auction protocol. In *Proceedings of Fifth International Financial Cryptography Conference (FC-01)*, 2001.

15. P. Klemperer. Auction theory: A guide to the literature. *Journal of Economics Surveys*, 13(3):227–286, 1999.

16. K. Kobayashi, H. Morita, K. Suzuki, and M. Hakuta. Efficient sealed-bid auction by using one-way functions. *IEICE Trans. Fundamentals*, E84-A(1), 2001.

17. V. Krishna. *Auction Theory*. Academic Press, 2002.

18. M. Kudo. Secure electronic sealed-bid auction protocol with public key cryptography. *IEICE Trans. Fundamentals*, E81-A(1), 1998.

19. H. Lipmaa, N. Asokan, and V. Niemi. Secure Vickrey auctions without threshold trust. In *Proceedings of Sixth International Financial Cryptography Conference (FC-02)*, pages 87–101, 2002.

20. J. McMillan. Selling spectrum rights. *Journal of Economics Perspectives*, 8(3):145–162, 1994.

21. M. Naor, B. Pinkas, and R. Sumner. Privacy preserving auctions and mechanism design. In *Proceedings of the First ACM Conference on Electronic Commerce (EC-99)*, pages 129–139, 1999.

22. K. Omote and A. Myaji. An anonymous auction protocol with a single non-trusted center using binary trees. *Proceedings of ISW2000*, pages 108–120, 2000. LNCS 1975.

23. K. Omote and A. Miyaji. A second-price sealed-bid auction with the discriminant of the p-th root. In *Proceedings of Sixth International Financial Cryptography Conference (FC-02)*, pages 57–71, 2002.

24. E. Rasmusen. *Games and Information*. Blackwell, 1989.

25. M. H. Rothkopf, T. J. Teisberg, and E. P. Kahn. Why are Vickrey auctions rare. *Journal of Political Economy*, 98(1):94–109, 1990.

26. M. H. Rothkopf, A. Pekeč, and R. M. Harstad. Computationally manageable combinatorial auctions. *Management Science*, 44(8):1131–1147, 1998.

27. K. Sako. Universally verifiable auction protocol which hides losing bids. *Proceedings of Public Key Cryptography 2000*, pages 35–39, 2000.

28. K. Sakurai and S. Miyazaki. A bulletin-board based digital auction scheme with bidding down strategy. *Proceedings of 1999 International Workshop on Cryptographic Techniques and E-Commerce*, pages 180–187, 1999.

29. T. Sandholm. An algorithm for optimal winner determination in combinatorial auction. In *Proceedings of the Sixteenth International Joint Conference on Artificial Intelligence (IJCAI-99)*, pages 542–547, 1999.

30. J. Shneidman and D. C. Parkes. Rationality and self-interest in peer to peer networks. In *Proceedings of Second International Workshop on Peer-to-Peer Systems (IPTPS-2003)*, 2003.

31. S. G. Stubblebine and P. F. Syverson. Fair on-line auctions without special trusted parties. *Proceedings of Third International Financial Cryptography Conference (FC-99)*, 1999.

32. K. Suzuki, K. Kobayashi, and H. Morita. Efficient sealed-bid auction using hash chain. *Proceedings of International Conference Information Security and Cryptology 2000 (LNCS 2015)*, pages 183–191, 2000.
33. K. Suzuki and M. Yokoo. Secure combinatorial auctions by dynamic programming with polynomial secret sharing. In *Proceedings of Sixth International Financial Cryptography Conference (FC-02)*, Lecture Notes in Computer Science 2357, pages 44–56. Springer, 2002.
34. K. Suzuki and M. Yokoo. Secure Generalized Vickrey Auction using homomorphic encryption. In *Proceedings of Seventh International Financial Cryptography Conference (FC-03)*, 2003.
35. H. R. Varian. Economic mechanism design for computerized agents. In *Proceedings of the First Usenix Workshop on Electronic Commerce*, 1995.
36. W. Vickrey. Counter speculation, auctions, and competitive sealed tenders. *Journal of Finance*, 16:8–37, 1961.
37. Y. Watanabe and H. Imai. Reducing the round complexity of a sealed-bid auction protocol with an off-line TTP. In *Proceedings of ACM Conference on Computer and Communications Security 2000*, pages 80–86, 2000.
38. A. C. Yao. How to generate and exchange secrets. In *Proceedings of IEEE Symposium on Foundations of Computer Science*, pages 162–167, 1986.
39. M. Yokoo, Y. Sakurai, and S. Matsubara. Robust combinatorial auction protocol against false-name bids. *Artificial Intelligence*, 130(2):167–181, 2001.
40. M. Yokoo, Y. Sakurai, and S. Matsubara. The effect of false-name bids in combinatorial auctions: New fraud in Internet auctions. *Games and Economic Behavior*, 46(1):174–188, 2004.
41. M. Yokoo and K. Suzuki. Secure multi-agent dynamic programming based on homomorphic encryption and its application to combinatorial auctions. In *Proceedings of the First International Conference on Autonomous Agents and Multiagent Systems (AAMAS-2002)*, pages 112–119, 2002.

Electronic National Lotteries

Elisavet Konstantinou[1,2], Vasiliki Liagkou[1,2], Paul Spirakis[1,2],
Yannis C. Stamatiou[1,3,4], and Moti Yung[5]

[1] Research and Academic Computer Technology Institute,
P.O. Box 1122, 26110 Patras, Greece
[2] Department of Computer Engineering and Informatics,
University of Patras, 26500 Patras, Greece
{konstane,liagkou,spirakis}@ceid.upatras.gr
[3] Department of Mathematics, University of the Aegean,
Karlovassi, 83200, Samos, Greece
stamatiu@aegean.gr
[4] Joint Research Group (JRG) on Communications and Information Systems
Security (University of the Aegean and Athens University of Economics and Business)
[5] Computer Science, Columbia University, New York, NY, USA
moti@cs.columbia.edu

Abstract. We describe the design and implementation of secure and
robust protocol and system for a national electronic lottery. Electronic
lotteries at a national level are a viable cost effective alternative to mechanical ones when there is a business need to support many types of
"games of chance" and to allow increased drawing frequency. Electronic
lotteries are, in fact, extremely high risk financial application: If one dis-
covers a way to predict or otherwise claim the winning numbers (even
once) the result is huge financial damages. Moreover, the e-lottery process
is complex, which increases the possibility of fraud or costly accidental
failures. In addition, a national lottery must adhere to auditability and
(regulatory) fairness requirements regarding its drawings. Our mechanism, which we believe is the first one of its kind to be described in
the literature, builds upon a number of cryptographic primitives that
ensure the unpredictability of the winning numbers, the prevention of
their premature leakages and prevention of fraud. We also provide measures for auditability, fairness, and trustworthiness of the process. Besides
cryptography, we incorporate security mechanisms that eliminate various risks along the entire process. Our system which was commissioned
by a national organization, was implemented in the field and has been
operational and active for a while, now.

1 Introduction

Generating numbers for the support of lotteries is a utility that needs to produce *unpredictable numbers* with additional protection (e.g., against premature
disclosure) and a secure system supporting various sorts of fraud prevention
mechanisms throughout the entire lottery process. A huge amount of money is
at stake for the lottery operator in case of malicious intervention in the number

A. Juels (Ed.): FC 2004, LNCS 3110, pp. 147–163, 2004.
© IFCA/Springer-Verlag Berlin Heidelberg 2004

drawing mechanism or anywhere else in the system (e.g., introducing a winning coupon "after the fact"). Thus, what we need is assurances of robustness that will make sure the desired unpredictability properties while facing a new set of attacks perhaps by insiders or other parties with access to various partial relevant data. In the real world, achieving these aims can be traditionally accomplished with mechanical lotteries performed live on TV with a certified auditor present. However, due to recent business needs, the use of such lotteries is not suitable. For instance, there may be a requirement for very frequent drawings (every 5 minutes in KENO-like games) or drawings that should be accomplished within a very short time interval. In such cases the use of electronic lotteries is inevitable. Also, dynamically games may change as new games are introduced and the cost of new mechanical device for each game is quite large, whereas an electronic device producing random bits is much more easily adapted to new games, merely by re-interpretation of the random stream of bits. Regarding the consumer side, auditability is required and acceptable assurances are required to make sure that the lottery result is fair. Assuring that the process is indeed a "game of chance" may also be required by regulation. This is in contrast with "Internet casino sites" that rather than playing a fair game (with some agreed upon bias, perhaps), might secretly study specific user behavior and tune their games accordingly, to maximize profit.

Related Work

A number of designs that seem to lack scalability (which is a must in a national lottery game) are available in the literature. In [9], a lottery protocol is presented that allows the support of e-casinos with secure remote gambling. An interesting feature of the protocol is that the initial randomness (seeds) is chosen through the collaboration of two or more players in such a way that the final choice is essentially random to all of them. The protocol also includes various auditing functions that build trustworthiness between the casino owner and the players. However, the need for collaboration of players and the overhead in the required protocol steps make it rather unsuitable for large scale electronic lotteries with a large expected player participation and a requirement for fast operation. The paper also present some interesting practical issues pertaining to the design and operation of remote electronic lotteries. In [6], another electronic lottery protocol is proposed based on the concept of *delaying functions*. A delaying function is a function that cannot be computed in time less than a predetermined time limit. Although these functions ensure fairness and public verifiability of the whole process, the time required for the verification is as long as the time to compute the function and this can be unacceptably low in applications where the drawings are frequent. Also, the status of the best time to compute a function may change as our knowledge changes (due to lack of solid lower bounds in complexity theory), thus the delay may not be robust enough over time (one can, of course, always adjust the parameters to handle algorithmic advances but it requires awareness of the advances on the designers' side). In addition, the protocol puts an upper bound on the number of lottery coupons one can buy which is unacceptable in a scalable nation-wide design. In [24], a protocol based on a bit-commitment scheme where a secret (the winning numbers) is committed to and can be read by the lottery players only after a predetermined amount of time. This still can be unacceptable in applications that require frequent drawings and unsuitable for large scale lotteries. In [22], a protocol for Internet based lotteries is presented. It generates the winning numbers using the played coupons with cryptographic primitives such as hash functions. This protocol is actually incorporated in a tool that supports user-initiated drawings and verification of the generation process. However, this cannot be used in large-scale lotteries with many participating users where each user is part of the auditing function. In [13] a protocol is presented that involves a bit-commitment scheme on the part of the electronic lottery so that the chosen seed cannot later be changed. It allows users to participate in the drawing of numbers indirectly by incorporating their numbers in the chosen seed. A scalability issue with this protocol is that it requires some computation steps that need to be performed by the players so that they can decide whether they win or not.

In [26], another protocol is presented whose main features are the preservation of the anonymity of the players and the existence of a mechanism for paying the winners. However, this protocol still requires the users to participate in the identification of the winners and, also, adds the complication of payments that usually is not an issue since the winners can claim their prizes later at the lottery organization or some designated bank out of band. In essence this protocol is about the front end user handling over the Internet, whereas we concentrate on the back end support (that can be augmented to include a front end over the Internet). The protocol presented in [12] uses as primitives a bit-commitment scheme and a hash function and it is suitable for a large-scale Internet operation (but it is essentially a protocol for Internet betting rather than lottery). It attempts to minimize the transactions between involved parties for security and efficiency reasons. The protocol mainly addresses Internet security and it focuses on resolution of conflicts among parties as well as prevention of collaboration among them towards forgery. Thus, it does not focus on the crux of the system, namely on the number generation process.

Finally, practical ideas and techniques on the frequently neglected but highly critical issue of generating and managing securely the "true" randomness necessary for various components of cryptographic applications can be found in [10] and the references contained therein, as well as Chapter 10 of the book of Ferguson and Schneier [7].

Our Design

The protocol we describe in this paper has been implemented in a real nationwide electronic lottery environment that requires *frequent* drawings per day with *strict* drawing times. Thus, the large number of expected players and the hard timing constraints essentially preclude the explicit participation of users in the number generation and winner identification processes. Our design is scalable, since it is a nationwide application that is alive. In contrast with all previous approaches, to build up people's trust in the electronic lottery we have done the following:

1. We focused on the core number generation process and our protocol incorporates several interacting cryptographic primitives that ensure the credibility of the process. Each element of the generation combines various independent technologies concurrently to assure **cryptographic robustness**.
2. We provided protection against various manipulations of the process assuring the necessary security level, so as to avoid a huge financial loss for the lottery organization if one manages to interfere with or prematurely learn the process. We used bit commitments, signatures and encryptions to protect various pieces of information and bind the results to the bidding data. We protected the process against premature or future manipulation by binding it to the system's state via a process we call **state stamping.**
3. We designed extensive real-time auditing facilities. We made sure that some independent processes will monitor/ audit other critical components as much as possible, so that actions can be verified after the fact due to logging, signing, etc.
4. We took into account performance (time constraint) requirements.
5. We incorporated security mechanisms (since cryptography alone is never a complete security solution). We isolated parts of the network and employed network security tools, and designed for independent actions and logs to take place. We also took care of physical and operational security.
6. In addition, since delays or cancellations of the drawings may damage the reputation of the lottery organization, there is a provision for replication (fault tolerance) at all system levels (hardware and software) in order to increase reliability and achieve high-availability.
7. We assured modularity, enabling the protocol to be suitable plug-in component in, e.g., as part of an Internet lotteries that also take care of many interacting parties such as banks, lottery organization, coupon sellers, etc.

In what follows, we will describe the protocol by describing its basic primitives and the way they interact with each other. In Section 2 we motivate and discuss the requirements posed by an electronic lottery design. In Section 3 we provide a design proposal to meet the set requirements. In Section 4 we provide a high-level functional description of the components and the drawing protocol used by the electronic lottery. In Section 5 we provide the details of the implementation of each of the components. Finally, in Section 6 we summarize the main feature of the electronic lottery protocol and discuss possible practical improvements and extensions of a real implementation of the protocol.

We believe that this work will serve as a starting point for triggering thoughts and proposals on how application-driven protocols for the production of random numbers should be designed, in terms of security, robustness and efficiency, for use in other electronic lottery settings and similar scenarios "where true pseudorandomness counts."

2   Operational Environment and Requirements

2.1   The Environment

The operational context in which the electronic lottery operates is the following (see Figure 1). The players submit their coupons (on which they mark their number choices) at one of 6000 lottery agencies. Then the agencies send (via telephone lines) the coupon data to the central computer of the lottery organization where the support software stores them in a special coupon file. Exactly 5 minutes before the predetermined time of the next the drawing, no more coupons are permitted in the system and the bidding stops. Note that in the future the agencies and phone lines can be augmented with Internet servers that collect coupons from individual Internet users in another lottery distribution channel (the rest of our mechanism constituting the back-end and result publication component stay as is).

At this stage, the electronic lottery is initiated by the central computer and produces the numbers at the exact time of the drawing, sending them over to the TV channel as well as to the central computer. Every element in the system has an independent backup and many channels are replicated. Various auditing and monitoring is performed on-line. Reliability is another issue we provide, which implies replication of components.

In more details, due to high-availability and security requirements, the electronic lottery is composed of three components: two computers, the generators, interconnected in a master-slave configuration so as the slave automatically takes over in case of failure of the master plus one computer, the verifier, that acts as an intermediate between these computers and the central computer. The generators are totally isolated from the environment and they only communicate with the verifier, to which they send the numbers plus other auditing information. Then the verifier checks the integrity of the drawing and if all checks are successful then the numbers can be safely transmitted to the central computer. Moreover, for auditing purposes, the generators send the numbers also to a printer and a computer monitor placed at a supervisor's office for cross-checking and they store them on CD-recorder and hard disk for later verification.

Finally we assure physical security. The electronic lottery system (i.e the two generators plus the verifier) is enclosed in a shielded room with biometric access control system which is under a 24-hour per day camera surveillance (and there is a plan for periodically updating the physical protection).

2.2   Sets of Requirements for the Electronic Lottery

The great financial risks involved in the building and operation of the electronic lottery necessitated a very careful consideration of all possible security aspects as well as environmental factors that may disturb the normal operation of the lottery (e.g. power and network failures).

Generally speaking, the main "operational requirements" placed on a system capable of supporting any lottery can be summarized in the following:

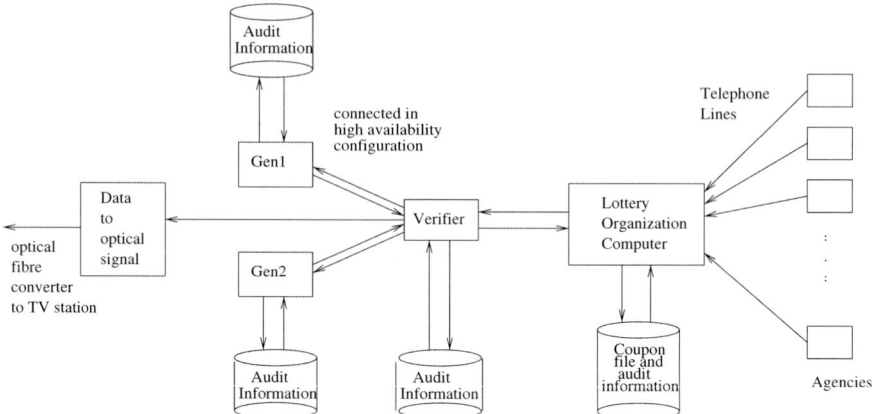

Fig. 1. An overview of the system

1. The produced numbers should obey the uniform distribution over their intended range.
2. It should be infeasible for anyone (either the lottery operator, the lottery designers or the players) to guess the next number of the lottery, given all the lottery history, with chances better than if the next number was to be chosen at random.
3. It should be infeasible for anyone (either the lottery operator, the lottery designers or the players) to interfere with the drawing mechanism and with the choice of winners (even after the drawn numbers are known and published). In case such an interference eventually occurs, then this fact is detectable.
4. The drawing mechanism should be designed so as to obey a number of standards and, in addition, there should also be a process through which it can be officially certified (by a lottery designated body) that these standards are met by the chosen mechanism.
5. The drawing mechanism should be under constant scrutiny (by a lottery designated body) so as to detect and rectify possible deviations from either of the above requirements or potential tampering with it.
6. The details of the operation of the drawing mechanism should be publicly available to people so as to ensure their trust and interest in the games. In addition, this ensures a publicly open lottery auditing protocol (which may be required by regulations).

Ensuring these requirements is accomplished (under a reasonable physical model) through the use of the traditional drawing mechanism of balls that are shuffled by some random physical process and then chosen from within an urn, where this entire process is performed publicly and with auditors present and is pre-authorized by a state authority. This appears to achieve all requirements set above plus people's satisfaction that the whole mechanism is trustworthy and fair to them.

The situation changes dramatically, however, if business requirements necessitate the use of electronic means as is our case. There are many reasons why one would prefer this option over the traditional drawing mechanism. For example, to increase players' interest for participation in lottery games, many lottery organizations (such as the one using the protocol we describe in this paper) desire to perform many drawings each day instead of the traditional end-of-the week drawing. This is done in KENO-like games where drawings may be performed as frequently as every 5 minutes, increasing the lottery organization's chances for profits. This is because people play more frequently since they are attracted by the fact that if the do not win at the current draw, they may well be winners at the next draw in a few minutes. Another reason for not using the traditional drawing mechanism could be the fact that the lottery organization desires the introduction of a variety of games with numbers drawn in different ways (e.g. repetitions allowed or not, different ranges, etc.), a thing that would require building many drawing machines with high cost and construction time. Indeed, in our case, the lottery organization desired the introduction of two *different* games, one with the selection of three numbers from 0 to 9 (repetitions allowed) and another one with the selection of 5 numbers from 1 to 35 (repetitions not allowed). Also, there was a requirement for four electronic drawings per day at predetermined times. In addition, for publicity and publication (as well as marketing) benefits, each drawing should be sent over to a private TV channel that displays the numbers in real time at the lower third of the screen. The publication method integrity is assured on-line. The numbers are also sent over to the computer that stores the played coupons so that the winner can be selected and various statistics calculated.

Finally, a very important requirement with regard to all the entities involved, was the *high-availability* of the electronic lottery. No delay or cancellation of a drawing was acceptable due to failures of the electronic lottery as this would jeopardize the success of the new games as well as the reputation of the entities.

From the above considerations, it is clear that traditional drawing mechanisms are costly and cumbersome, if not impossible, to use and support the business operational requirements.

Taking into account the above discussion on the "security and safety requirements" of the whole system, the security requirements for our application can be described more precisely as follows:

1. Confidentiality: Information should be disclosed only to the intended recipients and no leaks of information occur before predetermined time points. Confidentiality can be achieved through encryption methods as well as secure random number sources that prevent estimation of their evolution.
2. Integrity: No unauthorized changes should be made, both in stored and transmitted data. Integrity of data can be achieved through the use of computation of hash and MAC functions.
3. State stamping: The lottery outcome is a function of a given state representing all the coupons of the current drawing and the internal (randomly chosen) state of the lottery mechanism, some of it secret. The system should stamp the state using cryptographic tools so that no future modifications are possible without detection.

4. Availability: The system should be ready for operation any time it is needed and should not turn down authorized service requests (subject to given service/ performance requirements). Availability can be achieved through component and data path replication.
5. Accountability: All access to, or modification of, specific information in the system should be detected and, possibly, traced to specific sources (this also include identification schemes). Non-repudiation of an action is the lack of capability of an actor to deny an action, and as a security property, it is closely related to accountability. These requirements can be achieved using mechanisms of electronic signing and commitment.

In the next section we will provide the design of the electronic lottery and justify the design choices.

3   Design Considerations

In this section we will discuss the components of the solution to the drawing process. We explain how we met the security requirements, confidentiality, state stamping, integrity, availability and accountability described above. More specifically, we describe the specific electronic lottery choices we made, indicating for each of them the specific requirement it meets. We employed numerous cryptographic primitives and protocols at the low level of the generation making it robust according to the requirements.

3.1   Randomness Sources

One component of the confidentiality requirement concerns the use of a good source of random numbers. There are three approaches, other than the traditional one, for producing sequences of numbers: (i) Using an appropriate algorithmic scheme – *pseudorandom number generator*, (ii) Using some physical process such as, for example, semi-conductor noise – *truly random number generators*, and (iii) Using a combination of (i) and (ii). There is much debate going on as to which is the best approach. Approach (i) has been subjected to the criticism, that an algorithm has a limited, although huge, number of possible states and, as it follows a well defined set of steps, it may be amenable to some clever educated guess attack. Although the introduction of, the so called, *cryptographically secure* pseudo-random number generators can handle this criticism the fact remains that an algorithm is deterministic and, thus, its output can always be guessed in principle, given the initial state. Approach (ii) on the other hand receives the criticism that physical processes often obey specific distribution laws that may enable one to limit the range of possible future evolutions of a generator based on them. In addition, physical devices often malfunction or deviate from their initial statistical behavior depending on environmental factors such as temperature, humidity, magnetic fields etc. This may, also, enable one to easily interfere with the number generation process. In addition, physical randomness, if not backed-up correctly (for auditing purposes), is hard to reproduce and, thus, check appropriately. Finally, according to approach (iii), software-based pseudorandomness and truly random generators are both used (as a hybrid) in a way that amplifies their advantages and diminishes their disadvantages. It is exactly this approach that, we believe, is the most beneficial for designing a system for the needs of a lottery and this is the approach we followed and describe below. We also replicate generators of both types, and combine streams of independent generators to achieve cryptographic robustness, in case some method or technology fails.

Of course, approach (iii) alone is not, by itself, sufficient to guarantee that the lottery system obeys all the requirements. We still have to consider the exclusion of many possible threats such as post-betting, malicious intervention, system observation, system access protection and many more.

3.2 Seed Commitment and Reproduction of Received Numbers

An issue that arises when a drawing is performed is whether the seeds claimed to have been used by the generation process were actually used. Ensuring that the seeds were actually used, entails the use of a bit-commitment protocol and is related to the integrity and accountability requirements. The commitment is performed by the number generator and the related information is transmitted to the verifier that performs the necessary checking. This commits to a verifiable state, yet keeps the confidentiality of the seed to prevent premature leakage.

3.3 State Stamping: Prevention of Post-betting

A major requirement from the random number generation protocol was to be in position to detect post-betting, i.e. to detect whether a coupon was inserted into the coupon file after the current drawing is closed. This meets the integrity and accountability requirements as it guards against illicit coupon file modification. In addition, when this especially bad situation is detected, the protocol should be terminated immediately and report it, essentially canceling the current drawing. One way to detect post-betting is to use a fingerprint (hash value) of the coupon file after the bidding time is over and check that it still has the same value. If not, an error condition is raised and a supervisor is notified.

3.4 Seed Processing

We used the Naor-Reingold pseudorandom function (see [20]) for processing the combination of the seeds that are obtained from the physical random number generators with the hash value of the coupons file. The NR function is initially seeded with a strong random key. With the use of the NR function the resulting processed seeds is made not directly dependent on the on-line drawn physical bits, an act which guards against malfunctioning of the physical randomness sources by "rectifying" deviations (and makes the process independent of the manufacturers of the physical devices).

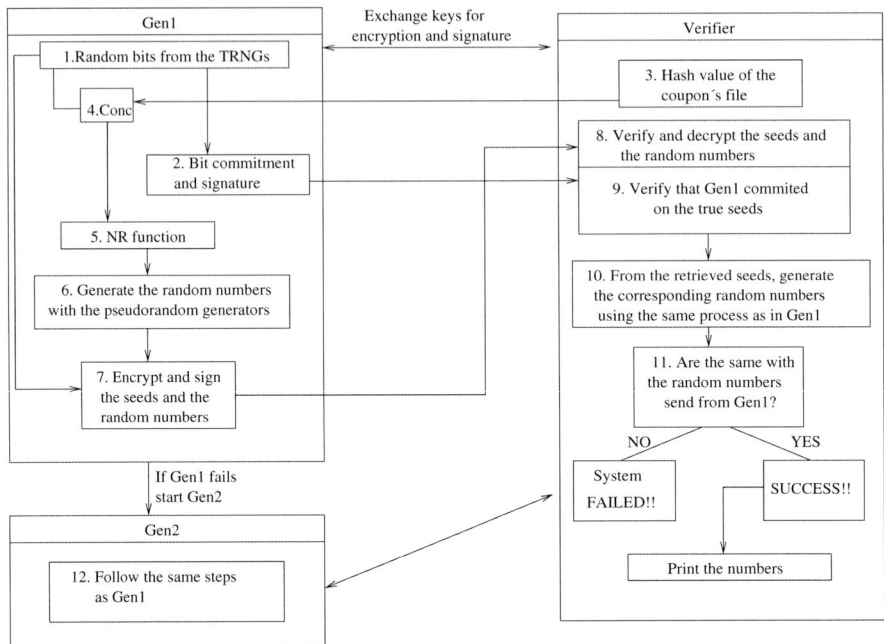

Fig. 2. The architecture of the random number generation system

3.5   Signing and Authenticating

To boost confidentiality and accountability, each time a drawing is performed the seeds and the produced numbers sent over from the generation source, should be signed by the source (using, e.g., a public key cryptographic scheme) and verified by the recipient. In this way, the source of the drawing is authenticated and the drawing can be considered valid.

4   A High-Level Description of the Protocol of the Electronic Lottery

Before we detail each component of the protocol, it will be useful to give a high-level description of these components as well as their interaction as summarized in Figure 2. The protocol is based on two basic interacting agents: the Generator and the Verifier. The Generator is replicated for high-availability purposes. (Of course, other components can be replicated as well, but this is easy to do since they are mainly general purpose computers whereas the generator is a complex and highly secured component that we replicated.) First, the Generator and the Verifier execute a key-exchange protocol in order to end-up sharing a secret key to enable secure communication between them. They also generate a private/public key pair for signature purposes. At this point, the Generator starts idling and waits for a drawing initiation signal from the Verifier. The Verifier knows the times of the daily drawings since they are communicated to it by the central computer. Only coarse time synchronization is needed since there is enough time for all time-based operations in the system, since the mechanism operates four times a day. The following are the steps in generation (see Figure 2):

1. Upon initiation, the Generator first draws a sequence of truly random bits as seeds from a set of physical random numbers sources (reseeding occurs at sufficiently frequent time intervals).

2. Then the Generator executes a bit-commitment protocol on the seed bit sequence and signs it. The packet that results from these actions is sent over to the Verifier. As a result the seeds are committed to and the commitment is signed.

3. The Verifier, in turn, gives the Generator the hash of the file of coupons.

4. Next, the Generator mixes the random bits produced by the physical random number generators with the hash value of the file containing all the coupons played up to the allowed time (contained in the coupon file) in order to inextricably bind together the seed with the coupon file. This mixing can be effected by simply concatenating the random bits with the hash value given by the Verifier, essentially "freezing" the coupon file (this is the state stamping for post-betting prevention). Since the randomness is committed to and signed (and verified) and the coupon file hash is a commitment to the file, this is a state stamping which is present and logged at the Verifier.

5. The first portion of the initially produced (i.e. bits from the physical randomness s ources with concatenated hash value of the coupon file) bit-sequence is then fed through the Naor-Reingold (pseudorandom) function as a post-processing precaution to further decouple any direct biases of the random sources (provided by external manufacturers) from totally influencing the randomness (based on separation of duties principle). The result is interpreted as a bit stream.

6. The bit stream result of the previous stage is XORed with a second portion of the initially produced bit-sequence (to mix a physical stream and a pseudorandom stream for cryptographic robustness). Then, this final bit sequence is used as the seed to a set of software based pseudorandom generators, in order to stretch the seed and assure that enough random numbers are generated. In our protocol we are currently using algebraic as well as block cipher based generators. We employed the algebraic pseudorandom number generators RSA and BBS (which have a proof of security in the literature) and two generators based on the block ciphers DES and AES. These generators can operate alone or in various output combinations. Although we have used the specific generators (as they are widely known or accepted within the cryptographic community) any number or type of secure software random number generators could be used instead. Note that basing our final generation on variety of functions adds to cryptographic robustness.

7. Then the Generator executes a bit de-commitment (opens the initial physical random seed bits). The seed and the numbers are encrypted and their encrypted form is signed. The packet that results from these actions is sent over to the Verifier and the Generator stops.

8. The Verifier first authenticates the packet (using the public key of the Generator), decrypts the received packet and recovers the numbers plus the seed presumably used by the Generator to produce these numbers.
9. Then, the Verifier checks that the Generator has committed to the sent seed.
10. Then, the Verifier checks that the seed was used properly by repeating the same generation process used by the Generator and interpreting the outcome in the range of numbers to announce.
11. If the produced numbers match the numbers sent by the Generator then the drawing is considered successful and the drawing is completed by announcements of the winning numbers. This check against the commitment and the hash of the file of coupons verifies that no interference occurred in the drawing process in the Generator. If the numbers do not match the numbers sent, then an alarm is raised, the drawing is canceled and the Verifier initiates it again (or some other action is taken to assure integrity and continuity). In this way the Verifier acts as an auditor of the entire drawing process.
12. If the system fails the Verifier activates the second Generator, that repeats the process of the first one.

Finally, we also included a provision for *on-line statistical testing* that estimate the entropy of sources and long sequences of (i) the produced random numbers, and (ii) the hardware random number generators. Algorithms implemented in software need only be checked once, at the system installation phase (assuming the entire system is not being changed since no one gets access to it). However, given the fact that physical random number generators are vulnerable to environmental conditions or even subject to aging and physical malfunctions, one can never be certain that they are operating properly once installed on a computer. A very informative discussion on testing (on-line as well as off-line) physical random number generators can be found in [23] where a number of tests are prescribed for such generators able to meet their special requirements. These considerations discussed in that paper are already incorporated in the German AIS 31 national standard (as well as prerequisite for device approval) for testing physical random number generators.

5   Implementation Choices

5.1   Randomness Sources

The software random number generators. Our decision to incorporate several different algorithms for the generation of the numbers was to base the whole design on generators relying on different principles of operation and security so as to increase the difficulty of attacks aiming at guessing the number sequence. Different security principles imply that an attacker would face more difficulties in guessing as it would be necessary to break all of these principles. All the cryptographic primitives that will be described are fully reconfigurable in terms of their key sizes (i.e. the sizes modifiable at the implementation level). These sizes can be changed sufficiently frequently, depending on cryptanalytic advances.

We included two algebraic generators. One of them, BBS was proposed by Blum, Blum, and Shub (see [3]) is one of the most frequently used cryptographically strong pseudorandom number generators. The second generator involved in the random number generation protocol is the RSA/Rabin generator and it is based on the RSA function (see in [1]). These works have shown proof of security, but these are typically too slow in many applications, but we had enough time to include them in our mix.

The other two secure generators we used are based on the encryption algorithms DES and AES which are more often used. We used the implementations provided by version 2.5.3 of the mcrypt library (available at [18]). The key sizes were 64 bits for DES (56 bits effective) and 192 bits for AES. In order to have number generators from the encryption algorithms, DES and AES are used in their CFB (Ciphertext Feed-Back) mode and they operate as follows: an initial random vector is constructed from a seed processed as described in Section 4 and then DES and AES are invoked as many times as the bytes we wish to generate. In particular, every time the encryption function is called, a byte with all zeros is encrypted (always in CFB mode, which means re-encrypting the ciphertext) and the encryption result is the output of the generator. The cryptographic strength of the two generators is based on their encryption counterparts assuming the entire block is unpredictable.

We further employed two techniques that are used to fortify and increase variability of weak generators (even though our generators are strong). One of them employs two shuffling algorithms for combining the output of the random number generators: *Algorithm M*, proposed by MacLaren and Marsaglia [15] and *Algorithm B* proposed by Bays and Durham [2]. Algorithm M takes as input two sequences X_n and Y_n, and outputs a more random sequence. The algorithm actually is shuffling the sequence X_n using elements of the sequence Y_n as indexes into the sequence X_n. Thus, the elements of the new sequence are the same with those of X_n but in different order. Algorithm B is similar to M, but it requires only one sequence as input. The output is, again, a shuffled instance of the input. Both algorithms are described in detail in Knuth's book [11].

Another technique for achieving extended variability in the lottery is to combine the four generators (which are viewed as "independent functions") using the bit-wise XOR operation, and to allow the protocol to swap, periodically (according to some predetermined internal schedule), to different sub-set combinations of the generation of the random numbers.

Physical random number generators. The seeds of any software random number generator must, eventually, be drawn from a physical source of randomness. After considering the various physical sources of randomness within a computer (e.g. /dev/random in LINUX, fluctuations in hard disk access times, timing crystal frequency jitter, etc.) and evaluating the trade-off between easiness in using and quality of output, it was decided to use commercial hardware generators known to pass a number of demanding statistical test (e.g. DIEHARD). Moreover, it was important to include more than one physical sources (with outputs XORed) as it is not uncommon to have, after some time, harmful deviations in the physical characteristics of the devices from which noise is drawn. These fluctuations, in turn, may cause the appearance of detectable biases in the produced number sequences. XORing, however, a biased physical source with a good one helps decreasing the bias.

The component of the implementation responsible for physical randomness generation is actually comprised of three separate hardware-based random number generators: (i) One based on the phase differences of the clocks of the computer's motherboard. These differences are tapped by the function VonNeumannBytes(), written by Adam L. Young, which produces a stream of random bytes based on these phase differences. As their authors state, this function is based on truerand() by M. Blaze, and J. Lacy, D. Mitchell, and W. Schell [14] (ii) A commercial device placed on one of the ISA slots of a computer that produces random bits on demand via appropriate system calls: this device is the ZRANDOM random number generator built by of the German company Westphal Electronics (for product overview, consult [25]), and (iii) The commercial device SG100, which is a hardware random number generator connected to the serial port of the computer. It is provided by the Swedish company Protego Information AB (for product overview consult [21]). We used three sources of physical randomness for increased security and in order to guard against malfunction of any one of them.

5.2   State Stamping

We needed to assure that the drawing is based on a given random seed independent of the coupons, yet that no modification of state would be acceptable. A simple way to meet this requirement was to mix the coupon file as is with the truly random (and committed to) seeds drawn from the hardware devices and *then* drive the software generators. As the coupon file is, generally, too big to be combined in a usable way with the seeds drawn from the physical random number generators, we used its much smaller hash value instead (see Figure 2, Gen1). The hash function we used is RIPEMD-160 (see [5]). The Verifier can later check that the right random bits (committed to earlier) were used in this mixing. The commitment makes the mixing non-malleable in the sense that the system's state cannot be changed given the record at the Verifier.

5.3   Seed Processing

As we mentioned above (Section 3.4), we used the Naor-Reingold function, or NR for short, for processing the seeds to assure that whatever biases still exist, a pseudorandom function will process the random seed. (This assumes that we made sure at the start that seeding the NR function key is done with very strong random bits). The seed processing via a pseudorandom function seed can be common to the Generator and the Verifier who both possess the NR key. The Verifier can privately make sure the function was applied correctly. This check can also be done via a non-interactive zero-knowledge proof. We further note that an alternative approach to this stage can be the use of the more recent "verifiable (pseudo)random functions" as defined in [19], where audit of the correctness of a pseudorandom function can be checked as a public verification utility.

Regarding the NR function, a key for it is a tuple $\langle P, Q, g, \boldsymbol{a} \rangle$, where P is a large prime, Q is a large prime divisor of $P - 1$, g is an element of order Q in Z_P^* and $\boldsymbol{a} = \langle a_0, a_1, \ldots a_n \rangle$ is an uniformly distributed sequence of $n + 1$ elements in Z_Q. For every input x of n bits, $x = x_1 \ldots x_n$, the NR function is defined as:

$$\tilde{f}_{P,Q,g,\boldsymbol{a}} = (g^{a_0})^{\prod_{x_i=1} a_i} \bmod P.$$

In our implementation, the size of P is 1000 bits and the size of Q is 200 bits. Note that we applied a pseudorandom function for this both randomizing the result and so that this serves as a commitment that based on its inputs its outputs can be checked if and when an internal audit is required (one can verify the output based on given inputs, directly relying on the security of the verifier. As mentioned above, alternatively, audit can be achieved in a zero-knowledge fashion, given the NR function's public description). Since the NR function is pseudorandom, revealing input-output relationships does not hurt its security in this case. The portion processed via a pseudorandom function, is combined with a physical random source portion in order to take advantage of physical randomness as well, in case it is the best source we have.

5.4   Encryption, Signing and Authenticating

The Generator and the Verifier, are each equipped with an RSA key pair. At start-up they construct this pair and exchange their public keys. Then the commitments, the sets of numbers, as well as the seeds, that originate from the Generator are first encrypted and then signed using the shared secret key. This keeps any transmission private within the mechanism as a layer of protection. Before the encryption, however, we used the *Simplified Optimal Asymmetric Encryption Padding*, or SAEP [4]. With the SAEP protocol, a padding on the bits of the message packet is performed aiming at achieving semantic security and chosen ciphertext security (in the random oracle model). Note that typically, a hybrid encryption is used in applications, but given our performance requirements and the specific nature of our messages within the application, we can afford using public key encryption. A possible key size for the encryption is 1000 bits and for the signature 2000 bits. The number of zeros in the SAEP protocol can be equal to 100 and the random number required can, also, have 100 bits. Note that signatures are performed over committed encrypted (thus random) values. The Verifier, after receiving the packet, decrypts it using the same secret key and verifies that it originated from the legal Generator. This avoids the risks associated with authentication through, e.g., IP address checking, password phrase exchange etc. The RSA pairs used for signing can be refreshed after a drawing is completed. This is perhaps an exaggerated precaution due to the large key sizes. In general, refreshment can be less granular. Note that a new public RSA key can be certified by being signed with the old keys this achieves forward secrecy (namely, when the system is compromised past signatures are valid).

5.5   Seed Commitment and Reproduction of Received Numbers

In order to ensure that the Generator actually used the seeds it claims to have used for the current drawing, the Generator and the Verifier execute a bit-commitment protocol based on the RSA encryption scheme and the hash function RIPEMD-160. After this processing, the commitment is sent to the Verifier and then the Generator can get the hash of the file of coupons and then the Generator produces and sends to the Verifier the seed and the resulting numbers of the current drawing. Upon receipt of the numbers, the Verifier uses the seed to which the Generator committed itself to in order to reproduce the received drawn numbers. If the reproduced numbers match the ones sent by the Generator, the numbers are deemed legal and are made public. Otherwise, the protocol stops and issues a warning.

6   Discussion

In this paper we have described a general protocol for the support of a national electronic lottery system. To the best of our knowledge this is the first publicly described system focusing on the core number generation and auditing process.

We have argued why electronic lotteries are an exceptionally challenging type of financial applications, and that there are many factors that should be considered for a robust protocol designed to support an electronic lottery. The generation of sequences that are exceptionally difficult to guess is only one such factor, but one should take measures against many possible attacks on the generation as well as on the entire system operation and management process.

References

1. W. Alexi, B. Chor, O. Goldreich, and C. Schnorr, RSA and Rabin Functions: Certain Parts are as Hard as the Whole, *SIAM J. Computing* **17(2)**, pp. 194–209, April 1988.
2. C. Bays and S.D. Durham, Improving a Poor Random Number Generator, *ACM Trans. Math. Software* **2(1)**, pp. 59–64, March 1976.
3. L. Blum, M. Blum, and M. Shub, A Simple Unpredictable Pseudo-Random Generator, *SIAM J. Computing* **15(2)**, pp. 364-383, May 1986.
4. D. Boneh, Simplified OAEP for the RSA and Rabin Functions, in: *Proc. Crypto '01*, LNCS 2139, pp. 275–291, Springer-Verlag, 2001.
5. H. Dobbertin, A. Bosselaers, and B. Preneel, RIPEMD-160: A Strengthened Version of RIPEMD, in: *Proc. Fast Software Encryption 1996*, LNCS 1039, pp. 71–82, Springer Verlag, 1996.
6. D.M. Goldschlag and S.G. Stubblebine, Publicly Verifiable Lotteries: Applications of Delaying Functions, in: *Proc. Financial Cryptography 98*, LNCS 1465, pp. 214–226, Springer Verlag, 1998.
7. N. Ferguson and B. Schneier, *Practical Cryptography*, John Wiley & Sons, 2003.
8. M.P Ford and D.J. Ford, Investigation of GAUSS' Random Number Generators, a report prepared for Aptech Systems, Inc., *FORWARD Computing and Control Pty. Ltd.*, NSW Australia, 2001.

9. C. Hall and B. Schneier, Remote Electronic Gambling, in: *Proc. 13th ACM Annual Computer Security Applications Conference*, pp. 227-230, 1997.

10. M. Jakobsson, E.A.M. Shriver, B. Hillyer, A. Juels, A Practical Secure Physical Random Bit Generator, in: *Proc. of the 5th ACM Conference on Computer and Communications Security 1998*, pp. 103–111, 1998.

11. D.E. Knuth, *Seminumerical Algorithms*, Third Edition, Addison-Wesley, 1997.

12. K. Kobayashi, H. Morita, M. Hakuta, and T. Nakanowatari, An Electronic Soccer Lottery System that Uses Bit Commitment, in: *IEICE Trans. Inf. & Syst.*, Vol. E 83-D, No. 5, pp. 980–987, 2000.

13. E. Kushilevitz and T. Rabin, Fair e-Lotteries and e-Casinos, in *Proc. CT-RSA 2001*, LNCS 2020, pp. 100–109, Springer Verlag, 2001.

14. J.B. Lacy, D.P. Mitchell, and W.M. Schell, CryptoLib: Cryptography in Software, in *Proc. 4th USENIX Security Symposium*, USENIX Assoc., pp. 237–246, 1993.

15. M.D. Maclaren and G. Marsaglia, Uniform Random Number Generators, *JACM* **12(1)**, pp. 83–89, January 1965.

16. G. Marsaglia, A current view of random number generators, keynote address in: *Proc. 16th Symposium on the Interface between Computer Science and Statistics*, pp. 3–10, 1985.

17. G. Marsaglia, DIEHARD: A battery of tests for random number generators, available at http://stat.fsu.edu/~geo/diehard.html

18. Mcrypt cryptographic library: ftp://mcrypt.hellug.gr/pub/crypto/mcrypt

19. S. Micali, M. Rabin, and S. Vadhan, Verifiable Random Functions, in: *Proc 40th IEEE Symp. on Foundations of Cumputer Science*, pp. 120–130, 1999.

20. M. Naor and O. Reingold, Number-theoretic constructions of efficient pseudorandom functions, *Proc. 38th IEEE Symp. on Found. of Computer Science*, 1997.

21. Protego, product information, http://www.protego.se/sg100_en.htm

22. K. Sako, Implementation of a digital lottery server on WWW, in: *Proc. CQRE '99*, LNCS 1740, pp. 101–108, Springer Verlag, 1999.

23. W. Schindler and W. Killmann, Evaluation criteria for true (physical) random number generators used in cryptographic applications, in *Proc. 4th International Workshop on Cryptographic Hardware amd Embedded Systems (CHES 2002)*, pp. 431–449, 2002.

24. P. Syverson, Weakly Secret Bit Commitment: Applications to Lotteries and Fair Exchange, in: *Proc. IEEE Computer Security Foundations Workshop (CSFW11)*, pp. 2–13, 1998.

25. Westphal Electronics, product information, http://www.westphal-electronic.de

26. J. Zhou and C. Tan, Playing Lottery on the Internet, in: *Proc. ICICS 2001*, LNCS 2229, pp. 189-201, Springer Verlag, 2001.

Identity-Based Chameleon Hash
and Applications

Giuseppe Ateniese and Breno de Medeiros

Department of Computer Science
The Johns Hopkins University
{ateniese,breno}@cs.jhu.edu

Abstract. Chameleon signatures are non-interactive signatures based on a hash-and-sign paradigm, and similar in efficiency to regular signatures. The distinguishing characteristic of chameleon signatures is that their are non-transferable, with only the designated recipient capable of asserting its validity. In this paper, we introduce the first identity-based chameleon hash function. The general advantages of identity-based cryptography over conventional schemes relative to key distribution are even more pronounced in a chameleon hashing scheme, because the owner of a public key does not necessarily need to retrieve the associated secret key. We use the identity-based chameleon hashing scheme to build the id-based chameleon signature and a novel sealed-bid auction scheme that is robust, communication efficient (bidders send a single message), and secure under a particular trust model.

Keywords: Digital signatures, secure hash functions, chameleon hashing, sealed-bid auctions

1 Introduction

Chameleon signature schemes were introduced in [1]. A distinguishing feature of chameleon signature schemes is that they are *non-transferable,* i.e. a signature issued to a designated recipient cannot be validated by another party. While not universally verifiable, chameleon signatures provide *non-repudiation*: If presented with a false signature claim, the signer can prove that the signature is forged, while incapable of doing so for legitimate claims. Accordingly, the signer's refusal to invalidate a signature is considered equivalent to her affirmation that the signature is valid.

Unlike *undeniable signatures* [2–6], which also provide non-repudiation and non-transferability, chameleon signatures are non-interactive protocols. More precisely, the signer can generate the chameleon signature without interacting with the designated recipient, and the latter will be able to verify the signature without interacting with the former. Similarly, if presented with a forged signature, the signer can deny its validity by revealing certain values. These values will revoke the original signature and the forged one simultaneously, and the revocation can be universally verified. In other words, the forged-signature denial

A. Juels (Ed.): FC 2004, LNCS 3110, pp. 164–180, 2004.

protocol is also non-interactive. There also exist non-interactive versions of undeniable signatures [7]. Chameleon signatures are considerably less complex, at the sacrifice of not conferring the signer the ability to engage in non-transferable secondary proofs of signature (non-)validity.

Chameleon signatures are based on the well established hash-and-sign paradigm, where a *chameleon hash function* is used to compute the cryptographic message digest. A chameleon hash function is a trapdoor one-way hash function: Without knowledge of the associated trapdoor, the chameleon hash function is resistant to the computation of pre-images and of collisions. However, with knowledge of the trapdoor, collisions are efficiently computable.

When a chameleon hash function is used within a hash-and-sign signature scheme, it permits the party with knowledge of the trapdoor to re-use the signature value to authenticate other messages of choice. In particular, if the hash function is part of the recipient's public key, then the signature is publicly verifiable by no one other than the intended recipient. On the other hand, if the recipient re-uses the hash value to obtain a signature on a second message, the signer can prove knowledge of a hash collision, since the original signed message and the claimed signed message have the same hash value. Because computing hash collisions is infeasible for the signer, possession of such a collision is seen as proof of forgery by the signature recipient.

1.1   ID-Based Chameleon Hashing

In this paper, we propose the first ID-based chameleon hashing scheme. ID-based cryptography is an alternate form of public-key cryptography that does not use certification authorities or certificates. Instead, an ID-based scheme defines "identity strings", which are nothing more than a special string format to describe real entities (persons or machines). For instance, an identity string could be an e-mail address, a URL, a person's address, or any other unambiguous reference. The public keys are derived from these identity strings by means of a public algorithm, which is part of the scheme description. Any entity that can be described with an identity string (as specified in the particular scheme) has automatically a public key. Since the identity string is a 'natural' way to refer to the entity, anyone who knows the entity will also be able to compute the entity's public key, without having to look it up in a key distribution center. Instead, the owner of the key is responsible for contacting an escrow server to obtain the secret key associated to his public key. Identity-based cryptography was originally introduced in the classical paper [8], which described id-based identification and signature schemes. Despite several efforts, id-based encryption eluded researchers until recently [9, 10].

As with other cryptographic primitives, such as encryption and regular digital signatures, there are considerable advantages to be gained from employing an ID-based chameleon hash scheme over a regular scheme. For instance, a signer can sign a message to an intended recipient, without having to first retrieve the recipient's certificate; in fact, the signer can sign a message to the recipient before the recipient has registered with the system and obtained the secret key.

This reduces the negative network effects that make it hard to deploy public key infrastructures.

One limitation of the original chameleon signature scheme ([1]) is that signature forgery results in the signer recovering the recipient's trapdoor information. Such feature has some advantages: For instance, since with the knowledge of the trapdoor the signer can compute other collisions, she can prove knowledge of a collision *without revealing the original message signed*. This *message hiding* permits the signer to deny forged messages without the onus of confirming the original signature. However, the signer can use this trapdoor information to deny *other* signatures given to the recipient, whether or not the recipient tried to re-use the corresponding hash values. In the worst case, the signer could collaborate with other individuals to invalidate any signatures which were designated to be verified by the same public key. This creates a strong disincentive for the recipient to forge signatures, partially undermining the concept of non-transferability. If a third party is aware of the potential damage to the recipient that would result from the forgery of a signature, she will likely believe the authenticity of a recipient's claims.

Non-transferability is more convincing if the scheme is such that forgery of a hash value does not compromise the long-term key of the recipient. Clearly, this can be accomplished in any chameleon hashing scheme if the public keys are changed often. However, one now has a key distribution problem. The signer must be able to retrieve the most recent public key for the recipient, most likely by interacting with the recipient itself. The protocol then ceases to be non-interactive, at least in a practical sense.

The scheme we present permits the signer to use a different public key for each transaction with a recipient, without having to retrieve a new certificate: The signer concatenates the recipient's identification information with a string which uniquely identifies the transaction. Notice that the recipient *does not need to retrieve the associated secret key to verify the signature's validity. Only if the recipient wishes to compute a collision and a forgery does he need to recover the secret key.* Clearly, the key escrowing function is provided by the scheme manager for the bona fide reason that non-transferability, i.e., the ability of the recipient to forge signatures, is a property of the scheme that protects the legitimate signer. We remark that collision-forgery still results in the trapdoor information – now associated to a single transaction key – being recovered. Therefore, if the recipient produces a hash collision, the signer may deny the original message by providing a different collision, still enjoying the message hiding property. She will not be capable, however, of denying signatures on any other messages.

1.2   Our Results

To summarize, chameleon signature schemes introduced in [1] have the following properties.

- Non-repudiation: The signer cannot deny legitimate signature claims.
- Non-transferability or non-universal verifiability.

- Non-interactive.
- Practical and efficient: The algorithms have costs comparable with those of standard signature schemes.
- Semantic security: The hash value does not reveal information about the message signed.
- Message hiding: The signer does not have to reveal the original message to deny the validity of a forgery.
- Convertibility: A variant of the chameleon signature can be transformed into a regular signature by the signer.

The scheme we present in this paper enjoys all the attributes above, with the added characteristics of being ID-based:

- ID-based: Parties can sign messages for recipients, even if these recipients do not yet have the corresponding secret keys. Also, signers do not need to retrieve public key certificates of the intended recipient.
- Lightweight key distribution/refreshment: Public keys do not need to be distributed after a refreshment. Secret key retrieval is optional for recipients.
- Stronger non-transferability: The penalty for the recipient for engaging in forgery can be restricted to the loss of the original signature.

We describe in later sections some applications which make use of these extra properties of the ID-based scheme. These applications are not meant to be the only motivation for the primitive we are introducing, but only illustrative examples of its potential uses.

2   ID-Based Chameleon Hashing

We assume that all system users are identifiable by a bit-string easily derivable from public knowledge about the individual. For instance, it could be the user's e-mail address, augmented by some information such as an expiration-date. We call such a string an *identity* string. Formally, an ID-based chameleon hashing scheme is defined by a family of efficiently computable algorithms:

Setup: A trusted party, the key escrow, runs this efficient, probabilistic algorithm to generate a pair of keys $\mathcal{SK}$ and $\mathcal{PK}$ defining the scheme. It publishes $\mathcal{PK}$ and keeps $\mathcal{SK}$ secret. The input to this algorithm is a security parameter(s).

Extract: An efficient, deterministic algorithm that, on inputs $\mathcal{SK}$ and an identity string S, outputs the trapdoor information B associated to the identity.

Hash: An efficient, probabilistic algorithm that, on inputs $\mathcal{PK}$, an identity string S, and a message m, outputs a hash value h.

Forge: An efficient algorithm that, on inputs $\mathcal{PK}$, an identity string S, the trapdoor information B associated with S (i.e., the output of **Extract**($\mathcal{SK}, S$)), a message m', and a hash value h of a message m, outputs a sequence of random bits that correspond to a valid computation of **Hash**($\mathcal{PK}, S, m'$) yielding the target value h.

Repeating a computation of the hash function involves knowledge of the random choices made by the algorithm. We use also the notation $\mathsf{Hash}(S, m, r)$ to denote the *deterministic* algorithm that takes as inputs an identity string, a message and a string of random bits. (This notation leaves implicit the public key of the trusted party.) In practice, the **Forge** algorithm needs as input the random string r leading to a valid computation of $h = \mathsf{Hash}(S, m, r)$ and then can output a second $r' \neq r$ such that also $h = \mathsf{Hash}(S, m', r')$. We denote the deterministic algorithm by $\mathsf{Forge}(S, B, m, r, h, m')$, where $B = \mathsf{Extract}(\mathcal{SK}, S)$.

2.1   Security Requirements

In establishing the security of a chameleon hashing scheme, one may consider vulnerabilities against different attacks. A total break would be an attack resulting in the recovery of the secret key $\mathcal{SK}$ of the trusted party. This would permit the attacker to obtain the trapdoor information associated to any given identity string.

A lesser powerful attack model involves extracting the trapdoor information of some identity string, not necessarily a meaningful string, chosen by the attacker, i.e., an existential attack on the extract protocol. In this case, the string very probably does not correspond to the identity of any real-world party. Such an attack is dangerous inasmuch as it can lead to an advantage in forging hash collisions for hash values published by real-world entities.

Any attack is said to be successful if it accomplishes *collision forgery*.

Definition 1. (Collision forgery): *A collision-forgery strategy is an efficient, probabilistic algorithm that, given identity string S, message m, and random bits r, outputs another message m' and random bits r', such that $\mathsf{Hash}(S, m, r) = \mathsf{Hash}(S, m', r')$, with non-negligible probability.*

We say that the hashing scheme is *secure against existential collision forgery by passive attacks* if no collision-forgery strategy against it exists. However, to model an active attacker that could compromise various users and obtain their secrets, we must also allow oracle queries to the **Extract**($\cdot$) algorithm as part of the collision-forgery strategy. (Clearly, querying **Extract**($\cdot$) on the identity string of the target is not permitted.)

Definition 2. (Resistance to collision forgery by active attacks): *Let S be a target identity string. Let m be a target message. The chameleon hashing scheme is secure against (existential) collision forgery by active attacks if, for all four-tuples of non-constant polynomials $f_1(\cdot)$, $f_2(\cdot)$, $f_3(\cdot)$, $f_4(\cdot)$, and for large enough k, there is no probabilistic algorithm A which runs in time less than $f_1(k)$, makes at most $f_2(k)$ queries to an **Extract**($\cdot$) oracle (on identity strings other than S), and succeeds with probability larger than $\frac{1}{f_3(k)}$ in computing integers r and r', and binary string m', where $m' \neq m$, such that $\mathsf{Hash}(S, m, r) = \mathsf{Hash}(S, m', r')$, where $\mathsf{Hash}(\cdot)$ is an instance of the scheme with security parameter $f_4(k)$.*

The chameleon hashing scheme must also be semantically secure. From the hash value it is infeasible to determine which message is likely to have resulted in such value by an application of the hash algorithm.

Definition 3. (Semantic security): *The chameleon hashing scheme is said to be semantically secure if, for all identity strings S, and all pairs of messages m and m', the probability distributions of the random variables* Hash(S, m, r) *and* Hash(S, m', r) *are computationally indistinguishable.*

Note that the semantic security of a chameleon hashing scheme implies the non-transferability of the corresponding chameleon signature scheme.

3   The Scheme

Let τ and κ be security parameters. The scheme fixes a secure hash function $\mathcal{H} : \{0,1\}^* \rightarrow \{0,1\}^{2\tau}$, mapping strings of arbitrary length to strings of fixed length 2τ. Reasonable choices for an implementation of the scheme are $\tau = 80$ and SHA-1 for $\mathcal{H}(\cdot)$.

The setup algorithm is similar to an RSA key generation step. The trusted party T generates two prime numbers p and q in the set $\{2^{\kappa-1}, \ldots, 2^{\kappa} - 1\}$. Let $n = pq$. The bit-length of n, $\ell(n)$, is no less than 2κ. Let $\mathcal{C} : \{0,1\}^* \rightarrow \{0, \cdots, 2^{2\kappa-1}\}$ be a secure deterministic hash-and-encode scheme mapping arbitrary bit-strings to integers less than n. For instance, it is possible to use the deterministic version of EMSA-PSS encoding defined in [11, 12][1]. T then generates a random prime integer v s.t. $v > 2^{2\tau}$, and such that $\text{GCD}(v, (p-1)(q-1)) = 1$, i.e., v is relatively prime to the order $\phi(n)$ of the multiplicative residues modulo n. Applying the extended Euclidean algorithm for the GCD, T computes w and z such that $wv + z(p-1)(q-1) = 1$.

T's public key is (n, v). Its secret key is (p, q, w).

We can now describe the extraction algorithm. Let S be the identity string associated to some party. First we apply the deterministic hash-and-encode scheme to obtain the element $J = \mathcal{C}(S)$ in $\mathbf{Z}_n$. The secret key is extracted as $B = J^w \bmod n$. Notice that being able to compute B from S should be infeasible. In particular, if $\mathcal{C}$ is chosen as the EMSA-PSS encoding, then B is a *secure* RSA signature on the string S, under the public key (n, v).

The Hash$(\cdot)$ algorithm is:

$$\text{Hash}(S, m, r) = J^{\mathcal{H}(m)} r^v \bmod n,$$

where, again, $\mathcal{H}(\cdot)$ is the secure hash function, and $J = \mathcal{C}(S)$.

The Forge algorithm is:

$$\text{Forge}(S, B, m, r, h, m') = r' = rB^{\mathcal{H}(m) - \mathcal{H}(m')} \bmod n.$$

---

[1] Clearly, any deterministic encoding method would suffice. However, EMSA-PSS is recommended because the security of its deterministic version (when `seedLen=0` [11]) is shown to be *loosely* reducible to the security of the RSA function in the random oracle model.

Note indeed that

$$\begin{aligned}
\mathsf{Hash}(S, m', r') &= J^{\mathcal{H}(m')} r'^v \\
&= J^{\mathcal{H}(m')} r^v B^{v(\mathcal{H}(m) - \mathcal{H}(m'))} \\
&= J^{\mathcal{H}(m')} J^{vw(\mathcal{H}(m) - \mathcal{H}(m'))} r^v \\
&= J^{\mathcal{H}(m')} J^{\mathcal{H}(m) - \mathcal{H}(m')} r^v \\
&= J^{\mathcal{H}(m)} r^v \\
&= \mathsf{Hash}(S, m, r).
\end{aligned}$$

3.1   Security Analysis

As remarked above, the extraction algorithm requires knowledge of the trapdoor; obtaining the secret key from the private key without knowledge of the trapdoor requires forgery of a *secure* RSA signature. We now extend this argument to the other security requirements.

Theorem 1. *The chameleon hashing scheme is resistant to forgery under active attacks, provided that the* secure *RSA signature scheme is similarly resistant.*

The proof is simple, so we sketch it here. Given a collision, $\mathsf{Hash}(S, m, r) = \mathsf{Hash}(S, m', r')$, it is possible to extract the secret key B associated to the public key $J = \mathcal{C}(S)$.

$$J^{\mathcal{H}(m)} r^v = J^{\mathcal{H}(m')} r'^v \Longrightarrow (r'/r)^v = J^{\mathcal{H}(m) - \mathcal{H}(m')} \Longrightarrow r'/r = B^{\mathcal{H}(m) - \mathcal{H}(m')}. \quad (1)$$

Now, each hash value is the binary representation of a positive integer of value smaller than $2^{2\tau}$, and so the absolute value of $\Delta = \mathcal{H}(m) - \mathcal{H}(m')$ is also smaller than $2^{2\tau}$. Since v is a prime integer larger than $2^{2\tau}$, it follows that these values are relatively prime, i.e. $\gcd(\Delta, v) = 1$. Using the Extending Euclidean algorithm for the GCD, one computes α and β such that $\alpha \Delta + \beta v = 1$. B can now be extracted:

$$(r'/r)^\alpha J^\beta = B^{\alpha \Delta + \beta v} = B. \quad (2)$$

Recall that he secret key B is a *secure* RSA signature on the identity string S, as remarked above. Hence, being able to compute collision forgeries for target strings implies in the capability of computing *secure* RSA signatures on messages of choice. $\square$

Theorem 2. *The chameleon hashing scheme is semantically secure.*

This is because all elements of the RSA ring are v-powers when v is relatively prime to the factors of the modulus n. Thus, given a hash value z and any message m, there is exactly one random integer r, with $0 \leq r < (p-1)(q-1)$, such that $\mathsf{Hash}(S, m, r)$ equals z, namely r is equal to the v-th root of $zJ^{-\mathcal{H}(m)}$. $\square$

4   ID-Based Chameleon Signatures

Our hash function shares all the benefits of any ID-based construct (such as ID-based encryption or signature schemes), in particular:

- There is no need to retrieve the certificate of the intended recipient. The hash function can be computed from publicly available identity information (e.g., the recipient's email address).
- The hash function can be computed under a recipient's identity even if such recipient does not even exist or will join the system at a later time.
- Exposure of secret keys can be minimized by customizing the identity information under which the hash is computed (e.g., by concatenating time information to the identity of the recipient).

A chameleon signature scheme ([1]) is a signature computed over a chameleon hash function. The recipient can verify that the signature of a certain message m is valid but cannot prove to others that the signer actually signed m and not another message. Indeed, the recipient can find collisions of the chameleon hash function, thus finding a message different from m which would pass the signature verification procedure.

An ID-based chameleon signature on m consists of a traditional signature scheme, such as RSA or DSA, computed over the ID chameleon hash of m under the hashed identity J of the intended recipient. In particular, the signer generates a random r and computes:

$$S_{ID} = \{Sign(S, \mathsf{Hash}(S, m, r)), m, r\},$$

where $\mathsf{Hash}(S, m, r) = J^{\mathcal{H}(m)} r^v \bmod n$ is the id-based chameleon hash function computed for $J = \mathcal{C}(S)$.

As suggested in [1], an authenticated description of the hash function should also be added whenever such a description is not publicly available. As already mentioned, $Sign(\cdot)$ can be any standard signature scheme. In particular, it can also be implemented as any identity-based signature scheme, such as the Fiat-Shamir [8] or Guillou-Quisquatter [13]. This way, the verification process would be also ID-based since the signature can be verified from the identity of the signer.

The above signature could be repudiated by a malicious signer who claimed that the recipient had forged the signature. But a trusted third party, or judge, could intervene to settle the dispute by asking the signer to provide a pair of values, different from (m, r), which would pass the signature verification procedure. If the signer does not provide such a pair then the signature on m is considered valid. If the signer does provide a different pair $(m', r') \neq (m, r)$, which passes the signature verification procedure, then the judge can conclude that the recipient has cheated and the signature on m is marked as invalid.

As with all identity-based schemes, only the trusted third party can extract the secret key – the value B such that $J = B^v \bmod n$. One fundamental feature of an identity-based chameleon signature scheme, computed under a hashed identity J, is that the recipient does not have to know the secret B unless he wants to forge the signature. Interestingly, this adds a new flavor to the identity-based cryptography in general: *The user does not have to retrieve the secret to terminate a transaction unless he wants to diverge from the basic scheme.* This is somehow different from the identity-based encryption where one has to necessarily retrieve the secret in order to decrypt messages or from identity-based signatures where one has to have the secret in order to start signing messages. In our case, the recipient may never ask for the secret but still successfully complete all transactions. However, the recipient can *potentially* obtain the secret from the trusted third party at any time which makes the original signature non-transferable. (A verifier does not know whether the recipient queried the trusted third party or not.)

4.1   Message Hiding

When a dispute takes place, it is often desirable to protect the confidentiality of the original message even against the judge. As suggested in [1], whenever the recipient cheats, the judge can solve any dispute without knowing the message originally signed by the signer. Indeed, it would be enough to reveal any collision of the chameleon hash function to convince the judge that the recipient cheated. This can be easily accomplished since the secret trapdoor information associated to the recipient's public key is revealed whenever a collision of the chameleon hash function is known. For instance, suppose the signer computes the signature on the pair (m, r) and the recipient finds a collision and claims that the signature is on (m', r'). During the dispute resolution, the judge reveals (m', r'), enabling the signer to compute the trapdoor, as follows: First, the signer calculates $r'/r = B^{\mathcal{H}(m)-\mathcal{H}(m')}$. Then, B is extracted given that $J = B^v$ is known and that $GCD(\mathcal{H}(m) - \mathcal{H}(m'), v) = 1$ always holds. For details, see section §3.1 and the proof of Fact 1.

Once the signer knows B, she can use the recipient's **Forge**($\cdot$) algorithm to compute a new collision (m'', r'') and provide it to the judge, proving that the recipient cheated while keeping the original pair (m, r) private.

4.2   Customized Identities

Notice that anyone knowing a collision can find the recipient's secret B. Similarly, this happens with the original scheme in [1] where the secret key corresponding to the public key used for the hash computation is revealed. This works as a deterrent to forging. However, if the recipient is unwilling to forge a signature, in order to avoid exposing his secret key, the non-transferability property of chameleon signature schemes is somewhat weakened. Third-party verifiers may be inclined to consider valid any signatures proposed by the recipient, upon knowing his hesitation in forging them. Would a recipient forge a signature when this might jeopardize all other transactions involving his public key? The identity-based chameleon hash function offers a natural way to solve this problem without requiring the recipient to interact with the signer. Indeed, the hash can be computed under a *customized* identity J; for instance, J could be the result of applying a hash-and-encode function $\mathcal{C}(\cdot)$ to the identity of the recipient, concatenated with the identity of the signer, plus some transaction identifier:

$$J = \mathcal{C}(identity\_recipient \parallel identity\_signer \parallel transaction\_ID).$$

In this case, the scheme should stipulate that the secret key B will be provided only to the recipient, identified as the person whose identity prefixes the string used to form the public key J.

Whenever public keys are employed, one should in principle check whether a public key has been revoked or not. The use of properly customized identities eliminates this need. If the customized identity is unique to each message signed, the signer is certain that the corresponding secret has never been exposed since it has not even been computed by the trusted authority. In this regard, we stress again that the recipient does not have to retrieve the secret key to verify the signature. In a practical system, recipients would be eventual signers, and thus would have an interest in recovering secret keys occasionally, to ensure that the trusted party works correctly and that the non-transferability property holds. Clearly such frequency could be considerably lower than the frequency of transactions the recipient participates in.

4.3   Message Recovery

In case of forgery, the recipient's key compromise results in the signer being capable of claiming any message as the one originally signed. Moreover, it becomes impossible for the signer to prove which message was the original one. In some applications, this may not be an acceptable outcome. Circumstances may be such that the signer has an interest in being capable to affirm the original signature if she so desires. This situation has been addressed in [1], and the solution can be applied to our scheme. The *convertible* variant of the basic scheme provides the signer with a non-interactive algorithm to transform any instance of the chameleon signature into a universally verifiable instance.

A different possibility is that the application requires that the original message be recoverable even without the signer's cooperation. In these cases, it may be necessary to add to the signature some additional information about the message itself. One possibility is to include in the signature an encryption of the pair (m, r) computed under the public key of the judge. That is, the signature becomes:

$$S_{ID} = \{Sign(S, \mathsf{Hash}(S, m, r), PK[(m, r)]), m, r\},$$

where the public-key encryption is assumed to be semantically secure[2]. In practice, one would sign a hash of the encryption, so as to compute the signature on parameters of fixed size.

---

[2] This is required to maintain the non-transferability of the signature once augmented by the encrypted message. Informally, a semantically secure encryption is a randomized encryption that protects all the bits of the plaintext. In particular, if one of two publicly known messages is encrypted, no-one can tell which of the two was encrypted by just looking at the ciphertext.

The above construction eliminates the need for the signer to store signatures in order to repudiate forgeries, shifting the storage burden onto the recipient, as in regular (digital) signatures. With this scheme, the signer is protected against a malicious recipient that produces a forgery and then prevents the signer from participating in the adjudication of the claim – a denial-of-service attack on the signer. This scheme does *not* provide the recipient with a mechanism for adjudicated convertibility, because the recipient has no guarantee that the signer has encrypted the correct information during the signing step. It only protects the recipient against a later "change of heart" by the signer.

5   Sealed-Bid Auction System

In this section, we describe a very simple sealed-bid auction scheme based on ID-based chameleon signatures. We stress that this application is not meant to be the sole motivation for the primitive we are introducing, but only an illustration of some of its potential uses and benefits.

In public seller auctions, also called English or forward auctions, bidders compete by announcing successive bids, with the highest offer acquiring the good being auctioned. Alternatively, public buyer auctions (also called reverse auctions) are used by the Government and by businesses to procure supplies and services. In reverse auctions the lowest bid wins.

By contrast, in sealed-bid auctions (whether forward or reverse), bidders are allowed to submit a single, sealed bid. The seller stipulates a period for accepting bids, at the end of which the bids are unsealed and compared. The winning bid is revealed so that all competitors can ascertain its winning merits.

The Internet has transformed the auctioning business. Auction systems were some of the earliest success stories in the commercial Internet, and continue to grow profitably. While the site eBay© is a household name, multiple other sites cater to the vast segment of business-to-business procurement. The auction type (forward/reverse) varies but proxy bidding is commonly found. Proxy bidding-based auctions are intermediate between open and sealed-bid auctions. As in public auctions, the current winning price is openly determined, constantly changing while the auction is ongoing. However, in similarity with closed auctions the maximum bid (or minimum bid in a reverse auction) is not known to competitors.

Proxy bidding has a few characteristics that makes it less desirable than sealed-bid auctions, at least in some circumstances. For instance, late bidders (those who submit their bids closest to the auction closing time) are at an advantage, raising both questions of fairness to all bidders and of possible underestimation of the market value of the product being auctioned, which is unfair to the seller. As the value, variety, and complexity of items auctioned online increase, it is possible that some markets will favor auction systems that optimize for factors such as efficiency and fairness, for instance by featuring sealed-bid auctions [14].

5.1   Closed Auction System Models

Standard models for sealed-bid auction systems require that the following properties hold:

Correctness: The correct winner and clearing price are determined in each auction.
Confidentiality: Bids remain hidden before the action ends.
   (Optionally): Only the winning bid and the clearing price are revealed. Losing bids remain private.
Fairness: Bidders do not learn information about competing bids before the auction closes, neither can they change their bid after the closing of the auction.
Non-repudiation: The winner cannot repudiate his bid.
Robustness: No party, whether or not a legitimate party in the auction, may maliciously or accidentally compromise the correct functioning of the system.

There has been considerable research on secure, closed e-auction systems, such as [15–21]. Most of these systems are fairly complex, employing techniques such as secure multi-party evaluation of predicates on encrypted bids. The general idea is that the bidders submit encrypted bids. The auctioneer, or other bidders, cannot determine from the encrypted values the original bids, but can cooperate to determine the highest bid value and the auction winner. It is necessarily true that only systems based on encrypted bids can achieve the strongest possible security guarantees. In particular, without keeping the bids encrypted before the auction closing time, it is not possible to provide fairness without making some additional trust assumptions, because if a bid is ever available as clear-text its content could be communicated to competitors. Similarly, losing bids must never be decrypted if full privacy is desired.

In practical applications one must consider the optimal trade-off between security properties and other worthwhile goals such as lower communication complexity (reducing the number of messages sent greatly simplifies system design as a whole), computational costs and administrative ones (such as key management issues). Our approach considers the design of a system that is extremely practical. The design goals are as follows:

Thin clients: The client software/hardware (assisting the bidder function) should be of minimal complexity. Optimally, it should consist of a non-customized (or minimally customized) web browser or even a text-messaging application.
Stateless clients: A stateless protocol is much easier to implement correctly and to analyze for its security properties. Moreover, less state information results in greater robustness.
Low communication: The communication complexity of a distributed protocol can be defined either as the number of bits sent or the number of messages sent. From a practical perspective, the number of messages influences the complexity of protocol implementation and analysis, while the number of bits is important whenever network bandwidth is at a premium.

Asynchronous communication model: The only timeliness constraint is that auctioneer and bidders can agree on whether a bid is submitted after or before the closing of an auction.

Auction rule flexibility: This is an important requirement for a general-purpose auction system. Different auction styles require different methods to determine the clearing price for the item(s). For instance, a $(k + 1)$-auction is one in which k items are auctioned. The k-th highest bidders claim items, all at the same clearing price, which corresponds to the $k + 1$-st highest bid.

5.2   The Auction Scheme

We present a sealed-bid auction protocol satisfying all the above design goals, while providing only partially the security guarantees of the general model. We first describe a straightforward protocol, which provides non-repudiation:

1. *Each bidder sends a single signed message to the auctioneer, containing the bid information.*
2. *The auctioneer publishes a receipt for each bid received.*
3. *The auctioneer publishes the winning bid. (After auction closes.)*

The above protocol also reaches correctness, if the following conditions hold:

- All bids submitted before the auction closes are accepted by the auctioneer. In particular, this implies that all parties can agree on the auction closing time – a soft synchronization requirement.
- *Consistency of view* of the published information must be assured.

We remark that both conditions are required of any *robust* protocol. We assume that the underlying communication channel between bidders and the auctioneer is such that both properties above hold, as the techniques for achieving such guarantees are well understood and can be achieved in practice. Under such assumption, the above protocol is robust.

On the other hand, this protocol achieves neither *fairness* or *privacy* unless the auctioneer can be trusted not to publish any undue information. As alluded to before, fairness and absolute privacy can only be achieved by performing all computations (such as clearing price and auction winner determination) on encrypted bids. Use of encryption increases the communication complexity (once to collect bids and another to perform decryptions) and makes robustness harder to achieve. (For instance, one must ensure that encryption keys can be recovered for the winning bid or else there is no robustness of the non-repudiation guarantee.) This poses the question of whether partial *fairness* and *privacy* guarantees can be achieved without resorting to computation on encrypted information.

Our approach is to simplify the trust model. Clearly, if the auctioneer is entirely trusted then privacy and fairness can be achieved simply by protecting the bid-submission channel. If the auctioneer may arbitrarily collude with bidders then complex cryptographic techniques are required to ensure fairness or privacy. These are not the only two possible trust models. Alternatively, the auctioneer might not be trusted to keep the bids privately and yet also untrusted by dishonest bidders to provide the correct information about competitors' bids. *This model does not protect against auctioneer-bidder collusions but can accommodate situations in which a hacker or malicious insider breaks into the system and tries to peddle the information to a suspectful bidder.*

Notice that the simple scheme described above is still vulnerable under this restricted trust model. An insider could easily convince a suspicious bidder of the correctness of the peddled information because the bids are signed. However, if the bids were to be signed using a chameleon-hashing scheme that would not be the case. As the signature on bids are non-transferable, the suspicious insider cannot be assured of the correctness of the reported bid value. We now describe this in some detail. The final protocol is simply:

---

1. *Each bidder sends a single signed message to the auctioneer. The message contains the bid terms, signed using the identity-based chameleon signature scheme.*
2. *The auctioneer publishes a receipt for each bid received.*
3. *The auctioneer publishes the winning bid. (After auction closes.)*

The bids are submitted to the auctioneer in the clear, but since they are signed using chameleon signatures, their validity can only be determined by the auctioneer. The auctioneer publishes the signatures on each bid, which acts as a receipt on the bid, but does not publish the value of the bids themselves. If the auctioneer were to cheat and reveal to a bidder some of the competitors' bids, that bidder would have no means to determine whether or not the auctioneer is telling the truth. Yet, since chameleon signatures are non-repudiatable, the bid winner must make good on her offer: In case of disputes, a judge would determine the validity of the bid.

An important point is that it be believable that the auctioneer might cheat. If regular chameleon signatures are used, it is unlikely that an auctioneer would cheat by forging bids because, by cheating, it would reveal a collision of the chameleon hash function. This in turn discloses its long-term secret key, affording the colluding bidder to repudiate his bid during any later auctions as well as during the current one. However, the non-transferability of a chameleon signature comes from the fact that the recipient of such a signature may be willing to forge it. If such an event is unlikely then the chameleon signature behaves, de facto, much like a traditional signature scheme.

An alternative solution would be for the auctioneer to generate temporary public keys, perhaps one for each item being auctioned. At the highest level of granularity, the auctioneer might issue a different public key for each potential bidder on the item. Clearly, such public keys cannot be pre-computed in large systems with millions of users such as eBay[©]. That implies that a bidder must first contact the auctioneer about a particular auction and request the respective key. While correct, this solution requires a second round of communication when compared to the previous one. Instead, an identity-based scheme allows the bidder to generate a signature under a customized hashed identity J of the following form:

$$J = \mathcal{C}(auctioneer\_id \,\|\, bidder\_id \,\|\, item\_id).$$

This can be done without interacting with the auctioneer and would offer the highest level of granularity. The auctioneer does not have to retrieve the secret corresponding to J unless he wants to forge the signature. In case of forgery and subsequent dispute, only the secret related to a particular transaction from a specific bidder is revealed, leaving the rest of the transactions valid. This makes any signed bids completely useless for other bidders and non-transferable.

Our identity-based scheme allows users to participate in digital auctions that interface with real world. For instance, items for bidding can be labeled by reference strings. Unlike regular public keys, reference strings can be mnemonic, facilitating entry by potential buyers. For instance, realtors could put a sign in front of houses available on the market with a realtor identity and a number identifying the property. Auctioneers could advertise items for auction in public newspapers, including item reference strings. (Today, in the US, government-seized property auctions and foreclosure-related auctions must be advertised in newspapers to comply with the law.) Potential buyers would view the property and could type that information into an e-mail or text-messaging capable computing device to submit a bid. Not needing to download a public key simplifies the process, adding convenience: System users would be able to submit bids from low-bandwidth communication devices such as cell phones and PDAs. The above scheme is even more convenient if clients, such as cell phones, take advantage of an architecture of strong authentication (permitted by the device smartcard, in the case of cell phones) to eliminate the need for dedicated cryptographic software and key management on the client side. The bids could be forwarded to a proxy signature server (for instance, the site of the mortgage banker) which would chameleon-sign the bid on behalf of the user.

To summarize we have designed a very simple e-auction protocol that achieves correctness and non-repudiation in all cases, and which achieves fairness and privacy only under certain trust assumptions: The auctioneer is allowed to malfunction or to be dishonest, and the same is allowed of bidders, but the model does not handle the case when bidders and the auctioneer may collude. However, the simplicity and convenience afforded by the proposed scheme would be of considerable practical significance. In particular, we would like to point out the statelessness of clients and the fact that protocol requires the sending of a *single message* by bidders. Notice that the identity-based properties of the chameleon signature are essential to enable the single-message feature within this trusted model: Alternative methods would require schemes for delivering temporary keys, for instance. The use of an identity-based scheme eliminates the need of a certificate distribution architecture.

Apart from (and partly because of) being very efficient, and achieving the lowest possible message complexity, the protocol is quite robust. We believe that the importance of robustness has been overlooked in some of the existing protocols. Without robustness, the strong fairness and privacy conferred by some of the protocols based on encryption cannot be achieved in practice, because in any realistic implementation one must consider how a protocol performs under attacks or when parties malfunction.

6   Conclusions

Krawczyk and Rabin introduced in [1] the concept of chameleon hashing. In this paper, we extended their work by introducing an ID-based chameleon hash function. ID-based cryptography in general enjoys advantages relative to key distribution over conventional schemes. In the case of chameleon hashing these advantages are multiplied by the fact that the owner of a public key does not necessarily need to retrieve the associated secret key. Therefore, ID-based chameleon hashing can support single-use public keys very efficiently. We exploit this feature to design a novel application of chameleon signatures to e-auction schemes that enjoys efficiencies difficult to achieve with other cryptographic techniques.

Acknowledgments

Many thanks to the anonymous referees for their insightful comments. This work was partly funded by a NSF grant.

References

1. Krawczyk, H., Rabin, T.: Chameleon signatures. In: Proceedings of NDSS 2000. (2000) 143–154
2. Chaum, D., Antwerpen, H.: Undeniable signatures. In: Advances in Cryptology – CRYPTO'89. Volume 435 of LNCS., Springer-Verlag (1991) 212–216
3. Chaum, D.: Zero-knowledge undeniable signature. In: Advances in Cryptology – EUROCRYPT'90. Volume 473 of LNCS., Springer-Verlag (1990) 458—464
4. Boyar, J., Chaum, D., Damgård, I.B., Pedersen, T.P.: Convertible undeniable signatures. In: Advances in Cryptology – CRYPTO'90. Volume 537 of LNCS., Springer-Verlag (1990) 189–205
5. Chaum, D., van Heijst, E., Pfitzmann, B.: Cryptographically strong undeniable signatures, unconditionally secure for the signer. In: Proc. of Advances in Cryptology – CRYPTO'91. Volume 576 of LNCS., Springer-Verlag (1991) 470–ff
6. van Heijst, E., Pedersen, T.: How to make efficient fail-stop signatures. In: Proc. of Advances in Cryptology – EUROCRYPT'92. Volume 658 of LNCS., Springer-Verlag (1993) 366–377
7. Jakobsson, M., Sako, K., Impagliazzo, R.: Designated verifier proofs and their applications. In: Proc. of Advances in Cryptology – EUROCRYPT'96. Volume 1070 of LNCS., Springer-Verlag (1996) 143–ff
8. Shamir, A.: Identity-based cryptosystems and signature schemes. In: Advances in Cryptology – CRYPTO'84. Volume 196 of LNCS., Springer-Verlag (1984) 47–53

9. Boneh, D., Franklin, M.: Identity-based encryption from the Weil pairing. In: Proc. of CRYPTO'01. Volume 2139 of LNCS. (2001) 213 ff.

10. Cocks, C.: An identity based encryption scheme based on quadratic residues. (http://www.cesg.gov.uk/technology/id-pkc/media/ciren)

11. Bellare, M., Rogaway, P.: PSS: Provably secure encoding method for digital signature. IEEE P1363a: Provably secure signatures. `http://grouper.ieee.org/-groups/1363/p1363a/pssigs.html` (1998)

12. RSA Labs: RSA Cryptography Standard: EMSAPSS – PKCS#1 v2.1. (2002)

13. Guillou, L.C., Quisquater, J.J.: A practical zero-knowledge protocol fitted to security microprocessor minimizing both transmition and memory. In: Proc. of Advances in Cryptology – EUROCRYPT'88. Volume 330 of LNCS., Springer-Verlag (1988) 123–128

14. Chin, S.: Chip trade group calls for better governing of reverse auctions. In: `http://www.ebnonline.com/showArticle.jhtml?articleID=12803165`. EBN Online (2003)

15. Franklin, M., Reiter, M.: The design and implementation of a secure auction service. In: Proc. IEEE Symp. on Security and Privacy, Oakland, CA, IEEE Computer Society Press (1995) 2–14

16. Lipmaa, H., Asokan, N., Niemi, V.: Secure Vickrey auctions without threshold trust. In: Proc. of the 6th Annual Conference on Financial Cryptography. (2002)

17. Baudron, O., Stern, J.: Non-interactive private auctions. In: LNCS. Volume 2339., Springer-Verlag (2002) 364 ff

18. Harkavy, M., Tygar, J.D., Kikuchi, H.: Electronic auctions with private bids. In: 3rd USENIX Workshop on Electronic Commerce. (1998) 61–74

19. Naor, M., Pinkas, B., Sumner, R.: Privacy preserving auctions and mechanism design. In: Proc. of the 1st conf. on Electronic Commerce, ACM (1999) 129–139

20. Cachin, C.: Efficient private bidding and auctions with an oblivious third party. In: 6th ACM Conference on Computer and Communications Security (CCS), ACM Press (1999) 120–127

21. Kikuchi, H.: $(m+1)$st-price auction protocol. In Syverson, P., ed.: Financial Cryptography – Fifth International Conference. LNCS, Springer-Verlag (2002)

22. Fiat, A., Shamir, A.: How to prove yourself: Practical solutions to identification and signature problems. In: Advances in Cryptology – CRYPTO'86. Volume 263 of LNCS., Springer-Verlag (1987) 186–194

Selecting Correlated Random Actions

Vanessa Teague[*]

Stanford University, Stanford CA 94305, USA
vteague@cs.stanford.edu

Abstract. In many markets, it can be beneficial for competing firms to coordinate their actions. However, such arrangements usually have the problem that nobody has an incentive to adhere to the agreement. In this paper we investigate a way for two companies to communicate together and agree on a coordinated strategy in such a way that both participants have an incentive to keep to the agreement.

We provide a more efficient solution to the game theoretic problem solved by Dodis, Halevi and Rabin in [DHR00]: two selfish rational parties want to select one of a list of pairs, according to some probability distribution, so that one party learns the first element and the other learns the second, and neither gains any other information. In game theory terms, the problem is to achieve a correlated equilibrium without the trusted mediator. Our solution is more efficient than [DHR00] in terms of the probability distribution.

1 Introduction

The Internet is composed of participants who are often neither malicious nor perfectly honest, but are selfish and (reasonably) rational just like the traditional game theory players. This paper is part of a growing body of work (including for example [AET01], [FPSS02], [FPS01], [NPS99], [NR01], [RT02]) that aims to consider both the agents' computational limitations and their incentives when solving problems. In this case, we solve an existing problem in game theory by making computational assumptions and using cryptography. Our solution is more efficient than the one in [DHR00] in terms of one of the parameters (a probability distribution).

Consider for example two competing furniture stores, selling roughly the same secondhand chairs from failed dot-coms for roughly the same prices. Each week, the CEO of each store may choose either to retain the usual prices or to have a special sale and discount the chairs substantially. They must choose in advance (so they can't just wait to see what the other does). If both decide to retain their usual higher prices then both make a moderate amount of money that week. If one retains the normal prices but the other goes on sale, then the latter will have far more customers and make more money than in a normal week, while the former will make less. However, if both decide to have a sale

---

[*] Supported by OSD/ONR CIP/SW URI "Software Quality and Infrastructure Protection for Diffuse Computing" through ONR grant N00014-01-1-0795.

Table 1. Payoffs and probabilities for the game

Payoffs		
	No Sale	Sale
No Sale	9, 9	5, 12
Sale	12, 5	0, 0

Probabilities		
	No Sale	Sale
No Sale	5/11	3/11
Sale	3/11	0

at the same time then this is a disaster because they will not get many more customers than usual but they will receive much less money per customer. An example of the possible payoffs is shown in Table 1, where the first number of each pair is the payoff of the row player and the second is that of the column player. The state with the highest average income (per store) is the one in which neither offers a sale. Unfortunately, there is a reason to expect that the stores will not remain in this state: if either side is confident that the other will not offer a sale, then it has an incentive to offer one itself, thus gaining 12 instead of 9. In game theory terms, (No Sale, No Sale) is not a Nash equilibrium. Indeed, there is no Nash equilibrium better than the ones where one player offers a sale and the other doesn't.

A Nash equilibrium might be *mixed*, meaning that each player randomizes among several different actions. In a (mixed) Nash equilibrium, the players' random choices must be independent. However, in some games (such as this one) the players can earn a higher average payoff by randomizing according to some correlated joint distribution. The idea of *correlated equilibrium* is that there is a trusted party who helps the players to do the correlation. It chooses a particular move for each player from a commonly-known distribution over pairs of actions, then it tells each player what action to take. (More precise definitions of Nash and correlated equilibria are given in section 2.)

It is natural for cryptographers (and game theorists) to ask whether the players can achieve the same payoff without the trusted party. That is, if the players are allowed to talk amongst themselves before the game, can they correlate their random choices without giving away any information that will destroy the equilibrium? In the game theory literature, Barany [Bar92] showed that this was possible for four or more players, but impossible for two computationally unbounded players (except in some uninteresting cases). Dodis, Halevi and Rabin [DHR00] have shown that by making computational assumptions, it is possible to solve this problem for two players using cryptography. It is a Nash equilibrium for the players to execute the cryptographic protocol that simulates the trusted party correctly and then choose the appropriate move. (There is also a solution by Urbano and Vila [UV02], but their cryptographic protocol has security flaws.) The contribution of this paper is to provide a protocol that solves the same problem as [DHR00] and is more efficient in terms of the probability distribution required.

Although the protocol presented in [DHR00] is very efficient in terms of the security parameter, it is designed for uniform distributions and is not efficient in terms of the probability distribution that the parties are supposed to be taking their moves from. The protocol presented in this paper is much more efficient in this parameter. (The form of the protocol that is designed for selfish agents is less efficient than [DHR00]'s in terms of the security parameter, which is itself a function of the end-of-game payoffs.) Although most examples of correlated equilibria in game theory textbooks (for example, [OR94] and [FT91]) do use a uniform distribution, there is no particular reason to expect that most correlated equilibria should be uniform or nearly uniform. For example, the game in Table 1 has a correlated equilibrium with the distribution given in the table. It also has a correlated equilibrium based on a uniform distribution among the same three pairs of actions, but that equilibrium has a lower average payoff. Section 2 contains proofs of these claims.

In the following section we give some background game theory and explain the problem more carefully. In section 3 we present a protocol that is secure against honest-but-curious players, and in section 4 we show how to compile the protocol for security against one malicious player. We then show that two selfish players would execute the protocol correctly.

2   Definitions and Game Theory Background

In this section we provide enough background to explain the problem that we are trying to solve.

Definition 1. *A* Game *for two players consists of:*

- *for each player $i \in \{0,1\}$ a nonempty set A_i of actions, and*
- *for each player $i \in \{0,1\}$ a utility function $u_i : A_1 \times A_2 \to \mathbb{R}$.*

The utility function represents how happy a player is with a certain outcome. The larger its value, the better-off the player. Players may randomize their actions. A *strategy* in a strategic game is a probability distribution over actions. (The notion of strategy will be broadened for extended games later in this section.) A *Nash equilibrium* is a self-enforcing agreement by each agent to choose a certain strategy. Given the agreement, neither player has an incentive to deviate from it unilaterally. The main restriction is that the random choices made by the two players must be independent.

Definition 2. *A* Nash equilibrium *of a game G is a pair of independent strategies (σ_1^*, σ_2^*) such that for any $a_1 \in A_1$ and $a_2 \in A_2$, we have $u_1(\sigma_1^*, \sigma_2^*) \geq u_1(a_1, \sigma_2^*)$ and $u_2(\sigma_1^*, \sigma_2^*) \geq u_2(\sigma_1^*, a_2)$.*

The idea of a correlated equilibrium is that there is a trusted third party who recommends an action to each player before the game. It chooses the pair of actions according to a probability distribution that is common knowledge. Hence the recommended action gives each player some information about its opponent's action, since it knows the distribution of what will be recommended to its opponent conditioned on its own recommended action. Each player's recommended action should be its best strategy, given this information. This gives us a generalization of Nash equilibrium in which the players' random choices may be correlated.

We write $\sigma_2^*|a_1^*$ for the probability distribution on the action recommended to player 2, conditioned on action a_1^* being recommended to player 1. The utility $u_1(a_1, \sigma_2^*|a_1^*)$ is player 1's expected utility for choosing action a_1, assuming that player 2 acts according to the distribution $\sigma_2^*|a_1^*$. Similarly, $u_2(\sigma_1^*|a_2^*, a_2)$ is player 2's expected utility for a_2, given its information.

Definition 3. *A* correlated equilibrium *is a pair of strategies* $s^* = (\sigma_1^*, \sigma_2^*)$ *such that for any* (a_1^*, a_2^*) *in the support of* s^*, *for any* $a_1 \in A_1$ *and* $a_2 \in A_2$, *we have* $u_1(a_1^*, \sigma_2^*|a_1^*) \geq u_1(a_1, \sigma_2^*|a_1^*)$ *and* $u_2(\sigma_1^*|a_2^*, a_2^*) \geq u_2(\sigma_1^*|a_2^*, a_2)$.

It is easy to see that for any Nash equilibrium there is a correlated equilibrium with the same distribution on pairs of actions (and therefore the same average payoff). Correlated equilibrium payoffs can be outside the convex hull of Nash equilibrium payoffs. For example, consider the game in Table 1. We first show that the probabilities given in the table produce a correlated equilibrium. Since the game is symmetric, we need only consider the incentives of player 2, the column player, given what it has been told to play. The conditional probabilities for player 1's action given what has been recommended to player 2 are:

$$Pr\,(a_1 = \text{No Sale}|a_2 = \text{No Sale}) = \frac{5/11}{3/11 + 5/11}$$
$$= 5/8$$
$$Pr\,(a_1 = \text{Sale}|a_2 = \text{No Sale}) = 3/8$$
$$Pr\,(a_1 = \text{No Sale}|a_2 = \text{Sale}) = 1$$
$$Pr\,(a_1 = \text{Sale}|a_2 = \text{Sale}) = 0$$

Suppose the column player is told to play Sale. Then it can be certain that the row player has been told to play No Sale, so the column player gets its maximum possible payoff, namely 12, for doing as it is told. Suppose instead that the column player is told to play No Sale. Then its expected payoff for being obedient and playing No Sale is $9Pr\,(a_1 = \text{No Sale}|a_2 = \text{No Sale}) + 5Pr\,(a_1 = \text{Sale}|a_2 = \text{No Sale}) = 7\frac{1}{2}$. If it decides to disobey and play Sale instead, its expected payoff is $12Pr\,(a_1 = \text{No Sale}|a_2 = \text{No Sale}) = 7\frac{1}{2}$, so it has no incentive to deviate. Hence this is a correlated equilibrium.

There are two pure-strategy Nash equilibria, (No Sale, Sale) and (Sale, No Sale), both of which have an average payoff per player of $8\frac{1}{2}$. There is also a mixed Nash equilibrium in which each player plays No Sale with probability $5/8$. This gives an average payoff of $7\frac{1}{2}$. The correlated equilibrium in the table gives the players an average payoff of $9 \times 5/11 + 12 \times 3/11 + 5 \times 3/11 = 8\frac{8}{11}$, which is better than any Nash equilibrium.

Furthermore, a correlated equilibrium with a non-uniform distribution can give a strictly higher average payoff than any with a uniform distribution in the same game. For example, in the game in Table 1, the uniform distribution over (Sale, Sale), (Sale, No Sale), (No Sale, Sale) also gives a correlated equilibrium, but this has an average payoff of $(5 + 12 + 9)/3 = 8\frac{2}{3}$ which is lower than the $8\frac{8}{11}$ achieved with the non-uniform distribution in the table.

It is interesting to wonder what happens for an arbitrary game when the trusted party is allowed to send more informative messages, rather than just informing each player of the action it is supposed to take. Upon first glance it seems that this might increase the set of equilibria, but it is a standard result in game theory (see [OR94] prop. 47.1) that it doesn't. For every equilibrium that is based upon some complicated messages from the trusted party, there is another that has the same distribution on action pairs (and therefore the same payoffs) in which the trusted party tells each player what action to choose and nothing else. This is why we adopt Definition 3 instead of a more complicated variant.

An *extended game* is a game preceded by a period of unrestricted communication among the parties. This is called "cheap talk" in the game theory literature, because the talk doesn't directly affect anyone's utility – the payoffs for the extended game are just the payoffs for the standard game that is played in the last step. A *strategy* in such a game consists of both a way of conducting the "cheap talk" (which may be randomized and may depend on messages received from others) and a choice of action afterwards.

One technical difficulty is defining such standard notions as Nash equilibrium given computational assumptions. We follow [DHR00] in assuming that players ignore any improvements in their utility that are negligible in the security parameter. For example, they don't bother trying to guess each other's private keys, because they know they have only a negligible probability of success.

Definition 4. *[DHR00, Definition 3] A computational Nash equilibrium of a game is a pair of independent strategies (σ_1^*, σ_2^*) such that*

- *both σ_1^* and σ_2^* are PPT computable.*
- *for any other PPT computable strategies σ_1 and σ_2, there exists a negligible function μ such that on security parameter k, we have $u_1(\sigma_1^*, \sigma_2^*) \geq u_1(\sigma_1, \sigma_2^*) + \mu(k)$ and $u_2(\sigma_1^*, \sigma_2^*) \geq u_2(\sigma_1^*, \sigma_2) + \mu(k)$.*

The idea now is to devise a cryptographic protocol that selects a pair of actions from some distribution and reveals to each player what action it should take and nothing else. We will call this the *correlated element selection* problem. It should be a computational Nash equilibrium of the extended game for each player to execute the protocol correctly during the "cheap talk" phase and then choose the action that is recommended by it.

Dodis *et al.* present an efficient protocol for solving the correlated element selection problem with the uniform distribution. They show how to augment this protocol to make it secure against malicious parties, which is enough to make it a computational Nash equilibrium for selfish parties to execute the protocol and then take the action that they are supposed to, assuming the uniform distribution was indeed a correlated equilibrium. Their protocol is very efficient for uniform distributions, but the solution for non-uniform distributions is to repeat some of the pairs until choosing uniformly from the resulting list gives the correct distribution. This has an asymptotic efficiency on the order of the least common multiple of the denominators of the probabilities. Our contribution is a protocol for solving the same problem that is more efficient in terms of the probability distribution: its asymptotic efficiency is on the order of the inverse of the smallest non-zero probability. This is always smaller (except in the uniform case and some other simple cases, when it is equal), because the inverse of a number in $(0, 1]$ is smaller than or equal to the denominator, so the smallest of the inverses is smaller than or equal to the least common multiple of the denominators.

In both protocols, the longest message is a list sent in the first step. For example, for the game in Table 1 our protocol uses a list of length $\lceil 11/3 \rceil = 4$ while the one in [DHR00] uses one of length l.c.m $\{11, 11, 11\} = 11$. If we wanted a correlated equilibrium that consisted of choosing one pair of actions with probability $1/100$, one with probability $1/99$ and another with probability $1 - 1/99 - 1/100$, then Dodis et al's protocol would use a list of 9900 messages, while our protocol would use 100. In the uniform case, the lists have the same length for both protocols. However, our messages are larger by a constant factor (about 3).

2.1   Summary: How the Protocol Fits in to the Game

The traditional cryptographic assumption is that at most one player is *malicious*, meaning that it might deviate from the protocol in any computationally feasible way, while the other is completely honest. The protocol must either produce the correct answer and reveal no other information, or stop early without revealing information (See [Gol03] for a more precise statement). However, in this case we can't assume that one player is honest. The usual game theoretic assumption is that both players are *rational*. We assume that each player might deviate from the protocol (in any computationally feasible way) if this increases its expected utility (by a non-negligible amount).

In cryptography, it usually suffices to show that the honest player will notice if a malicious player tries to cheat. However, in our setting both players still have to choose an action after the protocol, so we must describe what action they should choose after detecting that the other has cheated. We follow [DHR00]: if player 1 detects that player 2 has cheated, it punishes 2 by choosing the action a_1 that minimizes $\max_{a_2}\{u_2(a_1, a_2)\}$. This is called player 2's minimax action. Likewise, if player 2 catches player 1 cheating, it minimaxes 1. It is shown in [DHR00] that the cheating player's minimax utility is always smaller than its correlated equilibrium payoff, so it has an incentive to be honest as long as its probability of being caught when cheating is sufficiently large. We use standard cryptographic techniques to make sure this is the case.

Consider the extended game defined by a period of "cheap talk" followed by the playing of a game. Let $\mathcal{P}$ be the protocol for correlated element selection given in section 4, parameterized for a particular correlated equilibrium of the game. Let S_{honest} be the strategy, "follow $\mathcal{P}$ until you detect the other player cheating. If you reach the end without detecting cheating, choose the action output at the end of $\mathcal{P}$. Otherwise, punish your opponent to its minimax level."

A precise statement of our main result is:

Theorem 1. *It is a computational Nash equilibrium of the extended game for each player to follow strategy S_{honest}.*

This result means that two selfish players could be expected to implement the protocol correctly and then choose the recommended moves, thus achieving a correlated equilibrium without the trusted party.

While both players following strategy S_{honest} is a computational Nash equilibrium, it is not subgame perfect because it involves an "incredible threat". A player may have no incentive to punish the other even if it is caught cheating, since the minimax state may hurt the punisher as much as the cheater. Such incredible threats are allowed in Nash equilibria because we assume that each player chooses its strategy in advance and does not maintain control of the algorithm. However, for some games a subgame perfect equilibrium is possible: if the original (unextended) game has, for each player, a Nash equilibrium that gives that player a sufficiently small payoff, then that state can be used as punishment rather than a minimax. In that case, a rational player that detects the other cheating and can still control what move to make will have no incentive not to punish the other correctly.

3   Protocol for Honest-but-Curious Players

We present a protocol for the correlated element selection problem that is efficient in terms of both the security parameter and the required probability distribution. This protocol has message size and computation time linear in the security parameter and linear in the inverse of the smallest probability in the distribution on pairs of actions. This protocol is secure in the honest-but-curious model, meaning that the players are allowed to record everything they know about the interaction and try to learn from it, but they are not permitted to deviate from the protocol in any other way, including the tossing of fair coins. In then next section, we will show how to make the protocol secure against one malicious player or two selfish players. There may be interesting applications for this protocol other than finding correlated equilibria.

We first describe a useful cryptographic primitive used in [DHR00] and also in our protocol. Blindable encryption allows someone who knows only the public key to transform a ciphertext of a message m into a random ciphertext of $m+m'$, for any value of m' that it chooses. (In the following definition, when we want to write the random inputs to a function explicitly, we separate them from the non-random inputs with a semicolon).

3.1   Blindable Encryption

Definition 5. *[DHR00, Definition 4]. A public key encryption scheme $\mathcal{E}$ with public key pk is* blindable *if there exist (PPT) algorithms Blind and Combine such that for every message m and every ciphertext $c \in Enc_{pk}(m)$:*

– For any message m' (also referred to as the "blinding factor"), $Blind_{pk}(c, m')$
produces a random encryption of $m + m'$.
– If r_1, r_2 are the random coins used by two successive "blindings", then for
any two blinding factors m_1, m_2,

$$Blind_{pk}(Blind_{pk}(c, m_1; r_1), m_2; r_2) = Blind_{pk}(c, m_1 + m_2; Combine_{pk}(r_1, r_2))$$

Two blindable encryption schemes are ElGamal and Goldwasser-Micali
[GM84].

Blindable encryption provides an easy way for player 1 to ask player 2 to
decrypt a message encrypted with 2's public key, without player 2 learning anything about what it has decrypted. Player 1 simply chooses a random blinding
factor, blinds the ciphertext, asks player 2 for the decryption and then subtracts
the blinding factor from the result. We will use this idea twice in this protocol.
Blindable encryption also provides a useful way to make a given ciphertext unrec-
ognizable. Suppose there are several encryptions of the same message. Someone
who knows the public key can blind a ciphertext by zero, producing a random
encryption of that message. Even someone who knows the private key cannot
tell which encryption of the message the new ciphertext was derived from.

3.2   The Protocol

Figure 1 describes the improved protocol for correlated element selection. There
is a longer explanation in the following text. We assume that all numbers are
expressed to $\hat{k} = \Theta(k)$ bits of precision, where k is the security parameter.
Choosing a random number from a real interval means choosing randomly from
among the (finitely many) $\hat{k}$-precision numbers in that interval.

The protocol is a variation on Dodis $et\ al.$'s protocol for correlated element
selection. The common input is a list of triples $\{(a_i, b_i, p_i)\}_{i=1}^n$, meaning that the
pair of actions (a_i, b_i) should be chosen with probability p_i. The output is an
action a_i for the chooser and the corresponding action b_i for the preparer. Let $\hat{p}_i$
denote $\sum_{j=1}^i p_j$. We assume $\hat{p}_n = 1$. The probabilities divide the interval $[0, 1)$
into n intervals $[0, \hat{p}_1), [\hat{p}_1, \hat{p}_2), \ldots, [\hat{p}_{n-1}, 1)$, with each interval corresponding to
a pair of actions.

(a_1, b_1)	(a_2, b_2)	$\cdots$	(a_{n-1}, b_{n-1})	(a_n, b_n)
0 $\quad$ $\hat{p}_1$	$\hat{p}_2$	$\hat{p}_{n-2}$	$\hat{p}_{n-1}$	1

$Preparation.$ The preparer generates a random number $r_0 \in [0, 1)$ and shifts the
probability intervals along by adding r_0 to each and "wrapping" back around to
zero for those sums that are greater than 1. That is, let $i^* = \min\{i | r_0 + \hat{p}_i > 1\}$.
The preparer creates new intervals $[0, \hat{p}_{i^*} + r_0 - 1), [\hat{p}_{i^*} + r_0 - 1, \hat{p}_{i^*+1} + r_0 -
1), \ldots, [\hat{p}_{n-1} + r_0 - 1, r_0), [r_0, \hat{p}_1 + r_0), \ldots, [\hat{p}_{i^*-1} + r_0, 1)$. It shifts the corre-
sponding action pairs along with the intervals, so for $i < i^*$ the action pair
(a_i, b_i) corresponds to the interval $[\hat{p}_{i-1} + r_0, \hat{p}_i + r_0)$, while for $i > i^*$, (a_i, b_i)
corresponds to the interval $[\hat{p}_{i-1} + r_0 - 1, \hat{p}_i + r_0 - 1)$ and the action pair (a_{i^*}, b_{i^*})
is split over the two intervals $[0, \hat{p}_{i^*} + r_0 - 1)$ and $[\hat{p}_{i^*-1} + r_0, 1)$.

Protocol CES

Common inputs: List of pairs of actions with probabilities $\{(a_i, b_i, p_i)\}_{i=1}^n$, public key pk, security parameter k.

Preparer knows: secret key sk.

Outputs: With probability p_i, C outputs a_i and P outputs b_i.

All calculations are done with $\Theta(k)$ bits of precision.

P: **1. Shift and encrypt**

    Choose a random $r_0 \in [0,1)$.

    Choose minimum l s.t. $1/l \leq \min_i\{p_i\}$ and divide $[0,1)$ into l equal-sized blocks.

    Let $\hat{p}_i$ denote $\sum_{j=1}^i p_j$, and $frac(x)$ the fractional part of x

    For $\lambda = 1 \ldots l$ make block λ as follows:

        If there is an i with $frac(\hat{p}_i + r_0) \in [(\lambda - 1)/l, \lambda/l)$, make block

        $((Enc_{pk}(a_i), Enc_{pk}(b_i)), Enc_{pk}(frac(l(\hat{p}_i + r_0))/l), (Enc_{pk}(a_{i+1}), Enc_{pk}(b_{i+1}))$

        Otherwise, choose a random $q_\lambda \in [0, 1/l)$ and make block

        $((Enc_{pk}(a_j), Enc_{pk}(b_j)), Enc_{pk}(q_\lambda), (Enc_{pk}(a_j), Enc_{pk}(b_j))$

        (where $j = \min\{j' | frac(\hat{p}_{j'} + r_0) > (\lambda - 1)/l\}$)

    Send the list of blocks to C.

C: **2. Choose and blind**

    Choose a random block $((c_{a_1}, c_{b_1}), c_p, (c_{a_2}, c_{b_2}))$ from the list.

    Choose a random blinding factor β_1

    Send $c'_p = Blind_{pk}(c_p, \beta_1)$ to P.

P: **3. Blindly decrypt probability**

    Send $p' = Dec_{sk}(c'_p)$ to C.

C: **4. Choose actions**

    Let $p = p' - \beta_1$.

    Generate a new random number β_2.

    With probability lp, set $(e, f) = (Blind_{pk}(c_{a_1}, \beta_2), Blind_{pk}(c_{b_1}, 0))$

    Otherwise set $(e, f) = (Blind_{pk}(c_{a_2}, \beta_2), Blind_{pk}(c_{b_2}, 0))$

    Send (e, f) to P.

P: **5. Decrypt and output**

    Set $\tilde{b} = Dec_{sk}(e)$. Send $\tilde{b}$ to C.

    Output $Dec_{sk}(f)$.

C: **6. Unblind and output**

    Set $b = \tilde{b} - \beta_2$. Output b.

Fig. 1. A protocol for correlated element selection in the honest-but-curious model

The preparer then chooses the smallest $l \in \mathbb{N}$ so that $1/l \leq \min_i\{p_i\}$, and divides the interval $[0,1)$ into l intervals of equal size, which will be called "blocks". (This is why the resulting message length is linear in the inverse of the smallest probability.) Some blocks fall entirely within one of the shifted probability intervals (and hence correspond to only one pair of actions), while others overlap the border between two (and hence correspond to two pairs of actions). No block corresponds to three or more pairs of actions because the size of a block is chosen to be smaller than the smallest interval that one pair occupies.

The idea is that the chooser will choose one of these blocks randomly and uniformly and will then choose randomly (but *not* uniformly) one of the actions represented by the block. Let $frac(x)$ denote the fractional part of x. The preparer prepares the blocks in the following way: if the λ-th block overlaps two shifted probability intervals (say that the block contains the value $frac(\hat{p}_i + r_0)$ for some i), it normalizes $frac(\hat{p}_i + r_0)$ by subtracting integer multiples of $1/l$ to get the value $\bar{p}_\lambda = frac(l(\hat{p}_i + r_0))/l$ in $[0, 1/l)$. It then separately encrypts $\bar{p}_\lambda$ and all four actions with its own public key, maintaining their pairing and order. Blocks that fall entirely within one shifted probability interval are easier to prepare, but must be made indistinguishable from the other kind of block: for these blocks, the preparer generates a random number $q_\lambda \in [0, 1/l)$ for the λ-th block, encrypts it and then encrypts the pair of actions twice with different randomness. When all blocks are prepared, the preparer sends the list of blocks to the chooser.

Decryption. We use a semantically secure encryption scheme, so it is infeasible for the chooser to tell whether the two pairs of actions in a block are actually the same pair or not. It chooses one of the l blocks uniformly at random and gets the preparer to blindly decrypt its probability p (that is, the chooser blinds the encrypted p with a random value, asks the preparer to decrypt the result and then subtracts the blinding value). The chooser then chooses the leftmost pair of actions with probability lp and the rightmost otherwise. The chooser blinds its own action (the first one in the chosen pair) with a random value and blinds the preparer's action with 0, then sends the result to the preparer. The preparer decrypts its own action (without knowing which of the blocks containing that action has been chosen) and the chooser's blinded action. It sends the blinded value back to the chooser (without knowing what the unblinded value is). The chooser subtracts the blinding value to get the result.

We need to prove that this protocol produces the right outputs with the correct probabilities, and that neither side gains any extra information.

Lemma 1. *Protocol CES securely computes the function of correlated element selection in the honest-but-curious model, with a negligible error in the probability of selecting any pair.*

Proof. **Correctness:** We will show that for all $i \in \{1, \ldots, n\}$, the action pair (a_i, b_i) is chosen by the protocol with probability p_i. This is true even given a fixed r_0. Suppose that $\hat{p}_i + r_0 < 1$. (The other cases are similar.) Let $int(x)$ denote the integer part of x. Then the number of blocks in which both pairs are (a_i, b_i) is $int(l(\hat{p}_i + r_0)) - int(l(\hat{p}_{i-1} + r_0)) - 1$. (Since $1/l < p_i$ this is always non-negative.) There is one block in which (a_i, b_i) is the leftmost pair only and another block in which it is the rightmost pair only. The probability of C choosing the leftmost pair in the former block is $frac(l(\hat{p}_i + r_0))$; the probability of it choosing the rightmost pair in the latter block is $1 - frac(l(\hat{p}_{i-1} + r_0))$. Therefore the chooser's probability of selecting (a_i, b_i) is

$$
\begin{aligned}
Pr\left(\text{Get } (a_i, b_i)\right) &= \left[int(l(\hat{p}_i + r_0)) - int(l(\hat{p}_{i-1} + r_0)) - 1\right]/l + frac(l(\hat{p}_i + r_0))/l \\
&\quad + \left[1 - frac(l(\hat{p}_{i-1} + r_0))\right]/l \\
&= \left[l(\hat{p}_i + r_0) - l(\hat{p}_{i-1} + r_0)\right]/l \\
&= p_i
\end{aligned}
$$

So if the protocol is followed correctly then it produces action pairs according to the correct distribution.

Secrecy: Informally, the preparer receives only three values: blinded encryptions of the chooser's action and the probability p_i that it is using, and a random encryption of its own action b_i. The first two provide no information because they are blinded by a random value that the preparer does not know. The last provides no information other than b_i, because any of the encryptions of b_i that were sent to the chooser are equally likely to have produced that ciphertext after blinding with zero. The chooser learns only four (unencrypted) values: the index of the block chosen, the probability of choosing the leftmost pair in that block, which pair (leftmost or rightmost) was chosen, and its output action a_i. The probability reveals no information, even combined with the index of the chosen block, because it is either a randomly chosen number independent of the input, or it is blinded by the factor r_0 which the chooser does not know. The choice of leftmost or rightmost pair also reveals no information because each pair of actions appears exactly the same number of times on the left and right sides.

More formally, the preparer's view can be simulated given its input and output b_i by sending it the encryptions of random values in place of the blinded action and probabilities, and sending it a random encryption of b_i in step 5. This produces a distribution identical to that of the protocol run.

The chooser's view can be simulated given its input and output a_i by sending it a "prepared list" of the right form which may actually include encryptions of anything. When it chooses a blinding factor β_1 for the probability, the simulator replies with a random value in $[0, 1/l)$. When the chooser chooses a blinding factor β_2 for its action, the simulator chooses an action pair (a_i, b_i) according to the correct distribution and sends $a_i + \beta_2$ to the chooser. This produces a distribution computationally indistinguishable from that of the protocol run. A distinguisher of the two distributions can defeat the semantically secure encryption scheme.

We now need to enhance the protocol to make it very unlikely that either player can cheat in a way that improves its utility without being detected by the other.

4   Protocol Secure against One Malicious or Two Selfish Players

We use zero knowledge proofs adapted from [DHR00] and a cut-and-choose protocol to transform the protocol from section 3 into one secure against a malicious player. After each step of the honest-but-curious protocol, the sender of the last message "proves" to the receiver that it has constructed the message correctly. The cryptographers' view is that if one player is malicious it cannot gain an advantage over an honest opponent. More importantly for our purposes, it is an equilibrium for two selfish players to execute the protocol correctly, because any deviation is either unhelpful or likely to be detected and punished by the other.

4.1   Probability Distribution Is Correct with One Faulty Player

The only protocol steps that can't be checked using zero-knowledge proofs or a cut-and-choose protocol are those that involve making some random choice according to a specified probability distribution. Since players can't prove to each other that they have done this correctly, we will use the standard trick of arguing that as long as one of the players makes its random choices correctly, the outcome will be correct (which in this case means that the final pair of actions is chosen according to the correct probability distribution). The game theory view is that it is an equilibrium for both players to toss their coins fairly, since unilateral deviation makes no difference to the outcome.

Lemma 2. *Suppose that the players are allowed to deviate from the protocol only by altering their random coin tosses. Then if at least one player tosses its coins correctly, the final pair of moves is selected according to the correct probability distribution.*

Proof. If the chooser chooses its randomness correctly, then it is easy to see that the resulting distribution is correct. For the other case, suppose that the preparer correctly chooses r_0 uniformly at random from $[0, 1)$ but that the chooser chooses its block according to a non-uniform distribution and chooses the leftmost pair of actions according to a (possibly randomized) function $\text{CH}()$ that depends on the block chosen and the probability p decrypted by the preparer. $\text{CH}()$ outputs either L (for left) or R (for right). Since the encryption algorithm used is semantically secure, the distribution on blocks must be independent of the choice of r_0. More importantly, $\text{CH}()$ is independent of r_0 and the preparer's other coin tosses given p. We will show that for all p, for all choices of the block, the probability (given p) that the chooser chooses a particular pair of actions is exactly what it should be. Fix the value of p and the chooser's choice of block (call it λ). Let P_i be the probability that the i-th action pair (a_i, b_i) is chosen. We need to prove that $P_i = p_i$. Let r_P denote the random coin tosses of the preparer (apart from r_0) and let r_{CH} denote the random coin tosses of the $\text{CH}()$ algorithm. Let $P_{lt} = Pr_{r_{\text{CH}}}(\text{CH}(p, \lambda) = L)$ and $P_{rt} = Pr_{r_{\text{CH}}}(\text{CH}(p, \lambda) = R)$. Recall that all the computations are done to $\hat{k}$ bits of precision. Then

$$P_i = Pr_{r_0, r_P, r_{\text{CH}}}[(\text{Left pair is } (a_i, b_i) \text{ and } \text{CH}(p, \lambda) = L)$$
$$\text{or } (\text{Right pair is } (a_i, b_i) \text{ and } \text{CH}(p, \lambda) = R)]$$
$$= P_{lt} Pr_{r_0, r_P} (\text{Left pair is } (a_i, b_i)) + P_{rt} Pr_{r_0, r_P} (\text{Right pair is } (a_i, b_i))$$
$$= P_{lt} Pr_{r_0, r_P} (r_0 = (\lambda - 1)/l + p - \hat{p}_i \vee (r_0 \in [(\lambda/l - \hat{p}_i, (\lambda - 1)/l - \hat{p}_{i-1}) \wedge q_\lambda = p))$$
$$+ P_{rt} Pr_{r_0, r_P} (r_0 = (\lambda - 1)/l + p - \hat{p}_{i-1} \vee (r_0 \in [\lambda/l - \hat{p}_i, (\lambda - 1)/l - \hat{p}_{i-1}) \wedge q_\lambda = p))$$
$$= P_{lt} \frac{1/2^{\hat{k}} + (p_i - 1/l)l/2^{\hat{k}}}{l/2^{\hat{k}}} + (1 - P_{lt}) \frac{1/2^{\hat{k}} + (p_i - 1/l)l/2^{\hat{k}}}{l/2^{\hat{k}}}$$
$$= p_i$$

The first equation is given by the independence of CH() from r_0 and the other coin tosses of the preparer, given p. The second is just the definition of what it means to have (a_i, b_i) in the left or right part of the λ-th block. The third gives the probabilities for r_0 being in the required ranges, given p – the denominator is the *a priori* probability of getting a particular value for p.

This shows that, as long as one party tosses its coins correctly, the output probability distribution is correct.

4.2   Preventing Deviation from the Protocol

We use the same techniques as [DHR00] to prevent players from deviating from the protocol in ways other than making their random choices wrongly. After each round of the honest-but-curious protocol (except the first), the sender proves to the recipient in Zero Knowledge that it produced the message correctly. We can use the same proofs as [DHR00] for proving truthful decryption and proving that a certain ciphertext is truly a blinding of one from the original list. The only place where we must do this in an inefficient manner (differently to the method used in [DHR00]) is in the first message that the preparer sends to the chooser. Here we use a "cut-and-choose" protocol: the preparer prepares several candidate lists and the chooser selects one of them to be used in the protocol. The preparer must decrypt the rest, thereby proving to the chooser that they were prepared correctly. Of course, if the prover makes one incorrect list there is some chance that it will succeed in fooling the chooser. There is a known upper bound on the profit that the preparer can make by cheating (its greatest payoff in the game minus its equilibrium payoff), so the number of candidate lists must be large enough that its expected gain from trying to cheat is negative. This means that the length of the first message is linear in the payoffs of the game. The protocol in [DHR00] is actually logarithmic in the payoffs, because their security parameter needs to be at least long enough that the probability of the cryptography failing (either in the zero knowledge proofs or in encryptions) is a constant fraction of the game's payoffs. Hence their methods for preventing protocol deviation are more efficient than ours in terms of the game's payoffs.

We can now prove Theorem 1, that it is a computational Nash equilibrium for everyone to execute the protocol correctly and minimax the other if it cheats. We have shown that a player that cheats (except by tossing its coins wrongly) will be detected and punished with high enough probability that it has no incentive to do so. We have also shown that a player that cheats by tossing its coins wrongly has no effect on the outcome if the other is honest, so there is no incentive for that kind of cheating either. Hence the "honest" strategy is a computational Nash equilibrium. Two competing, selfish and rational firms could use this to attain any correlated equilibrium payoff without using a trusted mediator.

5   Conclusion

There is a lot of interesting overlap between cryptography and game theory. In this paper we have given an efficient way of implementing a game theoretic solution concept that is impossible to implement without either cryptography or a trusted third party. This could be used by participants in all sorts of markets to coordinate their actions for their mutual benefit. We expect cryptography to be a useful tool for solving many other practical game theoretic problems that relate to the careful distribution of information.

Acknowledgements

Thanks to Yevgeniy Dodis for helpful feedback on an earlier version of this work, to Adam Cagliarini for thinking up examples of correlated equilibria with non-uniform distributions, to Bob McGrew for some pointers to literature, to John Mitchell for helpful comments on a draft of this paper, and to Andrew Conway for suggesting many interesting practical applications of this protocol, and for encouraging me to write this paper.

References

[AET01]   Aaron Archer and Éva Tardos. Truthful mechanisms for one-parameter agents. In *Proceedings of the 42nd IEEE Symposium on Foundations of Computer Science*, pages 482–491, 2001.

[Bar92]   I. Barany. Fair distribution protocols or how the players replace fortune. *Mathematics of Operations Research*, 17(2):327–340, 1992.

[DHR00]   Y. Dodis, S. Halevi, and T. Rabin. A cryptographic solution to a game theoretic problem. In *Proceedings of CRYPTO*, 2000.

[FPS01]   Joan Feigenbaum, Christos Papadimitriou, and Scott Shenker. Sharing the cost of multicast transmissions. *Journal of Computer and System Sciences*, 63:21–41, 2001. Special issue on Internet Algorithms.

[FPSS02] Joan Feigenbaum, Christos Papadimitriou, Rahul Sami, and Scott Shenker. A bgp-based mechanism for lowest-cost routing. In *Proceedings of the 21st Symposium on Principles of Distributed Computing*, pages 173–182, New York, 2002. ACM Press.

[FT91]   Drew Fudenberg and Jean Tirole. *Game Theory*. MIT Press, Cambridge, Massachusetts, 1991.

[Gol03]   O. Goldreich. Draft of a chapter on general protocols: Extracts from a working draft for volume 2 of foundations of cryptography. Available at `http://www.wisdom.weizmann.ac.il/~oded/`, 2003.

[GM84]   S. Goldwasser and S. Micali. Probabilistic encryption. *Special issue of Journal of Computer and Systems Sciences*, 28(2):270–299, 1984.

[NPS99]   M. Naor, B. Pinkas, and R. Sumner. Privacy preserving auctions and mechanism design. In *Proceedings of the 1st ACM conf. on Electronic Commerce*, 1999.

[NR01]   N. Nisan and A. Ronen. Algorithmic mechanism design. *Games and Economic Behavior*, 35:166–196, 2001.

[OR94]   M. Osborne and A. Rubinstein. *A course in Game Theory*. MIT Press, 1994.

[RT02]   T. Roughgarden and É. Tardos. How bad is selfish routing? *Journal of the ACM* 49(2):236–259, March 2002.

[UV02]   A. Urbano and J. Vila. Computational complexity and communication: coordination in two-player games. *Econometrica*, 70(5):1893–1927, September 2002.

An Efficient and Usable Multi-show Non-transferable Anonymous Credential System*

Giuseppe Persiano[1] and Ivan Visconti[2,**]

[1] Dipartimento di Informatica ed Applicazioni
Università di Salerno
via S. Allende – 84081 Baronissi (SA), Italy
giuper@dia.unisa.it
[2] Département d'Informatique
École Normale Supérieure
rue d'Ulm - 75230 Paris Cedex 05, France
ivan.visconti@ens.fr

Abstract. In an anonymous credential system a user can prove anonymously the possession of credentials to a service provider. Multi-show and non-transferability are two important properties of such systems. More precisely, in a *multi-show* system the same credential can be used more than once without threatening anonymity, moreover, lending of non-transferable credentials is *inconvenient*. In this paper we give a construction for multi-show non-transferable credentials for which the owner can prove that the credentials satisfy access control policies expressed by means of linear boolean formulae.

1 Introduction

Privacy enhancing technologies focus on the deployment of infrastructures that protect user privacy in the digital world. Currently many services that are fundamental for the worldwide economy are available on the Internet and many others are going to be supported. Several services are not accessible anonymously from everybody, but a form of access control is performed in order to distinguish qualified users (i.e., the ones that have enough rights to access the service) and unqualified ones. Current standard technologies implement such access control policies by requiring user identification (e.g., by using username and password or X509 [1] digital certificates), by retrieving user's credentials from a local database and then by checking that user's credentials satisfy a given access control policy. Such a typical scheme is secure, efficient, practical and guarantees that unqualified users do not get access to a restricted service. However such a scheme does not deal at all with user privacy protection since in each transaction between

---

* Work partially supported by NoE ECRYPT.
** Work done while Ivan Visconti was a temporary researcher at the Dipartimento di Informatica ed Applicazioni of the Università di Salerno.

a user and a service provider the user reveals his identity, the transaction can be logged and an accurate dossier of all activities performed by the user can eventually be extracted from the logs.

In an *anonymous credential system* we have three types of players: organizations, users and service providers. Typically, a user gets a credential certificate encoding the user credentials from an organization and uses the credentials to access services. Each service provider specifies which users are qualified to access the service as a function of the credentials of the user. Thus, before accessing the service the user and service provider engage in a protocol in which the user proves possession of (a credential certificate encoding) credentials sufficient for the service in question. In an anonymous credential systems it is desired that the service provider cannot link a request for the service with a specific user or with other past requests. Roughly, we now list the properties that an anonymous credential system should enjoy.

1. **Security:** it is hard for a coalition of users to get access to a service without having the requested credentials.
2. **Multi-show privacy:** a user during a transaction can prove possession of credentials and, at the same time, the service provider does not obtain any private user information. This holds even if the user interacts using the same credential certificate several times with the same (or other) service provider.
3. **Usability:** a user that possesses a credential certificate should be able to prove *general statements* (in our case the satisfaction of linear Boolean formulae) over the credentials while preserving multi-show privacy.
4. **Non-Transferability:** it should be inconvenient for a user to lend his credentials to another user.
5. **Efficiency:** the overhead in terms of communication and computation imposed by the anonymous credential system to users and service providers must not heavily affect their performance.

Related Work. An anonymous credential system can be based on the concept of proofs in which a user shows possession of some piece of information (the credentials) that satisfies some given conditions (e.g., the access control policy). A first implementation of these proofs, for the case in which the conditions are expressed by a monotone Boolean formula, can be traced back to the general results on statistical zero-knowledge proof systems by [2] with efficiency communication improvements given by [3]. In [4, 5] these techniques are further explored and their applicability to real-life scenarios shown. In particular, Brands [4] presented a Public Key Infrastructure in which a user can prove in zero knowledge that the credentials encoded by his certificate satisfy a given linear Boolean formula. Brands' constructions are efficient since only a few modular exponentiations (i.e., the number of modular exponentiations is linear in the number of encoded credentials) have to be performed in order to prove that the credentials encoded in the certificate satisfy a given linear Boolean formula. The main drawback of Brands' certificates is that they are *one-show* in the sense that using the same certificate in two distinct transactions links the two transactions as performed by the same user. As a consequence of this weakness, a user needs to obtain from the Certification Authority an impractically large batch of certificates so that no certificate is used twice.

In our construction we will be interested in *multi-show* certificates that can be used several times still guaranteeing unlinkability. We will base our construction on some techniques proposed in [4, 5] in order to achieve proofs of possession of credentials that satisfy a given linear Boolean formula and we extend such schemes in order to achieve the *multi-show* property.

The first implementation of anonymous credentials has been presented in [6] where a third party is necessary in order to achieve unlinkability. Lysyanskaya et al. [7] proposed a general credential system that, however, is impractical being based on general one-way functions and zero-knowledge proofs. Moreover, they also presented an efficient one-show construction. The same drawback affects the solution proposed in [8]. The work of Camenisch and Lysyanskaya [9] has improved these pioneering works. In [9] the authors proposed an anonymous credential system that is based on the strong RSA assumption and the DDH assumption. In the system of [9] it is possible to unlinkably prove possession of a credential supporting the multi-show property and the entities that release credentials can independently choose their cryptographic keys. More recently, Verheul [10] proposed a more efficient solution for multi-show credentials. The result is based on the assumption that for some groups the Decisional version of the Diffie-Hellman (DDH) problem is easy while its Computational version (CDH) is hard and on an additional *ad-hoc* assumption.

The property of Brands' constructions, by which general statements of the values encoded by a certificate can be proved, is not enjoyed by the works of [9, 10]. Indeed, in such systems it is necessary to have one ad-hoc credential for each specific access control policy otherwise more information than the minimal one needed in each transaction is disclosed.

Finally, in [11], Persiano and Visconti presented a non-transferable anonymous credential system that is multi-show and for which it is possible to prove properties (encoded by a linear Boolean formula) of the credentials. Unfortunately, their proof system is not efficient since the step in which a user proves possession of credentials (that needs a number of modular exponentiations that is linear in the number of credentials) must be repeated k times (where k is the security parameter) in order to obtain a satisfying soundness.

Thus, the state of the art presents efficient solutions that either require one credential certificate for each service [9, 10] but each can be used as many times as needed; or require one credential certificate for each time the user needs to access a service [4] but a certificate can be used for any service.

Our contribution. In this paper, we present an anonymous credential system that is secure, multi-show, usable, non-transferable and efficient. In our system a user needs to obtain only *one* certificate to be used as many times as necessary with any service provider since our system enjoys the multi-show property. Moreover, in our construction we show how to enforce the non-transferability property. The security property of our system is based on new computational assumptions derived from the ones used in [12–14].

2   The Model

Our model consists of three types of players:

1. The *organizations*, that release *credential certificates* to users.
2. The *users*, each with a set of credentials. A user receives a credential certificate encoding his credentials from an organization that he will then use to access services.
3. The *service providers*, that offer services and have access control policies for their services. We assume that the access control policy for each resource of each service is represented by a linear Boolean formula Φ over the required credentials.

A *credential system* $\mathcal{C}$ consists of the following five algorithms

$$(\texttt{SetUp}, \texttt{Enroll}, \texttt{IssueCred}, \texttt{ProveCred}, \texttt{VerifyCred}).$$

Next, we summarize how these algorithms interact and which of the parties executes each algorithm. In Section 4 we will present an implementation of such procedures.

1. **System set-up:** this step is performed only once by each organization in order to establish publicly verifiable parameters $\texttt{Pub}$ (that will be used by the other procedures) and consists in executing algorithm $\texttt{SetUp}$ on input the security parameter. The organization also obtains the private information $\texttt{Priv}$ which corresponds to the public information $\texttt{Pub}$ that she will use to release credential certificates.
   At the end of this phase, the organization is ready to release credential certificates.
2. **User enrollment:** this step is performed jointly by the user and by an organization and consists in executing the pair of algorithms ($\texttt{Enroll}, \texttt{IssueCred}$). The user has as input her credentials encoded by an m-tuple $(x_1, \cdots, x_m)$ and the public information published by the organization during the set up of the system.
   The organization verifies the credentials and then releases the credential certificate.
3. **Proving possession of credentials:** this step is performed by a user executing algorithm $\texttt{ProveCred}$ interacting with a service provider executing $\texttt{VerifyCred}$ in order to gain access to a service which is restricted to legitimate users.
   The user has as input her credential certificate, the credentials, the public information and the formula Φ that encodes the access control policy.

   Our anonymous credential system guarantees the following properties:

Usability: once a user has obtained a credential certificate $\texttt{CredCert}$ for credentials $(x_1, \cdots, x_m)$ from the organization then $\texttt{CredCert}$ can be used (as input to algorithm $\texttt{ProveCred}$) to successfully access any service with access control formula Φ such that $\Phi(x_1, \cdots, x_m) = 1$. In other words, the user has to interact only once with the organization in order to get her credential certificate. From then on, the *same* credential certificate can be used to access any service (provided that the credentials satisfy the access control formula).

Security: it is computationally infeasible for a coalition of users to access the system without having a credential certificate; moreover, it is not possible to generate a new credential certificate even knowing a polynomial number of other credential certificates.

We formalize the security property in the following way.

Definition 1. *Let* C=*(*SetUp, Enroll, IssueCred, ProveCred, VerifyCred*) be a credential system. We say that* C *is* secure *if for all probabilistic polynomial time algorithms* A *and for any formula* Φ *the probability that* A *on input the public information* Pub *and a sequence of credential certificates corresponding to credentials not satisfying* Φ *successfully interacts with algorithm* VerifyCred *on* Φ *is negligible.*

Multi-show privacy: no information about the credentials owned by a user is leaked by the protocol executed to prove possession of credentials other than the fact that the credentials satisfy the access control formula Φ. Moreover, two uses of the same credential certificate cannot be linked.

We formalize the property of multi-show privacy in the following way.

Definition 2. *Let* C=*(*SetUp, Enroll, IssueCred, ProveCred, VerifyCred*) be a credential system. We say that* C *is* multi-show private *if for any triple of adversarial algorithms (*SetUp*, IssueCred*, VerifyCred*) there exists an algorithm* S *running in expected polynomial-time such that for any linear Boolean formula* Φ*, for all* $(x_1, \cdots, x_m)$ *for which* $\Phi(x_1, \cdots, x_m) = 1$ *it holds that*

$$S(\mathtt{Pub}) = (\mathtt{ProveCred}(x_1, \cdots, x_m, \mathtt{CredCert}, \mathtt{Pub}, \Phi)$$
$$\leftrightarrow \mathtt{VerifyCred}^*(\mathtt{Priv}, \mathtt{Pub}, \Phi))$$

where $(\mathtt{Priv}, \mathtt{Pub}) \leftarrow \mathtt{SetUp}^*(1^k)$ *and* $\mathtt{CredCert} \leftarrow (\mathtt{Enroll}(x_1, \cdots, x_m, \mathtt{Pub}) \leftrightarrow \mathtt{IssueCred}^*(\mathtt{Priv}, \mathtt{Pub})).$

Roughly, the formalization above states that the interaction between a user possessing a certificate for credentials $(x_1, \ldots, x_m)$ and a service provider (that could be the same organization that releases credential certificates and thus take as input Priv) can be efficiently simulated by an algorithm that has as input the public information and black-box access to the service provider.

Moreover (formal definition omitted from this abstract) in our construction the multi-show privacy holds even if the same credential certificate is used a polynomial number of times for a polynomial number of different Boolean formulae.

Our construction also enjoys the *non-transferability* property: it is "inconvenient" for a legitimate user to share her credentials with other users.

Finally, our construction is particularly *efficient* in the amount of information to be stored and in the amount computation to be performed (see Section 4.6) when a large number of credentials is considered used.

3   Background

In this section we summarize the main cryptographic techniques that we use in our constructions. For further details see [15, 4, 13].

We start by reviewing the notions of discrete logarithm and discrete logarithm representation.

Definition 3. *Given a group G of order n, and two elements g and y of G, the discrete logarithm of y to the base g, if it exists, is the integer $0 \leq x \leq n-2$ such that $y = g^x$.*

We stress that the discrete logarithm of y to the base g exists if and only if y belongs to the subgroup generated by g. This is the case, for example, if G is a finite cyclic group and g is a generator of G; in this case computing the discrete logarithm is considered hard. The discrete logarithm is also considered hard in the group Z_n^* where n is a composite integer. Indeed, if the discrete logarithm problem in Z_n^* can be solved in polynomial time, then n can be factored in expected polynomial time.

Definition 4. *Let G be a group of order n and let $y, g_1, \ldots, g_m \neq 1$ be elements of G. A $(G, g_1, \ldots, g_m)$-DL representation of y is a tuple $(x_1, \ldots, x_m)$ such that $0 \leq x_i \leq n-1$ for $i = 1, \ldots, m$ and $y = g_1^{x_1} \ldots g_m^{x_m}$.*

Moreover, for $i = 1, \ldots, m$, we call x_i the g_i-part of the $(G, g_1, \ldots, g_m)$-DL representation $(x_1, \ldots, x_m)$ of y.

Definition 5. *Let e be an element of Z_n^* co-prime with $\phi(n)$. A (Z_n^*, e)-root of $y \in Z_n^*$ is an element $x \in Z_n^*$ such that $x^e \equiv y \pmod{n}$.*

Note that if the factorization of n is unknown then computing e-th roots in Z_n^* is assumed to be infeasible (this is the RSA assumption).

We introduce the notion of RSA representation that has also been used in some of the constructions of [4, 5].

Definition 6. *Let $e \in Z_n^*$ be co-prime with $\phi(n)$ and let $y, g_1, \cdots, g_m \neq 1$ be elements of Z_n^*. A $(Z_n^*, e, g_1, \cdots, g_m)$-RSA representation (RSAREP) of y is a tuple $(x_1, \ldots, x_m, x)$ such that $y \equiv g_1^{x_1} \cdots g_m^{x_m} x^e \pmod{n}$, $0 \leq x_i < e$ for $i = 1, \ldots, m$ and $x \in Z_n^*$.*

In [4] it is shown how to choose the parameters so that the RSA representation problem can be reduced to the RSA problem.

3.1   Proofs of Knowledge

We summarize the proofs of knowledge (PoKs) that will be used in our construction, for details see [13, 4, 16].

PoK of a discrete logarithm. On input (the description of) a cyclic group G of order n, a generator g of G, and an element $y \in G$, the prover P proves knowledge to the verifier V of x, the discrete logarithm of y to the base g.

PoK of a $(G, g_1, \ldots, g_m)$-DL representation. On input the description of a cyclic group G of order n and elements $y, g_1, \cdots, g_m$ of G, the prover P proves knowledge of a $(G, g_1, \ldots, g_m)$-DL representation $(x_1, \ldots, x_m)$ of y.

PoK of a $(Z_n^*, e, g_1, \ldots, g_m)$-RSA representation. On input $n, e, g_1, \ldots, g_m$ where (n, e) is an RSA public key and $g_1, \ldots, g_m$ are randomly chosen element of Z_n^*, the prover proves knowledge of a $(Z_n^*, e, g_1, \ldots, g_m)$-RSA representation $(x_1, \ldots, x_m, x)$ of $y \in Z_n^*$.

In such proofs of knowledge if the challenge of the verifier is in $\{0, 1\}^k$ and $k = O(\log \log n)$, then the proofs are statistical zero-knowledge proofs of knowledge with soundness probability 2^{-k}. This probability can be reduced by sequentially repeating the protocols. If instead $k = \Omega(\log n)$, then the protocols are statistical witness indistinguishable. In particular by using such proofs, at the cost of one exponentiation per base it is possible to prove in a witness indistinguishable manner knowledge of a discrete logarithm or of a DL-representation or of an RSA-representation and still have negligible error probability.

PoK of an e-th root of the h_1-part of a (G, h_1, h_2)-DL representation. In [13], when e is a small integer, an efficient PoK by which it is possible to prove knowledge of a root of a part of a DL representation is presented. More precisely, we have the following theorem.

Theorem 7. *[13] Let G be a cyclic group of order n where n is the product of two safe primes. There exists a statistical zero-knowledge proof of knowledge for the polynomial-time relation $((G, h_1, h_2, e, y), (x_1, x_2, x))$, where h_1, h_2 are two elements of G, e is co-prime with $\phi(n)$, $y \in G$, (x_1, x_2) is a (G, h_1, h_2)-DL representation of y and $x \in Z_n^*$ is the e-th root of $x_1 \in Z_n^*$.*

The PoK of the previous theorem requires a number of modular exponentiations which is linear in e and thus is particularly efficient when $e = 3$ (as in our construction).

Recently, in [17] such a PoK has been improved by requiring only a number of modular exponentiations that is logarithmic in e.

PoK of the discrete logarithm to a based g of the h_1-part of a (G, h_1, h_2)-DL representation. On input (the description of) a cyclic group G of order n, where n is the product of two safe primes, two elements h_1, h_2 of G, a large order element g of Z_n^* and an element $y = h_1^{g^{x_1}} h_2^{x_2} \in G$, the prover P proves knowledge to the verifier V of the discrete logarithm x_1 to the base g of the h_1-part of the (G, h_1, h_2)-DL representation of y to the bases h_1, h_2.

Such a PoK can be given by repeating the following steps:

1. P computes $t = h_1^{g^{r_1}} h_2^{r_2}$ with randomly chosen r_1, r_2 and sends t to V;
2. V sends a bit b to P;
3. if $b = 0$ then P computes $s_1 = r_1$ and $s_2 = r_2$, otherwise he computes $s_1 = r_1 - x_1$ and $s_2 = r_2 - x_2 g^{s_1}$ and sends s_1, s_2 to V;
4. V accepts if $t = h_1^{g^{s_1}} h_2^{s_2}$ and $b = 0$ or $t = y^{g^{s_1}} h_2^{s_2}$ otherwise.

Theorem 8. *Given a cyclic group G of order n where n is the product of two safe primes, two elements h_1, h_2 of G and an element $g \in Z_n^*$, the previous protocol is an honest-verifier zero-knowledge proof of knowledge of the discrete logarithm x_1 to the base g of the h_1-part of a (G, h_1, h_2)-DL representation (g^{x_1}, x_2) of an element $y \in G$.*

Proving knowledge of a special representation. In [4, 5], Brands presents PoKs by which the prover can prove knowledge of a DL representation that satisfies a given linear Boolean formula Φ, i.e., a Boolean formula where each atomic proposition is a relation that is linear in the values of the DL representation (e.g., $((x_1 + 3x_2 = 4)$ OR (NOT $(5x_1 + 4x_3 = 6)))$ AND $(8x_2 + 3x_3 = 12))$.

The protocol is based on the following technique. For a finite cyclic group G and for any linear Boolean formula Φ, knowledge of a $(G, g_1, \ldots, g_m)$-DL representation $(x_1, \ldots, x_m)$ of y for which $\Phi(x_1, \ldots, x_m) = 1$ is equivalent to knowledge of a $(G, g_1', \ldots, g_m')$-DL representation $(x_1', \cdots, x_m')$ of $y' \in G$. The values $g_1', \cdots, g_m'$ and y' only depend on the formula Φ and on $g_1, \ldots, g_m$ and y while $(x_1', \cdots, x_m')$ can be computed from $(x_1, \cdots, x_m)$. Thus, the prover and the verifier construct the auxiliary instance of the DL representation problem and run the protocol described above for proving knowledge of a DL representation. This implies that the above efficiency considerations regarding the PoK of a DL-representation apply also to the PoK in which knowledge of a DL-representation satisfying Φ is proved.

Theorem 9. *[4, 5] Let G be a finite cyclic group of order n and Φ be a linear Boolean formula, then there exists a statistical zero-knowledge proof of knowledge and a constant-round statistical witness indistinguishable proof of knowledge for the polynomial time relation $((G, u, g_1, \cdots, g_m, \Phi), (x_1, \cdots, x_m))$ such that $(x_1, \cdots, x_m)$ is a $(G, g_1, \cdots, g_m)$-DL representation of $u \in G$ and $\Phi(x_1, \cdots, x_m) = 1$.*

The same result can be extended also to the case in which we need to prove knowledge of an RSA representation and we have the following result.

Theorem 10. *[4, 5] Let Φ be a linear Boolean formula, (n, e) be an RSA public key, then there exists a statistical zero-knowledge proof of knowledge and a constant-round statistical witness indistinguishable proof of knowledge for the polynomial time relation $((Z_n^*, e, u, g_1, \cdots, g_m, \Phi), (x_1, \cdots, x_m, x))$ and it holds that $(x_1, \cdots, x_m, x)$ is a $(Z_n^*, e, g_1, \cdots, g_m)$-RSA representation of $u \in Z_n^*$ and $\Phi(x_1, \cdots, x_m) = 1$.*

4   Our Implementation of Credential Certificates

We first introduce a computational assumption on which we base our construction of credential certificates.

4.1   Computational Assumption

The security of a group signature scheme presented in [12] (based on the one presented in [13]) is based on the assumption that, on input an integer $n =$

$p_1 p_2$ where p_1 and p_2 are primes of the same length, an integer e such that $\gcd(e, \phi(n)) = 1$ and $a, c \in Z_n^*$, it is hard to find in probabilistic polynomial time a pair (v, x) such that $v^e = a^x + c \pmod{n}$. Moreover, in [12] it is assumed that such a pair (v, x) is hard to find even if several other pairs are known. This property is used in order to prove the unforgeability of their scheme even with respect to coalitions of users. The computational assumption on which we are going to the base the security of our construction is a generalization of the assumption of [12].

We start with the following definition.

Definition 11. *Given an RSA public key (n, e) and elements $g, c, g_1, \ldots, g_l \in Z_n^*$ such that $g_1, \ldots, g_l \in \langle g \rangle$, we say that a tuple $(x_1, \ldots, x_l, x, v, z, y)$ such that, for $i = 1 \ldots, l$, $0 \leq x_i < e$, $0 \leq y < e$, $v, x \in Z_n^*$ and is a good tuple with respect to $(n, e, g, c, g_1, \cdots, g_l)$ if $v^3 \equiv g^y g_1^{x_1} \cdots g_l^{x_l} x^e + c g^z \pmod{n}$. Moreover, if $(x_1, \ldots, x_l, x, v, z, y)$ is a good tuple then we say that $(x_1, \ldots, x_{l-1})$ is its prefix.*

Consider the following game in which a probabilistic polynomial-time algorithm $\mathcal{A}$ receives as input:

1. an integer n such that $n = p_1 p_2$ where $p_1 = 2q_1 + 1, p_2 = 2q_2 + 1$, q_1, q_2 are primes of length k, $3 \nmid (p_1 - 1)(p_2 - 1)$;
2. $e \in Z_n^*$ such that $3 \nmid e$, $e \nmid (p_1 - 1)(p_2 - 1)$;
3. large order elements $g, c \in Z_n^*$ and $g_1, \ldots, g_l$ for $l \geq 2$ that are elements of $\langle g \rangle$;
4. s such that $g \equiv s^3 \pmod{n}$;

and has access to an oracle $\mathcal{O}$ that, on input the sequence $(x_1, \ldots, x_{l-1})$ outputs a random good tuple $(x_1, \ldots, x_l, x, v, 0, 0)$ with prefix $(x_1, \ldots, x_{l-1})$ such that x_l is co-prime with both 3 and e.

We denote by $\mathrm{Succ}^{\mathcal{A}}(k)$ the probability that algorithm $\mathcal{A}$, running on the input described above, where n has length k, and having oracle access to $\mathcal{O}$ outputs a good tuple $(x_1', \ldots, x_l', x', v', z', y')$ whose prefix $(x_1', \ldots, x_{l-1}')$ is different from any of the queries made to the oracle by $\mathcal{A}$.

We have the following assumption.

Assumption 12. *For all efficient algorithms $\mathcal{A}$, for all constants η and for all sufficiently large k*

$$\mathrm{Succ}^{\mathcal{A}}(k) \leq k^{-\eta}.$$

Given a good tuple $(x_1, \ldots, x_l, x, v, 0, 0)$, the tuple $(x_1, \ldots, x_l, x, vs^y, y, y)$ is also good for any value of $0 \leq y < e$. Indeed we will use exactly this property in order to achieve the multi-show privacy. However, we stress that in order to break our assumption it is necessary to produce a new tuple in which the prefix $(x_1, \ldots, x_{l-1})$ (which in our system encodes the credentials) is different from that of each original sub-tuple.

4.2 Our Implementation

For the sake of simplifying the presentation, we now describe our system only for the case in which a credential certificate carries two credentials. We stress that modifying the system in order to support more than two credentials is straightforward.

System set-up. We now describe algorithm SetUp performed by an organization O.

Algorithm SetUp(1^k)

1. randomly pick two k-bit safe primes $p_1 = 2q_1 + 1, p_2 = 2q_2 + 1$ such that $\gcd(3, \phi(p_1 p_2)) = 1$, q_1, q_2 are primes and sets $n = p_1 p_2$;
2. randomly pick $e \in Z_n^*$ such that $\gcd(e, \phi(n)) = 1$ and $\gcd(3, e) = 1$;
3. compute $d \in Z_n^*$ such that $3d \equiv 1 \pmod{\phi(n)}$;
4. select element $g, c \in Z_n^*$ of large order;
5. randomly pick elements v_1, v_2, v_3 and set $g_1 \equiv g^{v_1}, g_2 \equiv g^{v_2}, g_3 \equiv g^{v_3} \pmod{n}$;
6. compute $s \equiv g^d \pmod{n}$;
7. compute a cyclic group G of order n in which computing the discrete logarithm is infeasible (e.g., G can be computed as a subgroup of Z_q^* for a prime q such that $n|(q-1)$), along with six elements $h_1, \ldots, h_6 \neq 1$ of G;
8. output public information Pub $= (n, e, g, s, c, g_1, g_2, g_3, G, h_1, \ldots, h_6)$ and private information Priv $= (q_1, q_2, d, v_1, v_2, v_3)$.

The bases g_1 and g_2 are used to encode the two credentials of a certificate, c, g_3 for the security of the system, g and s are used in order to achieve multi-show privacy, while $h_1, \ldots, h_6$ are used in order to compute commitments.

User enrollment. In this phase a user asks the organization for a credential certificate with encoded values x_1, x_2 of the two credentials. We assume that $0 \leq x_1, x_2 < e$. The organization returns a good tuple with prefix (x_1, x_2).

Protocol Enroll(x_1, x_2, Pub) $\leftrightarrow$ IssueCred(Pub, Priv)

1. the organization verifies the credentials (x_1, x_2) submitted by the user in observance to its policy;
2. the organization randomly chooses x_3 such that $0 \leq x_3 < e$, x_3 is co-prime with e and not multiple of 3, and $x \in Z_n^*$;
3. the organization sets $a \equiv g_1^{x_1} g_2^{x_2} g_3^{x_3} x^e \pmod{n}$, $b \equiv c \pmod{n}$, and computes $v \equiv (a+b)^d \pmod{n}$;
4. the organization sends the good tuple $(x_1, x_2, x_3, x, v, 0, 0)$ to the user;
5. the user verifies that the tuple received is a good tuple;
6. the user and the organization engage in zero-knowledge proofs in which the organization proves that n is the product of two safe primes and that g is a large-order element of Z_n^* (this is done using the protocols of [18]), that g_1, g_2, g_3, x are elements of $\langle g \rangle$ (this is done by proving knowledge of the discrete logarithms of g_1, g_2, g_3 to the base g).
   Such proofs have to be performed only once for each user, independently of the number of credential certificates that he receives.

Showing possession of credentials. In this phase a user proves to a service provider the possession of a good tuple with prefix (x_1, x_2) satisfying the linear Boolean formula Φ encoding the access control policy. More precisely, the following steps are performed by the user and the service provider.

Protocol ProveCred $\leftrightarrow$ VerifyCred

Common input to user and service provider: the public information Pub $= (n, e, g, s, c, g_1, g_2, g_3, G, h_1, h_2, h_3, h_4, h_5, h_6)$ and a linear Boolean formula $\Phi(\cdot, \cdot)$ encoding the access control policy.

Private input to user:

1. a good tuple $(x_1, x_2, x_3, x, v, 0, 0)$ such that $\Phi(x_1, x_2) = 1$.

Instructions for user and service provider:

1. the user sets $a \equiv g_1^{x_1} g_2^{x_2} g_3^{x_3} x^e \pmod{n}$, $b \equiv c \pmod{n}$, $m \equiv a + b \pmod{n}$;
2. the user picks a random y such that $0 \le y < e$;
3. set $\hat{m} \equiv g^y m \pmod{n}$, $\hat{v} \equiv s^y v \pmod{n}$, $\hat{a} \equiv g^y a \pmod{n}$ and $\hat{b} \equiv g^y b \pmod{n}$; thus we have $\hat{m} - \hat{a} - \hat{b} \equiv 0 \pmod{n}$;
4. the user computes commitments to $\hat{m}, \hat{a}$ and $\hat{b}$ by randomly choosing $r_1, r_2, r_3 \in Z_n$ and computing the following values (operations are performed in G):
   4.1. $\mathrm{Com}(\hat{m}) = h_1^{\hat{m}} h_2^{r_1}$;
   4.2. $\mathrm{Com}(\hat{a}) = h_3^{\hat{a}} h_4^{r_2}$;
   4.3. $\mathrm{Com}(\hat{b}) = h_5^{\hat{b}} h_6^{r_3}$;
5. the user sends to the service provider $\mathrm{Com}(\hat{m}), \mathrm{Com}(\hat{a}), \mathrm{Com}(\hat{b})$ and $\hat{a}$;
6. let $\mathrm{Com}(c) = \mathrm{Com}(\hat{m})\mathrm{Com}(\hat{a})\mathrm{Com}(\hat{b})$. Parties engage in proofs of knowledge:
   6.1. The user proves knowledge of a $(Z_n^*, e, g, g_1, g_2, g_3)$-RSA representation (u_g, u_1, u_2, u_3, u) of $\hat{a}$ such that $\Phi(u_1, u_2) = 1$. This is achieved by means of the PoK of Theorem 10 with (y, x_1, x_2, x_3, x) as witness.
   6.2. The user proves knowledge of $(u_1, \ldots, u_6)$, a $(G, h_1, \ldots, h_6)$-DL representation of $\mathrm{Com}(c)$ such that $(u_1 - u_3 - u_5 = 0) \wedge (u_3 = \hat{a})$. This is achieved by means of the PoK of Theorem 9 and with $(\hat{m}, r_1, \hat{a}, r_2, \hat{b}, r_3)$ as witness.
   6.3. The user proves knowledge of the $(Z_n^*, 3)$-root of the h_1-part of the (G, h_1, h_2)-DL representation of $\mathrm{Com}(\hat{m})$; that is, the user proves to know the third root $\hat{v}$ of $\hat{m}$. This is achieved by using the PoK of Theorem 7.
   6.4. The user proves knowledge of the discrete logarithm with base g of the h_5-part of the (G, h_5, h_6)-DL representation of $\mathrm{Com}(\hat{b})^{c^{-1}}$. Since $\hat{b} \equiv g^y b \equiv c g^y \pmod{n}$, then $y \pmod{n}$ can be used as witness for the PoK of Theorem 8.

4.3   Properties of Our Implementation

The usability property is obvious. For the proof of the security property we will use the following theorem.

Theorem 13. *The pair of algorithms* (ProveCred, VerifyCred) *is a PoK for the polynomial time relation of pairs* $((n, e, g, c, g_1, g_2, g_3), (x_1, x_2, x_3, x, v, z, y))$ *for which* $(x_1, x_2, x_3, x, v, z, y)$ *is a good tuple with respect to* $(n, e, g, c, g_1, g_2, g_3)$.

Proof. For the soundness, consider a knowledge extractor $\mathcal{E}$ that has black-box access to algorithm ProveCred* that interacts successfully with algorithm VerifyCred. Extractor $\mathcal{E}$ engages in the five statistical zero-knowledge proofs of knowledge of step 6 and for each proof of knowledge $\mathcal{E}$ extracts the witness used in the proof. Thus, $\mathcal{E}$ obtains

1. the $(Z_n^*, e, g, g_1, g_2, g_3)$-RSA representation (y, x_1, x_2, x_3, x) of $\hat{a}$ such that $\Phi(x_1, x_2) = 1$;
2. the values $\hat{m}, r_1, \hat{a}, r_2, \hat{b}, r_3$;
3. the third root $v = \hat{v}$ of $\hat{m}$;
4. the discrete logarithm z of $c^{-1}\hat{b}$ to base g;

Using the values extracted, $\mathcal{E}$ can compute a good tuple $(x_1, x_2, x_3, x, v, z, y)$ whose prefix satisfies Φ.   □

The theorem above thus shows that if an adversary successfully interacts with algorithm VerifyCred then she possesses (with very high probability) a good tuple whose prefix satisfies the access control formula. On the other hand, by our assumption, it is not computationally feasible for a polynomial-time adversary to construct a good tuple without the help of the organization (even if the adversary has access to a polynomial number of good tuples that do not satisfy Φ). Therefore we can conclude that the proposed credential system is secure.

For the multi-show privacy we consider a simulator S that has black-box access to a malicious service provider (that possibly has access to the organization private values). The simulator S receives as input the public information output by the organization and, for all (x_1, x_2) for which $\Phi(x_1, x_2) = 1$, outputs a view that is statistically close to the view of the interaction of a legitimate user that possesses credentials (x_1, x_2) with the service provider. Essentially the same simulator can be used to simulate any number of interactions with a service provider each interaction with a (possibly) different formula Φ.

The simulator starts by randomly choosing y such that $0 \leq y < e$, x_3 such that $0 \leq x_3 < e$, x_3 is co-prime with e and 3, $x \in Z_n^*$ and x_1', x_2' such that $0 \leq x_1', x_2' < e$, and $\Phi(x_1', x_2') = 1$ [1]. Then the simulator computes the values $\hat{a} \equiv g^y g_1^{x_1'} g_2^{x_2} g_3^{x_3} x^e \pmod{n}$, $\hat{b} \equiv cg^y \pmod{n}$ and $\hat{m} \equiv \hat{a} + \hat{b} \pmod{n}$ and commitments by randomly choosing $r_1, r_2, r_3 \in Z_n^*$ and setting $\mathrm{Com}(\hat{m}) = h_1^{\hat{m}} h_2^{r_1}, \mathrm{Com}(\hat{a}) = h_3^{\hat{a}} h_4^{r_2}, \mathrm{Com}(\hat{b}) = h_5^{\hat{b}} h_6^{r_3}$.

---

[1] For the sake of ease of exposition we are not addressing the problem of finding a tuple (x_1', x_2') that satisfies $\Phi(\cdot, \cdot)$. We will give details in the full version of the paper.

The simulator sends $\mathrm{Com}(\hat{m}), \mathrm{Com}(\hat{a}), \mathrm{Com}(\hat{b})$ and $\hat{a}$ to the verifier. Observe that the values computed by the simulator have the same distribution of the values sent by the prover (i.e., a legitimate user) in a real execution of the protocol.

For the proofs of knowledge of 6.1 to 6.4, we observe that the simulator has the witnesses for successfully performing proofs 6.1, 6.2, 6.4. However, since the proofs are statistical zero-knowledge (and hence statistical witness indistinguishable) the output of the simulator for this proofs is statistical indistinguishable from a proof performed by a legitimate user with credentials (x_1, x_2). Instead for proof 6.3, the simulator resorts to the simulator of the statistical zero-knowledge proof systems and thus again the output produced by the simulator is statistically close to the view of the verifier in a real execution.

We thus have the following theorem

Theorem 14. *The tuple of algorithms (*SetUp, Enroll, IssueCred, ProveCred, VerifyCred*) is a usable, secure and multi-show private credential system.*

4.4   Non-transferability

When a user shares his credential certificate with other users he has to give them the corresponding good tuple. In order to discourage such a sharing it is possible to add some credentials that typically are not shared by their owners. For example another base $g^* \in \langle g \rangle$ could be considered in order to encode a credit card number or a private key in a credential certificate. Using this mechanism each user that tries to use such a credential certificate needs to know the owner's credit card number or private key in order to successfully perform protocol ProveCred while interacting with the service provider running algorithm VerifyCred.

More precisely, a credential certificate can be lent by a user only if all credentials that are in the credential certificate are also released thus making the lending of credential certificates inconvenient.

4.5   Efficiency Improvement

The step 6.4 of protocol ProveCred $\leftrightarrow$ VerifyCred is the most expensive one of our protocol. We briefly suggest two possible improvements, details are omitted from this extended abstract.

1. Step 6.4 could be replaced by a proof of knowledge of a third root of a part of a representation, in this case the constant c has to be replaced by a value chosen by O that gives to the user the corresponding third root. In this case the complexity assumption need to be strengthened. One possible workaround is to add another (efficient) proof of knowledge on the value $\hat{a}$, for instance by setting $a = cg_0^w$ for a new base g_0, then the user should also prove knowledge of a square root of w and knowledge of the third roots of z_1, z_2 such that $\hat{a} = c_1 z_1 + c_2 z_2$ where c_1, c_2 are new constants. This can be achieved by considering a proof of knowledge of the square root of a committed value [16], since $\hat{a} = cg^y g_0^w$.

2. By using the subgroup of quadratic residues of Z_n^*, it is possible to extend both the system set-up and user enrollment phases by integrating the construction of [14] (obviously, the ability of the group manager of opening signatures must be removed). In such a case, each user obtains a triplet A^*, e^*, x^* such that $A^{*e^*} = g^{*x}g'$ and it is hard (strong RSA assumption) to generate a new valid triplet. By linking such a triplet to the value $g_1^{x_1}g_2^{x_2}g_3^{x_3}x^e$, then the user should prove knowledge of both a valid triplet and an RSA representation.

4.6   Efficiency of Our Scheme

In our proposed scheme, a user only needs one certificate to access any (polynomial) number of times any (polynomial) number of different services each with her access control policy encoded by a linear boolean formula. Previous schemes either required one certificate for each access and each service (e.g., [4, 5]) or one certificate for each type of service (e.g., [9, 10]). In Table 1 we show a general case in which a user is described by β attributes and wants to unlinkably access α different services each for δ times. Each service in general has a different access control policy (encoded via a linear boolean formula) that is based on the β credentials.

Table 1. Performance comparison.

Scheme	# Certificates	# Workload
This paper	1	$O(\beta)$
[10]	α	$O(\beta)$
[9]	α	$O(\beta)$
[4]	$\alpha\delta$	$O(\beta)$

Each row contains data for an anonymous credential system. The first column specifies the schemes. The second column specifies the number of certificates required to unlinkably access services. The last column specifies the number of modular exponentiations to be performed for each access.

The scheme of Brands (see [4, 5]) requires $\alpha\delta$ certificates since Brands' certificates are one-show and thus accesses that use the same certificate are linkable. Accessing a service require $O(\beta)$ modular exponentiations and these are due to a proof of knowledge of a discrete logarithm representation. The constant hidden by the O notation is small.

The schemes by Camenisch and Lysyanskaya [9] and the one by Verheul [10] are multi-show and thus the same certificate can be used more than once for gaining access to the same service. However, each service (with its own access control policy described by different formulae) requires a different certificate. This is due to the fact that the schemes of [9] and [10] do not allow to prove general statements on the credentials encoded by a certificate and thus the certificates themselves have to encode the access control policy. This has an important consequence. In the system of Brands and in our scheme the certificates can be obtained independently of the access control policies for which they will be used. Instead in the system of [9] and in the one of Verheul [10] the certificates depend on the access control formula. Therefore, should the access control policy of the service change, a new certificate suited for the new formula should be requested by the user. The number of modular exponentiations for accessing a service is linear in the number of credentials for both the constructions; however the system of [10] is efficient and the constant hidden in the O notation is small.

The scheme presented in this paper allows one to use the same certificate for accessing α services each δ times while preserving anonymity and unlinkability. In particular, this means that services can change their access control policies without requiring the users to get new certificates from the issuing organizations. This property is not obtained for free. Indeed the number of modular exponentiations for each access to a service is still linear in the number β of certificates and it is the sum of two factors: a factor (proportional to β with a small hidden constant) due to a proof of knowledge of an RSA representation that is very efficient and a constant factor due to one proof of knowledge of a double discrete log. The suggestions discussed in Section 4.5 improve such a constant factor. Notice that when the number of encoded credentials is large such a constant factor becomes negligible and the overhead inferred by our system decreases.

5   Conclusion

In this paper we have presented an efficient and usable non-transferable multi-show anonymous credential system. We have shown the advantages of our system with respect to the recent results of [9, 10, 4, 5] since it allows a user prove efficiently general statements on the credentials encoded in his certificate and, at the same time, it is multi-show and non-transferable.

References

1. Housley, R., Polk, W., Ford, W., Solo, D.: Internet X509 Public Key Infrastructure: Certificate and Certificate Revocation List (CRL) Profile. Network Working Group, RFC 3280 (2002)
2. De Santis, A., Di Crescenzo, G., Persiano, G., Yung, M.: On Monotone Formula Closure of SZK. In: Proceedings of the 35th Symposium on Foundations of Computer Science, (FOCS '94). (1994) 454–465
3. De Santis, A., Di Crescenzo, G., Persiano, P.: Communication-Efficient Anonymous Group Identification. In: Procedings of the 5th ACM Conference on Computer and Communications Security, ACM (1998) 73–82
4. Brands, S.: Rethinking Public Key Infrastructures and Digital Certificates; Building in Privacy. MIT Press (2000)
5. Brands, S.: Rapid Demonstration of Linear Relations Connected by Boolean Operators. In Fumy, W., ed.: Advances in Cryptology – Eurocrypt '97. Volume 1223 of Lecture Notes in Computer Science., Springer-Verlag (1997) 318–333

6. Chaum, D., Evertse, J.: A Secure and Privacy-Protecting Protocol for Transmitting Personal Information between organizations. In: Advances in Cryptology – Crypto '86. Volume 263 of Lecture Notes in Computer Science., Springer-Verlag (1987) 118–167

7. Lysyanskaya, A., Rivest, R., Sahai, A., Wolf, S.: Pseudonym Systems. In: Proceedings of Selected Areas in Cryptography. Volume 1758 of Lecture Notes in Computer Science., Springer-Verlag (1999) 184-199

8. Chen, L.: Access with Pseudonyms. In: Cryptography: Policy and Algorithms. Volume 1029 of Lecture Notes in Computer Science., Springer-Verlag (1995) 232–243

9. Camenisch, J., Lysyanskaya, A.: An Efficient Non-Transferable Anonymous Multi-Show Credential System with Optional Anonymity Revocation. In: Advances in Cryptology – Eurocrypt '01. Volume 2656 of Lecture Notes in Computer Science., Springer-Verlag (2001) 93–118

10. Verheul, E.: Self-Blindable Credential Certificates from the Weil Pairing. In Boyd, C., ed.: Advances in Cryptology – Asiacrypt '01. Volume 2248 of Lecture Notes in Computer Science., Springer-Verlag (2001) 533–551

11. Persiano, P., Visconti, I.: An Anonymous Credential System and a Privacy-Aware PKI. In: Proceedings of the 8th Australasian Conference on Information Security and Privacy, (ACISP '03). Volume 2727 of Lecture Notes in Computer Science., Springer-Verlag (2003) 27–38

12. Ateniese, G., Tsudik, G.: Some Open Issues and New Directions in Group Signatures. In Franklin, M., ed.: Financial Cryptography. Volume 1648 of Lecture Notes in Computer Science., Springer-Verlag (1999) 196–211

13. Camenisch, J., Stadler, M.: Efficient Group Signature Schemes for Large Groups. In: Advances in Cryptology – Crypto 97. Volume 1294 of Lecture Notes in Computer Science., Springer-Verlag (1997) 410–424

14. Ateniese, G., Camenisch, J., Joye, M., Tsudik, G.: A Practical and Provably Secure Coalition-Resistant Group Signature Scheme. In: Advances in Cryptology - Crypto '00. Volume 1880 of Lecture Notes in Computer Science., Springer-Verlag (2000) 255–270

15. Menezes, A., van Oorschot, P.C., Vanstone, S.A.: Handbook of Applied Cryptography. CRC Press (1996)

16. Ateniese, G., De Medeiros, B.: Efficient Group Signatures without Trapdoors. In: Advances in Cryptology – Asiacrypt '03. Lecture Notes in Computer Science, Springer-Verlag (2003) 246-268

17. Bresson, E., Stern, J.: Proofs of Knowledge for Non-Monotone Discrete-Log Formulae and Applications. In: Proceedings of International Security Conference (ISC '02). Volume 2433 of Lecture Notes in Computer Science., Springer-Verlag (2002) 272-288

18. Camenisch, J., Michels, M.: Proving in Zero-Knowledge that a Number is the Product of Two Safe Primes. In: Advances in Cryptology – Eurocrypt '99. Volume 1592 of Lecture Notes in Computer Science., Springer-Verlag (1999) 106–121

The Ephemeral Pairing Problem*

Jaap-Henk Hoepman

Department of Computer Science, University of Nijmegen
P.O.Box 9010, 6500 GL Nijmegen, the Netherlands
jhh@cs.kun.nl

Abstract. In wireless ad-hoc broadcast networks the *pairing problem* consists of establishing a (long-term) connection between two specific physical nodes in the network that do not yet know each other. We focus on the *ephemeral* version of this problem. Ephemeral pairings occur, for example, when electronic business cards are exchanged between two people that meet, or when one pays at a check-out using a wireless wallet. This problem can, in more abstract terms, be phrased as an *ephemeral key exchange* problem: given a low bandwidth authentic (or private) communication channel between two nodes, and a high bandwidth broadcast channel, can we establish a high-entropy shared secret session key between the two nodes without relying on any a priori shared secret information.

Apart from introducing this new problem, we present several ephemeral key exchange protocols, both for the case of authentic channels as well as for the case of private channels.

Keywords: Authentication, identification, pairing, key exchange.

1   Introduction

In wireless ad-hoc broadcast networks like Bluetooth[1] or IrDA[2] there is no guarantee that two physical nodes that want to communicate with each other are actually talking to each other. The *pairing problem* consists of securely establishing a connection or relationship between two specific nodes in the network that do not yet know each other[3]. For example, to insure that a newly bought television set is only controllable by *your* old remote control, the two need to be paired first. Because this pairing is performed only once (or a few times) during the lifetime of any pair of nodes, the pairing procedure can be quite involved. The importance of pairing, and the security policies governing such long-term paired nodes, is described by Stajano and Anderson [SA99].

---

* $Id : pairing.tex, v1.112003/11/2411 : 34 : 49 hoepman Exp$

[1] See http://www.bluetooth.com

[2] See http://www.irda.org

[3] Note the subtle difference with authentication: in the pairing problem we are not interested in the actual identity of any of the nodes. In fact, in a wired network the problem is easily solved by checking that a single wire connects both nodes.

A. Juels (Ed.): FC 2004, LNCS 3110, pp. 212–226, 2004.

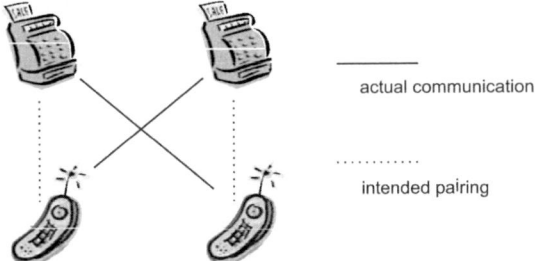

actual communication

intended pairing

Fig. 1. Unwanted exchange of information between unpaired nodes.

Sometimes, pairings may have to be performed much more frequently, and should only establish a relationship for the duration of the connection between the two nodes. Such *ephemeral pairings* occur, for example, when exchanging electronic business cards between two people that happen to meet, or when paying at a check-out using a wireless wallet on your mobile phone. Because such pairings may happen many times a day, the pairing procedure should be fast and the amount of user intervention should be limited. On the other hand, a high level of trust in the pairing may be required. Therefore, the pairing should be established in such a way that a high level of security is achieved even with minimal user interaction. Additionally, privacy may be a concern. Finally, the pairing should be made on the spot, preferably without any preparations.

To achieve such pairings, we do not wish to rely on any secret information shared a priori among the nodes. For the large scale systems where we expect the ephemeral pairings to play a part, such a secure initialisation might be costly and carry a huge organisational burden. Instead, we allow the nodes in the system to exchange *small* amounts of information reliably and/or privately. Several realistic methods for doing so are briefly discussed in this paper.

The importance of correctly pairing nodes becomes apparent if we study the two examples just given in slightly more detail (see Fig. 1). If some people in a crowd start exchanging business cards that may also contain quite personal information, the business cards surely should not be mixed up by the wireless network. Similarly, if two people are about to pay using a wireless wallet at two adjacent check-outs in a supermarket, the system should make sure that both are paying the right bills. In fact, similar problems plague smart card purse based systems like the Common Electronic Purse Specifications (CEPS [Cep01]), see [JW01] for details.

The ephemeral pairing problem can also be phrased in more abstract terms as a key exchange problem. Suppose we are given a low bandwidth authentic (or private) communication channel between two nodes, and a high bandwidth broadcast channel, can we establish a high-entropy shared secret session key between the two nodes without relying on any a priori shared secret information? We call this problem the *ephemeral key exchange* (denoted by φKE) problem. Here, the low bandwidth channel models the (implicit) authentication and limited information processing capabilities of the users operating the nodes.

1.1   State of the Art

The ephemeral key exchange problem is related to the encrypted key exchange (EKE) problem introduced by Bellovin and Merritt [BM92, BM93]. There, two parties sharing a low entropy password are required to securely exchange a high entropy session key. For φKE, the two parties do not share a password, but instead can use a small capacity authentic and/or private channel. EKE protocols are not suitable for this setting directly, most certainly not when only authentic channels are available. However, using private channels and with some minor additions they can be used to solve the φKE problem. This relationship is explored further in Sect. 3.

Jablon [Jab96] thoroughly discusses other solutions to the EKE problem. This paper also contains a good overview of the requirements on and a comparison among different EKE protocols. A more rigorous and formal treatment of the security of EKE protocols was initiated by Lucks [Luc97], and expanded on by several authors [BMP00, BPR00, Sho99, CK01, GL03]. This was followed by several more new proposals for EKE protocols secure in this more formal sense, cf. [Mac01, KOY01].

1.2   Contribution and Organisation of This Paper

We first introduce and define the ephemeral pairing problem and the ephemeral key exchange problem, and show how both are related. To the best of our knowledge, both problems have never before been studied in the literature. Next, in Sect. 3, we present ephemeral key exchange protocols both for the case where the nodes are connected through authentic channels and when the nodes are connected using private channels. In Sect. 4 we discuss how such authentic and private channels could be implemented in practice. We discuss our results in Sect. 5.

2   The Ephemeral Pairing Problem

Consider n physically identifiable nodes communicating over a broadcast network[4], each attended by a human operator. The operators (and/or the nodes they operate) can exchange *small* amounts of information reliably and/or in private.

The ephemeral pairing problem requires two of these nodes (to be determined by their operators) to establish a shared secret such that

(R1) both nodes are assured the secret is shared with the correct physical node,
(R2) no other node learns (part of) the shared secret, and
(R3) the operators need to perform only simple, intuitive steps.

The shared secret can subsequently be used to set up a secure channel over the broadcast network between the two nodes. The generalised ephemeral pairing

---

[4] In general the wireless network may not be completely connected and may change dynamically during the course of the protocol; we can safely ignore these cases, because they do not change the essence of the problem.

problem among $m < n$ nodes requires m nodes to establish a shared secret. We do not study that problem here. A weaker version of the ephemeral pairing problem requires only one node (the *master*) to be assured that the other node (the *slave*) actually shares the secret with it. This is called the *one-sided* ephemeral pairing problem[5].

2.1   Using Channels to Define the Problem

As explained in the introduction, this problem can be seen in more abstract terms as an ephemeral key exchange (φKE) problem. In this case, Alice and Bob share a low bandwidth communication channel over which they can exchange at most η bits of information per message[6]. This channel is either

authentic, meaning that Bob is guaranteed that a message he receives actually was sent by Alice (but this message may be eavesdropped by others), or
private, meaning that Alice is guaranteed that the message she sends is only received by Bob (but Bob does not know the message comes from Alice).

These guarantees may hold in both directions, or only in one direction[7]. We note that the low-bandwidth restriction of both the authentic and the private channel is important in practice. For instance, an authentic channel could be implemented by a terminal showing some small number on its public display, that must entered manually on the other terminal. Sect. 4 discusses more examples of such authentic and private channels.

Alice and Bob are also connected through a high bandwidth broadcast network (see Fig. 2). In this paper, we assume that for the correct delivery of broadcast messages, and to separate message streams from different protocol instances, the nodes on the network have unique identities. Messages on the broadcast channel carry a small header containing the identity of both the sender and the receiver. Clearly, the adversary has full control over the contents of these header fields as well. Given these connections, Alice and Bob are required to establish an authenticated and shared σ bits secret (where $\sigma \gg \eta$). They do not share any secrets a priori, and do not have any means to authenticate each other, except through the low bandwidth channel.

The adversary may eavesdrop, insert and modify packets on the broadcast network, and may eavesdrop on the authentic channel or insert and modify packets on the private channel. Note that, by assumption, the adversary cannot

---

[5] This applies to the case where the slave is unattended by an operator. A typical scenario would be paying with a wireless wallet (the master) at a vending machine (the slave). Note that now the slave has no clue (physically) with whom it shares the secret.

[6] We require that the number of messages exchanged over the channel in a single protocol run is constant, and small. This, together with the small size of η formalises requirement (R3) above.

[7] Note that in the case of an unidirectional authentic channel for solving the one-sided φKE problem, the channel runs from the slave to the master. See Sect. 4 for concrete examples.

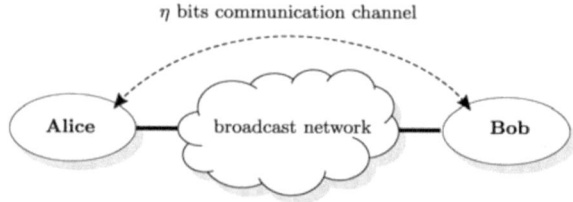

Fig. 2. The ephemeral key exchange system model.

insert or modify packets on the authentic channel. Also, the adversary may subvert any number of nodes and collect all the secret information stored there.

2.2   Model and Definitions

We prove security of our protocols in the encrypted key exchange model developed by Bellare *et al.* [BPR00]. For self containment reasons, we briefly summarise this model here.

There is a fixed set of principals, that either behave as clients or as servers. Each principal p may engage in the protocol many times. Each time this creates a new, unique, instance Π_p^i. Instances of a single principal share the global state maintained by that principal. This state is not accessible to the adversary (but see below).

Communication over the network is assumed to be controlled completely by the adversary. Interaction of the adversary with protocol instances of a principal is modelled by giving the adversary access to oracles for those instances. Let P be the protocol under consideration. For each instance Π_p^i the following oracles exist.

$\mathrm{Send}(p, i, m)$ Sends or broadcasts message m to instance Π_p^i. Any responses or output according to P are given to the adversary.

$\mathrm{Execute}(p, i, q, j)$ Executes a complete protocol run of P between client Π_p^i and server Π_q^j. The adversary learns all the messages exchanged between the instances, and whether they accept or not.

$\mathrm{Reveal}(p, i)$ Reveals the session key generated by instance Π_p^i to the adversary.

$\mathrm{Test}(p, i)$ Can be called only once at any time in each execution. A bit b is flipped at random, and depending on the outcome the adversary is given either a random session key (when $b = 0$), or the session key generated by instance Π_p^i (when $b = 1$).

An execution of the protocol P is defined as a sequence of oracle calls performed by the adversary. Two instances are called paired[8] if they jointly ran protocol P. For a correct protocol, two paired instances must share the same session key.

---

[8] Formally, pairing can be defined as follows. Let the trace of an instance be the concatenation of all messages sent and received by that instance. Then two instances are paired when their traces are equal.

The aim of an adversary $\mathcal{A}$ attacking protocol P is to correctly guess whether the call to the Test(p, i) query returned the session key of that instance or just a random session key (or, in other words, to guess the value of the coin flip b used in the query). Let $S_{\mathcal{A}}^{P}$ denote the event that adversary $\mathcal{A}$ correctly guesses the value of the bit when attacking protocol P. Then the advantage of an adversary $\mathcal{A}$ attacking protocol P is defined as follows:

$$\mathsf{Adv}_{\mathcal{A}}^{P} = 2\,\mathbf{Pr}\left[S_{\mathcal{A}}^{P}\right] - 1\ ,$$

(where $\mathbf{Pr}\left[X\right]$ denotes the probability of event X). To make this a non trivial task, the adversary is restricted in the the sense that it is not allowed to call the Test(p, i) query if it called the Reveal query on Π_{p}^{i} or on the instance paired with it.

Each protocol is actually a collection of protocols that must be instantiated using a particular value for its security parameter. In the case of φKE protocols there are actually two security parameters. There is a large security parameter s (that roughly corresponds to the size of the session key to be established, and that mostly determines the advantage of a passive adversary), and there is a small security parameter t (that roughly corresponds to the capacity of the channel between two principals, and that mostly determines the advantage of an active adversary).

In our analysis we will bound the advantage of the adversary for a particular protocol using s, t and the number of Send queries (denoted by q_s) performed by the adversary. We work in the random oracle model, and assume hardness of the Decisional Diffie Helman problem.

We use the following notation throughout the paper. In the description of the protocols, ac is the authentic channel, pc is the private channel, and bc is the broadcast channel. Assignment is denoted by :=, and $\xleftarrow{R}$ means selecting an element uniformly at random from the indicated set. Receiving messages from the channel or the broadcast network can be done in a blocking fashion (indicated by **receive**) or in a non-blocking fashion (indicated by **on receiving**).

In message flowcharts, $\xrightarrow{m}$ denotes sending m on the private or authentic channel, while $\xRightarrow{m}$ denotes broadcasting m on the broadcast channel. The receiving party puts the message in the indicated variable v at the arrowhead.

3   Ephemeral Key Exchange Protocols

In this section we present φKE protocols, for varying assumptions on the properties of the low bandwidth channel between Alice and Bob. We start with the case where the channel between Alice and Bob is unidirectional and private as well as authentic. Then we discuss the case where the channel is bidirectional. We present a protocol for just private channels, and finish with a protocol where the channel is only authentic.

In some of the protocols, an EKE protocol [BM92, KOY01] is used as the basic building block. This EKE protocol is assumed to broadcast its messages over the broadcast channel instead of sending them point to point.

if client
    then $p \xleftarrow{R} \{0, \ldots, 2^t - 1\}$
        send p **on** pc
    else receive p **from** pc
$k := \text{EKE}(p)$

Protocol 3.1: φKE for unidirectional private and authentic channel.

3.1 φKE for an Unidirectional Private and Authentic Channel

In the unidirectional private and authentic channel case, existing EKE protocols can easily be used as a building block. The channel is simply used to reliably send a random password from the client to the server, after which the EKE protocol is run to exchange the key. This is laid down in Prot. 3.1. The security parameters are set by $t = \eta$ and $s = \sigma$.

Analysis. We assume the underlying EKE protocol is correct and secure. If Alice and Bob want to exchange a key, it is straightforward to show that in an honest execution of Prot. 3.1, at the end of the protocol they do actually share the same key.

Next we show this protocol is secure.

Theorem 3.1. *The advantage of an adversary attacking Prot. 3.1 is at most the advantage of any adversary attacking the basic EKE protocol.*

Proof. Suppose an adversary attacks a run of protocol Prot. 3.1 with advantage a. Because by assumption, the adversary cannot control or gain information from the messages sent over the private and authentic channel, the advantage of the adversary would still be a when given this run where all messages sent over the channel are random, independent, values. But this is a run over the basic EKE protocol, with additional random values added to it. Hence the adversary can attack the basic EKE protocol with advantage a by adding random values to it and treating it as a run over Prot. 3.1.   □

Note that each execution of the EKE protocol is given a fresh password. This is unlike the typical case for EKE protocols, where each pair of nodes use the same password each time they wish to connect. This negatively impacts the upper bound for φKE protocols on the advantage of the adversary, in that the advantage of the adversary increases too quickly with the number of times he tries to guess the password. Because Prot. 3.1 uses a fresh password for each execution of the EKE protocol, the upper bound could be improved slightly if we consider one particular instance of an EKE protocol in our analysis.

3.2 φKE for a Bidirectional Private Channel

If the channel is bidirectional and private (without being authentic), existing EKE protocols can also be used as a building block. If the channel is bidirectional,

$$p \stackrel{R}{\leftarrow} \{0, \ldots, 2^t - 1\}$$
send p **on** pc
receive q **from** pc
$r := p \oplus q$
$k := \text{EKE}(r)$

Protocol 3.2: φKE for bidirectional private channel.

Alice and Bob simply generate two short t bit passwords, exchange them over the private channel, and subsequently run an EKE protocol using the exclusive OR[9] of both passwords as the EKE password to establish the shared session key. Security of this protocol is based on the observation that although anybody can try to set up a session with Bob by sending him a password, Bob will only divulge his own password to the person he wants to connect to, i.e., Alice. Therefore, only Alice is capable of generating the EKE password that will be accepted by Bob. In other words, Alice's authenticity is verified by the fact that she knows Bob's password. The protocol is detailed in Prot. 3.2. Again, the security parameters are set by $t = \eta$ and $s = \sigma$.

Analysis. It is again straightforward to show that if Alice and Bob want to exchange a key using Prot. 3.2, they will actually share the same key in an honest execution thereof, if we assume the underlying EKE protocol is correct.

Next we prove security of the protocol.

Theorem 3.2. *The advantage of an adversary attacking Prot. 3.2 is at most the advantage of any adversary attacking the basic EKE protocol.*

Proof. Suppose in a run of Prot. 3.2, an adversary attacks this run with advantage a. The password used by an instance depends on a value received on the private channel, xor-ed with a private random value that is also sent privately to the other party. Because by assumption the adversary cannot gain information from the messages sent over the private channel, the password used in an instance of the basic EKE protocol is independent of the values exchanged over the private channel. Hence by similar reasoning as in theorem 3.1, the advantage of the adversary attacking the basic EKE protocol is at least a. $\square$

3.3 φKE for a Bidirectional Authentic Channel

For the φKE protocol for a bidirectional authentic channel we use a different approach, not using an EKE protocol as the basic building block. The idea behind the protocol (presented as protocol 3.3) is the following.

To establish a shared session key, Alice and Bob will use a Diffie-Helman type key exchange [DH76]. To avoid man-in-the-middle attacks, the shares must be

---

[9] Using the exclusive OR instead of concatenation makes the resulting EKE password as long as the φKE short security parameter. Moreover, it makes the protocol for Alice and Bob symmetric.

Commit
    pick random x
    broadcast $h_1(g^x)$ **on** bc
    receive α **from** bc
Authenticate
    send $h_2(g^x)$ **on** ac
    receive β **from** ac
Key exchange
    broadcast g^x **on** bc
    receive m **from** bc
    if $h_1(m) = \alpha$ and $h_2(m) = \beta$
        then $u := m$
        else abort
Key validation

$$j := \begin{cases} 0 & \text{if client} \\ 1 & \text{if server} \end{cases}$$

    broadcast $h_{4+j}(u^x)$ **on** bc
    receive m **from** bc
    if $h_{5-j}(u^x) = m$
        then $k = h_3(u^x)$
        else abort

Protocol 3.3: φKE for bidirectional authentic channel.

authenticated. However, the capacity of the authentic channel is too small to do so directly. Instead, Alice and Bob proceed in four phases. In the first phase (the *commit phase*) Alice and Bob commit to their shares without revealing them. Then in the *authentication phase* they will send a small authenticator of their share to each other over the authentic channel. In the *key exchange phase*, both will reveal their share. Only shares committed to will be accepted, and the share matching the authenticator will be used to compute the shared session key. The key is verified in the final *key validation phase* to ensure that Alice and Bob indeed share the same session key, using the mechanism described in [BPR00]. Only if the validation phase is successful the protocol will accept.

Note that we must first commit to a value before revealing either the value or the authenticator, or else the adversary can trivially (in an expected $2^{\eta-1}$ number of tries) find a share of his own that matches the authenticator that will be sent by Alice.

In Prot. 3.3, the security parameters are determined by the size of the session key established and the capacity of the authentic channel. We set $s = \sigma$ and $t = \eta$. G is a group of order at least 2^{2s} with generator g for which the Decisional Diffie Helman (DDH) problem is hard. A possible candidate is the subgroup of order q in $\mathbb{Z}_p^*$ for p, q prime and $p = 2q + 1$ [Bon98]. Naturally, exponentiations like g^x are computed in the group G.

Furthermore, we use two hash functions $h_1 : G \mapsto G$ and $h_2 : G \mapsto \{0, 1\}^{\eta}$, that satisfy the following property.

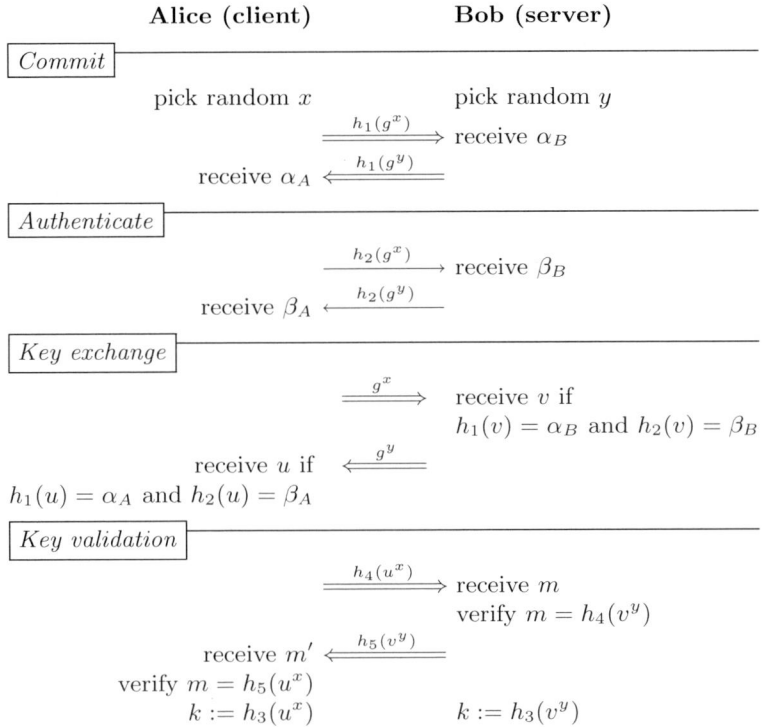

Fig. 3. Message flow of φKE for a bidirectional authentic channel.

Property 3.3. Let X be a uniformly distributed random variable over G, and let $a \in \{0,1\}^\eta$ and $b \in G$ be arbitrary. We assume that the two hash functions h_1, h_2 satisfy

$$\mathbf{Pr}\,[h_2(X) = a\,|\,h_1(X) = b] = \mathbf{Pr}\,[h_2(X) = a] = 2^{-\eta}\,.$$

Finally, pairwise independent hash functions $h_3, h_4, h_5 : G \mapsto \{0,1\}^\sigma$ are used as well. In practice, these hash functions can be derived from a single hash function h using the equation $h_i(x) = h(x \parallel i)$ (where $\parallel$ denotes concatenation of bit strings).

Analysis. It is straightforward to show that in an honest execution of Prot. 3.3, if Alice and Bob want to exchange a key, at the end of the protocol they do actually share the same key.

Security of Prot. 3.3 is proven as follows. We use the following result presented by Boneh [Bon98], which holds under the assumption that the Decisional Diffie Helman problem over G is hard.

Proposition 3.4. *Let the order of G be at least 2^{2s}, and let $h_3 : G \mapsto \{0,1\}^s$ be a pairwise independent hash function. Then the advantage of any adversary* *distinguishing $h_3(g^{ab})$ from a random element of $\{0,1\}^s$, when given g^a, g^b is a most $O(2^{-s})$.*

Using this proposition we are able to prove the following theorem.

Theorem 3.5. *The advantage of an adversary attacking Prot. 3.3 using at most q_{send} send queries is at most*

$$O(1 - e^{-q_{send}/2^t}) + O(2^{-s}) .$$

Proof. We split the proof in two cases. We first consider the case where the session key k generated by an oracle is not based on a share g^a sent by the adversary and derived from a value a of his own choosing, and then consider the case where the adversary manages to convince the oracle to use such a share of his own choosing.

If the session key generated by an oracle is not based on a share g^a sent by the adversary and derived from a value a of his own choosing, then k depends on private random values x, y unobserved by the adversary and publicly exchanged shares g^x and g^y using a Diffie-Helman (DH) key exchange. Any adversary attacking Prot. 3.3 can be converted to an adversary attacking a basic DH key exchange, by inserting the necessary hashes $h_i(g^x)$ and $h_j(g^y)$ (for $i, j \in \{1, 2, 3\}$) and random values for $h_4()$ and $h_5()$ (this is possible due to the random oracle model and Prop. 3.4) in the run of the basic DH key exchange before analysing the run. Hence the advantage of the adversary to distinguish the session key cannot be higher than its advantage in breaking the Diffie-Helman key exchange, which is at most $O(2^{-s})$ by Prop. 3.4.

In the other case, in order to convince an oracle of A to use the share g^a of the adversary in the third phase of the protocol, the adversary must ensure that

- $h_1(g^a) = \alpha$, and
- $h_2(g^a) = \beta$

for values α, β used in this oracle. Note that β is unknown in the commit phase. Moreover, property 3.3 guarantees it is independent of values exchanged during the commit phase. Therefore, for any value g^a committed by the adversary in the commit phase, the probability that $h_2(g^a) = \beta$ is $2^{-\eta}$.

For each send query then the probability of success is $2^{-\eta}$. Success with one instance is independent of success in any other instance. Hence, with q_{send} send queries, the probability of success becomes (cf. [Fel57])

$$1 - (1 - 2^{-\eta})^{q_{send}} \approx 1 - e^{-2^{-\eta} q_{send}}$$

With $t = \eta$ this proves the theorem.   □

Note that in fact the advantage of the adversary attacking the φKE protocol is strictly less than the advantage of the adversary attacking password based EKE protocols, like the protocol of Katz et al. [KOY01] whose advantage is bounded by

$$O(q_{send}/2^t) + O(2^{-s}) ,$$

where, loosely speaking, q_{send} is the number of times the adversary tries to guess the password. The difference is caused by the fact that in the EKE setting, multiple instances of the protocol use the same password[10].

4   Applications

Beyond those mentioned in the introduction, there are many other situations that involve ephemeral pairing.

- Connecting two laptops over an infrared connection, while in a business meeting.
- Buying tickets wirelessly at a box office, or verifying them at the entrance.
- Unlocking doors using a wireless token, making sure the right door is unlocked.

For all these applications it is very important that the burden of correctly establishing the right pairing should not solely rest on the user. The user may make mistakes, and frequent wrong pairings will decrease the trust in the system. This is especially important for applications that involve financial transactions. On the other hand, some user intervention will obviously always be required. The trick is to make the user actions easy and intuitive given the context of the pairing.

In the next section, we describe how a low bandwidth authentic or private channel can be implemented in quite practical settings. These are of course merely suggestions. There are probably many more and much better ways to achieve the same effect. The point here is, however, to merely show that such channels can be built in principle.

4.1   Implementing the Low Bandwidth Authentic or Private Channel

To implement an authentic or private channel in practice, several solution strategies are applicable.

- Establishing physical contact, either by a wire, through a connector, or using proximity techniques.
- Using physical properties of the wireless communication link, that may allow 'aiming' your device to the one you wish to connect to.
- Using fixed visible identities, either using explicitly shown unique names on devices, or using the unique appearance of each device.
- Using small displays that can either be read by the operator of the other device or read directly by the other device.

Which strategy to select depends very much on the specific application requiring ephemeral pairing. We will discuss each of these strategies briefly.

---

[10] This could be overcome by allowing only the first z connections to use the password alone, and using parts of the previously established shared secrets to generate new, longer, passwords. Then the bound on the advantage of the adversary essentially becomes equal to ours.

Physical Contact. The easiest way to solve ephemeral pairing is to connect both nodes (temporarily) physically, either by a wire, or by making them touch each others conductive pad. The resulting physical connection can be used as the private or authentic channel in the previous protocol. Or it can be used to exchange the shared secret directly, of course.

Fixed Visible Identities. Here one could use for example numbers, or the physical appearance. Each node holds a unique private key, and the physical identity is bound to the corresponding public key using a certificate generated by the certification authority (CA) managing the application.

The main drawback is that these solutions require a central Certification Authority. Moreover, the a priori distribution of secrets is contrary to the spirit of the φKE problem.

A variant (described in [Mob01]) uses the fixed identity of nodes in the following way. Any node wishing to connect can do so. Each connection is assigned a unique and small connection number, which is shown on a display. The user mentions the number to the merchant, who then initiates a payment over the indicated connection. The problem with this setup is that it is vulnerable to man-in-the-middle attacks.

Physical Link Properties. Depending on the properties of the physical link, one could reliable aim a device at another, or safely rule out connections to/from other far away devices.

Operator Read Displays. In this scheme, each node has a small display and a way to select several images or strings from the display (through function keys or using a touch pad). An authentic channel can be implemented as follows. To send a η bit string, it is converted to a simple pattern that is shown on the display of the sender. The receiver enters the pattern on its device, which converts it back to the η bits.

5   Conclusions

We have formulated the ephemeral pairing problem, and have presented several ephemeral key exchange protocols showing that this problem can be solved using small capacity, and mostly bidirectional, point to point channels and a broadcast network with identities to separate communication streams.

More work needs to be done to develop φKE protocols using only unidirectional channels, or on truly anonymous broadcast networks.

It would be interesting to develop protocols that are correct under less strong assumptions, i.e., ones that do not require to assume either the random oracle model or hardness of the Decisional Diffie Helman problem (or both). The same holds for the assumption on the authentic channel that adversary cannot modify or inject messages of his choice at all. More research is needed to investigate the effects on the advantage of the adversary if he can modify or inject messages on the authentic channel with low success probability.

Acknowledgements

This work was inspired by the work of Yan Yijun on a payments architecture for mobile systems, under the supervision of Leonard Franken of the ABN AMRO bank and myself. I would like to thank Yan and Leonard for fruitful initial discussions on this topic.

References

[BPR00] BELLARE, M., POINTCHEVAL, D., AND ROGAWAY, P. Authenticated key exchange secure against dictionary attacks. In *EUROCRYPT 2000* (Bruges, Belgium, 2000), B. Preneel (Ed.), LNCS 1807, Springer, pp. 139–155.

[BM92] BELLOVIN, S. M., AND MERRITT, M. Encrypted key exchange: Password-based protocols secure against dictionary attacks. In *IEEE Security & Privacy* (Oakland, CA, USA, 1992), IEEE, pp. 72–84.

[BM93] BELLOVIN, S. M., AND MERRITT, M. Augmented encrypted key exchange: A password-based protocol secure against dictionary attacks and password file compromise. In *1st CCS* (Fairfax, VA, USA, 1993), ACM, pp. 244–250.

[Bon98] BONEH, D. The decision Diffie-Hellman problem. In *Proc. of the 3rd Algorithmic Number Theory Symp.* (1998), LNCS 1423, pp. 48–63.

[BMP00] BOYKO, V., MACKENZIE, P., AND PATEL, S. Provably secure password-authenticated key exchange using Diffie-Hellman. In *EUROCRYPT 2000* (Bruges, Belgium, 2000), B. Preneel (Ed.), LNCS 1807, Springer, pp. 156–171.

[CK01] CANETTI, R., AND KRAWCZYK, H. Analysis of key-exchange protocols and their use for building secure channels. In *EUROCRYPT 2001* (Innsbruck, Austria, 2001), B. Pfitzmann (Ed.), LNCS 2045, Springer, pp. 453–474.

[Cep01] CEPSCO. Common Electronic Purse Specifications: Technical specification, version 2.3, 2001. http://www.cepsco.com.

[DH76] DIFFIE, W., AND HELLMAN, M. E. New directions in cryptography. *IEEE Trans. Inf. Theory* **IT-11** (1976), 644–654.

[Fel57] FELLER, W. *An Introduction to Probability Theory and Its Applications*, 2nd ed. Wiley & Sons, New York, 1957.

[GL03] GENNARO, R., AND LINDELL, Y. A framework for password-based authenticated key exchange. Tech. rep., IBM T.J. Watson, 2003. Abstract appeared in EUROCRYPT 2003.

[Jab96] JABLON, D. P. Strong password-only authenticated key exchange. *Comput. Comm. Rev.* (1996). http://www.std.com/~dpj and www.integritysciences.com.

[JW01] JÜRJENS, J., AND WIMMEL, G. Security modelling for electronic commerce: The common electronic purse specifications. In *First IFIP conference on e-commerce, e-business, and e-government (I3E)* (Zürich, Switzerland, 2001), Kluwer.

[KOY01] KATZ, J., OSTROVSKY, R., AND YUNG, M. Efficient password-authenticated key exchange using human-memorable passwords. In *EUROCRYPT 2001* (Innsbruck, Austria, 2001), B. Pfitzmann (Ed.), LNCS 2045, Springer, pp. 475–494.

[Luc97]   LUCKS, S. Open key exchange: How to defeat dictionary attacks without encrypting public keys. In *The Security Protocol Workshop '97* (1997), pp. 79–90.

[Mac01]   MACKENZIE, P. More efficient password-authenticated key exchange. In *Topics in Cryptography (CT-RSA)* (2001), LNCS 2020, Springer, pp. 361–377.

[Mob01]   MOBILE ELECTRONIC TRANSACTIONS. Solution to Bluetooth multiuser problem using method of tokens. Tech. rep., 2001.
`http://www.mobiletransaction.org/`.

[Sho99]   SHOUP, V. On formal models for secure key exchange. Tech. Rep. RZ 3120 (#93166), IBM, 1999. Invited talk at ACM Computer and Communications Security conference, 1999.

[SA99]   STAJANO, F., AND ANDERSON, R. The resurrecting duckling: Security issues for ad-hoc wireless networks. In *Security Procotols, 7th Int. Workshop* (1999), B. Christianson, B. Crispo, and M. Roe (Eds.), LNCS, pp. 172–194.

Mixminion:
Strong Anonymity for Financial Cryptography

Nick Mathewson and Roger Dingledine

The Free Haven Project
{nickm,arma}@freehaven.net

Systems Track

Abstract. Anonymous communication is a valuable but underused tool for securing financial communications. As early as the first commercial telegraph codes, businesses have recognized the value of cryptography to protect their communication from prying eyes. But cryptography alone still allows adversaries to discover confidential business relationships by performing traffic analysis to reveal the *presence* of such communication. Mixminion is an open source, deployed system under active development. It resists known forms of traffic analysis, allowing parties to communicate without revealing their identities.

Keywords: anonymity, privacy, traffic analysis, corporate espionage

1 Introduction: Anonymity and Digital Commerce

In this paper, we argue that strongly anonymous (traffic analysis resistant) communications are valuable to the business and finance community, and we present Mixminion, an anonymous communication system in active development.

As early as when the first business-related telegrams were received by an untrusted telegraph operator, businesses have recognized the importance of encrypting messages on communications networks. Less well-recognized, however, is the importance of protecting business communications against traffic analysis.

Whenever data travels over public networks, an eavesdropper can usually link messages to their senders and receivers with little difficulty. Although this linkage might initially seem of little interest, there are many circumstances under which the volume of communication between two sites can reveal sensitive information. For example, linking senders and recipients can reveal:

- Whether (and how often) the CEO of a Fortune 500 corporation has been exchanging email with the CEO of a rumored buyout partner.
- Which suppliers' websites a given purchaser is visiting.
- Which prospective customers a vendor has emailed and which of them responded via email.
- In some digital cash designs, the volume and frequency of transactions between participants and between participants and banks.

A. Juels (Ed.): FC 2004, LNCS 3110, pp. 227–232, 2004.
© IFCA/Springer-Verlag Berlin Heidelberg 2004

When an organization is geographically distributed, its internal communications can become a target of traffic analysis. In this way, an eavesdropper may learn:

- Which locations have employees working late.
- Which locations have employees consulting job-hunting websites.
- Which research groups are communicating with a company's patent lawyers.
- What volume of communication an R&D group is exchanging with a production line.

While firewalls or virtual private networks can conceal a network's interior view, they do not provide any further privacy against traffic analysis attacks.

These attacks are certainly feasible today. On the simplest level, corporate website administrators routinely survey logs to learn which competitors and customers have viewed which parts of their websites, and how often. The more sophisticated attacks are almost certainly within the capabilities of a nation able and inclined to use signals intelligence resources for economic goals, as the US has (probably) done with the NSA-backed ECHELON system. Finally, in between the threat of unsophisticated analysis and the threat of mid-sized foreign governments, is the potentially more compelling threat of espionage from competing companies. The risk of a competitor bribing an employee at a nearby telecom, or sneaking eavesdropping equipment into a colocation facility, is not well explored in the public literature.

Traffic analysis resistance is also a critical component to more advanced financial cryptography systems, such as anonymous digital cash schemes and private auctions: without anonymous transport, these schemes provide very little of the privacy that they promise.

1.1 Background

David Chaum launched the study of anonymous communications in 1981, with his design for a network of anonymizing servers or *mixes* [5]. In Chaum's design, message senders iteratively wrap their messages in the public keys of a sequence of mixes, then send the messages to the first mix in the sequence. Each mix in turn removes a layer of encryption from the messages, waits until enough messages have been received, then re-orders the messages and sends them to the next mix in the sequence. If any mix in the sequence correctly hides the correlation between incoming and outgoing messages, an eavesdropper should not be able to connect senders to recipients.

The first widespread public implementations of mixes were produced by contributors to the Cypherpunks mailing list. These "Type I" *anonymous remailers* were inspired both by the problems surrounding the anon.penet.fi service [10], and by theoretical work on mixes. Hughes wrote the first Cypherpunk anonymous remailer [12]; Finney followed closely with a collection of scripts that used Phil Zimmermann's PGP to encrypt remailed messages. Later, Cottrell implemented the Mixmaster system [11], or "Type II" remailers, which added message padding, message pools, and other mix features lacking in the original Cypherpunk remailers. Unfortunately, Mixmaster does not support replies or anonymous recipients. Thus, people who need *bidirectional* anonymous communication must use the older and less secure Cypherpunk network.

In parallel with the evolution of mix nets for mail-like communication, other work has progressed on systems suitable for faster communication. These systems range from the simple centralized Anonymizer [2], to distributed sets of servers like Freedom [4] and Onion Routing [8], to designs for totally decentralized peer-to-peer networks like Tarzan [9] and MorphMix [13]. But while these systems are more suitable than mixes for low-latency applications such as web browsing, chatting, and VoIP, they are more vulnerable to certain attacks than are traditional high-latency mix-net designs. Specifically, if an eavesdropper can observe both sides of the communication, the timing of message sending and delivery will quickly link senders and recipients. Although these systems block certain kinds of traffic analysis, they cannot defend against an adversary with significant eavesdropping abilities.

2   Mixminion: Open Source Strong Anonymity

Mixminion is the reference implementation of the Type III mix-net, which was first designed between 2001 and 2002 to address weaknesses in Type II and also to reintroduce reply messages in a secure manner, thus allowing us to retire the (insecure) Type I network. Mixminion's design was first published in [7]; its specification is publicly available [6].

The Type III mix-net design improves on previously deployed designs:

- **Secure single-use reply blocks, with indistinguishable replies.** In order to prevent attacks on earlier systems in which multiple-use reply channels can be used to break anonymity, Type III supports only single-use reply channels. These replies are indistinguishable from forward messages to all parties except their senders and recipients.
- **Forward-secure, email-independent transfer protocol.** Integration with mail transfer agents (such as Sendmail) has made earlier remailer networks fragile. Type III uses its own TLS-based transfer protocol to relay messages between mixes. The protocol is forward-secure: that is, future mix compromises cannot compromise past traffic recorded by an eavesdropper.
- **Integrated directory design.** Earlier deployed mix-nets have left the issue of mix discovery to a set of unspecified, uncoordinated, out-of-band key-servers. Type III introduces synchronized directory servers to sign mix directories and avoid single-point-of-failure issues.
- **Integrated key rotation.** Under Type I and Type II, key rotation occurs out of band, when a mix's administrator publicly announces a new key and tries to persuade other mixes and users to stop using the old key. This process can take weeks to months. Type III's key rotation is more practical: mixes publish new keys to directories so that clients can retrieve them automatically.
- **Dummy traffic.** Type III introduces a simple cover traffic design to complicate traffic analysis within the network.

The first public version of Mixminion was released in December of 2002. Since then, we have grown a deployed network of 22 testing servers[1], operated by volunteers in the US, Canada, and Europe. (For comparison, the widely used Mixmaster network currently has about 30 working mixes.) The current codebase implements anonymous messages, anonymous replies, erasure-correcting fragmentation and reassembly, address blocking, reliable message delivery, and an automated server directory with key rotation.

3   Future Work

Before Mixminion is ready for broad-scale user adoption, more work remains, both in research and in implementation. The largest areas ahead are, broadly:

- **Usability and client implementation.** For an anonymity system to hide its users' communications, it must have many users to hide them among: thus usability directly affects security [1,3]. The current Mixminion client runs only from a command line on Unix-like platforms, though a Windows32 client is planned within the next few months. For maximum user acceptance, more work is needed to integrate Mixminion with existing email applications.
- **Distributed directory design.** It is essential that all users of the Type III network have an identical view of which servers are available, reliable, and trustworthy. The current implementation uses a centralized directory, which gives the entire network a single point of failure. Our design calls for a more distributed directory implementation.
- **Pseudonymity.** Currently, there is no practical way to maintain a long-term pseudonymous identity via Type III reply blocks. Although we have a specification for a workable pseudonym server, the server is not yet implemented.
- **Abuse prevention.** One of the best ways to attack users' anonymity is by mounting a denial of service (DoS) attack against some or all of the Type III mix-net, in order to force users onto compromised servers, or to force them to use other (less secure) channels. At the same time, we need a way to let uninterested recipients opt out of anonymous mail, without letting them deny service to legitimate users. We need more research on how much impact these DoS opportunities can have on anonymity.
- **Enterprise integration.** The current implementation, because of its volunteer roots, assumes that most installations are for a single computer. In an enterprise environment, however, it could be more reasonable to integrate a single Mixminion node as a part of the outgoing email server. This *enclave firewall* model allows the enterprise's security administrators to do their jobs while still protecting the company's activities from outside observers.

Beyond software development and research, much exploration remains within the broader financial cryptography community to discover appropriate applications and economic models for anonymous communication channels. Despite the

---
[1] As of 8 September 2003.

potential applications of strong traffic analysis resistance in the business world, little effort has been spent in solving usability and scalability problems faced by these users.

There is reason for hope. The incentive structure of anonymity systems strongly argues against in-house measures to block traffic analysis: an organization using a "private" anonymity system cannot hide its traffic among traffic from other organizations. Thus, finance organizations that need to resist traffic analysis have an incentive to seek common solutions that not only meet their own needs, but that will attract as many users as possible.[1] The same reasoning gives non-business users an incentive to construct their systems to meet the needs of business and financial communities.

Mixminion aims to be the first deployed anonymous communication system that provides strong traffic analysis resistance, emphasizes usability, supports bidirectional communication, and can be sustained for the long term. These goals require more research on anonymity designs, more work on human/computer interaction and interfaces, and more awareness of the need for privacy around the world. We feel that pushing the envelope on all fronts and exploring the relationships between these requirements is the best way to bring the world closer to ubiquitous securable communications.

References

1. Alessandro Acquisti, Roger Dingledine, and Paul Syverson. On the Economics of Anonymity. In Rebecca N. Wright, editor, *Proceedings of Financial Cryptography (FC '03)*. Springer-Verlag, LNCS 2742, January 2003.
   http://freehaven.net/doc/fc03/econymics.pdf.
2. The Anonymizer. http://www.anonymizer.com/.
3. Adam Back, Ulf Möller, and Anton Stiglic. Traffic analysis attacks and trade-offs in anonymity providing systems. In Ira S. Moskowitz, editor, *Information Hiding (IH 2001)*, pages 245–257. Springer-Verlag, LNCS 2137, 2001.
   http://www.cypherspace.org/adam/pubs/traffic.pdf.
4. Philippe Boucher, Adam Shostack, and Ian Goldberg. Freedom systems 2.0 architecture. White paper, Zero Knowledge Systems, Inc., December 2000.
   http://freehaven.net/anonbib/#freedom2-arch.
5. David Chaum. Untraceable electronic mail, return addresses, and digital pseudonyms. *Communications of the ACM*, 4(2), February 1981.
   http://www.eskimo.com/~weidai/mix-net.txt.
6. George Danezis, Roger Dingledine, and Nick Mathewson. Type III (Mixminion) mix protocol specifications. http://mixminion.net/minion-spec.txt.
7. George Danezis, Roger Dingledine, and Nick Mathewson. Mixminion: Design of a Type III Anonymous Remailer Protocol. In *Proceedings of the 2003 IEEE Symposium on Security and Privacy*, May 2003.
   http://mixminion.net/minion-design.pdf.
8. Roger Dingledine, Nick Mathewson, and Paul Syverson. Tor: The Second-Generation Onion Router, November 2003.
   http://freehaven.net/tor/tor-design.pdf.

9. Michael J. Freedman and Robert Morris. Tarzan: A peer-to-peer anonymizing network layer. In *Proceedings of the 9th ACM Conference on Computer and Communications Security (CCS 2002)*, Washington, DC, November 2002. http://pdos.lcs.mit.edu/tarzan/docs/tarzan-ccs02.pdf.

10. J. Helsingius. `anon.penet.fi` press release. http://www.penet.fi/press-english.html.

11. Ulf Möller, Lance Cottrell, Peter Palfrader, and Len Sassaman. Mixmaster Protocol – Version 2. Draft, July 2003. http://www.abditum.com/mixmaster-spec.txt.

12. Sameer Parekh. Prospects for remailers. *First Monday*, 1(2), August 1996. http://www.firstmonday.dk/issues/issue2/remailers/.

13. Marc Rennhard and Bernhard Plattner. Introducing MorphMix: Peer-to-Peer based Anonymous Internet Usage with Collusion Detection. In *Proceedings of the Workshop on Privacy in the Electronic Society (WPES 2002)*, Washington, DC, USA, November 2002. http://www.tik.ee.ethz.ch/~rennhard/publications/morphmix.pdf.

Practical Anonymity for the Masses
with MorphMix

Marc Rennhard and Bernhard Plattner

Swiss Federal Institute of Technology, Zurich, Switzerland
Computer Engineering and Networks Laboratory
{rennhard,plattner}@tik.ee.ethz.ch

Abstract. MorphMix is a peer-to-peer circuit-based mix network to provide practical anonymous low-latency Internet access for millions of users. The basic ideas of MorphMix have been published before; this paper focuses on solving open problems and giving an analysis of the resistance to attacks and the performance it offers assuming realistic scenarios with very many users. We demonstrate that MorphMix scales very well and can support as many nodes as there are public IP addresses. In addition, we show that MorphMix is indeed practical because it provides good resistance from long-term profiling and offers acceptable performance despite the heterogeneity of the nodes and the fact that nodes can join or leave the system at any time.

Keywords: anonymity, peer-to-peer mix networks, collusion detection

1 Introduction

MorphMix is a peer-to-peer *circuit-based mix network* [6] to enable anonymous Internet usage for low-latency applications such as web browsing. Unlike traditional circuit-based mix systems such as Onion Routing [14], the Freedom Network [5], JAP[1], and the Anonymity Network [19], MorphMix does not consist of a relatively small set of dedicated mixes that serve many users. Rather, every MorphMix user is also a mix at the same time.

The main goal of MorphMix is to provide practical anonymous Internet access for the masses, i.e. for millions of users. Traditional mix systems – operated commercially or not – may not be the best option to fulfil this task [18]: the experience with the commercial Freedom network has shown it is difficult to offer such a service in a profitable way and systems with mixes run by volunteers may fail to acquire enough mixes for cost reasons and due to potential political and legal pressure. In general, having many mixes operated by independent institutions or persons located in several different geographical and jurisdictional areas is good to increase the resistance to certain attacks because (1) it is difficult for even a well-funded adversary to run a significant portion of all mixes himself and (2) legal attacks are much harder to carry out.

---

[1] http://anon.inf.tu-dresden.de

A. Juels (Ed.): FC 2004, LNCS 3110, pp. 233–250, 2004.
© IFCA/Springer-Verlag Berlin Heidelberg 2004

The basic ideas behind MorphMix have been published before [17]. In this paper, we answer the questions that were left open (mainly about the threat model, peer discovery, and scalability) and present a full analysis to demonstrate MorphMix is indeed practical system to provide anonymity for the masses. With practical, we mean that it (1) offers acceptable performance despite the heterogeneity of the nodes and the fact that nodes can join or leave the system at any time, and (2) provides good resistance to a realistic adversary. Especially the first property is very important because in anonymity, usability is an essential requirement: hardly anybody will use a system that offers poor performance no matter how well it protects from attacks. But without any users, there is no anonymity at all [2, 1].

In the next Section, we provide a brief overview of MorphMix. Section 3 states the threat model and Section 4 briefly repeats the collusion detection mechanism. Section 5 discusses the peer discovery mechanism and Section 6 discusses why MorphMix scales very well. In Section 7, we analyze the collusion detection mechanism. The performance MorphMix users may expect is evaluated in Section 8 before we compare MorphMix with similar systems in Section 9. Finally, we conclude our work in Section 10. Due to the limited space, we can only present the most important results of our analyses. For a more thorough discussion, refer to the technical report [16].

2   MorphMix Overview

MorphMix is made up of an open-ended set of nodes. A node i is identified by its IP address ip_i and has an RSA key-pair generated locally when a node is started for the first time, consisting of a secret (or private) key SK_i and a public key PK_i. A node that is part of MorphMix is *connected* to other MorphMix nodes, which are its *neighbors*. Two nodes that are connected share a symmetric key, which is exchanged using their public keys.

Basically, MorphMix is a circuit-based mix network and to access Internet hosts anonymously, a node establishes a circuit, which we name *anonymous tunnel*, via some other nodes. The first node in a tunnel is the *initiator*, the last node the *final node*, and the nodes in between are *intermediate nodes*. The total number of nodes in a tunnel is the *tunnel length*. Sending data along a tunnel works similar as in other circuit-based systems such as Onion Routing [14] and makes use of *layered encryption* and *fixed-length cells*. Anonymous tunnels can be used to contact several hosts subsequently or in parallel. To do so, *anonymous connections* that are only visible to the initiator and final node are transported within anonymous tunnels. It should be noted that setting up tunnels is a background process in the sense that when a host should be contacted anonymously, there are always a few tunnels ready to be used (see Section 8).

One key feature of MorphMix is that when setting up a tunnel, each node along the tunnel selects its successor node. This has the advantage that a node only has to manage its local environment consisting of its current neighbors, which is nearly independent of the system size. Neighbors can directly communicate with each other and exchange control information to learn which nodes have spare resources to accept further anonymous tunnels.

We only give a sketch of the protocol to set up a tunnel because it has already been provided and analyzed in [17] and has only been slightly adapted [16]. The initiator a picks the first intermediate node b among its current neighbors and establish a symmetric key with it that is used for the layered encryption. Then, a tells b to append a node. To prevent b from easily picking any next hop it likes, b must offer a *selection* of possible next hops among its neighbors to a, which selects one of them. This selection plays an important role in the collusion detection mechanism (see Section 4). Assuming a has picked node c, a and c establish a symmetric key via b to be used for the layered encryption. Since a learns c's public key from b as part of the selection, a cannot simply choose a key and encrypt it with c's public key, because this could easily be exploited by b by carrying out a man-in-the middle attack on the layer of encryption between a and c. To prevent this attack, a picks a *witness* w from the nodes it currently knows (see Section 5) and encrypts the key first for c and then for w. The resulting data are sent to b, which sends them to w. Node w decrypts the data and forwards them to c, which decrypts the data again to extract the symmetric key. Appending additional nodes works in exactly the same way until a decides the tunnel is long enough.

3   Threat Model

We assume the adversary wants to link communication partners in as many cases as possible to accumulate and possibly sell dossiers about Internet users. Consequently, the goal of MorphMix is to provide very good protection from long-term profiling instead of guaranteeing the anonymity of every single transaction. In fact, considering the open and asynchronous nature of the Internet and powerful attacks on mix systems [2–4, 11, 13, 21, 22], operating such a system such that it is both practical and resistant to powerful adversaries is a very challenging problem. In particular, if a user is suspected to communicate anonymously with a host, then a targeted attack by monitoring both the data sent and received by the user's computer and the host should make it possible to link the two communication partners in most cases by means of traffic confirmation. Cover traffic may protect from such attacks, but especially in mix networks for low-latency applications, they tend to introduce vast amounts of data overhead. In general, the benefit of dummy traffic is still not really understood and therefore, MorphMix does not employ any such mechanisms at this time. However, since MorphMix is essentially a mix network, we state that if efficient cover traffic mechanisms that significantly increase the protection from attacks low will be ever developed, they should be easily applicable to MorphMix.

We say an anonymous tunnel is *malicious* or *compromised* if an adversary manages to link the initiator and the host(s) that are contacted through this tunnel. Since MorphMix does not employ any cover traffic, we assume that a tunnel is compromised if (1) an external observer eavesdrops on both the link

between initiator and first intermediate node and on the route between final
node and host(s), or (2) an adversary operating some nodes himself controls
both the first intermediate and the final node. Note that in practice, this is not
always easy because the chances of the adversary depend on the amount of data
exchanged between initiator and host. In addition, one property of MorphMix
is *plausible deniability*, i.e. the first intermediate node does not know if the
previous node in the tunnel is the initiator or if that node is merely relaying
the data for yet another node. However, by analyzing the timing patterns of
cells exchanged between initiator and first intermediate nodes and because of
the fact that the tunnel length will be a reasonably small number in practice,
the first intermediate node should often be able to guess its position in the
tunnel. Nevertheless, our assumption about compromised tunnels is a worst case
assumption because anything else is difficult to quantify.

An adversary that observes a fraction of 0.1 of all MorphMix traffic succeeds
in compromising a fraction of $(0.1)^2 = 0.01$ of all tunnels on average. While
large backbone ISPs may indeed be capable of observing so many data, we state
the threat from external observers is quite small. Increasing the protection from
this adversary depends on the development of efficient cover traffic mechanisms.
On the other hand, due to the openness of the system, an internal active attacker controlling a subset of all nodes and compromising a significant fraction
of all tunnels is a real threat. Consequently, we must assume there are *honest*
nodes, which are nodes that do not try to break the anonymity of other users
and there are *malicious* nodes, which may collude with other malicious nodes to
break the anonymity of honest users. We have analyzed many different attack
strategies [16] for an internal attacker that aims at compromising as many tunnels as possible. Since every node in a tunnel selects its successor node, we have
come to the conclusion that the most effective attack to control both the first
intermediate and the final node in a tunnel is the one where malicious nodes
offer many or only other malicious nodes in their selections during the tunnel
setup (see Section 2).

To defend against the internal attacker, MorphMix employs a *collusion detection mechanism* (see Section 4), which exploits the fact that usually, only
contiguous ranges of IP addresses are under a single administrative control. We
say that all IP addresses with the same 16-bit prefix belong to the same */16
subnet*[2]. Leaving out reserved and multicast addresses, there are exactly 56559
public /16 subnets in the Internet. An adversary owning an entire class B network can still run 65533 MorphMix nodes, but from the point of view of the
collusion detection mechanism, they all belong into the same /16 subnet. Controlling nodes in many different /16 subnets is much more difficult than in a
single subnet. Even an adversary owning an entire class A network has easy access to only 256 different /16 subnets. Consequently, we assume the adversary
can operate nodes only in a small subset of all /16 subnets. It is difficult to specify an upper limit, but we do not believe it is realistic a single adversary will ever
be able to run nodes in significantly more than 1000 /16 subnets because even

---

[2] We have developed a similar concept to support IPv6 [16]

the largest ISPs do not control addresses in so many /16 subnets. The adversary could also try to run nodes in subnets he does not possess, either by himself or by private persons. Again, running nodes in much more than 1000 subnets is very difficult, in particular if the adversary wants to avoid that his activities become public.

4   Collusion Detection Mechanism

The collusion detection mechanism bases on the assumption that the most effective attack is that malicious nodes offer many or only malicious nodes in their selections, i.e. they offer nodes from a relatively small spectrum of all /16 subnets. Honest nodes, on the other hand, choose their neighbors and therefore also the nodes in their selections more or less randomly from all /16 subnets that contain nodes (see Section 5). We name the selections offered by honest nodes *honest selections* and the selections from malicious nodes *malicious selections*. Each node maintains a *extended selections list* L_{ES} that contains the k_{ES} (see Section 6) most recently received *extended selections*. The extended selection is the combination of the 16-bit prefixes of the IP addresses in a selection and of the node that offered the selection. For each new extended selection, the initiator computes a *correlation* by comparing it with all other extended selections in L_{ES}. We do not describe this algorithm here because this has already been done in detail in the original paper [17] and only repeat the main result that this correlation is in general relatively big if the new extended selection contains many or only colluding nodes and relatively small otherwise.

A node remembers the correlations it has computed over time and represents them as a *correlation distribution*. This correlation distribution is used by a node to determines a *correlation limit*, which has the property that if the correlation of a new extended selection is smaller than this limit, then the node that offered the corresponding selection is honest with a high probability. During the setup of a tunnel, the initiator gets an extended selection from each intermediate node. If at least one yields a correlation larger than the correlation limit, the tunnel is considered as *malicious* and is not used. Otherwise, it is considered as *good* and can be used to contact hosts anonymously.

5   Peer Discovery and Selecting Nodes

For the collusion mechanism to work correctly, honest nodes must pick the nodes they offer in their selections as randomly as possible from the set of all /16 subnets that contain at least one node. To do so, honest nodes must (1) frequently change their neighbors and (2) new neighbors must be selected as randomly as possible, which is exactly what the peer discovery mechanism should support.

Once a node is participating in MorphMix and starts setting up anonymous tunnels, it learns about a variety of other nodes through the selections it receives. It remembers these nodes and arranges them in a *most recently seen subnets list* L_S. There is at most one entry in the list per /16 subnet and each entry contains the corresponding 16-bit prefix and a *most recently seen nodes list* $L_{N,S}$, which contains information about nodes in this subnet that have been received in selections. An entry in $L_{N,S}$ contains the IP address, port, public key, and node level (see Section 7) of the corresponding node. When the initiator learns about a new node, it moves the corresponding entry in L_S to the first position of the list, or inserts an entry at the first position if the /16 subnet has not yet been in the list. Then, the information about the new node is inserted at the first position of the corresponding $L_{N,S}$. If $L_{N,S}$ already contains information about the node, the old entry is simply removed from $L_{N,S}$. Furthermore, to limit the memory requirements, the length of every $L_{N,S}$ is limited to ten entries.

Organizing the information about other nodes in this way has two properties: (1) the nodes belonging to the same /16 subnet are ordered in their respective $L_{N,S}$ such that the more recently a node has been seen, the closer to the first position in $L_{N,S}$ it is, and (2) the subnets in L_S themselves are ordered such that the more recently a node has been seen, the closer the corresponding subnet is to the first position in L_S. After a node has been participating in MorphMix for a while, its L_S will contain entries for nearly all subnets that contain at least one node. Since nodes may join and leave the system at any time a node never knows about all other nodes. However, this is no problem because for honest nodes, it is sufficient to know about nodes in nearly all /16 subnets (e.g. 80%) that contain at least one node to pick them as their neighbors and offer them in selections from a much wider spectrum of /16 subnets than malicious nodes do.

To pick a new neighbor, the initiator randomly selects a subnet from L_S and gets (and removes) the information about the first node in the corresponding $L_{N,S}$. If the node can be contacted and is willing to accept further anonymous tunnels, it is used as a new neighbor. Otherwise, the same is tried using the next node in $L_{N,S}$. If this fails for all nodes in the selected subnet, the subnet is removed from L_S and another subnet is tried. This guarantees honest nodes pick their neighbors, and therefore the nodes they offer in their selections, from a wide variety of /16 subnets that contain MorphMix nodes. Note that witnesses (see Section 2) are basically selected using the same method, but to make sure that a high percentage of attempts to set up an anonymous tunnel succeed, it is desirable that the witnesses the initiator selects are online with high probability. Witnesses should therefore be picked "close" to the first position in L_S, i.e. from the nodes that have been inserted more recently.

The nodes in newly arriving selections are only inserted into the most recently seen subnets list if the corresponding correlation is not above the correlation limit. So we have actually combined peer discovery and collusion detection to minimize the number of malicious nodes in the list. For the adversary to compromise an anonymous tunnel, controlling the first intermediate node is a requirement. To make sure that the nodes he controls are selected as often as possible as first intermediate nodes, he needs to include many or only malicious nodes in the selections. But since the collusion detection mechanism detects these malicious selection with high probability, the adversary cannot advertise malicious nodes as aggressively as he would like.

6   Scalability

The key to scalability in MorphMix bases on the fact that although there may be as many participating nodes as there are public IP addresses, the number of /16 subnets has a strict upper bound.

Our measurements [16] have shown that the effectiveness of the collusion detection mechanism depends on both the number of nodes offered in a selection (n_{sel}) and the number of extended selections in L_{ES} (k_{ES}). Using experiments, we have derived reasonable values for both sizes. They depend on the number s of different /16 subnets that contain MorphMix nodes. The selection size to be used is defined by $n_{sel} = \max(3, \lceil 7.75 \cdot \log_{10} s - 17 \rceil)$. Assuming there are MorphMix nodes in every public /16 subnet, the maximum selection size is given by $n_{sel,max} = \lceil 7.75 \cdot \log_{10} 56559 - 17 \rceil = 20$. This also implies it is sufficient for a node must have at least 20 neighbors that are willing to accept further anonymous being routed through them at any time. If $\overline{n_{sel}}$ is the average number of nodes in a selection, the number of extended selections in L_{ES} is defined by $k_{ES} = \lceil 2 \cdot \frac{s}{\overline{n_{sel}}} \rceil$. There is also an upper bound for the size of L_{ES}, which is given by $k_{ES,max} = \lceil 2 \cdot 56559/20 \rceil = 5656$. We carried out some performance tests on a system with a 1GHz AMD Athlon CPU and 256 MB RAM. With both n_{sel} and k_{ES} set to their maximum values, it takes about 50 ms to compute the correlation of a new extended selection. Assuming an initiator sets up one anonymous tunnel every two minutes (see Section 8) and the tunnel length is five, this only consumes about 0.125% of the computing power available on the system mentioned above, which can be neglected. Similarly, the maximum size of L_{ES} is 5656 entries with 21 IP addresses each, corresponding to less then 0.5 MB memory space, which is hardly an issue for state-of-the-art computers.

Peer discovery also scales well because L_S has at most 56559 entries. The information about a node includes four bytes for the IP address, two bytes for the port, 256 bytes for the RSA modulus, and one byte for the node level. Since there may be up to ten entries in every $L_{N,S}$, the maximum size of L_S is about 150 MB. While this is not insignificant, it can well be handled by modern systems. In addition, there is always the possibility to reduce the number of entries in a $L_{N,S}$ to reduce the memory requirements.

7   Analysis of the Collusion Detection Mechanism

Results from our earlier paper [17] have shown that it is not advisable for the adversary to always include only malicious nodes in malicious selections because such a selection is virtually always detected by the collusion detection mechanism. Including fewer malicious nodes makes malicious selections more similar to honest selections and less detectable. We name the number of malicious nodes the adversary offers in malicious selection the *attack level*. We have analyzed several strategies [16] an adversary may employ by varying the attack level depending on the position of a malicious node in a tunnel and have come to the conclusion that the most effective way is to attack always with the same attack level, i.e. malicious nodes always offer the same number of malicious nodes in their selections. The main reason is that the adversary can get all information to carry out this attack optimally, because observing the system tells him the approximate number of different /16 subnets with nodes in the system, which tells him the optimal attack level. Note that there are strategies that are slightly more effective in theory, for instance attacking only if the adversary controls the first intermediate tunnel. However, these attacks requires a malicious nodes to correctly "guess" its position in a tunnel during the setup, which is very difficult in practice, in particular if the initiator introduces random delays of several seconds between receiving a message and forwarding the next during tunnel setup.

Since MorphMix aims at providing anonymity for a large number of users, we analyze the performance of the collusion detection mechanism when there are nodes in nearly all public /16 subnets. We also take different capabilities of the nodes into account, i.e. some nodes have slow dial-up connections and can only relay few tunnels of others, which means they are chosen less frequently as neighbors (see Section 5) and therefore also offered less frequently in selections. Then there are nodes with very good network connectivity that can relay many data for others. As a basis for the kind of nodes that may participate in MorphMix, we use a measurement study [20] about the peers in the Napster and Gnutella file sharing systems. One main result of the study is the distribution of the bandwidths of the peers, and based on these results, we define a distribution for the bandwidths of MorphMix nodes that we assume to be realistic. To do so, we define six *node levels* and nodes are categorized according to their bandwidths. Depending on the node level, we define acceptance probabilities, which is the probability a node accepts relaying further anonymous tunnels when it is contacted as a new neighbor by another node. The left half of Table 1 illustrates the node levels and their up- and down-stream bandwidths, the distribution of MorphMix nodes over the node levels, and the acceptance probabilities. Note that these assumptions are only valid for honest nodes. We describe a different model for malicious nodes below.

Table 1. Assumed realistic bandwidth distribution of MorphMix nodes and acceptable intermediate and final nodes.

node level	bandwidth (Kb/s) up/down-stream	frac. of all nodes	acc. prob.	acceptable intermediate and final nodes					
				ISDN	ADSL$_{256}$	ADSL$_{512}$	DSL$_{512}$	T1	T3
ISDN	64/64	10	0.05	•	•	•	•	•	•
ADSL$_{256}$	64/256	0.25	0.1		•	•	•	•	•
ADSL$_{512}$	128/512	0.25	0.2			•	•	•	•
DSL$_{512}$	512/512	0.25	0.5				•	•	•
T1	1544/1544	0.1	0.8				•	•	•
T3	4632/4632	0.05	0.95				•	•	•

Looking at Table 1, we can see that we assign ISDN nodes a very small acceptance probability of 0.05, which implies that these nodes are only capable of accepting anonymous tunnels in one out of 20 cases when they are picked as a new neighbor by another node. Conversely, we assume fast nodes can nearly always accept being selected as a neighbor and we therefore assign T1 and T3 nodes an acceptance probability of 0.8 and 0.95, respectively. Note that we have not explicitly listed nodes with Cable connections because the bandwidths they offer are the same as ADSL or DSL connections. Therefore, the ADSL and DSL nodes in Table 1 also include nodes with Cable connections.

A second valuable result from the measurement study are the up-times of the peers. It shows that the probability a peer is connected to the Internet at any time is nearly evenly distributed between zero and one, with the exception that hardly any peer is nearly never or nearly always online. Applied to MorphMix, it is reasonable to assume that dial-up nodes are online and participating in MorphMix for only a relatively short time and the fast T1 and T3 nodes are nearly always up. We therefore model the up-times of honest nodes as follows:

- ISDN nodes are online during one hour a day, which means their up-time probability is $1/24$.
- T1 and T3 nodes have an up-time probability of 0.9.
- All other nodes get randomly an up-time between $1/24$ and 0.9.

To be most effective, the adversary makes sure that the malicious nodes are participating in MorphMix as often as possible. In addition, to be involved in as many anonymous tunnels as possible, the malicious nodes should always accept further anonymous tunnels, We therefore assign all malicious nodes per default an acceptance probability and an up-time probability of one.

Taking into account nodes with very different bandwidths, we must think about the quality of the nodes along an anonymous tunnel. Basically, the slowest node in a tunnel determines the maximum throughput of the tunnel: if one intermediate node is an ISDN node and all the others, including the initiator, are T3 nodes, the throughput of the tunnel will be at most 64 Kb/s. This is a significant problem because hardly any user is willing to sacrifice her fast Internet connection for anonymity if all she gets is the equivalent of a slow dial-up connection. The only way to cope with this problem is to make sure no slow nodes are present along tunnels of fast initiators. In practice, this means that the initiator specifies a minimum node level for the nodes it accepts and intermediate nodes offer only nodes in selections that meet or exceed this minimum level. The right half of Table 1 specifies reasonable acceptable node levels for the intermediate and final nodes depending on the node level of the initiator.

We analyze how well the collusion detection mechanism copes with the realistic acceptance and up-time probabilities defined above. We look at two scenarios: one system with 100000 honest nodes in 50000 subnets and a large system with 1000000 honest nodes in 50000 subnets. We assume the adversary manages to operate 10000 malicious nodes that are located in 1000, 2000, 5000, or 10000 different subnets that also contain honest nodes. We always set up 10000 tunnels, starting with an empty extended selections list, and use a tunnel length of five. Our main measure to assess the effectiveness of the collusion detection mechanism is the percentage p_{a_m} of malicious tunnels among the accepted tunnels. Besides p_{a_m}, we also show the percentage of *false positives*, i.e. the percentage of good tunnels that were wrongly classified as malicious. The data are represented as a rolling average over the 200 most recently set up anonymous tunnels. Figure 1 illustrates the results for both scenarios with malicious nodes in 1000, 5000, and 10000 subnets, respectively. The table below the graphs give the optimal attack level (oal) and p_{a_m} with and without collusion detection for malicious nodes in 1000, 2000, 5000, and 10000 subnets. We assume the initiator belongs to the four fastest types of nodes in Table 1, which corresponds to the worst case since the spectrum of nodes that can be offered in selections is smallest. The figures in parenthesis give p_{a_m} if no tunnel optimization according to the right half of Table 1 were made, i.e. if every node would accept every other node in its tunnel.

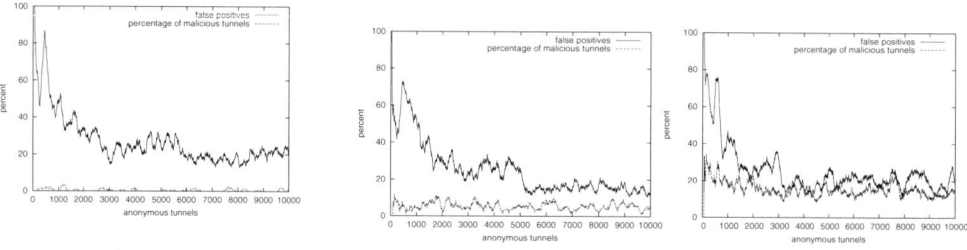

a) 100000 honest nodes, malicious nodes in 1000, 5000, and 10000 subnets

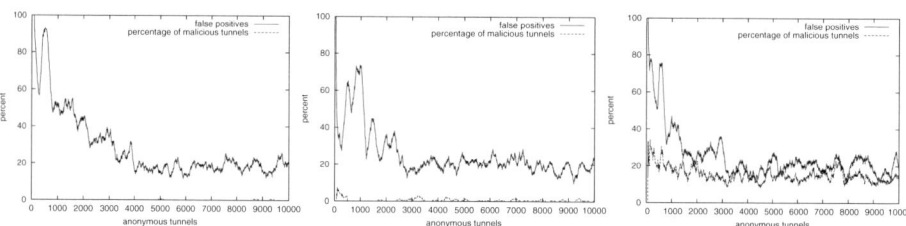

b) 1000000 honest nodes, malicious nodes in 1000, 5000, and 10000 subnets

subnets with mal. nodes	100000 honest nodes			1000000 honest nodes		
	oal	p_{a_m} with collusion detection	p_{a_m} without collusion detection	oal	p_{a_m} with collusion detection	p_{a_m} without collusion detection
1000	4	0.45 (0.28)%	5.74 (5.34)%	7	0.05 (0.05)%	1.79 (1.71)%
2000	5	1.13 (0.91)%	11.26 (10.04)%	8	0.18 (0.14)%	3.16 (2.95)%
5000	7	5.23 (4.47)%	24.04 (22.90)%	11	0.60 (0.52)%	5.71 (5.50)%
10000	10	14.17 (12.42)%	44.64 (42.54)%	14	2.37 (2.20)%	9.51 (9.23)%

Fig. 1. 100000 (a) and 1000000 (b) honest nodes; 10000 malicious nodes.

Figure 1 delivers several interesting results. First of all, it takes setting up about 4000 anonymous tunnels until the rate of false positives reaches and remains at approximately 20%. The reason for this is that the collusion detection mechanism works conservatively in the beginning to keep p_{a_m} small, but at the cost of more false positives. To make sure this learning phase happens only once, the extended selections list is periodically stored on disk and reloaded in case a node has been offline for a while. We also see that for the adversary, it is much better to operate only one or a few nodes in as many different subnets as possible than several nodes in a smaller number of subnets. This exactly what we wanted to achieve with the collusion detection mechanism operating on the 16-bit prefixes rather than the IP addresses themselves. In addition, Figure 1 illustrates that increasing the number of honest nodes makes the system significantly more resistant to attacks. This can be explained with the way honest nodes pick their neighbors (see Section 5): with 100000 honest nodes, only very few honest nodes are stored in the $L_{N,S}$ per subnet and the probability a malicious node is picked is much larger than with 1000000 honest nodes.

Finally, the measures to improve the throughput of anonymous tunnels only marginally increase the adversaries chances to compromise an anonymous tunnel. At first, this seems surprising because DSL_{512}, T1, and T3 account for only 40% of all nodes, which means the effective number of honest nodes for fast initiators is much smaller because slow nodes are no longer offered in selections to them. But actually, not so much has changed because looking at the acceptance probabilities in Table 1 shows that slow nodes accept relaying tunnels infrequently compared to the fast nodes, which means that even if they were accepted by fast initiators, they would be present in their tunnels rather infrequently. This implies that by requesting a minimum quality for the nodes offered in selection for fast nodes, we have merely removed occasional occurrences of slow nodes in these selections.

Assuming our threat model and looking at the results presented in this section, we conclude that the collusion detection mechanism works indeed well for large systems. It significantly reduces p_{a_m} compared to the case if no such mechanism were employed and it is very difficult for an adversary to compromise a significant percentage of all anonymous tunnels. Even optimizing the throughput of anonymous tunnels must not be paid with a significant increase in the number of compromised tunnels. In large systems, the task for the adversary becomes very complicated, because he cannot simply run many nodes in a few subnets but must be present in a large number of different subnets. Of course it could be the case that the adversary owns a part of the public IP address space, for instance a whole class A network. But this only gives him full control over 256 /16 subnets, which only enables him to compromise very few tunnels. To be effective, the adversary must have nodes under his control in very many different /16 subnets. Assuming a large system with honest nodes in nearly all public /16 subnets, the adversary must control nodes in several 1000 subnets to compromise more than 1% of all anonymous tunnels.

8   Simulation Results

To analyze the expected performance MorphMix offers to its users, we implemented our own simulator, mainly because existing generic network simulators simulate the underlying network protocols in great detail and are therefore not capable of simulating a large number of nodes (e.g. 1000) over a large simulated time period (several hours) within a reasonable execution time. Our simulator simulates the entire MorphMix protocol and is described in [16].

We use web browsing based on HTTP 1.1 for our analysis. The lengths of web requests and replies are modelled using appropriate values from traffic modelling and simulation literature. Web requests have a length of 300 bytes with a probability of 0.8 and 1100 bytes with a probability of 0.2 [12]. The lengths of web replies follow a ParetoII distribution with parameters $k = 2.4$ and $\alpha = 1.2$, resulting in average object size of 12 KB; the number of embedded objects per page also follow a ParetoII distribution with parameters $k = 0.8$ and $\alpha = 1.2$, resulting in an average of four embedded objects per page [9]. Finally, the reading time is defined by the time it takes between having completely downloaded a web page and initiating the next request and is also modelled by a ParetoII distribution with $k = 10$ and $\alpha = 2.0$, resulting in an average of ten seconds.

We have made several assumptions to reflect a realistic scenario. The time it takes for the data to travel between two neighboring nodes or a node and a web server and is selected randomly between 20 and 150 ms for each link. To force nodes to frequently change their neighbors, a newly selected neighbor may be offered in selection for only 30 minutes. The tunnel length is five, and every node sets up a new tunnel every two minutes on average. A tunnel may be used for at most ten minutes after it has been established, which means that at any time, a node has about five tunnels that are ready to be used. We assume it takes ten ms to process a cell in a node; if processing of data includes a DH or RSA operation, we add an additional 100 ms to the processing delay.

There are 1000 nodes in the system. More nodes are possible but the simulation time grows linearly with the number of nodes. However, we argue that even a system with 1000 nodes delivers reasonable information about how a very large system would perform if certain parameters are set accordingly. To do so, we will always use the maximum selection size of 20 (see Section 6), which implies the messages to set up a tunnel have their maximum length. We also make sure that at any time, every node has at least 30 neighbors that are willing to relay more anonymous tunnels, which implies that 20 nodes can easily be offered in selections at any time. So even if the system consisted of a million nodes, the tunnel setup messages would not be longer and the local environment every node has to handle would not be larger. The nodes' capabilities and up-times are chosen according to Section 7. For ISDN nodes, we assume their owners are browsing the web whenever the nodes are online. For all other nodes, we assume their owners browse the web during two hours a day. If the system were ten times bigger, there would also be ten times as much traffic, but also ten times as many nodes to handle it. Since the distribution of the nodes' capabilities and up-times would be unchanged, we could expect the simulation results to be very similar.

We analyze the download times for a complete web page depending on whether the web server is accessed directly or through MorphMix. In the latter case, we also compare the results with and without tunnel quality optimization according to Table 1. We simulate four hours of real time. Since the page download time is nearly linearly dependent on the page size, we use linear regression to plot the graphs. Figure 2 illustrates the results.

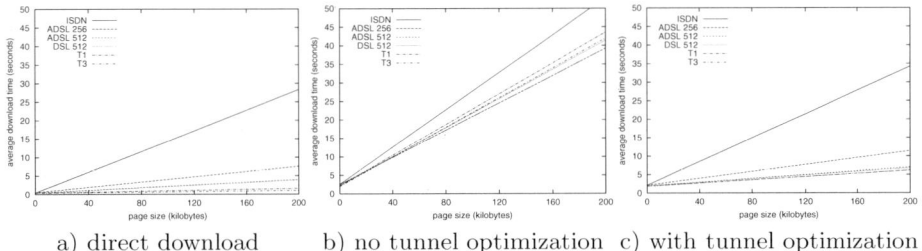

a) direct download   b) no tunnel optimization c) with tunnel optimization

Fig. 2. Download times when accessing the web server directly and through MorphMix.

The results are split into the six node levels defined in Table 1. Comparing Figures 2(a) and (b), we see that the download times get significantly longer if the web server is accessed through MorphMix without tunnel optimization. In particular, the end-to-end performance of any node drops below the performance ISDN nodes experience if the web server is contacted directly. We strongly believe that a performance loss so significant would be unacceptable for most users with reasonably fast Internet connections and hinder MorphMix from acquiring a critical mass.

Using tunnel optimization and looking at Figure 2(c), the end-to-end performance could be significantly improved. We can also clearly state that the benefits from optimizing the throughput of anonymous tunnels greatly outweighs the small increase in the number of compromised tunnels (see Figure 1). Compared to Figure 2(a), the download times have increased about 20% for ISDN nodes and about 50% for $ADSL_{256}$ nodes. All other nodes only accept nodes with at least DSL_{512} speed in their tunnels and the performance they experience is therefore approximately equal. Their download times are now about 50% longer than those of $ADSL_{512}$ or DSL_{512} nodes when the web server is contacted directly. Since Figure 2 does not take the time to completely display a page in the browser into account, the actual performance loss experienced by the user should be even smaller. We believe that for many users, this is an acceptable price for getting anonymity.

We now analyze the bandwidth usage and the data overhead of MorphMix assuming the web browsing scenario above. We distinguish between six different types of data: (1) web requests sent and web replies received at the initiator, which corresponds to the the data sent and received if the web server is contacted directly. (2) Cell headers and padding bits to generate fixed-length cells. (3) Forwarding of cells containing web requests and replies for other nodes. (4) Tunnel setup overhead, which includes all data sent and received to establish and tear down anonymous tunnels. (5) End-to-end (e2e) ping/pong overhead from regularly testing the quality of a tunnel. (6) Link message overhead, which includes all messages exchanged between two neighbors to set up a link and exchange keys, for link status information, and for flow control messages.

The first three types of data are needed to fulfil the prime task of a mix network: to send and receive user data through anonymous tunnels. We therefore do not count the cell headers and padding bits to generate fixed-length cells from the user data and forwarding these cells along anonymous tunnels as overhead, because they are essential properties of any mix system. We collectively identify these three types of data as *tunnel data* The other three types are needed to provide the anonymous tunnel infrastructure and are therefore *data overhead*.

We first analyze how much of the available bandwidth is actually used by MorphMix using the scenario in Figure 2(c). We distinguish between data sent and received and between tunnel data and overhead. Figure 3(a) shows the bandwidth usage for all nodes together and for the different node types.

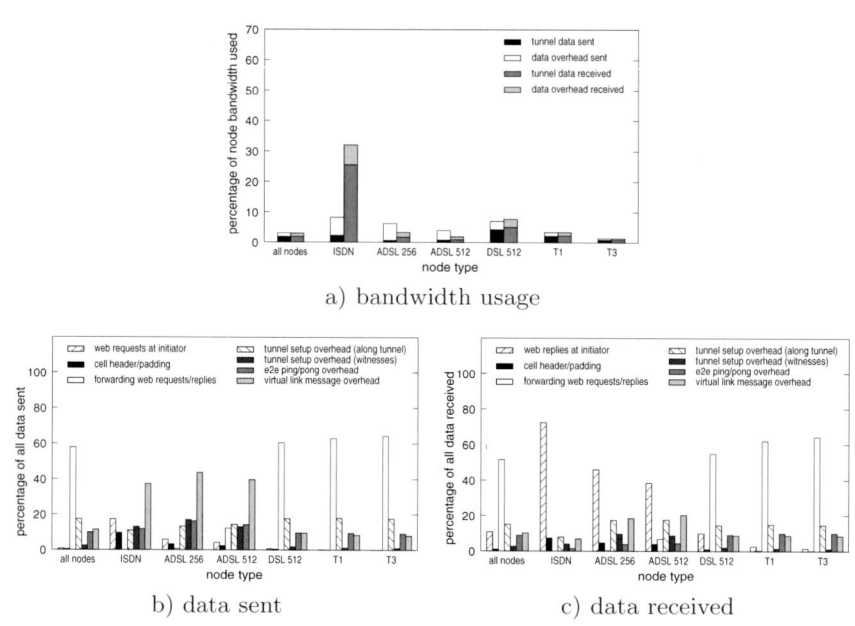

a) bandwidth usage

b) data sent   c) data received

Fig. 3. Bandwidth usage and data sent and received by the nodes.

Overall, about 3% of the total bandwidth available is used by MorphMix. This is quite a small total burden and Figure 3(a) shows that all nodes with at least a $ADSL_{256}$ connection can easily run a node without noticing a significant drop in terms of network performance for other applications. The reason why relatively much of the down-stream bandwidth of ISDN nodes is used is that their bandwidth is generally quite small and that we assume that ISDN users are always browsing when they are online. About 61% of all data are tunnel data and 39% are overhead. The overhead is therefore relatively large but since the total load on the nodes is so small, it can easily be dealt with.

To analyze the data sent and received by the nodes in more detail, Figures 3(b) and (c) illustrate how much of the used bandwidth is spent on which type of data. The biggest part – about 55% – is spent on forwarding the web requests and replies of other nodes and only relatively little is spent to handle the own data, which is reasonable. Tunnel setup and teardown overhead is responsible for about half of all overhead and for about 19% of all all data. About 16.5% stem from the nodes along the tunnel and 2.5% from the witnesses when appending a node. End-to-end ping/pong messages are responsible for about 9% and the various link messages exchanged between neighbors for about 11% of all data. Looking at the different node types, the bandwidth that is spent for handling the data of other nodes gets the bigger the faster the Internet connection to the node is. This is reasonable because according to our assumptions about realistic capabilities and up-times in Section 7, faster nodes accept relaying anonymous tunnels more frequently and are online more often.

We have also analyzed the impact of nodes that frequently crash or that can temporarily not be reached for any reason because this renders the corresponding tunnels useless and therefore also stops ongoing web page downloads along these tunnels. Without going into the details [16], we only state that MorphMix is still able to deliver satisfactory performance for application such as web browsing, although a small percentage of the web pages must be requested again.

For our analyses in this section, we have assumed that all nodes relay data for others. However, many peer-to-peer systems, especially those for file sharing, suffer from the "free rider" problem because there is often no real incentive to provide services to others because everything is for free and the systems seem to work well enough even if most users are free riders. If 90% of all MorphMix nodes were free riders the, load on the other 10% them could get quite high and the performance may suffer. However, the advantage of MorphMix compared to other peer-to-peer systems is that MorphMix provides incentive to relay the data of others. This has to do with the fact that the first intermediate node in a tunnel cannot easily learn that it is the first intermediate because no such information is leaked during the setup of the anonymous tunnel. So if a node is accused of having contacted a host anonymously, its operator can claim she only relayed the data for another node (plausible deniability). Traditional mix systems do not have this property because the clients and mixes are strictly separated. On the other hand, if a node a is a free rider in MorphMix, other nodes can learn about this by trying to pick a as a new neighbor. If this always fails or if a never accepts relaying tunnels, it can be concluded with very high probability that all data sent or received by a belong to tunnels of which a is the initiator. This implies that a cannot plausibly deny being the initiator of a tunnel and reduces a's anonymity compared to other nodes that relay the data of others.

9   Comparison with Similar Systems

We compare MorphMix with two other peer-to-peer based system aiming at anonymous low-latency Internet access: Crowds [15] and Tarzan [10].

Crowds requires a centralized lookup server to keep track of the nodes. This is a major drawback, first of all because it provides a single point of failure and attack and second because the lookup server must inform all participating nodes about any membership changes. The latter makes Crowds not well suited to support many nodes (e.g. several 1000s) that come and go. Crowds also neither employs layered encryption nor a collusion detection mechanism. Assuming the requester picks a malicious node to which it forwards the request and that node can find out that its predecessor is indeed the requester, it has broken the anonymity. To protect from this attack in the case of web browsing, the last node in the circuit retrieves the page including all embedded objects before sending it back to the requester. This prevents the malicious node from easily making use of a timing attack to learn whether it is directly following the requester or not because embedded objects would be requested by the browser automatically. The disadvantage is that the last node must parse HTML objects to get all embedded objects, which is impossible if HTTPS is used. There are additional possibilities for a requester to leak information (clicking on a hyperlink, HTTP redirects) that can be used for a timing attack by the node directly following the requester. The Crowds' designers propose to introduce random delays to complicate this attack, but this reduces the end-to-end performance and could refrain potential users from using the system. In general, it is always possible to introduce such application-dependent measures, but they also imply limiting the capabilities of the system a bit. The collusion detection mechanism as employed in MorphMix is a much cleaner solution because it tries to guarantee that anonymous tunnels are "secure" with high probability *before* any information about hosts to be contacted anonymously are revealed to the final node. Consequently, no such measures as employed by Crowds are required.

Tarzan builds an universally verifiable set of neighbors (the mimics) for every node, which requires a node lookup mechanism that can keep track of all nodes currently participating in Tarzan. This makes it unlikely Tarzan can function well in a large and dynamic environment where nodes come and go. Apart from this drawback, the fact that every node selects its neighbors in a pseudo-random way means all nodes along a circuit are also chosen pseudo-randomly from the set of all nodes. Consequently, when we talk about *collusion detection* in MorphMix, we can identify the mechanism employed by Tarzan as *collusion prevention*. However, this also means there is only little room for throughput optimization because the potential next hop nodes are limited to a node's mimics.

10   Conclusions

We have shown that MorphMix indeed provides practical anonymity for low-latency applications for a large number of users. In particular, MorphMix offers acceptable performance and provides good protection from long-term profiling. An important advantage of MorphMix compared to similar peer-to-peer based systems is that it does not rely on a lookup service that must keep track of all nodes that are currently participating, which makes it highly robust to membership fluctuations. In addition, MorphMix scales very well because every node handles only its local environment, which is nearly independent of the number of nodes in the system. Finally, the collusion detection mechanism also scales well because its complexity is bounded by the maximum number of /16 subnets.

As always, some open issues remain. Since nodes tend to fail or disappear more often than the mixes in traditional mix systems, MorphMix is less well suited for applications using long-standing TCP connections such as remote logins. Possible solutions are to bypass nodes that have failed but doing so could enable an attack where malicious nodes claim that their honest successor node along a circuit has failed. Another problem is exit abuse. What if a Yahoo account is accessed through MorphMix to send a threatening e-mail message? Will the last node in the chain be accused? This problem seems more significant in peer-to-peer-based than in traditional mix systems, because in the latter, the operator can "more plausibly" argue about not having sent the message himself. One way to solve this problem are exit policies using blacklists, but it is difficult to keep them up-to-date. Another potential problem are DoS attacks by malicious nodes that simply do not forward data for others. To solve this problem, one could couple MorphMix with a reputation system. Research on reputation systems is still in its infancy, but initial studies to make mix networks more reliable through reputation have been carried out [7, 8]. Finally, a lot of research remains to be done to develop efficient cover traffic mechanisms that significantly increase the protection from targeted attacks.

References

1. Alessandro Acquisti, Roger Dingledine, and Paul Syverson. On the Economics of Anonymity. In Rebecca N. Wright, editor, *Proceedings of Financial Cryptography (FC '03)*. Springer-Verlag, LNCS 2742, January 2003.
2. Adam Back, Ulf Möller, and Anton Stiglic. Traffic Analysis Attacks and Trade-Offs in Anonymity Providing Systems. In *Proceedings of 4th International Information Hiding Workshop*, Pittsburg, PA, USA, April 2001.
3. Oliver Berthold and Heinrich Langos. Dummy Traffic Against Long Term Intersection Attacks. In *Proceedings of the 2nd Workshop on Privacy-Enhancing Technologies*, San Francisco, CA, USA, April 14–15 2002.
4. Oliver Berthold, Andreas Pfitzmann, and Ronny Standtke. The Disadvantages of Free MIX Routes and how to Overcome them. In H. Federrath, editor, *Proceedings of Designing Privacy Enhancing Technologies: Workshop on Design Issues in Anonymity and Unobservability*. Springer-Verlag, LNCS 2009, July 2000.
5. Philippe Boucher, Adam Shostack, and Ian Goldberg. Freedom Systems 2.0 Architecture. White Paper, http://www.homeport.org/~adam/zeroknowledgewhitepapers/Freedom_System_2_Architecture.pdf, December 2000.
6. David L. Chaum. Untraceable Electronic Mail, Return Adresses, and Digital Pseudonyms. *Communications of the ACM*, 24(2):84–88, February 1981.
7. Roger Dingledine, Michael Freedman, David Hopwood, and David Molnar. A Reputation System to Increase MIX-net Reliability. In *Proceedings of 4th International Information Hiding Workshop*, pages 126–141, Pittsburg, PA, USA, April 2001.
8. Roger Dingledine and Paul Syverson. Reliable MIX Cascade Networks through Reputation. In *Proceedings of Financial Cryptography 2002*. Springer-Verlag, March 2002.
9. Anja Feldmann, Anna C. Gilbert, Polly Huang, and Walter Willinger. Dynamics of IP Traffic: A Study of the Role of Variability and the Impact of Control. In *Proceeding of SIGCOMM '99*, Massachusetts, USA, September 1999.

10. Michael J. Freedman and Robert Morris. Tarzan: A Peer-to-Peer Anonymizing Network Layer. In *Proceedings of the 9th ACM Conference on Computer and Communications Security (CCS 2002)*, Washington, D.C., USA, November 2002.
11. Dogan Kesdogan, Dakshi Agrawal, and Stefan Penz. Limits of Anonymity in Open Environments. In Fabien Petitcolas, editor, *Proceedings of Information Hiding Workshop (IH 2002)*. Springer-Verlag, LNCS 2578, October 2002.
12. Bruce A. Mah. An Empirical Model of HTTP Network Traffic. In *Proceeding of Infocom 1997*, pages 592–600, Kobe, Japan, April 1997.
13. Jean-François Raymond. Traffic Analysis: Protocols, Attacks, Design Issues and Open Problems. In H. Federrath, editor, *Proceedings of Designing Privacy Enhancing Technologies: Workshop on Design Issues in Anonymity and Unobservability*. Springer-Verlag, LNCS 2009, July 2000.
14. Michael Reed, Paul Syverson, and David Goldschlag. Anonymous Connections and Onion Routing. *IEEE Journal on Selected Areas in Communications*, 16(4):482–494, May 1998.
15. Michael K. Reiter and Aviel D. Rubin. Crowds: Anonymity for Web Transactions. *ACM Transactions on Information and System Security*, 1(1):66–92, November 1998.
16. Marc Rennhard. Anonymity for the Masses with MorphMix (available at `http://www.tik.ee.ethz.ch/~rennhard/publications/morphmix_tr2.pdf`). TIK Technical Report Nr. 159, TIK, ETH Zurich, Zurich, CH, May 2003.
17. Marc Rennhard and Bernhard Plattner. Introducing MorphMix: Peer-to-Peer based Anonymous Internet Usage with Collusion Detection. In *Proceedings of the Workshop on Privacy in the Electronic Society*, pages 91–102, Washington, DC, USA, November 21 2002.
18. Marc Rennhard and Bernhard Plattner. Practical Anonymity for the Masses with Mix-Networks. In *Proceedings of the IEEE 8th Intl. Workshop on Enterprise Security (WET ICE 2003)*, Linz, Austria, June 9–11 2003.
19. Marc Rennhard, Sandro Rafaeli, Laurent Mathy, Bernhard Plattner, and David Hutchison. An Architecture for an Anonymity Network. In *Proceedings of the IEEE 6th Intl. Workshop on Enterprise Security (WET ICE 2001)*, pages 165–170, Boston, USA, June 20–22 2001.
20. Stefan Saroiu, P. Krishna Gummadi, and Steven D. Gribble. A Measurement Study of Peer-to-Peer File Sharing Systems. In *Proceedings of Multimedia Computing and Networking 2002 (MMCN '02)*, San Jose, CA, USA, January 2002.
21. Paul Syverson, Gene Tsudik, Michael Reed, and Carl Landwehr. Towards an Analysis of Onion Routing Security. In H. Federrath, editor, *Proceedings of Designing Privacy Enhancing Technologies: Workshop on Design Issues in Anonymity and Unobservability*. Springer-Verlag, LNCS 2009, July 2000.
22. Matthew Wright, Micah Adler, Brian Neil Levine, and Clay Shields. An Analysis of the Degradation of Anonymous Protocols. In *Proceedings of ISOC Network and Distributed System Security Symposium (NDSS 2002)*, San Diego, USA, February 2002.

Timing Attacks in Low-Latency Mix Systems
(Extended Abstract)

Brian N. Levine[1], Michael K. Reiter[2], Chenxi Wang[2], and Matthew Wright[1]

[1] University of Massachusetts, Amherst, MA, USA
{brian,mwright}@cs.umass.edu
[2] Carnegie Mellon University, Pittsburgh, PA, USA
{reiter,chenxi}@cmu.edu

Abstract. A mix is a communication proxy that attempts to hide the correspondence between its incoming and outgoing messages. Timing attacks are a significant challenge for mix-based systems that wish to support interactive, low-latency applications. However, the potency of these attacks has not been studied carefully. In this paper, we investigate timing analysis attacks on low-latency mix systems and clarify the threat they pose. We propose a novel technique, defensive dropping, to thwart timing attacks. Through simulations and analysis, we show that defensive dropping can be effective against attackers who employ timing analysis.

1 Introduction

A *mix* [6] is a communication proxy that attempts to hide the correspondence between its incoming and outgoing messages. Routing communication through a chain of mixes is a powerful tool for providing unlinkability of senders and receivers despite observation of the network by a global eavesdropper and the corruption of many mix servers on the path. A mix can use a variety of techniques for hiding the relationships between its incoming and outgoing messages. In particular, it will typically transform them cryptographically, delay them, reorder them, and emit additional "dummy" messages in its output. The effectiveness of these techniques have been carefully studied (e.g., [4, 12, 18, 15, 13]), but mainly for high-latency systems, e.g., anonymous email or voting applications that do not require efficient processing. In practice, such systems may take hours to deliver a message to its intended destination.

Users desire anonymity for more interactive applications, such as web browsing, online chat, and file-sharing, all of which require a low-latency connection. A number of low-latency mix-based protocols for unlinkable communications have been proposed, including ISDN-Mixes [14], Onion Routing [16], Tarzan [10], Web Mixes [3], and Freedom [2]. Unfortunately, there are a number of known attacks

The work of Levine and Wright was supported in part by National Science Foundation awards ANI-0087482 and EIA-0080199. The work of Reiter, Wang, and Wright was supported in part by National Science Foundation award CCR-0208853 and a grant from the Air Force F49620-01-1-0340.

on these systems that take advantage of weaknesses in mix-based protocols when they are used for low-latency applications [19, 2, 20].

The attack we consider here is *timing analysis*, where an attacker studies the timings of messages moving through the system to find correlations. This kind of analysis might make it possible for two *attacker mixes* (i.e., mixes owned or compromised by the attacker) to determine that they are on the same communication path. In some systems, this allows these two attacker mixes to match the sender with her destination. Unfortunately, it is not known precisely how vulnerable these systems are in practice and whether an attacker can successfully use timing analysis for these types of attacks. For example, some research has assumed that timing analysis is possible when dummy messages are not used [20, 21, 19], though this has not been carefully examined.

In this paper, we significantly clarify the threat posed to low-latency mix systems by timing attacks through detailed simulations and analysis. We show that timing attacks are a serious threat and are easy to exploit by a well-placed attacker. We also measure the effectiveness of previously proposed defenses such as cover traffic and the impact of path length on the attack. Finally, we introduce a new variation of cover traffic that better defends against the attacks we consider, and demonstrate this through our analysis. Our results are based primarily on simulations of a set of attacking mixes that attempt to perform timing attacks in a realistic network setting.

We begin by providing background on low-latency mix-based systems and known attacks against them in Section 2. We present our system and attacker model in Section 3. In Section 4, we discuss the possible timing attacks against such systems and possible defenses. We present a simulation study in Section 5 in which we test the effectiveness of attacks and defenses. Section 6 gives the results of this study. We discuss the meaning of these results in light of different types of systems in Section 7 and we conclude in Section 8.

2   Background

A number of low-latency mix-based systems have been proposed, but systems vary widely in their attention to timing attacks of the form we consider here. Some systems, notably Onion Routing [19] and the second version of the Freedom [2] system, offer no special provisions to prevent timing analysis. In such systems, if the first and last mixes on a path are compromised, effective timing analysis may allow the attacker to link the sender and receiver identities [19]. When both the first and last mixes are chosen randomly with replacement from the set of all mixes, the probability of attacker success is given as $\frac{c^2}{n^2}$, where c is the number of attacker-owned mixes and n is the total number of mixes.

Both Tarzan [10] and the original Freedom system [2] use constant-rate cover traffic between pairs of mixes, sending traffic only between covered links. This defense makes it very difficult for an eavesdropper to perform timing analysis, since the flows on each link are independent. In Freedom, however, the attack is still possible for an eavesdropper, since there is no cover traffic between the

Initiator   Proxies   Responder

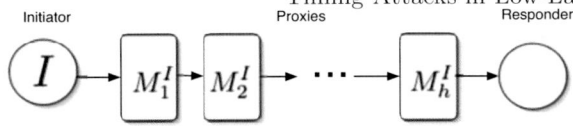

Fig. 1. A path P^I with an initiator I (leftmost) communicating with a responder (rightmost). M_1^I and M_h^I, the first and last mixes on the path originating at I, are controlled by attackers.

initiator and the first mix on the path, and between the last mix and the *responder*, the final destination of the initator's messages. This exposed traffic, along with the exposed traffic leaving the path, can be linked via timing analysis. Additionally, both systems are still vulnerable to timing analysis between attacker-controlled mixes. The mixes can distinguish between cover traffic and real traffic and will only consider the latter for timing analysis. This nullifies the effect of this form of cover traffic when attacker mixes are considered.

Web-Mixes [3], ISDN-Mixes [14], and Pipenet [7] all use a constant-rate cover traffic along the length of the path, i.e., by sending messages at a constant rate through each path. In these systems, it is unclear whether timing analysis is possible, since each initiator appears to send a constant rate of traffic at all times. An Onion Routing proposal for partial-path cover traffic is an extension of this idea [19]. In this case, the cover traffic only extends over a prefix of the path. Mixes that appear later in the path do not receive the cover traffic and only see the initiator traffic. Thus, an attacker mix in the covered prefix sees a very different traffic pattern than an attacker mix in the uncovered suffix. It is thus conceivable that the two mixes should find timing analysis more difficult.

3   System Model

Recall that our goal is to understand the threat posed by timing analysis attacks. In this section, we develop a framework for studying different analysis methods and defenses against them. We begin by presenting a system and attacker model. In the next section, we use this model to analyze attacks and defenses.

Figure 1 illustrates an initiator's path in a mix system. We focus on a particular initiator I, who uses a path, P^I, of mixes in the system. The path P^I consists of a sequence of h mixes that starts with M_1^I and ends with M_h^I. Although in many protocols the paths of each initiator can vary, to avoid cumbersome notation and without loss of generality, we let h denote the *last mix* in that particular path; our results do not assume a fixed or known path length. M_1^I receives packets from the initiator I, and M_h^I sends packets to the appropriate responders. We assume that each *link* between two mixes typically carries packets from multiple initiators, and that for each packet received, a mix can identify the path P^I to which the packet corresponds. This is common among low-latency mix systems, where when a path P^I is first established, every mix server on P^I is given a symmetric encryption key that it shares with I, and with which it decrypts (encrypts) packets traversing P^I in the forward (respectively, reverse) direction. We assume that M_h^I recognizes that it is the last mix on the path P^I. We also assume that mix M_1^I recognizes that it is the first mix on the path P^I and thus that I is, in fact, the initiator.

Though not shown in Figure 1, in our model we assume there are many paths through the system We are interested in the case where an attacker controls M_1^I and M_h^J on two paths P^I and P^J that are not necessarily distinct. The attacker's goal is to determine whether $I = J$. If $I = J$ and the attacker ascertains this, then it learns the responders to which I is communicating.

For these scenarios, we focus on the adversary's use of timing analysis to determine whether $I = J$. Packets that I sends along P^I run on a general-purpose network between the initiator I and M_1^I, and between each pair M_k^I and M_{k+1}^I. On this stretch of network there are dropped packets and variable transmission delays. Since these drops and delays affect packet behavior as seen further along the path, they can form a basis on which the attacker at M_1^I and M_h^J, for example, can infer that $I = J$. Indeed, the attacker may employ active attacks that modify the timings of packets emitted from M_1^I or intentionally drop packets at M_1^I, to see if these perturbations are reflected at M_h^J. For simplicity, we generally assume that the attacker has no additional information to guide his analysis, i.e., that there is no *a priori* information as to whether $I = J$.

4   Timing Attacks and Defenses

In this section, we describe the kinds of methods that an attacker in our model can use to successfully perform timing analysis. Additionally, we discuss defenses that can be used in the face of these kinds of attacks. In particular, we introduce a new type of cover traffic to guard against timing attacks.

4.1   Timing Analysis Attacks

The essence of a timing attack is to find a correlation between the timings of packets seen by M_1^I and those seen by an end point M_h^J. The stronger this correlation, the more likely $I = J$ and M_h^J is actually M_h^I. Attacker success also depends on the relative correlations between the timings at which distinct initiators I and J emit packets. That is, if M_1^I and M_1^J happen to see exactly the same timings of packets, then it is not be possible to determine whether the packet stream seen at M_h^J is a match for M_1^I or M_1^J.

To study the timing correlations, the most intuitive random variable for the attacker is the difference, δ_i, between the arrival time of a packet i and the arrival time of its successor packet. If the two attacker mixes are on the same path P^I, there should be a correlation between the δ_i values seen at the two mixes; for example, if δ_i is relatively large at M_1^I, then the δ_i at M_h^I is more likely to be larger than average. The correlation does not need to be strong, as long as it is stronger than the correlations that would occur between M_1^I and M_h^J, for two different initiators I and J.

Unfortunately, this random variable is highly sensitive to dropped packets. A dropped packet that occurs between M_1^I and M_h^I will cause later timings to be off by one. As a result, the correlation will be calculated between packets that are not matched – an otherwise perfect correlation will appear to be a mismatch.

Therefore, we extract a new random variable from the data that is less sensitive to packet drops. We use nonoverlapping and adjacent windows of time with a fixed duration W. Within instance k of this window, mix M maintains a count X_k^I of the number of packet arrivals on each path, P^I, in which M participates. Our analysis then works by cross correlating X_k^I and X_k^J at the two different mixes.

To enhance the timing analysis, the attacker can employ a more active approach. Specifically, the attacker can drop packets at M_1^I intentionally. These drops and the gaps they create will propagate to M_h^I and should enhance the correlation between the two mixes. Additionally, a careful placement of packet drops can effectively reduce the correlation between M_1^I and M_1^J for $I \neq J$.

4.2   The Defenses

A known defense against timing attacks is to use a constant rate of cover traffic along the length of the entire path [14,7]. This defense is useful, since it dramatically lowers the correlations between M_1^I and M_h^I. The lowered correlations may seem unexpected, since both nodes will now see approximately the same number of packets at all times. The difference is that the variations in packet delays must now be correlated: a long delay between two packets at M_1^I must match a longer-than-average delay between the same two packets at M_h^I for the correlation to increase. If the magnitude of variation between M_1^I and M_h^I dominates the magnitude of variation between I and M_1^I, this matching will often fail, reducing the correlation between the two streams.

This approach faces serious problems, however, when there are dropped packets before or at M_1^I. Dropped packets provide *holes* in the traffic, i.e., gaps where there should have been a packet, but none appeared. With only a few such holes, the correlation should increase for M_1^I and M_h^I, while the correlation between M_1^J and M_h^I should decrease. Packet drops can happen due to network events on the link between the initiator and M_1^I, or the attacker can have M_1^I drop these packets intentionally.

We now introduce a new defense against timing analysis, called *defensive dropping*. With defensive dropping, the initiator constructs some of the dummy packets such that an intermediate mix M_m^I, $1 \leq m \leq h$, is instructed to drop the packet. To achieve this, we only need one bit inside the encryption layer for M_m^I. If M_m^I is an honest participant, it will drop the dummy packet rather than sending it to the next mix (there will only be a random string to pass on anyway, but an attacker might try to resend an older packet). If these defensive drops are randomly placed with a sufficiently large frequency, the correlation between the first attacker and the last attacker will be reduced.

Defensive dropping is a generalization of "partial-path cover traffic," in which all of the cover traffic is dropped at a designated intermediate mix [19]. To further generalize, we note that the dropping need not be entrusted to a single mix. Rather, multiple intermediate mixes can collectively drop a set of packets. We discuss and analyze defensive dropping in depth in Section 7.

5   Simulation Methodology

We determined the effectiveness of timing analysis and various defenses using a simulation of network scenarios. We isolated timing analysis from path selection, *a priori* information, and any other aspects of a real attack on the anonymity and unlinkability of initiators in a system. To achieve this, the simulations modeled only the case when an attacker controls both the first and the last mix in the path – this is the key position in a timing attack.

We simulated two basic scenarios of mixes: one based on high-resource *servers*; and a second based on low-resource *peers*. In the server scenario, each mix is a dedicated server for the system, with a reliable low-latency link to the Internet. This means that the links between each mix are more reliable with low to moderate latencies, as described below. In the peer-based scenario, each mix is also a general purpose computer that may have an unreliable or slow link to the Internet. Thus, the links between mixes have more variable delays and are less reliable on average in a peer-based setting.

The simulation selected a drop rate for each link using an exponential distribution around an average value. We modeled the drop rate on the link between the initiator and first mix differently than those on the links between mixes. The link between the initiator and the first mix exhibits a drop rate, called the *early drop rate* (edr), with average either 1% or 5%. In the server scenario, the average *inter-mix drop rate* (imdr) is either 0%, meaning that there are no drops on the link, or 1%. For the imdr in the peer-based scenario, we use either 1% or 5% percent as the average drop rate. The lower imdr in the server case reflects good network conditions as can usually be seen on the Internet Traffic Report (http://www.internettrafficreport.com). For many test points on the Internet, there is typically a drop rate of 0%, with occasional jumps to about 1%. Some test points see much worse network performance, with maximal drop rates approaching 25%. Since these high rates are rare, we allow them only as unusually high selections from the exponential distribution using a lower average drop rate.

For the peer-based scenario, the average delay on a link is selected using a distribution from a study of Gnutella peers [17]. The median delay from this distribution is about 112ms, but the 98th percentile is close to 3.1 seconds, so there is substantial delay variation. For the server scenario, we select a less variable average delay, using a uniform distribution between 0ms and 1ms ("low" delay) or between 0ms and 100ms ("high" delay). Given an average delay for a link, the actual per-packet delays are selected using an exponential distribution with that delay as the mean. This is consistent with results from Bolot [5].

In addition to edr, imdr, and delays, the simulation also accounts for the length of the initiator's path and the initiator's communication rates. The path length can either be 5 or 8 or selected from a uniform distribution between these values. Larger path lengths are more difficult to use, since packets must have a fixed length [6].

Generating initiator traffic requires a model of initiator behavior. For this purpose, we employ one of four models for initiator behavior:

- **HomeIP:** The Berkeley HomeIP traffic study [11] has yielded a collection of traces of 18 days worth of HTTP traffic from users connecting to the Web through a Berkeley modem pool in 1996. From this study, we determined the distribution of times between each user request. To generate times between initiator requests during our simulation, we generate uniformly random numbers and use those to select from the one million points in the distribution.
- **Random:** We found that the HomeIP-based traffic model generated rather sparse traffic patterns. Although this is representative of many users' browsing behavior due to think times, we also wanted to consider a more active initiator model. To this end, we ran tests with traffic generated using an exponentially distributed delay between packets, with a 100ms average. This models an active initiator without any long lags between packets.
- **Constant:** For other tests, we model initiators with that employ constant rate path cover traffic. This traffic generator is straightforward: the initiator emits messages along the path at a constant rate of five packets per second, corresponding to sending dummy messages when it does not have a real message to send. (Equivalently, the Random traffic model may be thought of as a method of generating somewhat random cover traffic along the path.)
- **Defensive Dropping:** Defensive Dropping is similar to Constant, as the initiator sends a constant rate of cover traffic. The difference is that packets are randomly selected to be dropped. The rate of packets from the initiator remains at five packets per second, with a chosen drop rate of 50 percent.

Given a set of values for all the different parameters, we simulate the initiator's traffic along the length of her path and have the attacker save the timings of packets received at the first and last mixes. We generate 10,000 such simulations. We then simulate the timing analysis by running a cross correlation test on the timing data taken from the two mixes. We test mixes on the same path as well as mixes from different paths.

The statistical correlation test we chose works by taking adjacent windows of duration W. Each mix counts the number of packets X_k it receives per path in the k-th window. We then cross-correlate the sequence $\{x_k\}$ of values observed for a path at one mix, with the sequence $\{x'_k\}$ observed for a path at a different mix. Specifically, the cross correlation at delay d is defined to be

$$r(d) = \frac{\sum_i \left((x_i - \mu)\left(x'_{i+d} - \mu'\right)\right)}{\sqrt{\sum_i (x_i - \mu)^2}\sqrt{\sum_i \left(x'_{i+d} - \mu'\right)^2}}$$

where μ is the mean of $\{x_k\}$ and μ' is the mean of $\{x'_k\}$. We performed tests with $W = 10$ seconds and $d = 0$; as we will show, these yielded useful results for the workloads we explored.

Table 1. Equal error rates for simulations with path lengths between 5 and 8, inclusive. The rows represent the initiator traffic model and drop rate before reaching the first mix (edr). The columns represent the delay characteristics and drop rates (imdr) on each link between the first mix and the last mix. See Section 5 for details.

traffic pattern	imdr delay edr	0% low	0% high	1% low	1% high	1% gnutella	5% gnutella
HomeIP	1%	0.0000	0.0003	0.0007	0.0008	0.0026	0.0061
	5%	0.0001	0.0005	0.0008	0.0010	0.0039	0.0070
Random	1%	0.0000	0.0000	0.0000	0.0000	0.0002	0.0003
	5%	0.0000	0.0000	0.0000	0.0000	0.0004	0.0005
Constant	1%	0.0011	0.0346	0.0350	0.0814	0.1372	0.2141
	5%	0.0002	0.0079	0.0108	0.0336	0.0557	0.1014
Defensive Dropping	1%	0.1925	0.2424	0.2022	0.2506	0.2875	0.3117
	5%	0.0930	0.1233	0.1004	0.1289	0.1550	0.1830

We say that we calculated $r(0; I, J)$ if we used values $\{x_k\}$ from packets on P^I as seen by M_1^I and used values $\{x_k'\}$ from packets on P^J as seen by M_h^J. We infer that the values $\{x_k\}$ and $\{x_k'\}$ indicate the same path (the attackers believe that $I = J$) if $|r(0; I, J)| > t$ for some *threshold*, t. For any chosen t, we calculate the rate of *false positives*: the fraction of pairs (I, J) such that $I \neq J$ but $|r(0; I, J)| > t$. We also compute the *false negatives*: the fraction of initiators I for which $|r(0; I, I)| \leq t$.

6 Evaluation Results

Decreasing the threshold, t, raises the false positive rate and decreases the false negative rate. Therefore, an indication of the quality of a timing attack is the *equal error rate*, obtained as the false positive and negative rates once t is adjusted to make them equal. The lower the equal error rate, the more accurate the test is.

Representative equal error rate results are shown in Table 1. For all of these data points, the initiator's path length is selected at random between 5 and 8, inclusive. Not represented are data for fixed path lengths of 5 and 8; lower path lengths led to lower equal error rates overall.

Results presented in Table 1 show that the timing analysis tests are very effective over a wide range of network parameters when there is not constant rate cover traffic. With the HomeIP traffic, the equal error rate never rises to 1%. Such strong results for attackers could be expected, since initiators often have long gaps between messages. These gaps will seldom match from one initiator to another.

Perhaps more surprising is the very low error rates for the attack for the Random traffic flows (exponentially distributed interpacket delays with average delay of 100ms). One might expect that the lack of significant gaps in the data would make the analysis more difficult for the attacker. In general, however, the gaps still dominate variation in the delay. This makes correlation between unrelated streams unlikely, while maintaining much of the correlation along the same path.

When constant rate cover traffic is used, the effectiveness of timing analysis depends on the network parameters. When the network has few drops and low latency variation between the mixes, the attacker continues to do well. When imdr = 0% and the inter-mix delay is less than 1ms, meaning that the variation in the delay is also low, the timing analysis had an equal error rates of 0.0011 and 0.0002, for edr = 1% and edr = 5%, respectively. Larger delays and higher drop rates lead to higher error rates for the attacker. For example, with imdr = 1% drop rate and delays between 0ms and 100ms between mixes, the error rates become 0.0814 for edr = 1% and 0.0336 for imdr = 5%.

6.1   Effects of Network Parameters

To better compare how effective timing analysis tests are with different network parameters, we can use the rates of false negatives and false positives to get a Receiver Operator Characteristic (ROC) curve (see http://www.cmh.edu/stats/ask/roc.asp). Let fp denote the false positive rate and fn denote the false negative rate. Then fp is the x-axis of a ROC curve and $1 - $ fn is the y-axis. A useful measure of the quality of a particular test is the area under the curve (AUC). A good test will have an AUC close to 1, while poor tests will have an AUC as low as 0.5. We do not present AUC values. The relative value of each test will be apparent from viewing their curves on the same graph; curves that are closer to the upper left-hand corner are better. We only give ROC curves for constant rate cover traffic, with and without defensive dropping, as the other cases are generally too close to the axes to see.

We can see from the ROC curves in Figure 2 how the correlation tests perform with varying network conditions. The bottommost lines in Figures 2(a–b) show that the test is least accurate with imdr = 5% and the relatively large delays taken from the Gnutella traffic study. imdr appears to be the most significant parameter, and as the imdr lowers to 1% and then 0% on average, the ROC curve gets much closer to the upper left hand corner. Delay also impacts the error rates, but to a lesser extent. Low delays result in fewer errors by the test and a ROC curve closer to the upper-left-hand corner.

In Figure 2(c), we see how the correlation tests are affected by edr. edr's effect varies inversely to that of imdr. With edr = 5%, the area under the ROC curve is relatively close to one. Note that the axes only go down on the y-axis to 0.75 and right on the x-axis to 0.25. For the same imdr, correlation tests with edr = 1% have significantly higher error.

Figure 2(d) graphs the relationship between path length an success of the attackers. Not surprisingly, longer paths decrease the attackers success as there is more chance for the network to introduce variability in streams of packets.

We can compare the use of defensive dropping with constant rate cover traffic in Figures 2(e–f). It is clear that in both models, the defensive dropping ROC curves are much further from the upper-left-hand corner than the curves based

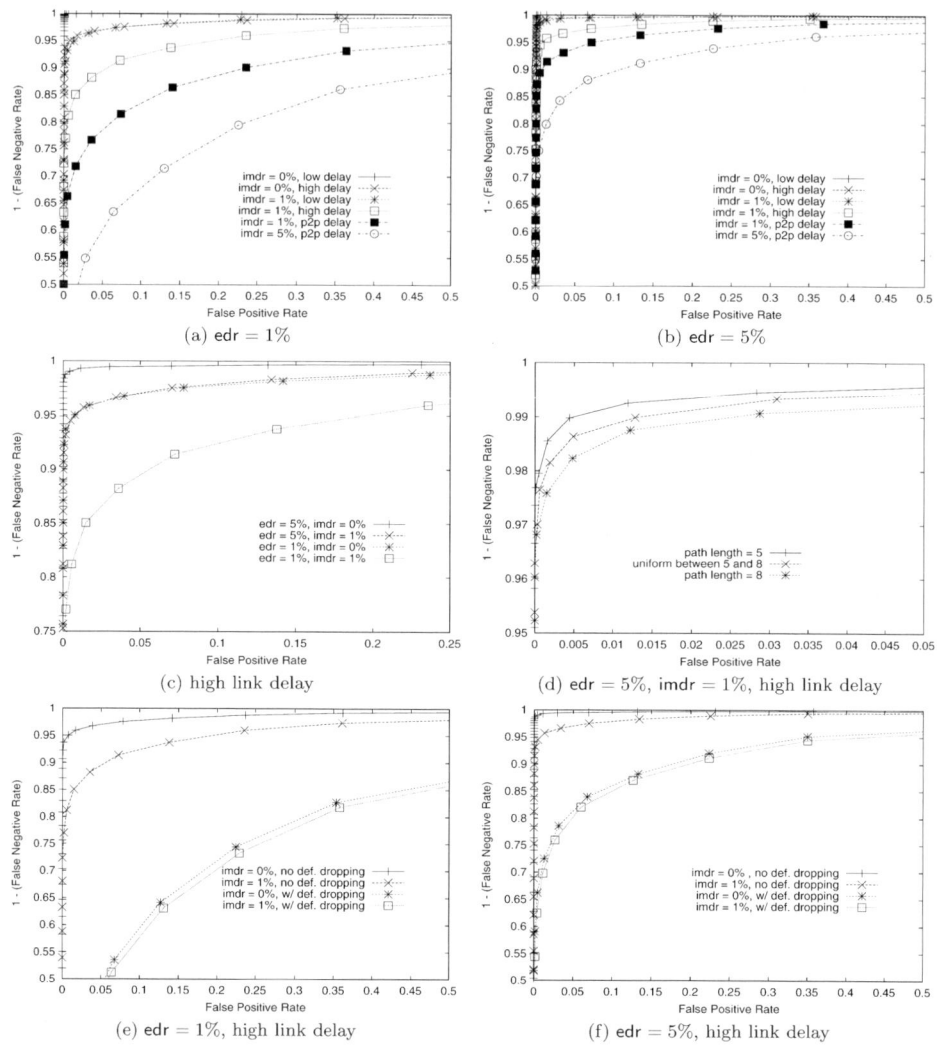

Fig. 2. ROC curves of simulation results.

on tests without defensive dropping. It makes a much larger difference than the imdr. From Figures 2(a–b), we know that imdr is an important factor in how well these tests do. Since defensive dropping has a much larger impact than imdr, we know that it does much better than typical variations in network conditions for confusing the attacker.

7   Discussion

Given that we have isolated the timing analysis apart from the systems and attacks, we now discuss the implications of our results. We first note that, rather than in isolation along a single path, timing analysis would occur in a system with many paths from many initiators. This creates both opportunities and difficulties for an attacker. We begin by showing how the attacker's effectiveness is reduced by prior probabilities. We then show how, when paths or network conditions change, and when initiators make repeated or long-lasting connections, an attacker can benefit. We then describe other ways an attacker can improve his chances of linking the initiator to the responder. We also examine some important systems considerations.

7.1   Prior Probabilities

One of the key difficulties an attacker must face is that the odds of a correct identification vary inversely with the number of initiators. Suppose that, for a given set of network parameters and system conditions, the attacker would have a 1% false positive rate and a 1% false negative rate. Although these may seem like favorable error rates for the attacker, there can be a high incidence of false positives when the number of initiators grows above 100. The attacker must account for the prior probability that the initiator being observed is the initiator of interest, I.

More formally, let us say that event $I \sim J$, for two initiators I and J, occurs when the attacker's test says that packets received at M_1^I and M_h^J are correlated. Assume that the *false positive rate*, $\mathsf{fp} = \Pr(I \sim J | I \neq J)$, and the *false negative rate*, $\mathsf{fn} = \Pr(I \nsim J | I = J)$, are both known. We can therefore obtain:

$$\Pr(I \sim J) = \Pr(I \sim J | I = J)\Pr(I = J) + \Pr(I \sim J | I \neq J)\Pr(I \neq J)$$
$$= (1 - \mathsf{fn})\Pr(I = J) + \mathsf{fp}(1 - \Pr(I = J))$$
$$= (1 - \mathsf{fn} - \mathsf{fp})\Pr(I = J) + \mathsf{fp}$$

Which leads us to obtain:

$$\Pr(I = J | I \sim J) = (\Pr(I = J \wedge I \sim J))/\Pr(I \sim J)$$
$$= (\Pr(I \sim J | I = J)\Pr(I = J))/\Pr(I \sim J)$$
$$= ((1 - \mathsf{fn})\Pr(I = J))/((1 - \mathsf{fn} - \mathsf{fp})\Pr(I = J) + \mathsf{fp})$$

Suppose $\Pr(I = J) = 1/n$, e.g., the network has n initiators and the adversary has no additional information about who are likely correspondents. Then, with $\mathsf{fn} = \mathsf{fp} = 0.01$, we get $\Pr(I = J | I \sim J) = (.99)/(.99 + .01(n - 1))$. With only $n = 10$ initiators, the probability of $I = J$ given $I \sim J$ is about 91.7%. As n rises to 100 initiators, this probability falls to only 50%. With $n = 1000$, it is just over 9%.

Contrast this to the case of $\Pr(I = J) = 0.09$, as the adversary might obtain additional information about the application, or by the derivation above in a previous examination of a different path for the same initiator I (if it is known that the initiator will contact the same responder repeatedly). Then, with $n = 1000$, the probability of $I = J$ given $I \sim J$ is about 90.7%.

The lessons from this analysis are as follows. First, when the number of initiators is large, the attacker's test must be very accurate to correctly identify the initiator, if the attacker has no additional information about the *a priori* probability of an initiator and responder interacting (i.e., if $\Pr(I = J) = 1/n$). In this case, defensive dropping appears to be an effective strategy in stopping a timing analysis test in a large system. By significantly increasing the error rates for the attacker (see Table 1), defensive dropping makes a timing analysis that was otherwise useful much less informative for the attacker. Second, *a priori* information, i.e., when $\Pr(I = J) > 1/n$, can be very helpful to the attacker in large systems.

7.2   Lowering the Error Rates

The attackers cannot effectively determine the best level of correlation with which to identify the initiator unless they can observe the parameters of the network. One approach would be to create fake users, generally an easy task [9], and each such user F can generate traffic through paths that include attacker mixes as M_1^F and M_h^F. This can be done concurrently with the attack, as the attack data may be stored until the attackers are ready to analyze it. The attacker can compare the correlations from traffic on the same path and traffic on different paths, as with our simulations, and determine the best correlation level to use.

In mix server systems, especially cascade mixes [6], the attacker has an additional advantage of being able to compare possible initiators' traffic data to find the best match for a data set taken at M_h^I for some unknown I. With a mix cascade in which n users participate, the attacker can guess that the mix with the traffic timings that best correlate to the timings taken from a stream of interest at M_h^I is M_1^I. This can lower the error rate for the attacker: while a number of streams may have relatively high correlations with the timing data at M_h^I, it may be that M_1^I will typically have the highest such correlation.

7.3   Attacker Dropping

Defensive dropping may also be thwarted by an attacker that actively drops packets. When an attacker controls the first mix on the path, he may drop sufficient packets to raise the correlation level between the first and last mixes. With enough such drops, the attacker will be able to raise his success rates. When defensive dropping is in place, however, the incidence of attacker drops must be higher than with constant rate cover traffic. Any given drop might be due to the defensive dropping rather than the active dropping. This means that the rate of drops seen by the packet dropping mix (or mixes) will be higher than it would otherwise be. What is unclear is whether such an increase would be enough to be detected by an honest intermediate mix.

In general, detection of mixes that drop too many packets is a problem of reputation and incentives for good performance [8, 1] and is beyond the scope of this paper. We note, however, that stopping active timing attacks requires very robust reputation mechanisms that allow users to avoid placing unreliable mixes at the beginning of their paths. In addition, it is important that a user have a reliable link to the Internet so that the first mix does not receive a stream of traffic with many holes to exploit for correlation with the last mix on the path.

7.4 TCP between Mixes

In our model, we have assumed that each message travels on unreliable links between mixes. This allows for dropped packets that have been important in most of the attacks we have described. When TCP is used between each mix, each packet is reliably delivered despite the presence of drops. The effect this has on the attacks depends on the packet rates from the initiator and on the latency between the initiator and the first mix.

For example, suppose that the initiator sends 10 packets per second and that the latency to the first mix averages 50 ms (100 ms RTT). A dropped packet will cause a timeout for the initiator, who must resend the packet. The new packet will be resent in approximately 100 ms in the average case, long enough for an estimated RTT to trigger a timeout. One additional packet will be sent by the initiator, but there will still be a gap of 100 ms, which is equivalent to a packet loss for timing analysis.

This effect, however, is sensitive to timing. When fewer packets are sent per second and the latency is sufficiently low, such effects can be masked by rapid retransmissions. However, an attacker can still actively delay packets, and a watchful honest mix later in the path will not know whether such delays were due to drops and high retransmission delays before the first mix or due to the first mix itself.

7.5 The Return Path

Timing attacks can be just as effective and dangerous on the path from M_h^I back to I as on the forward path. Much of what we have said applies to the reverse path, but there are some key differences. One difference is that I must rely on M_h^I to provide cover traffic (unless the responder is a peer using an anonymous reverse path). This, of course, can be a problem if the M_h^I is dishonest. However, due to the reverse layered encryption, any mix before M_1^I can generate the cover traffic and it can still be effective.

Because many applications, such as multimedia viewing and file downloads, require more data from the responder than from the initiator, there is a significant performance problem. Constant rate cover traffic can quickly become prohibitive, requiring a significant fraction of the bandwidth of each mix. For such applications, stopping timing attacks may be unattainable with acceptable costs.

When cover traffic remains possible, defensive dropping is no longer an option, as a dishonest M_h^I will know the timings of the drops. The last mix should not provide the full amount of cover traffic, instead letting each intermediate mix add some constant rate cover traffic in the reverse pattern of defensive dropping. This helps keep the correlation between M_h^I and M_1^I low.

8   Conclusions

Timing analysis against users of anonymous communications systems can be effective in a wide variety of network and system conditions, and therefore poses a significant challenge to the designer of such systems.

We presented a study of both timing analysis attacks and defenses against such attacks. We have shown that, under certain assumptions, the conventional use of cover traffic is not effective against timing attacks. Furthermore, intentional packet dropping induced by attacker-controlled mixes can nullify the effect of cover traffic altogether. We proposed a new cover traffic technique, defensive dropping, to obstruct timing analysis. Our results show that end-to-end cover traffic augmented with defensive dropping is a viable and effective method to defend against timing analysis in low-latency systems.

References

1. A. Acquisti, R. Dingledine, and P. Syverson. On the Economics of Anonymity. In *Proc. Financial Cryptography*, Jan 2003.
2. A. Back, I. Goldberg, and A. Shostack. Freedom 2.0 Security Issues and Analysis. Zero-Knowledge Systems, Inc. white paper, Nov 2000.
3. O. Berthold, H. Federrath, and M. Kohntopp. Project anonymity and unobservability in the internet. In *Proc. Computers Freedom and Privacy*, April 2000.
4. O. Berthold, A. Pfitzmann, and R. Standtke. The Disadvantages of Free Mix-Routes and How to Overcome Them. In *Proc. Intl. Workshop on Design Issues in Anonymity and Unobservability*, July 2000.
5. J. Bolot. Characterizing End-to-End Packet Delay and Loss in the Internet. *Journal of High Speed Networks*, 2(3), Sept 1993.
6. D. Chaum. Untraceable Electronic Mail, Return Addresses, and Digital Pseudonyms. *Communications of the ACM*, 24(2):84–88, Feb 1981.
7. W. Dei. Pipenet 1.1, August 1996. http://www.eskimo.com/ weidai/pipenet.txt.
8. R. Dingledine, N. Mathewson, and P. Syverson. Reliable MIX Cascade Networks through Reputation. In *Proc. Financial Cryptography*, 2003.
9. J. Douceur. The sybil attack. In *Proc. IPTPS*, Mar 2002.
10. M. Freedman and R. Morris. Tarzan: A Peer-to-Peer Anonymizing Network Layer. In *Proc. ACM Conference on Computer and Communications Security*, Nov 2002.
11. S. Gribble. UC Berkeley Home IP HTTP Traces. http://www.acm.org/ sigcomm/ITA/, July 1997.
12. M. Jakobsson. Flash mixing. In *Proc. Sym. on Principles of Distributed Computing*, May 1999.
13. D. Kesdogan, J. Egner, and R. Buschkes. Stop-and-go-mixes providing probablilistic anonymity in an open system. In *Proc. Information Hiding*, Apr 1998.
14. A. Pfitzmann, B. Pfitzmann, and M. Waidner. ISDNMixes: Untraceable Communication with Very Small Bandwidth Overhead. In *Proc. GI/ITG Communication in Distributed Systems*, Feb 1991.
15. C. Rackoff and D. R. Simon. Cryptographic defense against traffic analysis. In *Proc. ACM Sym. on the Theory of Computing*, May 1993.
16. M. Reed, P. Syverson, and D. Goldschlag. Anonymous Connections and Onion Routing. *IEEE JSAC Copyright and Privacy Protection*, 1998.

17. S. Saroiu, P. Krishna Gummadi, and S. Gribble. A Measurement Study of Peer-to-Peer File Sharing Systems. In *Proc. Multimedia Computing and Networking*, Jan 2002.

18. A. Serjantov, R. Dingledine, and P. Syverson. From a trickle to a flood: active attacks on several mix types. In *Information Hiding*, 2002.

19. P. Syverson, G. Tsudik, M. Reed, and C. Landwehr. Towards an Analysis of Onion Routing Security. In *Workshop on Design Issues in Anonymity and Unobservability*, July 2000.

20. M. Wright, M. Adler, B.N. Levine, and C. Shields. An Analysis of the Degradation of Anonymous Protocols. In *Proc. ISOC Sym. on Network and Distributed System Security*, Feb 2002.

21. M. Wright, M. Adler, B.N. Levine, and C. Shields. Defending Anonymous Communication Against Passive Logging Attacks. In *Proc. IEEE Sym. on Security and Privacy*, May 2003.

Provable Unlinkability against Traffic Analysis

Ron Berman*, Amos Fiat**, and Amnon Ta-Shma***

School of Computer Science, Tel-Aviv University
{bermanro,fiat,amnon}@tau.ac.il

Abstract. Chaum [1, 2] suggested a simple and efficient protocol aimed at providing anonymity in the presence of an adversary watching *all* communication links. Chaum's protocol is known to be insecure. We show that Chaum's protocol becomes secure when the attack model is relaxed and the adversary can control at most 99% of communication links.

Our proof technique is markedly different than previous work. We establish a connection with information theory - a connection we believe is useful also elsewhere, and which we believe supplies the correct language to attack the problem. We introduce "obscurant networks" - networks that can obscure the destination of each particular player, and we show almost all executions of the protocol include such a network.

The security guarantee we supply is very strong. It shows the adversary learns almost no information about any subset of players. Remarkably, we show that this guarantee holds even if the adversary has a-priori information about communication patters (e.g., people tend to speak less with those who do not understand their language). We believe this is an important issue in the real world and is a desirable property any anonymous system should have.

Keywords: Anonymity, Privacy, Traffic Analysis, Unlinkability, Peer to Peer networks.

1   Introduction

Chaum [1, 2] gave a general paradigmatic approach to anonymity. This includes the observation that one can restrict attention to traffic analysis and ignore message content, using encryption as the basic ingredient. These techniques are currently known as onion routing [3, 4]. Chaum also suggested to solve the traffic analysis problem even against an adversary who watches *all* communication links, using a cascade of mixes. Chaum's protocol is flawed and several attacks are known today. In 1993, Rackoff and Simon [5] showed that if all participants play at each time step, then these problems can be solved using secure computation.

* This research was supported by the Deutsch Institute.
** This research was supported by a grant from the European Community, Appol II.
*** This research was supported by the Dan David Prize Scholarship.

The requirement that each participant sends a message every time step, puts a large load burden on the system. Furthermore, if we think of a large peer to peer network, say the Internet, then it is inconceivable to require each participant to play each round. Unfortunately, it is not difficult to see that this requirement is necessary if the adversary controls *all* communication links. In this case, if at each time step only a fraction of the participants send a message then the well-known Mix flood attack [12] can isolate messages of any specific player. We therefore set on the task of finding the strongest adversary model, under which we can supply a provably anonymous system, and where the load burden on each player is small.

The model we come up with is one where the adversary can control most, but not all, of the communication links in the system, and the protocol we use is a simplification of Chaum's original protocol. We thus get a simple and efficient protocol (both in terms of delay and load) that is provably anonymous against an all powerful adversary that controls, say, at most 99% of communication links (for formal definitions and statements see Sect. 2). A comparison of our protocol with several other ones can be found in Table 1.

Table 1. Unlinkability protocols for a network of size N. Delay is how long it takes for an anonymous message to arrive after it's been initiated. Load is the number of messages actually sent per anonymous message delivered.

Protocol	Attack Model: Resources under adversary control	Delay	Load	Simple?	Attacks?
Chaum	$O(1)$ fraction of nodes All links	$\text{polylog}(N)$	$\text{polylog}(N)$	Yes	**Yes**
RS93 [5]	$O(1)$ fraction of nodes All links	$\text{polylog}(N)$	$\tilde{O}(N)$	No	–
This paper	$O(1)$ fraction of nodes $O(1)$ fraction of links	$\text{polylog}(N)$	$\text{polylog}(N)$	Yes	–

Our analysis is markedly different than previous work. Relaxing the attack model to one where the adversary does not control a fraction of the communication links makes mixing throughout layers possible. One then has to analyze the information the adversary gets in such a scenario.

Information theory provides a convenient language for expressing and dealing with the question. The notations and definitions used throughout this paper rely heavily on [17]. We show that anonymity can be defined in terms of the mutual information between the actual communication that took place, and the information the adversary knows about it. The mutual information function gives an estimate on how much knowledge can be deduced on one random variable, e.g., the matching of senders and receivers, from another partially correlated variable, e.g., the traffic information gathered by an adversary. We also show that this new definition is equivalent to previous definitions up to small factors.

Using information theory provides us with the language to attack the problem, but not the solution itself. For the proof, we show that with high probability, the information the adversary is missing contains within it communication edges that together form an "obscurant network" - a network that can obscure the destination of each particular player. The exact definition of a protocol execution containing a network is conceptually delicate, and the exact definition, given in Definition 9, is one of the main technical contributions of the paper. We then use information theory to show that this implies that the adversary learns almost no information about any *subset of players*. An alternate formulation of this statement is that the information gleaned by the adversary on the actual communications pattern is close to zero.

An added bonus is the treatment of unlinkability in a scenario where prior information is given to the adversary about the expected communication pattern. We believe this is a rather important issue as in the real world communication patterns are far from being random (*e.g.*, The a-priori probability of a message between two English speaking persons is much larger than that of a message between an English speaking person and a Chinese speaking person). Nevertheless, it seems all previous works avoided the issue. Using our tools, and a nice folding trick (and information theory again, of course), we show that no matter what the prior information is, the adversary learns almost no information from the communication it sees. We believe this result is rather strong and surprising, and is a desirable property any anonymous system should have.

1.1 Related Work

Rackoff and Simon [5] describe a simple protocol secure against passive adversaries (that do not deviate from the given protocol) that is based on sorting networks. Chaum [6] suggested the Dining-Cryptographer networks also secure against such an adversary. Both systems have some extra requirements (*e.g.*, DC require shared secret keys), most notable they both require all players to participate at each stage.

Implementations of Chaum's ideas appear in [13, 14, 4, 3, 8] and various attacks are described in [12, 15]. Other methods for anonymity appear in [7, 10, 11].

2   What Is Anonymity?

2.1   Our Attack Model

We have *nodes* and *communication links* in the system. We assume nodes hold data items which are all of the same length. Some nodes and links are under control of an adversary, others are not and are called *honest*. We distinguish between two types of adversaries. An adversary may instruct the nodes and links under his control to perform some arbitrary behavior based on the information he gathered so far. An *adaptive* adversary may instruct nodes and links under his control to initiate arbitrary new messages even not according to the protocol, but may not instruct to delete them. A malicious adversary may instruct such nodes to perform arbitrary behavior and in particular may delete messages. In this paper we only deal with adaptive adversaries.

We assume that a public key infrastructure (PKI) and a public key directory is widely available. The most significant assumption we make is that at least a constant fraction of the communication links are honest[1].

The delay of a protocol, also known as parallel time, is the number of rounds it takes until a message reaches its destination. The load of a protocol is the total number of messages transmitted throughout the protocol per anonymous message delivered. It is important to realize that a communication network in general, and the Internet in particular, may have a very large number N of potential users, while only very few actual active players at any given time. In particular, for an Internet protocol with only $K << N$ active players, one would hope for load that is $\tilde{O}(K)$ and not $\tilde{O}(N)$.

2.2   Defining Unlinkability

Say there are M active players and they wish to communicate with M distinct nodes[2]. Let π be the permutation that describes the communication pattern, i.e., player i communicates with node $\pi(i)$, and let Π be the random variable whose value is π. Now, let C be the random variable whose value is all the information available to the adaptive adversary, gathered from adaptive communication links and adaptive nodes. Specifically, C is a 0/1 matrix with rows indexed by time steps an columns indexed by edges and with $C_{t,e}$ being 1 iff there is some communication on edge e in time t. Simon and Rackoff require that (Π, C) is α–computationally close to some (Π, C') such that for all possible permutations $|\pi_1, \pi_2 |(C'|\Pi = \pi_1) - (C'|\Pi = \pi_2)|_1 \leq \alpha$. We now give an equivalent definition using the mutual information function. We define:

Definition 1. *Let $A = \{A_n\}, B = \{B_n\}$ be two families of distributions. We say $d(A, B)_P \leq \delta(n)$, if for every family of polynomial-size Boolean circuits $\{T_n\}$, for every large enough n, $| \Pr_{x \in A_n}[T_n(x) = 1] - \Pr_{x' \in B_n}[T_n(x') = 1] | \leq \delta(n)$.*

The following definition contains three alternative definitions:

Definition 2. *A family $\{(\Pi, C)\} = \bigcup_n (\Pi_n, C_n)$ is $\alpha(n)$–unlinkable if,*

- $d(\{(\Pi, C)\}, \{(\Pi, C')\})_P \leq \alpha(n)$ for some $\{(\Pi, C')\} = \cup_n(\Pi_n, C'_n)$, and,
- For every n, fix $\Pi = \Pi_n$, $C' = C'_n$ and $\alpha = \alpha(n)$. We require,
  · (Def 1 [5]): $\forall \pi_1, \pi_2 \in \Pi$, $|(C'|\Pi = \pi_1) - (C'|\Pi = \pi_2)|_1 \leq \alpha$.
  · (Def 2): $\Pr_{c \in C'}[|(\Pi|C' = c) - \Pi|_1 \geq \alpha] \leq \alpha$.
  · (Def 3): $I(\Pi : C') \leq \alpha$.

---

[1] Our results remain valid even when the adversary is allowed to eavesdrop *every* honest link 99% of the time, with the caveat that on a random 1% of the time, he fails to do so.

[2] If the M nodes are not distinct, then our protocol w.h.p. makes them distinct by adding a random identifier to each message.

We prove the three definitions are equivalent up to small multiplicative factors:

Lemma 3. *Let $\{(\Pi, C)\} = \bigcup_n (\Pi_n, C_n)$ be a family of arbitrary joint distributions, (Π_n, C_n) is distributed over some domain Λ_n.*

- *If $\{(\Pi, C)\}$ is $\gamma(n)$–unlinkable according to Def 1 (Def 2), then it is $\delta(n) = O(\log(|\Lambda_n|)\sqrt{\gamma(n)})$–unlinkable according to Def 3. Conversely, If $\{(\Pi, C)\}$ is $\delta(n)$–unlinkable according to Def 4, then it is $\gamma(n) = (2\ln 2 \cdot \delta(n))^{1/3}$–unlinkable according to Def 1 (Def 2).*

The formal proof will appear in the full version of the paper.

We now specialize to our case, and we define when a protocol is unlinkable. The thing to notice is that we allow the adversary a-priori knowledge on the honest player's communication pattern. Specifically this means that we do not require the a-priori distribution $\Pi_N(S_N)$ to be uniform. We say a protocol is $\alpha(N)$–unlinkable according to definition i, $i \in \{1, 2, 3\}$, if, for every N players, every choice of subsets S_N of honest players, and every distribution $\Pi_N(S_N)$ on their actual communication, which is the prior knowledge, if we let $C_N(S_N)$ be the correlated random variable that contains the information known to the adversary, then $\bigcup_N (\Pi_N(S_N), C_N(S_N))$ is $\alpha(N)$– unlinkable according to definition i.

We say a protocol P is *efficient* unlinkable protocol according to definition i, if for every possible error function $\alpha(N) \geq N^{-c}$,

- $P_{N,\alpha(N)}$ is $\alpha(N)$–unlinkable according to definition i, and
- $P_{N,\alpha(N)}$ takes $T(N) = O(\text{poly}(\log(\frac{N}{\alpha(N)})))$ rounds, and $O(M \cdot T(N))$ messages, when M is the number of players who wish to send a message at a time.

Because of the equivalence stated before, we have:

Theorem 4. *A protocol P is efficiently unlinkable according to any one definition iff it is efficiently unlinkable according to all definitions.*

Details of the proof will appear in the full version of the paper.

3   The Protocol

Our protocol is a variant of Chaum's protocol. We describe our protocol in a synchronous system. A wants to send a message $a \in \{0, 1\}^S$ to B and get back an answer $b \in \{0, 1\}^S$, where S is the length of data items in the system. A picks $T - 1$ random nodes $v_1, \ldots, v_{T-1}$, and sets $v_0 = A$, $v_T = B$. A also picks T random strings $r_i \in \{0, 1\}^S$, and $z_i \in \{0, 1\}^{\ell_i}$ where ℓ_i is a security parameter for the encryption schemes E_i. We let $E_1, \ldots, E_T$ be the public encryption methods of the T nodes. We denote

$$a_i = E_{i+1}(r_{i+1}, z_{i+1}, v_{i+2}, E_{i+2}(\ldots E_{T-1}(r_{T-1}, z_{T-1}, v_T, E_T(r_T, a))) \ldots)$$

for $i = 0, \ldots, T - 1$.

The way from A to B : A sends $(0, v_0, z_0, a_0)$ to v_1. In general, v_i sends (i, v_i, z_i, a_i) to v_{i+1} where $a_i = E_{i+1}(r_{i+1}, z_{i+1}, v_{i+2}, a_{i+1})$. v_{i+1} then decrypts a_i, and sends $(i + 1, v_{i+1}, z_{i+1}, a_{i+1})$ to v_{i+2}. It also records $v_i, v_{i+2}, z_i, z_{i+1}$ and r_{i+1}. $v_T = B$ recognizes it is the last on the path, and prepares an answer $b \in \{0, 1\}^S$ to the message a it receives.

The way back : $B = v_T$ sends (v_T, z_{T-1}, b_T) to v_{T-1} where $b_T = b \oplus r_T$. In general, v_i receives a message (v_{i+1}, z_i, b_{i+1}). v_i recognizes the value z_i, the link (v_{i-1}, v_i) that precedes (v_i, v_{i+1}) and the values r_i, z_{i-1} that are associated with it. It then sends $(v_i, z_{i-1}, b_i = b_{i+1} \oplus r_i)$ to v_{i-1}. Finally, $A = v_0$ receives $(v_0, z_0, b_0 = b_1 \oplus r_1)$ from v_1. The value $b_0 \oplus r_1 \oplus \ldots r_T$ is the desired value b.

We prove:

Theorem 5. *Assume the above protocol runs for T steps in a network with N nodes, $\binom{N}{2}$ communication links, some constant fraction of which are honest, and $T \geq \Omega(\log(N) \log^2(N/\alpha(N)))$. Then the protocol is $\alpha(N)$–unlinkable.*

The protocol can be adapted to the asynchronous setting as well, details to appear in the full version of this paper.

4   The Proof

4.1   Proof Sketch

Generally speaking, in order to prove that the above protocol is secure, a process of structuring is needed to be done to the communication patterns, to allow for easy analysis and calculations.

To perform this process a special communication network is constructed, an "Obscurant Network" (See Sect. 4.2). Apart from the data flow properties of this network that allows anonymity, this network has a highly static and structured communication pattern, compared with the patterns created by our protocol.

In order to analyze the amount of data the adversary gathers from the pattern created by our protocol, we show that this pattern has enough honest links within it that together contain an "embedded" obscurant network. After describing what an embedding is and an algorithm to find one in Sect. 4.3, we prove that our protocol's communication pattern contains, w.h.p., such an embedding in Sect. 4.4 for the case of no-prior information.

Our proof makes use of another interesting technique. During most steps of the analysis, information is purposely being revealed to the adversary regarding communication on links that are not under its control. This classifies the links in the network into two, ones where the adversary has full information of data flow, and ones where the adversary has absolutely no information about the flow of data. Showing both the existence of an embedding of an obscurant network as well as telling all other irrelevant data to the adversary allow for a simple proof in the case of no-prior information.

Prior information is dealt with in section 4.4. A folding trick is used to reveal yet some more information to the adversary about the connection between information flowing from the sources of the message and the information arriving at the final destinations of messages. This trick literally folds the communication pattern in half when observed from the adversary's point of view, reducing the analysis to the case of no-prior information, when the interesting layer of the protocol is the middle layer of communications. We then show that the middle layer does not convey enough information to the adversary, resulting in unlinkability. The result requires longer message paths in order to achieve a probable embedding of an obscurant network.

4.2   Obscurant Networks

A network is a layered directed circuit with the same number of vertices on each layer. We say a circuit is a crossover network, if every vertex has in-degree and out-degree one or two. An example is depicted in Fig. 1. We think of the following game: a pebble is put on some input vertex, say on the i'th vertex. If the vertex out-degree is one, we follow that link. Otherwise, we follow each of the crossover links with probability half. By the end of the game we get a distribution O_i over the output elements. We say the network ϵ–obscures the i'th input, if $|O_i - U_M| \leq \epsilon$, when U_M is the uniform distribution. We say a network ϵ-obscures inputs, if it ϵ-obscures every input. We call networks that obscure their inputs obscurant networks.

We now show an explicit construction of a simple shallow obscurant network that has depth $O((\log(M) + \log \epsilon^{-1}) \log(M))$ for M inputs.

Let Z be the largest power of two not larger than M. We use two components: a butterfly network B_Z, with comparators replaced with crossovers, and a network over $2k$ elements and two layers with k crossovers connecting vertex i in the first layer with both vertex i and vertex $k + i$ (mod $2k$) in the second layer, for $i = 1, \ldots, 2k$. We call this later network P_{2k}. We distinguish between two cases. If $Z = M$ we put B_Z on the Z inputs. Otherwise, $\frac{M}{2} < Z < M$. For the first level, we put B_Z on the Z rightmost elements. For the second level, We put B_Z on the Z leftmost elements. For the third level, We put $P_{2(M-Z)}$ on the $2(M - Z)$ rightmost elements. For the fourth level, we put B_Z on the Z leftmost elements. We then iterate the third and fourth levels $\log(M) + \log \epsilon^{-1}$ times (see Fig. 1).

We claim:

Lemma 6. *When using a depth of $O((\log(M) + \log \epsilon^{-1}) \log(M))$, the network is ϵ–obscurant.*

Proof. If $M = Z$, then for every input vertex i spans a tree. It follows that $O_i = U_M$ and the network is 0–obscurant.

Suppose $\frac{M}{2} < Z < M$. Let i be a starting vertex. Notice that B_Z gives equal weight to each of its Z outputs. When applying B_Z on the right followed by B_Z on the left, all the Z leftmost elements have one weight, ℓ_0, while the rest $M - Z$ rightmost elements have the same (possibly different) weight, r_0. One can observe that this property is an invariant that remains valid throughout the protocol, *i.e.*,

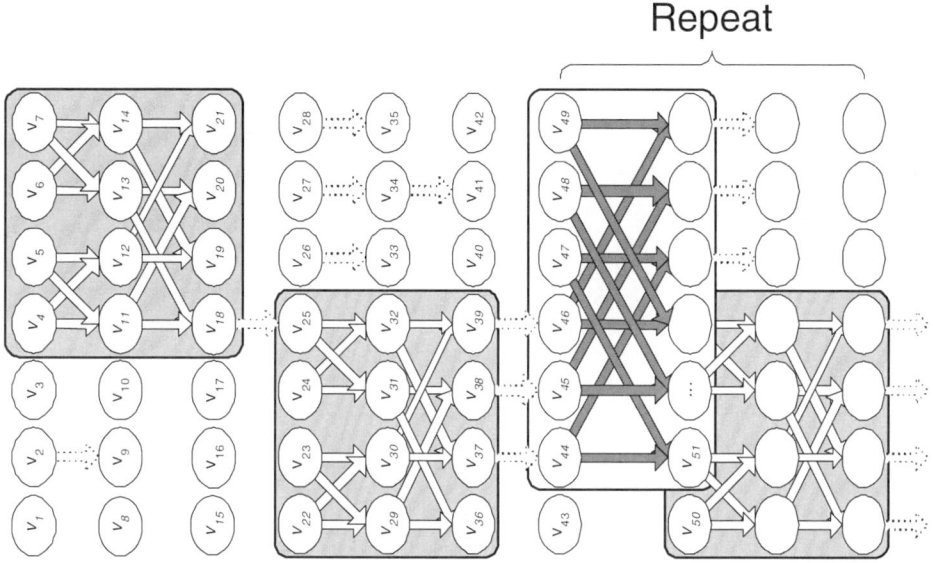

Fig. 1. *An obscurant network for $M = 7$, $Z = 4$. Simple connections are often omitted. The boxes with the grey background are B_4 butterflies. The other boxed sub-circuit is P_6.*

– The invariant: After applying the pair $P_{2(M-Z)}$ and B_Z i times, $i \geq 0$, the Z leftmost elements all have weight l_i and the $M - Z$ rightmost elements all have weight r_i.

– After applying $P_{2(M-Z)}$ of the $i + 1$'st pair, all the $2(M - Z)$ rightmost elements have one weight $r_{i+1} = (r_i + l_i)/2$ and all the remaining $M - 2(M - Z) = 2Z - M = K$, $1 \leq K < Z$, leftmost elements remain at weight l_i.

– After applying B_Z of the $i + 1$'st pair, all the Z leftmost elements have one weight $\ell_{i+1} = \frac{K \cdot l_i + (Z-K) \cdot r_{i+1}}{Z}$ and all the $M - Z$ rightmost elements remain at weight r_{i+1}.

Calculating, we see that $|\ell_{i+1} - r_{i+1}| < \frac{1}{2}|\ell_i - r_i|$, which leads to the fact that $|\ell_t - \frac{1}{M}| \leq \frac{(M-Z)}{M} 2^{-t}$. To conclude the proof we note that $|O_i^{(t)} - U_M|_1 \leq 2M \cdot |\ell_t - \frac{1}{M}| \leq 2(M-Z)2^{-t}$. As $M - Z < M/2 < M$, we get that $|O_i^{(t)} - U_M|_1 \leq M2^{-t} \leq \epsilon$, for $t = \log(M) + \log \epsilon^{-1}$. □

4.3   Finding Obscurant Networks in Protocol Executions

Say that M honest players start sending messages and that we have in mind an obscurant, crossover network G over M inputs and of depth D. Our goal is to show that if the M players run the protocol T steps, for some T large enough, then the network G, in a sense, appears as a subgraph of the protocol execution graph, which we call P. The precise notion of G appearing in P is somewhat delicate and we explain it in detail soon.

The basic fact that we know about our system is that at least an f fraction of the links are honest. The following combinatorial lemma asserts that no matter which edges are honest, if we choose four vertices a, b, c, d at random from V, then there is a crossover structure on the four vertices with probability at least f^4.

Fact 7 ([16], Corollary 2.1) Let $G = (V, E)$ be a graph and assume $|E| \geq f \cdot \binom{|V|}{2}$. Then $\mathrm{Pr}_{a,b,c,d \in V}$ [$\{(a, c), (a, d), (b, c), (b, d)\} \subseteq E$] $\geq f^4$.

Good Embeddings. We represent a crossover network G as $G = (V_G, \boxtimes_G, I_G)$ where V_G is the set of DM vertices of G, $\boxtimes_G$ is the set of all crossovers $(a, b; c, d)$ in G, and I_G is the set of all simple links in G (i.e., network edges of G not participating in any crossover). We represent a protocol P as $P = (V_P, T_P, C_P)$ where V_P is the set of TM vertices participating in the protocol, T_P is the set of all links carrying traffic in the execution of the protocol, and C_P is the set of all links that are under adversary control (whether used to carry traffic or not).

Definition 8. A function $\phi : V_G \times \{0, 1\} \to V_P$ is an embedding if:

- The mapping ϕ respects T_P. I.e.,
  - $\forall_{e=(v,w) \in I_G}$ $(\phi(v, 1), \phi(w, 0)) \in T_P$.
  - $\forall_{(a,b;c,d) \in \boxtimes_G}$ $\left| \left\{ \begin{array}{l} (\phi(a, 1), \phi(c, 0)), (\phi(a, 1), \phi(d, 0)), \\ (\phi(b, 1), \phi(c, 0)), (\phi(b, 1), \phi(d, 0)) \end{array} \right\} \cap T_P \right| = 2.$
- For every $v \in V_G$, $\phi(v, 0)$ and $\phi(v, 1)$ are connected in T_P.
- The adversary does not know any link in any crossover. I.e., for every $(v_1, v_2; w_1, w_2) \in \boxtimes_G$ and every $i, j \in \{1, 2\}$, $(\phi(v_i, 1), \phi(w_j, 0)) \notin C_P$.

We define $\phi_P(\boxtimes_G)$ to be the image of $\boxtimes_G$ under the embedding ϕ. I.e., the set of all $(u_1, u_2; u_3, u_4) \in V_P^4$ for which there exist $(v_1, v_2; v_3, v_4) \in \boxtimes_G$ s.t. $\phi(v_1, 1) = u_1$, $\phi(v_2, 1) = u_2$, $\phi(v_3, 0) = u_3$ and $\phi(v_4, 0) = u_4$.

A delicate point is that right now the embedding ϕ may depend on the actual communication P that took place. We therefore add the requirement that ϕ is independent of the communication that took place on the embedded copy of G. Formally this takes the following form:

Definition 9. Let G be defined as before. Let $\mathcal{P}$ be a protocol (e.g., the protocol of Sect. 3). An embedding strategy for the protocol, with ϵ error, is an algorithm that given an execution $P = (V_P, T_P, C_P)$ of the protocol, outputs a function $\phi_P : V_G \times \{0, 1\} \to V_P$ such that:

- $\mathrm{Pr}_{coins\ of\ P}[\phi_P$ is an embedding$] \geq 1 - \epsilon$, and,
- For every two protocol executions P and P' that use the same sets of vertices, if $T_{P'}$ agrees with T_P on all edges not participating in $\phi_P(\boxtimes_G)$ then $\phi_P = \phi_{P'}$.

A Good Embedding Exists. We prove:

Lemma 10. *Let G be any network over M inputs and of depth D. Let us run the protocol $\mathcal{P}$ of Sect. 3 for $T = 2Dk$ steps. Then there is an embedding strategy for $\mathcal{P}$ with $\epsilon = DM(1 - f^4)^k$ error.*

Proof. We first label each vertex v of G by $v_i^{(d)}$, where $0 \le d \le D$ is the depth of v, and i comes from an arbitrary labelling of the d'th layer with labels $\{1, \ldots, M\}$, such that all edges in G are either of the simple form $(v_i^{(d)}, v_i^{(d+1)})$ or of the crossover form $(v_i^{(d)}, v_j^{(d+1)})$ where $(v_i^{(d)}, v_j^{(d)}; v_i^{(d+1)}, v_j^{(d+1)}) \in \boxtimes_G$.

Algorithm 11 *(An algorithm for labelling V_P and constructing $\phi : V_G \to V_P$)*

Bottom layer: *The algorithm labels all the vertices in the bottom layer of P with $u_i^{(0)}$, where $i \in \{1, \ldots, M\}$ and the labels inside the layer are chosen arbitrarily (say, by lexicographic order on the identity of the vertex). We define $\phi(v_i^{(0)}, 0) = u_i^{(0)}$.*

Odd layer: *We reveal all communication on links going from a vertex in layer $2t$ to a vertex in layer $2t + 1$, for every $0 \le t \le \frac{T}{2}$. For every revealed edge $(u_i^{(2t)}, w) \in T_P$ we label w with $u_i^{(2t+1)}$.*

Even layer $t = d \cdot 2k + \ell$, $0 \le \ell < 2k$: *First, if $\ell = 0$ we set $ok(i) = false$ for every $i \in \{1, \ldots, M\}$. This tells us that we still have to take care of all vertices in the d'th layer of G. Otherwise, if $\ell \ge 2$ then for every $i \in \{1, \ldots, M\}$ we do the following:*

- *If $v_i^{(d)}$ belongs to a simple edge $(v_i^{(d)}, v_i^{(d+1)})$, we reveal the edge $(u_i^{(t-1)}, w)$ of T_P and we label w with $u_i^{(t)}$. Also, if $ok(i) = false$ then set $\phi(v_i^{(d)}, 1) = u_i^{(t-1)}$, $\phi(v_i^{(d+1)}, 0) = u_i^{(t)}$ and $ok(i) = true$.*

- *Otherwise, $v_i^{(d)}$ belongs to a crossover form $(v_i^{(d)}, v_j^{(d)}; v_i^{(d+1)}, v_j^{(d+1)}) \in \boxtimes_G$. Let w and z be the vertices such that $(u_i^{(t-1)}, w), (u_j^{(t-1)}, z) \in T_P$. If $ok(i) = true$ or if one of the edges $(u_i^{(t-1)}, w)$, $(u_i^{(t-1)}, z)$, $(u_j^{(t-1)}, w)$ or $(u_j^{(t-1)}, z)$ is in C_P we reveal all the above four edges. We also label w with $u_i^{(t)}$.*

  If, however, $ok(i) = false$ and all these four edges are honest, we label $\{w, z\}$ with the labels $\left\{ u_i^{(t)}, u_j^{(t)} \right\}$ in an arbitrary order (say, by the natural order on i and j as numbers) and we set $\phi(v_i^{(d)}, 1) = u_i^{(t-1)}$, $\phi(v_i^{(d+1)}, 0) = u_i^{(t)}$ and $ok(i) = true$. We also say, then, that we have found the crossover $(v_i^{(d)}, v_j^{(d)}; v_i^{(d+1)}, v_j^{(d+1)}) \in \boxtimes_G$ in P.

The first two conditions of Definition 8 hold directly from the way we choose the embedding ϕ. Also, let us say that we find G in P if we find every crossover of $\boxtimes_G$ in P. Whenever this happens the third condition also holds, because we then embed every crossover of G in V_P in a clean way.

To see that Algorithm 11 is an embedding strategy, fix two executions P and P' of the protocol that use the same sets of vertices, and that agree on all communication over links not in $\phi_P(\boxtimes_G)$. As P and P' differ only on crossovers, and the labelling of the vertices at the last layer of the crossover depends only on a pre-determined order, the labelling in P is the same as in P'. This means that $\phi_P = \phi_{P'}$.

To complete the argument we show that with high probability (over the random coins of the protocol $\mathcal{P}$ from Sect. 3) we find all crossovers of $\boxtimes_G$ in P.

Claim. For every crossover $(v_i^{(d)}, v_j^{(d)}; v_i^{(d+1)}, v_j^{(d+1)}) \in \boxtimes_G$, the probability we do not find it in an execution P of the protocol from Sect. 3 is at most $(1 - f^4)^k$.

Proof. Fix $(v_i^{(d)}, v_j^{(d)}; v_i^{(d+1)}, v_j^{(d+1)}) \in \boxtimes_G$. For every time step $t = 2kd + \ell$, $2 \leq \ell < 2k$, look at the vertices $u_i^{(t-1)}, u_j^{(t-1)}, u_i^{(t)}, u_j^{(t)}$. The vertices in each path are chosen at random, and we reveal all edges going from even layers to odd layers. Thus, the vertices in the $t - 1$ and t'th layers are chosen at random and independent of history. Specifically, the above four vertices are chosen at random, and independent of history. By Fact 7 we find a crossover with probability at least f^4. As different steps are independent, the probability we do not find a crossover in any of the k attempts is at most $(1 - f^4)^k$.   □

Using the union bound we see that:

Claim. Let G be any crossover network with M inputs and depth D. Let us run the protocol of Sect. 3 with M honest nodes and for $T = 2Dk$ steps. Let P be the resulting network. Then $\Pr[G \text{ does not appear in } P] \leq DM(1 - f^4)^k$.   □

4.4   The Unlinkability Proof

Our goal now is to prove that our protocol is unlinkable. We first deal with the no prior knowledge case, *i.e.*, when the a-priori distribution is uniform. We then show in section how the no prior knowledge case implies the general case.

We show that given knowledge of how players $1, \ldots, j$ behave, the adversary does not know how player $j + 1$ behaves. For every $j = 1, \ldots, M$, we display a *different* obscurant network G_j, over $M - j$ players, in the actual execution of the protocol.

Suppose there are M honest players sending messages in a network with N players, and let $\alpha(N) > N^{-c}$. Let $G = G_M$ be an ϵ-obscurant network over M inputs and of depth $D = O(\log(\frac{M}{\epsilon}) \log(M))$. Suppose we run the protocol for $T = 2Dk$ steps. We would like to set values for ϵ and k such that we receive $\alpha(N) - unlinkability$ with our protocol.

We define the following random variables:

X : X contains all the actual information generated throughout the protocol. *I.e.*, for every link $(v_i^{(t)}, v_j^{(t+1)})$ it contains the information whether there was traffic on that link or not.

Π : $\Pi(i)$ contains the actual destination of the i'th honest player. The random variable $\Pi = \Pi(1) \ldots \Pi(M)$ contains the actual communication pattern between the M honest players and the M destinations.

C' : C' contains all the traffic information the adversary knows. I.e., for every dishonest link $(v_i^{(t)}, v_j^{(t+1)})$ it contains the information whether there was traffic on that link during the t'th step or not.

Z : X and C' together determine whether the process described in section 4.3 finds the crossover network G in the protocol or not. If we do, we let Z contain all the information available on links that do not belong to $\phi_{X,C'}(\boxtimes_G)$. I.e., for every link $(v_i^{(t)}, v_j^{(t+1)})$ that does not belong to $\phi_{X,C'}(\boxtimes_G)$, it contains the information as to whether there was traffic on that link during the t'th step or not.

Notice that Z is correlated with X, Π and C'. Nevertheless, the chain rule for information ([17], Theorem 2.5.2, page 22) tells us that $I(\Pi : C') \le I(\Pi : C', Z)$. It would therefore suffice to show that $I(\Pi : C', Z) \le \alpha(N)$. Now comes the crux of the argument, and we do it in detail.

Suppose the embedding strategy finds G in an execution P of the protocol. By Definition 9, all executions P' of the protocol that use the same set of vertices and agree with P outside $\phi_P(\boxtimes_G)$ result in the same embedding. As all edges revealed are outside $\phi_P(\boxtimes_G)$, the random variable Z has the same value in both cases. Also, C' has the same value in both cases as $\phi_P(\boxtimes_G)$ contains only honest edges. Thus, the adversary can not distinguish P from P'. As the a-priori probabilities of the executions P and P' are the same, both are equally likely from the adversary point of view. I.e., any possible communication pattern on $\phi_P(\boxtimes_G)$ is equally likely.

Now, G is an ϵ-obscurant network. From the adversary point of view, any crossover is resolved to be identity with probability half, and a switch with probability half (because all possible communication patterns are equally likely), and so by the obscurant network properties $|(\Pi(1) \mid C', Z) - U_M|_1 \le \epsilon$.

Using lemma 10 it follows that $\Pr_{C',z}[|(\Pi(1)|C' = c', Z = z) - U_M|_1 \ge \epsilon] \le DM(1 - f^4)^k = \epsilon$, when k is set to $log_{\frac{1}{1-f^4}}(\frac{DM}{\epsilon})$.

We now continue with standard manipulations. From Lemma 3 we see that $I(\Pi(1) : C', Z) \le log(|\Lambda_N|) \cdot \sqrt{\epsilon} = O(TM^2\sqrt{\epsilon})$. Taking $\epsilon = \frac{\alpha^6(N)}{M^{12}}$, we receive $I(\Pi(1) : C', Z) \le O(\frac{\alpha(N)}{M})$.

Using the chain rule for information, $I(C' : \Pi) = I(C' : \Pi(1)) + I(C' : \Pi(2)|\Pi(1)) + \ldots + I(C' : \Pi(M)|\Pi(1), \ldots, \Pi(M-1))$.

We can bound the j'th term $I(C' : \Pi(j) \mid \Pi(j-1), \ldots, \Pi(1))$ in this equation, by adding to the adversary the knowledge of the communication paths of the first $j-1$ players. We then see that we get a new game with only $M-j+1$ players. Our analysis from before shows that $I(C', Z : \Pi(j) \mid \Pi(j-1), \ldots, \Pi(1)) \le O(\frac{\alpha(N)}{M})$. We therefore conclude that $I(C' : \Pi) \le M \cdot O(\frac{\alpha(N)}{M}) \le \alpha(N)$ as desired.

The Prior Information Case. In the general case the adversary knows that the actual communication that took place has a-priori distribution Π. The adversary may use this knowledge to deduce things about the next to last layer, the one preceding it and so forth. Thus, the information the adversary sees flows both from bottom up (because the adversary knows who initiates messages, and follows whatever links he can), and from top down (because the adversary has some partial information about who sent who a message, and he follows links from top down). We note that we would like to deal with priors that have extremely low probability in a uniform world. E.g., the adversary might know that residents of Kandahar tend to communicate with residents of Karachi.

The way we show our protocol works is by concentrating on the *middle* layer. This is intuitively natural because the adversary knows the permutation at the beginning, and has partial information about the final permutation (given by the prior), but the middle layer seems to be masked by the random choices made throughout the protocol. We let $\Pi^{(T/2)}$ be the random variable whose value is the actual permutation that took place between the first and middle layer. To show that even in the prior knowledge scenario the adversary does not learn much about the middle layer we give the adversary additional information so as to make the information flow only in one direction. Details follow.

Lemma 12. *Let Π be an arbitrary distribution. Suppose we run the protocol for $T = \Omega(\log(M)\log^2(\frac{M}{\alpha}))$ steps. Then $I(C' : \Pi^{(T/2)}) \leq \alpha$.*

Proof. We say a vertex $v^{(t)}$ from the t'th layer is associated with a vertex $w^{(T-t)}$ from the $T-t$'th layer, if the message that $v^{(t)}$ forwards eventually arrives at $w^{(T-t)}$. We also say the link (w, v) is associated with the link (v', w') if w is associated with w', and v is associated with v'.

We give the adversary the extra knowledge about which vertex at level t is associated with which vertex at level $T - t$, for every $0 \leq t \leq \frac{T}{2}$. We see that under this additional information the adversary gets to see M players playing our protocol for $T/2$ steps, and where a link $(v^{(t)}, v^{(t+1)})$ is honest iff both the link $(v^{(t)}, v^{(t+1)})$ and its associated link are honest.

Thus, the only difference from the case of no prior knowledge is that now the probability each link is honest is f^2 rather than f. We therefore can use the theorem for no prior-knowledge and conclude that $I(C' : \Pi^{(T/2)}) \leq \alpha$ as desired. $\square$

We now show that it must be the case that the adversary did not gain much information about the last layer. I.e.,

Lemma 13. $I(C' : \Pi^{(T)}) \leq I(C' : \Pi^{(T/2)})$.

Proof. We represent the random variable C' that contains the communication the adversary sees as $C' = (C_1, C_2)$ where C_1 is the communication seen throughout the first $T/2$ steps, and C_2 is the communication seen throughout the last $T/2$ steps.

$$I(\Pi^{(T)} : C_1, C_2) = I(\Pi^{(T)} : C_2) + I(\Pi^{(T)} : C_1 \mid C_2) =$$
$$I(\Pi^{(T)} : C_1 \mid C_2) \leq I(\Pi^{(T/2)} : C_1 \mid C_2) \leq I(\Pi^{(T/2)} : C_1, C_2)$$

The first equality and the last inequality are applications of the chain rule for information.

To see the second equality, notice that $(C_2|\Pi^{(T)} = \pi)$ is the same distribution for all permutations π that are valid values of $\Pi^{(T)}$. This is because we can think of the protocol as if the players first pick $\pi \in \Pi^{(T)}$, then pick the top $T-1$ levels at random, and then complete the first layer to implement π. Thus, $I(\Pi^{(T)} : C_2) = 0$.

The crux of the argument is the first inequality. For it, we use the data-processing inequality ([17], Theorem 2.8.1, page 32) and the probabilistic function $f(\sigma, c_2)$ that given $\sigma \in \Pi^{(T/2)}$ and $c_2 \in C_2$ chooses the permutation π with probability $\Pr(\Pi^{(T)} = \pi \mid \Pi^{(T/2)} = \sigma \wedge C_2 = c_2)$. The important thing to notice is that it suffices to know σ and c_2 alone to know the value of $f(\sigma, c_2)$.   □

5   Open Problems

We show an efficient protocol (both in terms of delay and load) secure against adaptive adversaries. However, in our opinion, this is only the beginning of a systematic study of unlinkability in anonymous networks. We mention a few interesting open problems:

- Our work (and most previous work) assume a complete communication network. In reality, the network is a low-degree graph. Simple calculations show that an adaptive adversary can easily isolate all messages that come from any specific user. Is there a reasonable relaxed attack model, that allows anonymous communication?
- Our work (and most previous work) assume the communication network (i.e., the vertices in the network, and which vertices and edges are honest) is fixed in advance. Can one design a protocol that handles dynamic changes in the topology (users joining and leaving) of the system?
- Our work (and most previous work) assumes each participant has full knowledge of the network topology, users' keys, etc. This does not conform, for example, with the fully distributed nature of peer to peer systems. Can we do better in this respect, and still retain efficiency and provable security?
- Extending the protocol to malicious adversaries.

Acknowledgements

We thank Benny Chor for enlightening discussions, and for insisting on prior knowledge. We thank the vibrant Hebrew University theory seminar for many important comments. We are especially indebted to Yonatan Bilu for pointing out, during the seminar, a fundamental mistake in an earlier version of the paper.

References

1. Chaum, D.: Untraceable electronic mail, return addresses, and digital pseudonyms. Thesis (M.S. in Computer Science), University of California, Berkeley, Berkeley, CA, USA (1979)

2. Chaum, D.: Untraceable electronic mail, return addresses, and digital pseudonyms. Communications of the Association for Computing Machinery **24** (1981) 84–88
3. Reed, M.G., Syverson, P.F., Goldschlag, D.M.: Anonymous connections and onion routing. IEEE Journal on Selected Areas in Communications **16** (1998) 482–494
4. Syverson, P.F., Goldschlag, D.M., Reed, M.G.: Anonymous connections and onion routing. In: 1997 IEEE Symposium on Security and Privacy. (1997) 44–54
5. Rackoff, C., Simon, D.R.: Cryptographic defense against traffic analysis. In: Proceedings of the Twenty-Fifth Annual ACM Symposium on the Theory of Computing, San Diego, California (1993) 672–681
6. Chaum, D.: The Dining Cryptographers Problem: Unconditional sender and recipient untraceability. Journal of Cryptology **1** (1988) 65–75
7. Reiter, M.K., Rubin, A.D.: Crowds: anonymity for Web transactions. ACM Transactions on Information and System Security **1** (1998) 66–92
8. Abe, M.: Mix-networks on permutation networks. In: Advances in Cryptology - ASIACRYPT '99, International Conference on the Theory and Applications of Cryptology and Information Security, Singapore, November 14-18, 1999, Proceedings. Volume 1716 of Lecture Notes in Computer Science. (1999) 258–273
9. Abe, M., Hoshino, F.: Remarks on mix-network based on permutation networks. Lecture Notes in Computer Science **1992** (2001) 317–324
10. Malkhi, D., Pavlov, E.: Anonymity without 'cryptography' (extended abstract). In: FC: International Conference on Financial Cryptography, LNCS, Springer-Verlag (2001)
11. Beimel, Dolev: Buses for anonymous message delivery. JCRYPTOL: Journal of Cryptology **16** (2003)
12. Raymond, J.F.: Traffic analysis: Protocols, attacks, design issues, and open problems. Lecture Notes in Computer Science **2009** (2001) 10–29
13. The anonymizer. (http://anonymizer.com)
14. Anonymous remailer information. (http://anon.efga.org/Remailers.)
15. Federrath, H., ed.: Designing Privacy Enhancing Technologies, International Workshop on Design Issues in Anonymity and Unobservability, Berkeley, CA, USA, July 25-26, 2000, Proceedings. In Federrath, H., ed.: International Workshop on Design Issues in Anonymity and Unobservability. Volume 2009 of Lecture Notes in Computer Science., Springer (2001)
16. Alon, N.: Testing subgraphs in large graphs. In: 42nd IEEE Symposium on Foundations of Computer Science. (2001) 434–439
17. Cover, T.M., Thomas, J.A.: Elements of Information Theory. Wiley Series in Telecommunications. John Wiley & Sons, New York, NY, USA (1991)
18. Nielsen, M., Chuang, I.: Quantum Computation and Quantum Information. Cambridge (2000)

Author Index